Understanding the Small Business Sector

This text analyses the key issues that influence the growth and development of small businesses. Looking at the context in which they operate, the book outlines the factors that are dominant in the sector and explores the effects it has on the economy.

Does training help small business managers? Is the creation of small businesses the answer to unemployment? Has the lowering of interest rates or taxation encouraged the self-employed to work harder? Have banks given small businesses a raw deal? These are just some of the questions raised and discussed as David Storey explains the issues of employment, finance and policy and the influences dictating failure or success.

This book is the first comprehensive introduction for those studying the nature of small businesses, providing a synthesis of the latest research and literature in the area. It will be relevant for all those taking courses in small business, enterprise and economics at undergraduate and MBA level.

David J. Storey is Director of the Centre for Small and Medium Sized Enterprises at Warwick Business School, University of Warwick.

Understanding the Small Business Sector

D.J. Storey

London and New York

First published 1994
by Routledge
11 New Fetter Lane, London EC4P 4EE

Simultaneously published in the USA and Canada
by Routledge
29 West 35th Street, New York, NY 10001

Typeset in Times by
Solidus (Bristol) Ltd, Bristol
Printed and bound in Great Britain by
Biddles Ltd, Guildford and King's Lynn

British Library Cataloguing in Publication Data
A catalogue record for this book is available from the British Library

ISBN 0–415–09626–X (hbk)
ISBN 0–415–10038–0 (pbk)

Library of Congress Cataloging in Publication Data
Storey, D.J.
Understanding the small business sector / David J. Storey.
p. cm.
Includes bibliographical references and index.
ISBN 0–415–09626–X. — ISBN 0–415–10038–0 (pbk.)
1. Small business—Government policy—Great Britain. 2. Small business—Government policy—Europe. 3. Small business—Government policy—United States. I. Title.
HD2346.G7S785 1994
338.6 ' 42 ' 094—dc20 94–1570
CIP

Contents

Figures

Tables

Preface

The genesis of this book extends back to approximately 1984. At that time a Conservative administration had been in power for five years in the United Kingdom. One of the pillars of its political agenda was the aim of making the United Kingdom a more enterprising society. The United Kingdom's prime funder of social science research, the Economic and Social Research Council (at that time the Social Science Research Council), recognised that the smaller enterprise sector in the United Kingdom was a key focus of public policy and yet one which seemed to generate little interest amongst the vast bulk of social scientists.

The Council therefore commissioned two studies to provide it with some guidance as to whether the topic was appropriate for research funding on a major scale. The first study was a review of existing research on 'job generation'. This was designed to assess the validity and implications of the work by David Birch in the United States, which had attempted to quantify the contribution to the US economy of different sizes of firms. It had been widely interpreted as showing that the small firm sector was the prime source of employment creation in the United States. The review, conducted by the current author and by Steve Johnson, concluded that the Birch work was correct in inferring that the small firm sector was a disproportionately large creator of new jobs. Even so, Birch had overestimated the significance of the small firm sector in job creation.

A second review was conducted by Tom Cannon, Sarah Carter, Wendy Faulkner and Stana Nenadic. They were commissioned to conduct an empirical investigation into the quality and utility of small business research in the United Kingdom. Their report was never published in full, but an abridged version is found in Rosa *et al.* (1989). They concluded, on the basis of questionnaires to researchers, citation analyses of leading publications and face-to-face discussions with academics, consultants and practitioners that, 'there is a general awareness of a want of quality and methodological rigour in the field'. Their conversations with public policy makers were even clearer:

> For those involved in policy formulation, problems of weak data, methodological rigour and what one civil servant described as 'a lack of intellectual equipment' produced what is perceived to be a disparate research field, prone to 'faddiness', which has yet to address the fundamental questions surrounding the small firm sector.

A tricky decision therefore faced the Economic and Social Research Council. Should it fund research in an area which, whilst of major political importance, appeared at that time to have a reputation for lacking 'intellectual equipment'?

In the event, the ESRC did decide to finance a programme of research. At the end of 1987 the current author was appointed as Programme Co-ordinator, with a structure in which three research centres would focus upon major themes, and a number of smaller projects would focus on specific, and generally narrower topics.

Part of the novelty of the programme was that there were sponsors of the programme in addition to ESRC. These sponsors were Barclays Bank, the SME Task Force (subsequently DG23) of the European Commission, the Department of Employment (subsequently the Department of Trade and Industry), and the Rural Development Commission.

The benefits of sponsorship were threefold. The financial contribution of these external sponsors increased the size of the research budget, in aggregate by almost 50 per cent. Secondly, the sponsors enjoyed a continuous opportunity over a four-year period to absorb the results of the research into the operations of their own organisation. Thirdly, it provided the researchers with personalised contact for data and information from within these organisations.

During 1988 decisions were made, following an invitation to tender, about the structure of the research. Three main centres were chosen, one at Kingston Polytechnic (now Kingston University) under the leadership of Jim Curran to look at the role of small firms in the service sector. The second was at the University of Cambridge, under the direction of Alan Hughes, to look at the economic contribution of small firms, and the third was under the direction of John Atkinson at the Institute of Manpower Studies, Sussex University, to look at small firms and the labour market. In addition, thirteen separate projects on a variety of different topics were commissioned. These research projects tended to be of a shorter duration than the three year studies undertaken by the centres. A full list of centres and projects is provided at the end of this preface.

Between 1989 and 1992 the centres and projects conducted their work mostly in the form of face-to-face, postal or telephone surveys with those owning or managing small firms. The table at the end of this preface shows that more than 10,000 small businesses participated in what, in aggregate, was the largest sample of small firms yet undertaken. The firms surveyed exhibited wide sectoral, geographical and size variability.

Over the three-year period, eleven workshops were held at which the researchers made presentations and discussed one another's work. Preliminary papers were presented, not only at these workshops, but also at conferences. Towards the end of the period the researchers' final material was appearing in print.

The programme was designed to provide not only an opportunity for researchers to publish and present material on their own specialisms, but also an overview of small business policy making in the United Kingdom. To this end there are four books which attempt to fulfil this role. Three are edited books on key topics: urban and rural issues (Curran and Storey 1993), employment (Atkinson and Storey 1993) and finance (Hughes and Storey 1994). The fourth book is the present volume, written by the Co-ordinator of the Programme and outlining his views of the research findings and policy issues. It is important to emphasise that these are not necessarily the views of any of the sponsoring organisations nor of the researchers.

In putting together this volume, it has not been possible – nor even desirable – to focus exclusively upon the research conducted as part of the ESRC initiative. This is primarily because, despite the scale of the exercise, not all relevant topics were covered. It would also be unreasonable to assume that the only work worthy of reference is that financed by ESRC.

Instead, the broad 'rule of thumb' employed by the author has been to utilise material from the ESRC programme where appropriate. To provide the reader with a balanced view of subject matter, it is essential to draw upon research material from outside the programme, where this exhibits methodological soundness. Indeed – perhaps inevitably – the bulk of references are to research which has not been funded as part of the ESRC programme.

In putting together this book I pay my thanks to a wide range of individuals. At ESRC in the early days I received valuable support from John Malin, Ann Marsden and Peter Southwood. Once the initiative began, Iain Jones, Helen Whitney and Phil Sooben all contributed to its management. Amongst the external sponsors, I particularly valued the contributions made by John Martin from Barclays Bank, Keith Lievesley from the Rural Development Commission, Martin Harvey from DG23 and Irene Brunskill from the DTI.

Frank Wilkinson, from the Cambridge Centre, once said to me that 'organising academics is a bit like herding cats!'. Whilst I understand what he means, I have to report that my experiences on this programme have been entirely positive. Attendance at workshops was consistently high, the level of debate good and delivery of manuscripts generally punctual – although that distribution does have a slight tail to it!

I particularly wish to thank those researchers who have taken the time to read and comment upon chapters in this volume. They have done so purely out of altruism and a desire to ensure that those who read my account of the results of their research in the years to come are informed accurately.

Throughout the four years of the ESRC initiative I have relied very heavily on the staff at the centres, such as Jim Curran and Robert Blackburn at Kingston, who have read and commented upon virtually the whole of this manuscript. I also have had help and comments from Alan Hughes and David Keeble at Cambridge and John Atkinson and Nigel Meager at Sussex. I really am most grateful to all of them.

Amongst project researchers who have been most generous with their time to me are David North and David Smallbone, Colin Mason, Michael Godwin and Judith Freedman, Bruce Lyons, Tim May and John McHugh, Peter Townroe, Will Bartlett, Hedley Rees and Alan McGregor.

Perhaps my greatest surprise has been the willingness of individuals, not financed under the ESRC initiative, to provide me with comments and opinions on my text. A list of their names almost reads like a list of the 'great and the good' in small business research. For example, Graham Bannock, the doyen of small business researchers, has been most generous, but so also have been many of the world's leading authorities on this topic – David Audretsch, Martin Binks, Dan Corry, Marc Cowling, Robert Cressy, David Deakins, Colin Gray, Peter Johnson, Arne Kalleberg, David de Meza, Gordon Murray, Paul Reynolds, Mike Scott and Robert Watson. Again I would stress that my opinions and theirs do not necessarily coincide, but that the text is, I believe, more robust as a result of their comments.

The material here has been presented in a number of seminars, meetings and workshops. My thanks go to those who have commented on this text at meetings at the CBI, HM Treasury, Department of Trade and Industry, DG23, Barclays Bank and London School of Economics. Presentations have also been made to academic audiences in Örebro (Sweden), Toronto (Canada), Parma and Milan (Italy).

Finally I would like to formally express my thanks to Glenda Hall, known to everyone in the research programme for organising workshops and 'herding the cats'. I calculate that there are approximately 170,000 words in this volume, all of which have been typed by her; bearing in mind that each has been changed at least three times, a considerable number of hours have been devoted to this topic with amazing good humour.

Thanks to all.

David Storey
SME Centre
University of Warwick

ESRC INITIATIVE – DEFINITIONS AND SAMPLE SIZE

Researcher	*Institution location*	*Definitions*	*Sectors*	*Sample no. of firms*	*Data source*	*Data collection*	*Response rate*	*Geography*
1. Curran *et al.*	Kingston University	'Grounded'	Services	350*	Yellow Pages, trade and local directories	Face-to-face/ telephone	56.1	Nottingham, Guildford, north-east Suffolk, Doncaster, Islington
2. Hughes *et al.*	Cambridge University	1–500 employees	Manufacturing and business services	2,028	Dun & Bradstreet	Postal	32.9	England, Scotland, Wales
3. Atkinson	Sussex University	Establishments with < 200 employees	All sectors	3,309	Business connections	Postal and face-to-face	29.8	North Cornwall, Shrewsbury, Brighton, Manchester, Newport, Slough
4. Townroe	Sheffield Hallam University	Small start-ups	All sectors	559	Rural Development Commission	Postal	23.3	Northumberland, Derbyshire, Norfolk, Devon
5. North *et al.*	Middlesex University	Independent and < 100 employees	Eight manufacturing sectors	306	Prior contact, Rural Development Commission, local directories	Face-to-face	–	London, Derbyshire, Hertfordshire, Essex, Cumbria, Lancashire (North), North Yorkshire
6. Owen	Sheffield Hallam University	< 300 employees	Manufacturing and mobile services	467	Local authority, chamber of commerce	Postal	25.5	Sheffield Hainaut (France/Belgium)
7. Rees	Bristol University	Self-employed	All sectors	N/A	General Household Survey	Government	N/A	UK
8. Bartlett	Bristol University	Co-ops and 'matched' private firms	All sectors	200	Business associations	Face-to-face	N/A	Emilia Romagna (Italy) Catalonia (Spain)

9. Jones *et al.*	Liverpool John Moores University	White, Asian, Afro-Caribbean owned firms	Retailing, wholesaling, manufacturing	403	Rateable valuation lists	Face-to-face	N/A	Wards in North, Midlands and south-east England
10. Freedman/ Godwin	Institute of Advanced Legal Studies	Incorporated & unincorporated firms (< £1m. turnover)	All sectors	429	Yellow Pages, companies register/ Jordans	Telephone, postal and face-to-face	29%	Bath, Sutton, Darlington, Derby
11. McGregor	Glasgow University	Community enterprises & firms in managed workspace	All sectors	346	–	Face-to-face	–	Belfast, Glasgow, Bristol, Manchester, London, Newcastle
12. Davies *et al.*	University of East Anglia	< 100 employees	Subcontractors	102	Benchmark	Postal	8%†	UK
13. Nenadic	Edinburgh University	Family-owned businesses 1861–1891	All sectors	781	Post Office directory	–	–	Edinburgh
14. Nayak	Birmingham University	< 10 employees	All sectors, engineering, electrical	200	Redditch Enterprise Agency	Face-to-face	–	West Midlands
15. May	Manchester Metropolitan University	< 100 employees	All sectors	294	Local authority	Telephone	73%	Oldham, Stockport
16. Mason/ Harrison	Southampton/ Ulster University	Users of informal venture capital	All sectors	297 (3 surveys)	VCR guide, brokers' contacts	Postal	12%†	Rural areas, Northern Ireland, Leicestershire, Hertfordshire, South Hampshire

Notes
*274 of these firms were reinterviewed in 1992 and 204 reinterviewed in 1993.
†Response rates do not take account of ineligible firms.

PARTICIPANTS IN ESRC SMALL BUSINESS PROGRAMME

Research centres

Local labour markets and small businesses in Britain

Mr J.S. Atkinson (with Mr N. Meager)
Institute of Manpower Studies
Mantell Building
University of Sussex
Falmer
Brighton BN1 9RF

Small enterprises in the service sector – a research programme

Professor J. Curran (with Dr R. Blackburn)
Midland Bank Professor of Small Business Studies
School of Business
Kingston University
Kingston Hill
Kingston upon Thames
Surrey KT2 7LB

Creation, survival and growth of small firms; determinants and constraints

Mr A. Hughes (with Dr D. Keeble)
Department of Applied Economics
University of Cambridge
Sidgwick Avenue
Cambridge CB3 9DE

Research projects

Subcontracting and the small business

Professor S.W. Davies (with Dr B. R. Lyons, Dr P. M. Townroe)
Economic Research Centre
School of Economic and Social Studies
University of East Anglia
Norwich NR4 7TJ

Legal form and taxation of small firms – a new regime?

Mrs J.A. Freedman (with Mr M. Godwin)
Law Department
London School of Economics and Political Science
University of London
Houghton Street
London WC2A 2AE

Small business initiative: ethnic minority business component

Mr T.P. Jones (with Professor D. McEvoy)
School of Humanities and Social Science
Liverpool John Moores University
Truman Street Building
15–21 Webster Street
Liverpool L3 2ET

Informal risk capital in the United Kingdom

Dr C.M. Mason (with Professor R.T. Harrison)
Department of Geography
University of Southampton
Southampton SO9 5NH

Stimulating and supporting small enterprises in hostile environments

Professor A. McGregor (with Dr A.A. McArthur)
Training and Employment Research Unit
Adam Smith Building
University of Glasgow
Glasgow G12 8RT

The relationship between the state representative groups and small businesses

Mr J. McHugh (with Mr T.C. May)
Social Science
Manchester Metropolitan University
Ormond Building
Lower Ormond Street
Manchester M15 6BX

The management information needs of small businesses

Mrs A.M. Nayak (with Dr S.M. Greenfield)
Accounting and Finance
University of Birmingham
P O Box 363
Birmingham B15 2TT

The family and the small firm: Edinburgh 1861 to 1891

Dr S. Nenadic (with Dr R.J. Morris)
Economic and Social History
University of Edinburgh
William Robertson Building
50 George Square
Edinburgh EH8 9JY

A longitudinal study of adjustment processes in mature small firms

Dr D.J. North (with Dr R. Leigh, Mr D.J. Smallbone)
Faculty of Social Science
Middlesex University
Queensway
Enfield
Middlesex EN3 4SF

Aid regimes and small businesses in the United Kingdom, France and Belgium

Mr G.W. Owen
Business Studies and Languages
Sheffield Hallam University
Pond Street
Sheffield S1 1WB

Cooperatives and small private firms in Mediterranean Europe

Dr G.F.M. Pridham (with Dr W.J. Bartlett)
Mediterranean Studies (CMS)
University of Bristol
12 Priory Road
Bristol BS8 1TU

The characteristics of the self-employed

Dr H.J.B. Rees (with Dr A.R. Shah)
Economics
University of Bristol
Alfred Marshall Building
8 Woodland Road
Bristol BS8 1TN

Characteristics of founders of rural small businesses

Professor P.M. Townroe
Urban and Regional Studies
Sheffield Hallam University
Pond Street
Sheffield S1 1WB

Chapter 1

Introduction

WHY DO LONG-TERM RESEARCH ON SMALL FIRMS?

'Four years?' said the incredulous small businessman. 'You're going to spend four years looking at the problems of small businesses and what government should do about it? You don't need to do that. I can tell you what the problems are and I can tell you today. I can also tell you now what government should do about it!'

That type of reaction is both understandable and frequently articulated by small business owners. So, what is the role of research on the small business sector, why should it be undertaken and why does it take so long?

This section identifies five reasons for undertaking long-term research on small firms. The first follows on from the businessman's statement. This illustrates the emphasis in small firms for an immediate solution to today's problems. Indeed, during this conversation the small business owner went on to say that any research which lasted a long time would be ineffective, since the nature of the problems facing his firm would have changed by the time the research was produced, hence making it out of date.

There used to be a phrase, common in the 1960s, that 'What's good for General Motors is good for the United States'. It may be the case today in the United Kingdom that the small business sector regards what is good for it as being good for the United Kingdom. Even the casual newspaper reader knows about the key role which small firms play in employment creation, their overall importance in the economy, their role in innovation, the importance which government attaches to 'enterprise', etc. But to provide guidance for public policy makers means that, as the small business sector grows in importance, it is even more necessary than in the past to examine its role in an economic, social and political framework. We have to see the role of small businesses in creating employment not only as part of employment policy, but also as part of urban and social policy. For example, one central question is whether efforts should be made to encourage the unemployed, many of whom may lack business skills, to create their own jobs by becoming self-employed. Is it reasonable to provide public funds to an individual living in a deprived inner-city area to start their own business as a way of creating employment for themselves, given that the risk if the business fails may be that they are saddled with a burden of debt which they are unable to service?

There is no better illustration of this scenario than the case of Lynne, as reported in MacDonald and Coffield (1991). She is a young mother with a child living on Teesside and is asked why she went into self-employment. This was her reply:

> 'It was something I had to try. I was getting nowhere. I couldn't see any future in what I was doing. I'd levelled off and I wanted to climb. I wanted self-esteem. Looking back it's been totally the opposite. I'd had two relationships that'd failed. My life has been a total failure since leaving college to now. I needed something to succeed. As it happens, I failed in that as well. Perhaps I'm just a born failure. But at least I've had the experience. I haven't just sat back moaning and on the dole. I've tried to get out of the poverty trap. Fine, it didn't work but at least I've gained the experience.
>
> 'So now a year later I have about £10,000 debts and I can't afford to declare myself bankrupt so that amount is rising with the interest. I got taken to the High Court by a supplier for £1,300. Then I had the County Sheriff on my doorstep with a possession order. Because he was a nice chap, and he could see I had a kid, he left the furniture but he had possession of them so if I took anything out of the house or sold it, I would be charged with theft. So he owns the furniture and I'm being charged interest on that at 27 pence a day and fees of 58 pence a day and that has been going on since last year. The taxman has also caught up with me and he wanted to take the furniture, but he couldn't 'cos it belonged to the County Sheriff. I'm between the devil and the deep blue sea. I'm totally in the dark at the moment about what I owe people but I can't phone them to find out in case that reminds them about it. I'm stuck – just waiting for the axe to fall. I could have the £10,000 hanging over me for the rest of my life.
>
> 'I went through hell mentally with it. Strait-jacket time, St Nicks' here I come.'[1]

The case of Lynne illustrates that small business policy is not to be conducted in a vacuum. Rather, it must be part of social and employment policy, and to place it in that context requires long-term research.

A second reason for conducting long-term research on smaller firms is that it is not always the case that the interests of the small business owner and those of society as a whole coincide. An example is where government imposes regulations upon businesses in order either to protect their workers or to protect the environment. Such regulations may be costly to business, but these costs are deemed to be more than offset by the benefits obtained by the rest of society. However, reaching an informed decision about the balance of regulation cannot simply involve consultation with the small business community. Clearly, wider social and economic considerations come into play, and a careful weighing of these takes time.

The third reason relates to the question of speed. 'Why', asked my small business owner, 'do you need to spend all this time doing it?' The reply has two elements: the first is that reaching a judgement on policy requires careful assessment of high-quality evidence. For example, small business lobbyists consistently argue that increased taxes are bad, because they constitute a major disincentive to entrepreneurs. 'Who is going to work the extra hour if it all goes to the government?' is a familiar theme. Yet research, conducted over a long period of time and reported in this volume suggests that, if anything, decreases in taxation have led the self-employed to work fewer hours, rather than more. This is because most business owners have an approximate level of income which they wish to achieve after tax. Reductions in marginal tax rates mean they have to work fewer hours, providing them with greater utility, even though output falls. Unfortunately, undertaking research of this type is extremely complex and much more time-consuming than, for example, conducting a straw poll of a non-random selection of small business owners and asking them whether they think tax rates on small firm owners should be cut. Hence the quickest research is not necessarily the best.

A second issue associated with speed, again emphasised by the small businessman, was that matters will have changed substantially by the time the research results are available. Such impatience is understandable amongst the small business community. Over a four-year period, around 40 per cent of the businesses which are trading at the start of this research will no longer be trading at the end of the research. A short time horizon is inevitable in organisations that are only able to pay the wages on the Friday if the bank has cleared a customer's cheque on the Thursday.

If there is important research which is going to influence government policy, and result in a healthier small business sector, then, of course, the results are needed as soon as possible. Yet reading historical accounts about small businesses heightens an awareness that, over long periods of time, so many issues remain remarkably similar. Nowhere is this better illustrated than in the financing of small businesses. For example, reading the newspapers today and listening to the clamour for the introduction of statutory interest on late payment might suggest this is a new problem. In fact, as Westhead (1993) shows, today's late payment problems are trivial compared with those of eighteenth century businesses in the UK. Westhead makes use of a quotation from Denyer (1991) *Traditional Buildings and Life in the Lake District* (Victor Gollancz, London):

> Analysis of the accounts for Troutbeck Park Quarries, located in the English Lake District has revealed late payment of bills was a problem during the 1750s. Out of eighty local transactions over five years only one

customer paid in less than six months and most took just over one year.
(Denyer 1991, p. 160).

In the more recent past, the Bolton Committee reported in 1971 about the difficulties which small firms experienced in obtaining relatively modest sums of equity capital. The MacMillan Committee more than sixty years ago reported upon similar problems. During that time there have been a number of attempts to overcome the problem, and it is certainly the case that the sums of equity capital which nowadays constitute the basis of any 'equity gap' are very much more modest than was the case sixty years ago. Nevertheless the basic issues remain the same, with small firms being associated with trading uncertainty.

Re-reading the Bolton Committee Report of 1971, whilst the economic environment has changed markedly, the agenda in those days was strikingly similar to that of today: financing, government intervention, the taxation system and macroeconomic policy. The real change is that, at the time of the Bolton Committee, the key issue was whether small firms were going to disappear from the scene altogether in the UK economy. Today, small firms are vastly more important than they were twenty years ago, and the key issue is how to nurture this development. Nevertheless the agenda items remain strikingly similar.

It is this continuity of so many of the problem areas for small firms, even if the firms themselves are constantly changing through birth and death, that is the third reason for the need to conduct long-term research.

A fourth reason is to provide an antidote to the 'knee-jerk' policy making which characterised the small firm environment in the UK during the 1980s. It continues to be the case today that intense lobbying takes place as the annual budget approaches, with each lobbyist attempting to persuade the Chancellor of the Exchequer to introduce 'pet' schemes. The casual sceptic could be excused for believing in 'Buggins's turn', whereby particular schemes are introduced in order to placate particular groups of powerful lobbyists. One central purpose of long-term research then, is to provide civil servants and others with evidence on the likely effectiveness or otherwise of particular initiatives.

An even more ambitious aim is for research to set the agenda for small firm policy making, rather than being used to evaluate policies which have already been implemented. One of the great benefits of developments during the 1980s is that much better data on small firms have become available and research on small firms, in many countries, has increased in quality and quantity. There is now a stock of information about which policies seem to be effective and which seem to be ineffective. The role of researchers has to be to use their information to influence policy towards a greater emphasis upon the 'successful' types of policy and to strongly oppose the ineffective. This book attempts to begin that process.

The fifth reason for undertaking long-term research is not directly related to policy making. It concerns the need to provide time for researchers to have the opportunity to make theoretical as well as empirical contributions. If policy makers can be criticised for a lack of considered coherence in developing small firm policy, then some small firm researchers may equally be criticised for a lack of theoretical development of their subject matter (Reid 1993a). Too often, the large-firm model is taken as given and the small firm is assumed to be a 'scaled-down' version of a large firm. Instead, as Wynarczyk *et al.* (1993) argue, theorists need to identify the characteristics of small firms, other than scale, which distinguish them from large firms and theorise on the implications of this. Wynarczyk *et al.*, strongly influenced by Casson (1982), argue these differences are the much greater roles played by uncertainty, by innovation and evolution amongst smaller firms. Reid (1993b) clearly illustrates this point by his efforts to reintroduce the role of the entrepreneur in economic theory as the individual who sees a market opportunity. The contribution of Reid is to apply this in an experimental laboratory context.

In some areas theorists have already made a major contribution to our understanding of small firm issues, but in others their contribution is much weaker. This is reflected within this volume, which attempts to use current theory as a context for discussing empirical results. In some contexts, such as the discussions of financing, the theoretical framework is well developed and accessible. In other areas – most notably small firm death and growth, it is much weaker.

To summarise, there are very strong reasons why long-term research on the small business sector needs to be undertaken. The remainder of the book attempts to lay out the results of such a review.

STRUCTURE OF THE BOOK

Chapter 2 provides an overview of the small firm sector in developed countries. It grapples with the familiar thorny question of the definition of a small firm, but its prime thrust is to demonstrate that, whatever definition is employed, small firms constitute the bulk of enterprises in an economy and are generally an increasingly important contributor to employment. The reasons for this are investigated, and an assessment is made of whether such trends are likely to continue into the future.

To obtain a better understanding of the factors which influence the number and size of small firms in an economy, it is appropriate to examine the influences on both the birth and death of firms. These are examined in Chapters 3 and 4 respectively. Chapter 3, which examines the factors influencing the birth rate of firms, briefly reviews theories of new firm births and then attempts to examine the extent to which these theories are accepted or rejected. A similar format is employed in Chapter 4 on the death of firms, although in both cases considerable space has to be devoted to an understanding of the strengths and weaknesses of available data in this area.

One persistent theme of the book is that, whilst the small firm sector exhibits very high rates of churning – births and deaths – a key element in small firm policy making is the extent to which small firms ultimately grow into medium and large-sized firms. In some senses small firms policy can be seen to be working towards its own demise, since an appropriate objective is to ensure that small firms grow to the extent that they are no longer small firms. It is this transition which is the focus of interest in Chapter 5.

Chapters 3, 4 and 5 may be considered to constitute an 'accounting' view of small firms, in the sense that the contribution of small firms may be considered as the joint effects of changes in the stock of firms (births minus deaths) and the contribution of the growth of firms. An alternative perspective is that pursued in Chapters 6 and 7, which focus upon the themes of employment and financing. As noted earlier, the prime reason for the upsurge of interest, particularly from politicians, in the small firm sector, is the research findings suggesting that smaller firms are significant sources of new job creation. This issue is addressed in Chapter 6. However, it is appropriate to ask not only what small firms do for the labour market, but to ask what the labour market does for small firms. This is a focus of the chapter.

Chapter 7 examines the question of financing of small firms, and here it is possible to anchor the empirics closely on existing theoretical developments. It enables a judgement to be reached on whether there is a 'gap' in the financing of small firms, and the extent to which there is a case for providers of finance and the small firms to be able to close this gap themselves.

The book places a heavy emphasis upon public policy making with respect to small firms. Chapter 8 reviews the role which governments play in promoting the sector and in seeing small firms as part of a wider economic and social framework. In conducting this analysis it is able to use not only the 'market failure' criteria of economists, but the notion of a 'policy community'. This enables us to understand better the choice of those small firm policy measures which were implemented during the 1980s in the United Kingdom.

Finally Chapter 9 provides a summary of the key findings and a basis for further action by small firms themselves, by financiers and by governments. It also highlights the areas where uncertainty remains.

Chapter 2

Small firms

Definitions, descriptions and patterns

INTRODUCTION

The casual reader of the high quality financial press – such as the *Financial Times*, the *Economist* or the *Wall Street Journal* – might be forgiven for believing that small firms hardly exist in the leading developed economies. Casual scrutiny of the *Financial Times*, on any day other than Tuesday, may fail to identify even a single article either about a business with less than fifty employees, or about the small firm sector more generally. Instead, perhaps fifty pages of the newspaper might well be exclusively concerned with very much larger firms, and with a particular focus upon those which are quoted on stock exchanges. This emphasis on large firms characterises virtually all financial and economic newspapers.

In some senses this is surprising, and in others it is not. It is not surprising that information needs to be publicly available and widely disseminated for quoted companies, to enable investors to make informed decisions regarding share purchases or sales. It is also the case, as we shall demonstrate in this chapter, that large firms produce the bulk of private sector output in most developed countries, and so a focus upon them is appropriate.

It *is* surprising in that politicians in many countries have emphasised, for at least a decade, the importance of small enterprises as a mechanism for job creation, innovation and the long-term development of economies. Perhaps the issue is really the scale of the 'imbalance' of the coverage in the financial press, where the emphasis is almost exclusively upon large firms. In its coverage of enterprises, more than 95 per cent of column space in the *Financial Times* is devoted to large firms, whereas in the European economy more than 95 per cent of firms are in fact small, and these small firms provide more than half of all jobs in the EC. It is this imbalance in coverage which is striking.

Our task in this chapter, however, is not to attempt to educate editors of major newspapers, but merely to draw attention to the fact that small firms, however they are defined, constitute the bulk of enterprises in all economies in the world. Such firms also make a major contribution to private sector output and employment, one which appears to be increasing over time.

The problem with making statements of this nature is that the reasonable question is posed as to what precisely constitutes a small firm. The next section of this chapter makes it clear there is no single definition of a small firm. Nevertheless, whether an upper range of 100 employees or only ten employees is selected, more than 95 per cent of all firms in the economies of the European Community are classified as 'small'. In short, it is the firm with more than 100 employees which is the exception rather than the rule in Europe.

The fact that there are so many small firms in most developed economies leads to further problems, most notably that of measuring precisely how many exist in the economy at any point in time. Many small firms deliberately do not register with the state authorities. Others have such a short lifespan that the state authorities do not have time to register their existence before the business ceases trading. Finally, many of the businesses are so small that the state does not deem it worthwhile to register their existence, and such enterprises are exempted from registration on grounds of size. This causes problems for those given the task of estimating the size of the small firm sector, its contribution to output and employment, estimating whether this has changed over a period of time and making comparisons with other countries.

For all these reasons, small firm statistics tend to be somewhat speculative. Whilst most of this chapter is focused upon addressing the above issues, the uncertainty of small business statistics in virtually all countries has to be in the forefront of the mind of the reader.

Despite these definitional problems, this chapter compares the size and contribution of the small firm sector in the UK with those of other major developed economies (pp. 21–5). Changes over time in the relative importance of small firms are also shown (pp. 25–34). Here we carefully assess the evidence which suggests that small firms became relatively more important in more developed economies during the 1970s and 1980s following, in many instances, several decades of relative decline. Such trends are clear in the United Kingdom, but are less apparent for other countries, apart from in self-employment. A series of 'explanations' for these changes are presented (pp. 34–43), followed by the conclusions to the chapter.

DEFINITIONS

There is no single, uniformly acceptable, definition of a small firm. This is because a 'small' firm in, say, the petrochemical industry is likely to have much higher levels of capitalisation, sales and possibly employment, than a 'small' firm in the car repair trades. Definitions, therefore, which relate to 'objective' measures of size such as number of employees, sales turnover, profitability, net worth, etc., when examined at a sectoral level, mean that in some sectors all firms may be regarded as small, while in other sectors there are possibly no firms which are small.

The Bolton Committee (1971) attempted to overcome this problem by formulating what they called an 'economic' definition and a 'statistical' definition. The economic definition regarded firms as being small if they satisfied three criteria:

- they had a relatively small share of their market place;
- they were managed by owners or part-owners in a personalised way, and not through the medium of a formalised management structure;
- they were independent, in the sense of not forming part of a large enterprise.

Given this 'economic' definition, Bolton then devised a 'statistical' definition which was designed to address three main issues. The first was to quantify the current size of the small firm sector and its contribution to economic aggregates such as gross domestic product, employment, exports, innovation, etc. The second purpose was to compare the extent to which the small firm sector has changed its economic contribution over time. Thirdly, the statistical definition, in principle, has to enable a comparison to be made between the contribution of small firms in one country with that of other nations.

The definitions used by the Bolton Committee are shown in Table 2.1. This illustrates the use of different definitions of a small firm in different sectors. It also shows that the criteria upon which the judgement of 'smallness' was made also varied sectorally. Thus in two groups of sectors – manufacturing and construction, and mining and quarrying – the criterion was employment, in three service sectors the criterion was sales turnover, in one sector – catering – it was based upon ownership. Finally, in road transport it was based upon the physical assets of the business – the number of vehicles.

Table 2.1 Bolton Committee definitions of a small firm

Sector	*Definition*
Manufacturing	200 employees or less
Construction Mining and quarrying	25 employees or less
Retailing Miscellaneous Services	Turnover of £50,000 or less
Motor trades	Turnover of £100,000 or less
Wholesale trades	Turnover of £200,000 or less
Road transport	Five vehicles or less
Catering	All excluding multiples and brewery-managed houses

Source: Bolton (1971)

Following the Bolton Committee there have been a number of criticisms of both its 'economic' and its 'statistical' definitions. Taking the 'economic' definition first, the Bolton criterion that a small business is 'managed by its owners or part owners in a personalised way, and not through the medium of a formal management structure' is almost certainly incompatible with its 'statistical' definition of small manufacturing firms which could have up to 200 employees. Whilst Bolton recognised that some smaller firms may 'have one or more intermediate layers e.g. supervisors or foremen to interpret their [owner-manager] decisions and transmit them to employees', it still regarded small firm owners as taking all the principal decisions and exercising the principal management functions. The work of Atkinson and Meager (1994), however, demonstrates that managerial appointments – not simply supervisors or foremen – are made when firms reach a size of between ten and twenty workers. At that size, owners are no longer the exclusive source of managerial decisions. By the time a business has in excess of 100 employees, the owners of businesses are starting to assemble significant teams of managers and have to devolve responsibilities to those teams. It therefore seems very unlikely that a firm with more than 100 employees could be managed in 'a personalised way'. This size of firm would certainly need a 'formal management structure', suggesting that the Bolton 'statistical' and 'economic' definitions are incompatible.

The second questionable aspect of the Bolton 'economic' definition is the emphasis upon the inability of the small firm to affect its environment – most notably its inability to influence, by changing the quantity which it produces, the price at which a product or service is sold in the market-place. In this respect Bolton is clearly influenced by the economist's concept of perfect competition. In practice, however, many small firms occupy 'niches'. They provide a highly specialised service or product, possibly in a geographically isolated area, and often do not perceive themselves to have clear competitors. As a result, in the short and possibly medium term, they can maintain higher prices and higher profits than the general industry 'norm'. Bradburd and Ross (1989) show that, in the United States, whilst large firms are generally more profitable than small, in heterogeneous industries – where niches are more likely to exist – this relationship is reversed.

An alternative 'economic' perspective on defining a small firm to that provided by Bolton is provided by Wynarczyk *et al.* (1993). Building upon the observation of Penrose (1959) that small and large firms are as fundamentally different from each other as a caterpillar is from a butterfly, they attempt to identify those characteristics of the small firm, other than size *per se*, which distinguish it from the larger enterprise. They argue there are three central respects in which small firms are different to large firms: uncertainty, innovation and evolution.

Three dimensions of uncertainty are identified:

- The first is the uncertainty associated with being a price-taker, which can be considered to be the inverse of the Bolton definition which emphasised the small share of the market-place.
- The second source of uncertainty for small firms is their limited customer and product base – the classic example of which is where small firms simply act as subcontractors to larger firms. Lyons and Bailey (1993) describe what they refer to as 'subcontractor vulnerability'. They argue this depends not only upon dependence on dominant customers, but also upon the extent to which output is specialised to particular customers, the specificity of investment decisions made and the probability that the customer will withdraw the custom. They clearly show that, even for subcontractors as a whole, the smaller firm clearly perceives itself to be more vulnerable than the large firm and, as we show later in this chapter, acts accordingly.
- The third dimension of uncertainty relates to the much greater diversity of objectives of the owners of small firms, compared with large. Many small business owners seek only to obtain a minimum level of income, rather than maximising sales or profits. Small business owners do not have to concern themselves with reporting their actions to external shareholders, and so 'performance monitoring' effectively does not exist. For a small firm, the relationship between the business and the owner is very much closer than it is between the shareholder and the large firm. The motivation of the owner of the small firm is therefore a key influence upon small firm performance. This contrasts with the large firm management literature, which emphasises the importance of control. Here the central issue is how the owners of the business ensure that the managers of the business act in their interest, and how senior managers exert control over more junior managers. This form of 'internal' conflict is absent in a small firm, where ownership and control are located in the hands of a few people, or possibly a single individual.

The central distinction between large and small firms, then, is the greater external uncertainty of the environment in which the small firm operates, together with the greater internal consistency of its motivations and actions.

A second key area of difference between small and large firms is their role in innovation. The glamorous role which Schumpeter (1934) saw small firms playing – that of initiating 'gales of creative destruction', through the introduction of totally new products, does have some basis in fact. Rothwell (1986) showed that the early development of the semi-conductor industry in California stemmed from the establishment of small firms which were able to grow extremely rapidly. Nevertheless, the much more conventional role which small firms play in innovation relates to their 'niche' role, discussed earlier. It is the ability of the smaller firm to provide something marginally different, in terms of product or service, which distinguishes it from the more standardised product or service provided by larger firms. The small firm, however, is also much less likely to undertake research and development than a large firm, and is less likely to have a high proportion of its staff concerned exclusively with research. Even so, small firms are more likely to introduce fundamentally new innovations than larger firms, this feature often being attributable to small firms having less commitment to existing practices and products (Pavitt *et al.* 1987).[1]

The third area of difference between large and small firms is the much greater likelihood of evolution and change in the smaller firm. We have already made reference to the transition which Penrose observed the small firm to make in becoming larger. She saw this as being comparable to the transition from a caterpillar to a butterfly, whereas management theorists have seen it to be not a single-stage change, but rather a multiple-stage change. Thus, small firms which become larger undergo a number of stage changes which influence the role and style of management and the structure of the organisation (Scott and Bruce 1987). The key point here is that the structure and organisation of the small firm is more likely to be in a state of change as the firm moves from one stage to another, than is the case for larger firms.

Wynarczyk *et al.* (1993) argue that the essential dimensions in which small firms differ from large relate to uncertainty, innovation and firm evolution. They argue that it is these dimensions which should be explored as a 'bottom-up' way of theorising about small firms, rather than implicitly assuming that a small firm is a 'scaled down' version of a large firm.

Turning now to the criticisms of the Bolton Committee 'statistical' definitions of small firms, five points emerge:

- The first, which was already noted from Table 2.1, is that there is no single definition, nor even any single criterion of 'smallness'. Instead, four different criteria are used in the definition – employees, turnover, ownership and assets.
- The second criticism is that three different upper limits of turnover are identified for the different sectors, and two different upper limits of employees are identified. These make the definitions too complex to enable comparisons to be made, either over time or between countries.
- The third criticism of statistical definitions based upon monetary units is that they make comparisons over time very difficult, since appropriate index numbers have to be constructed to take account of price changes. They also make international comparisons more difficult, because of currency value fluctuations.
- Fourthly, there are problems with employee-based criteria in comparing small and large firms over time. As Dunne and Hughes (1989) point out, output per head in constant prices varies according to firm size. They show that, using an index of net output per head where 1979 equals 100, by 1986 output per head in enterprises with less than 100 workers was

125.1, whereas that for enterprises with more than 1,000 workers was 132.8. Hence taking account of these increases in productivity over the last twenty years, the manufacturing upper limit for a small firm which was 200 in 1971, would be much closer to 100 in 1993.

- The fifth criticism of the Bolton Committee definitions is that they treat the small firm sector as being homogeneous. Even though the Committee, in their text, explicitly recognised that this was not the case, its single statistical definition for the smaller firm implies the existence of homogeneity.

To overcome a number of these problems, following the lead of the European Commission, the term 'small and medium enterprise' (SME) has been coined. The SME sector itself is disaggregated into three components:

- micro-enterprises: those with between 0 and 9 employees;
- small enterprises: those with 10 to 99 employees;
- medium enterprises: those with 100–499 employees.

The SME sector is therefore taken to be enterprises – except agriculture, hunting, forestry and fishing – which employ less than 500 workers. In several respects the EC definitions reflect the 'break points' in SME development which researchers have identified. We have already observed that Atkinson and Meager (1994) find the appointment of non-owning managers tends to take place when the firm has between ten and twenty employees. Lyons (1991) finds that subcontracting firms with less than ten employees are unlikely to have formal contracts with their customers, whereas this is much more likely when they have more than ten employees. Both these findings suggest that there is a marked shift to formality around the ten to twenty employee mark and that it is important to subdivide the SME sector in this way.

The major advantage of the EC definition is that, unlike Bolton, it does not use any criteria other than employment, and it does not vary its definition according to the sector of the enterprise. The only exception is that, at the EC level, a 'special' group of firms is identified – those in the craft trades. These are small-scale businesses which are heavily dependent on a handicraft, professional, traditional or artistic base. All European countries, with the exception of Spain and the United Kingdom, have some definition of craft trades, although the nature of that definition varies considerably from one country to another (ENSR 1993).

In almost all senses the EC definitions are currently more appropriate than those of the Bolton Committee.

- The EC definitions are exclusively based upon employment, rather than a multiplicity of criteria.
- The use of 100 employees as a small firm limit is more appropriate, given the rises in productivity which have taken place in the last two decades.

- The third benefit is that the EC definition recognises that the SME group is not homogeneous, in the sense that distinctions are made between micro, small and medium-sized enterprises.

However, the key remaining problem with the EC definition of an SME is that, for a number of countries, it is too 'all-embracing'. As will be shown, virtually all firms and the vast bulk of employment and output in countries such as Greece, Ireland, Spain and Portugal fall within the definition of SMEs. For 'internal' purposes, within these countries, the SME definition is not helpful. In these cases it is the categories within the SME definition which are most relevant.

Given these problems with official definitions of a small firm, we now review ways in which researchers have attempted to resolve these difficulties. Frequently their strategy has been to tailor or adjust a definition according to the particular topic of the research. One example is the work by Curran, Blackburn and Woods (1991) on small enterprises in the service sector. They argue that the use of a single size criterion leads to an exceptionally heterogeneous collection of businesses being included as small, yet where the owner-managers have little in common with each other in terms of the problems which they encounter or the business relations in which they engage. Curran *et al.* argue that 'smallness' is a multi-dimensional concept which is closely linked with legal independence, type of activity, organisational patterns, and economic activities. Their operational approach is to select enterprises as small on a 'grounded' definition. By this they mean that consultation takes place with owner-managers, industry representatives, trade associations, etc., and a consensus emerges as to what this group envisages as being a small enterprise within its particular sector.

The results shown in Table 2.2 are taken from Curran *et al.* (1991). It shows there are seven sectors, or groups of sectors, which the researchers investigated and which are shown as the rows of the table. It then identifies four criteria which, generally, vary from one sector to another, to identify the characteristics of the smaller firm. These four criteria are shown as the columns of the table and are the number of outlets, the upper employment limit, the lower employment limit, and special conditions. The table shows the maximum number of outlets is specified for only four of the seven major sectors and that, where specified, the number of outlets may be either one, two or three. In the second column the upper limit in terms of employment is specified for most, but not all, sectors; this upper limit may be either ten, twenty or twenty-five workers. The only consistency is that the minimum number of employees is a full-time equivalent of one worker other than the owner. Finally, the fourth column shows any special conditions which are imposed upon the firms in order that they should qualify as small.

Table 2.2 therefore demonstrates that a 'grounded' definition of a small firm has to be multi-dimensional. It illustrates that the 'statistical' definitions which apply a single criterion of, for example, maximum employment number, often cannot encapsulate the subtleties required by researchers investigating managerial and behavioural issues in small firms. On the other hand it would be virtually impossible to collect comprehensive data on smaller firms according to the 'grounded' definitions in Table 2.2, to enable comparisons to be made between countries and over periods of time. In short, 'grounded' definitions are appropriate for researchers to investigate managerial and behavioural aspects of small firms. The 'statistical' definitions constitute practical and operational approximations to the measurement of 'smallness'.

Finally, the table earlier in this book, at the end of the preface, showed the variety of different operational definitions of a small firm which were

Table 2.2 'Grounded' definitions of small firms in the services sector

	No. of outlets	*Employment limit (FTEs)*	*Minimum employment (FTEs)*	*Special conditions*
1. Free house	One	None	1	Not brewery-owned
Wine bar	One	10	1	Premises owned or rented
Restaurant	One	10	1	Premises owned or rented
2. Video hire	Up to three	None	1	–
Leisure services	One	10	1	–
3. Vehicle repair and servicing	Not specified	10	1	Car franchises excluded but other franchises allowed
4. Market research	One	25	1	
Advertising	One	25	1	Must not be in top 50 agencies
Design	One	25	1	Must not be in top 300 agencies
5. Employment	One or two	10	1	–
Secretarial	One or two	10	1	–
Training agencies	One or two	10	1	–
6. Computer services	Not specified	20	1	–
7. Plant, skip, equipment and vehicle hire	Not specified	10	1	–

Source: Curran, Blackburn and Woods (1991)
Note: FTE = full-time equivalent

employed by researchers on the ESRC Small Business Initiative. It demonstrates that, in practice, researchers have to tailor their definitions of a small firm according to the particular groups of small firms which are the focus of their interest. The factors which influence the inclusion of the firms are the nature of the premises in which they operate, or their use of certain types of finance, or their legal status. The same table also makes it clear that a wide variety of different sources of information are used to identify individual small firms – a point to be emphasised in the next section.

In summary, there is no uniformly satisfactory definition of a small firm. Nevertheless, the definitions employed by Bolton in 1971 can be seen to be no longer satisfactory, and have been effectively superseded by the EC definitions of a small and medium enterprise (SME), which has less than 500 employees. The value of the definition is that it uses only one criterion – employment – but can be subdivided into three categories – micro, small and medium-sized enterprises. Researchers, however, are likely to have to continue using their own definitions of small enterprises which are appropriate to their particular 'target' group.

Ultimately, debates about definition turn out to be sterile unless size is shown to be a factor which influences the 'performance' of firms. If it were possible to demonstrate that firms below a certain size clearly had a different performance from those above that band, then the definition has real interest. In practice, however, such clear 'breaks' are rare, and size appears to be a 'continuous' rather than a 'discrete' variable.

HOW MANY SMALL FIRMS ARE THERE IN THE UNITED KINGDOM?

Given the problems identified above in defining a small firm, it is perhaps not surprising that, in the United Kingdom, there is no single definitive statement about the total number of firms in the economy, or the proportion of those which, however defined, could be regarded as small. Part of the reason is a lack of consensus about what constitutes 'small'. Even more serious, however, is the absence of any single comprehensive data base covering all firms in the UK economy. This is not to say that data bases on UK firms do not exist – Daly and McCann (1992) noted that a study by Graham Bannock and Partners (1989), which reviewed existing official statistics, identified forty-four sources of information on firms which were categorised by size. Unfortunately none of these forty-four official sources were able to provide *comprehensive* coverage of all firms in the economy.

Table 2.3 identifies the seven main official data sources on employment and smaller firms in the United Kingdom. It shows that two of the data sources – the Annual Census of Production and the Census of Agriculture – are restricted sectorally, whilst the data on company accounts is limited to businesses choosing that particular legal form. Sectoral restrictions are also apparent, though less significant, for firms registering for VAT, since some sectors are tax-exempt. The bulk of the data sources underestimate the total number of firms, whereas others, such as companies data, are likely to over-estimate the total number of operational businesses since, as will be shown in Chapter 4, a large proportion of firms on the Register have either ceased trading and not been excluded, or never traded (Scott 1982).

The clear picture which emerges from Table 2.3 is that there is no data source which covers all firms in the economy and which is able to specify the proportion of total employment in the various size classes. The problems arise primarily for firms in the construction and service sector, where Curran and Burrows (1988) located almost 90 per cent of all UK small businesses employing between one and twenty-four workers.

To overcome these problems the Bannock and Partners (1989) study was the first to ingeniously attempt to 'sew together' elements from a number of the data sets in order to provide a more comprehensive picture of firms according to their size in the United Kingdom.

The prime building-block for the data set which Bannock and Partners construct is the VAT-based data. This is because, apart from certain sectoral exclusions, it is comprehensive for businesses with a turnover in excess of the minimum registration threshold, it distinguishes between different types of legal form, and it provides data on numbers of firms according to sales turnover. Its prime weakness, as Table 2.3 shows, is that no data are collected on employment.

Bannock and Partners then supplemented the VAT data by including firms which were too small to require VAT registration. The definition which Bannock uses of a firm corresponds closely to that of an 'enterprise' – defined as:

> [an] independent unit of control which, for a large firm, may include a number of establishments (places of work which are effectively reporting units), which may or may not be subsidiary companies (a subsidiary company would be regarded as part of the parent enterprise if 50 per cent or more of its equity capital is controlled by the parent).

For the VAT data, the term 'legal unit' is used, which includes an individual company, a sole trader or a partnership. The assumption made by Bannock is that VAT units are enterprises or firms.

To quantify the number of 'small' firms, one central decision is where to draw the line at the bottom end of the size distribution. Bannock and Partners choose to regard an individual who is self-employed – defined as where that individual's principal source of income is self-employment – as a firm if he or she operates as a sole proprietorship. If the individual indicates that their business is in the form of a partnership, then Bannock and Partners, taking Inland Revenue data on partnerships, assume that each partnership has 2.2 self-employed workers in it.

Table 2.3 Main official data sources on employment and smaller firms

Source	*Frequency*	*Measuring unit*	*Coverage (UK unless otherwise stated)*	*Data held*	*Classification SIC*	*Main exclusion*	*Main weakness*	*HMSO publication*
Census of Employment	Triennial sample (300,000) from 1978 to 1987	Reporting unit	PAYE scheme	Employees by FT/PT and by sex	1980	Self-employed. Firms without employees on PAYE	RU neither establishment nor firm	*DE Gazette*
Annual Census of Production	Annual sample (20,000)	Establishment enterprises	Divisions 1–5	Average employment, output, wages	1980	All 1–20 employees and 50 per cent of 20–40 employee establishments	Estimates of employment in smaller establishments	*Business Monitor PA 1002*
Census of Agriculture	Annual census	Individual holding	All agricultural holdings in UK	Numbers employed by FT/PT and by sex, whether family or hired		Minor holdings with no regular full-time workers, forestry and fisheries		*Agricultural Statistics*
New Earnings Survey	Annual sample (1 per cent)	Individual employee	Employees with NI number, members of PAYE	Industry, sex, hours worked, size of UK organisation (1979, 86 only)	1980	Part-time workers below NI earnings limit	No analysis of numbers of firms by size	*New Earnings Survey*
Labour Force Survey	Annual sample (0.5 per cent)	Adults (16+) in private households	All private households in Great Britain	Employment status, economic activity, size of workplace, industry, region	1980	Institutions	Self-assessment of employment status, size of workplace error-prone	*DE Gazette*
Company Accounts	Annual Sample (3,000)	Companies or groups of companies	Industrial and commercial companies in Great Britain	Employment, turnover financial variables	1980 (approx.)	Non-incorporated businesses	Employment data imputed for many small companies	*Business Monitor MA3*
VAT Register	Continuously updated register	Registered traders	Business above threshold plus voluntary registrations	Turnover, form of organisation	1968 (approx.)	Businesses below threshold (and not voluntarily registered)	Delays in registration and deregistration, turnover data not reliable and no employment information	*Business Monitor PA1003, British Business DE Gazette*

Source: Graham Bannock and Partners (1989)

Table 2.4 Number of businesses by legal status, 1986

Legal status	*VAT-registered firms*	*Unregistered*	*Total no.*	*%*
Sole proprietorships	603	748	1,351	54.7
Partnerships	398	235	633	25.6
Incorporated	459	–	459	18.6
Other	28	–	28	1.1
Total	1,488	983	2,471	100.0

Source: Graham Bannock and Partners (1989)

By making these assumptions, Bannock and Partners are able to estimate the number of businesses according to legal status in 1986. Their data are reproduced as Table 2.4. The first column relates only to those businesses registered for VAT, of which there were 1.488 million in 1986. The Labour Force Survey (LFS) for 1986 was then used to identify the total number of individuals claiming to be self-employed in that year. This figure was 2.744 million.

Given the assumptions noted above – most notably that partnerships on average have 2.2 self-employed workers, that sole proprietorships have one self-employed worker and that incorporated businesses have no self-employed workers – then VAT-registered firms accounted for 1.479 million of the self-employed. The remaining 1.265 million are assumed to be in unregistered businesses, none of which were incorporated. Assuming, then, that there are 2.2 self-employed workers in each partnership, and a ratio of sole proprietorships to partnerships which is the same as for the two smallest size VAT categories, Bannock and Partners calculate there were 2.471 million businesses in the United Kingdom in 1986. Of these, 1.488 million are VAT-registered, the remainder are unregistered. In total, about 55 per cent of UK businesses in 1986 were sole proprietorships, 26 per cent were partnerships and 19 per cent limited companies. By 1989, Daly and McCann (1992) estimated, the total number of businesses had risen to three million, broadly maintaining the same distribution of legal status.

The next task is to examine the sales turnover of these businesses by size grouping. This, in fact, presents few problems, since VAT-registered businesses are required to specify sales turnover and the unregistered are assumed to be exclusively located in the lowest three sales categories.

Far more problematic is the categorisation of UK businesses according to employment size since, as we have observed, such data are not collected as part of the VAT procedures. Bannock's initial approach was to utilise data collected in 1986 on a survey carried out in Paisley, Scotland (Leyshon 1987). The Leyshon study, which used saturation survey techniques for about 1,000 firms, collected data both on sales turnover and on employment, and focused particularly on firms with 200 employees or less.

The use of data of this type, in one small geographical area of the United Kingdom, as the best basis for converting sales turnover to employment for UK small businesses as a whole was unsatisfactory. It constituted a very serious indictment of government policy making in this area. Given the focus which the small business sector has had in public policy, as we shall observe in this volume, it almost beggars belief that UK researchers have had to rely until recently on a small survey in Paisley as a way of calibrating data, in order to provide information on the employment size distribution of firms in the whole UK economy, and so to enable comparisons to be made with other European countries. The fault lies not with Bannock and Partners, who demonstrate considerable ingenuity in their work, but on the successive reductions imposed by government on data collection services.

McCann (1993) has recently reported that Graham Bannock and Partners have made further useful improvements in their estimation procedures. Instead of relying on the Paisley data they are now able to use data from a survey of 3,000 firms to construct a transition matrix relating employment and turnover. Secondly, the analysis of estimating the number of enterprises through an examination of data on sole proprietorships, partnerships and limited companies now takes place on a sectoral basis, rather than for the economy as a whole. Thirdly, sectoral variations in the number of partnerships, sole proprietorships and limited companies are taken into account. Despite these improvements, statistics on numbers of UK enterprises and their distribution by employment size do reflect a substantial element of 'judgement' exercised by the statisticians.[2]

Given these assumptions, Table 2.5 presents the best available UK data on numbers of businesses and their share of employment according to employment size. Employment size categories are shown as the rows of the table, whilst the columns in the first group provide data on the total number of businesses expressed in thousands. The remaining two groups of columns show the share of number of businesses and employment according to firm size. The complexity of the table arises because it also presents this data for the three years 1979, 1986 and 1991.

The key point of Table 2.5 is to demonstrate that virtually two-thirds of UK firms throughout the 1980s had two employees or less. In 1979 it is estimated that 1.1 million firms had two employees or less, out of a total of 1.79 million firms – constituting 61 per cent of all businesses trading at that time. This proportion rose during the 1980s, so that by 1986 64 per cent of all UK businesses had two employees or less. This emphasises the key numerical importance of tiny businesses in the United Kingdom. Taking the EC definition of the micro-business – with ten workers or less – it can be seen that in 1991 this group constituted 92 per cent of all UK businesses.

The contribution of the micro-business to employment, however, is very much less than its contribution to the stock of business. Even so, in 1991

Table 2.5 Numbers of businesses, employment and turnover share by size band in the United Kingdom

Employment size band	*Numbers ('000)*			*Share of total (per cent)* *Businesses*			*Employment*		
	1979 †	*1986* †	*1991* *	*1979* †	*1986* †	*1991* *	*1979* †	*1986* †	*1991* *
1–2	1,099	1,595	1,735	61	64	64	7	11	11
3–5	319	535	565	18	22	21	6	10	10
6–10	179	178	196	10	7	7	7	7	7
11–19	109	84	97	6	3	4	8	6	6
20–49	46	56	65	3	2	2	7	8	9
50–99	16	16	20	1	1	1	5	6	7
100–199	15	9	10	1	–	1	10	7	8
200–499	5	5	6	–	–	–	8	10	9
500–999	2	2	2	–	–	–	8	7	6
1,000+	2	1	1	–	–	–	35	29	27
Total	1,791	2,481	2,697	100	100	100	100	100	100

Sources: *McCann (1993) †Daly and McCann (1992)

micro-businesses provided approximately 28 per cent of UK employment. This was also a significant increase compared with 1979, when micro-businesses provided only 20 per cent of employment.

This section has demonstrated that, whilst small firms in the UK economy are clearly numerous, our ability to specify their precise numbers remains weak. The fact that it is possible to construct a table such as Table 2.5 largely reflects the ingenuity of the researchers and their (sometimes heroic) assumptions, rather than the inherent quality of the underlying information. Even so, it is likely that there was an increase in the total number of firms in the UK economy in the 1980s, with the bulk of these being micro-enterprises with less than ten workers. Such enterprises dominate the UK stock of businesses, although they only provide just over a quarter of employment.

INTERNATIONAL COMPARISONS

The United Kingdom and Europe

Table 2.6 presents data for the twelve European Community countries, showing, not surprisingly, a wide variation in the total number of enterprises. When this is normalised by the number of inhabitants in the country, the EC average is 45 per 1,000 inhabitants, which is virtually the same as that for the United Kingdom. Countries with a higher number of enterprises per 1,000 inhabitants are Greece, Italy, Spain and Portugal, whereas those with a lower average number are the Netherlands, Denmark, France and Ireland. The third column of the table shows the average firm size, which is broadly inversely related to the number of enterprises per 1,000 inhabitants. It shows that the Netherlands, Luxembourg, Germany and Denmark have the highest average firm size. ENSR (1993) assert that these differences remain even when account is taken of differences in sectoral composition between countries. They also distinguish between large and small countries and countries in the central and in the peripheral regions of Europe. Their conclusion is that average firm size is higher in the large countries. Within the group of small countries, firm size is largest in the central countries and smallest in the peripheral European countries. It is also the case that it is the less developed countries of Spain, Greece and Portugal which have the largest number of enterprises per 1,000 inhabitants, so that numbers of small firms looks to be inversely related to level of economic development. This is most marked in comparing the smaller countries of the Netherlands, Belgium and Luxembourg with those of Greece and Portugal. In the former, more wealthy, countries the average number of employees per firm is more than double that of the latter, less wealthy, countries.

Figure 2.1 shows in graphical form the percentage distribution of employment by size class for each Community country in 1988. This is also shown, in part, in the final two columns of Table 2.6. It again emphasises the importance of micro-enterprises in economies such as Greece, Italy, Portugal and Spain.

Figure 2.1 is also interesting in that it enables direct comparisons to be

Table 2.6 EC enterprise by member states, 1988

Country	*Number of enterprises (× 1,000)*	*Number of enterprises per 1,000 inhabitants*	*Average firm size*	*Employment share 0–9 (%)*	*Employment share 0–499 (%)*
Belgium	530	53	5	28	69
Denmark	180	35	9	22	76
France	2,040	36	7	28	67
Germany*	2,160	35	9	17	62
Greece	670	67	3	59	91
Ireland	130	36	6	34	83
Italy	3,170	55	4	48	81
Luxembourg	20	43	9	23	74
Netherlands	420	28	10	28	72
Portugal	640	62	4	36	80
Spain	2,020	52	4	36	83
United Kingdom	2,630	46	8	26	65
Total EC	14,600	45	6	30	70

Source: ENSR (1993)
Note: *Former FRG only

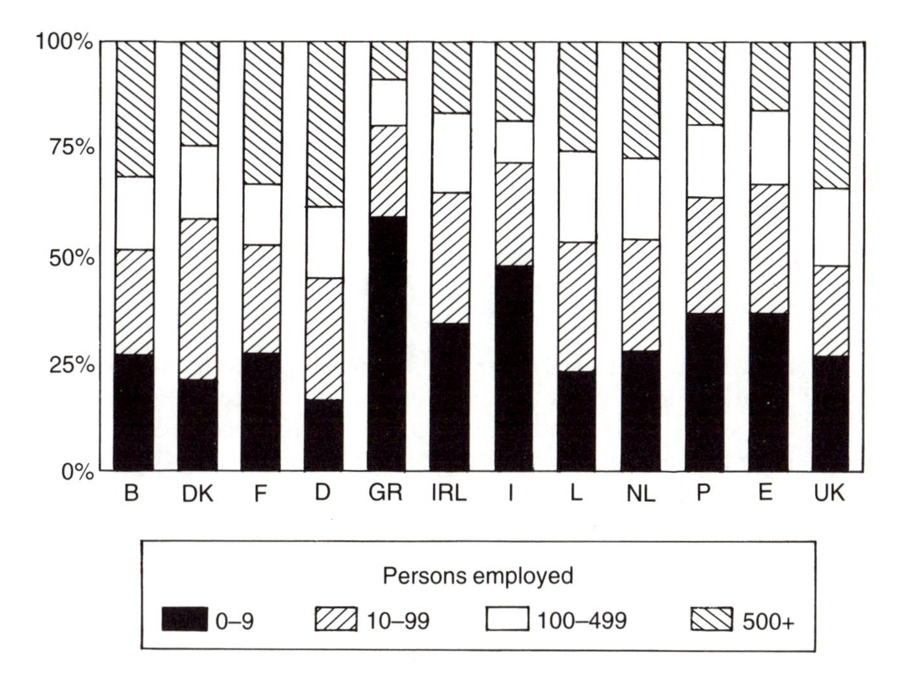

Figure 2.1 Percentage distribution of employment by size class for each country, 1988
Source: ENSR (1993)

made between the United Kingdom and Germany. A popular impression has been generated that the relatively poor performance of the UK economy in recent years is partly due to the relative absence in the United Kingdom of middle-sized businesses. For example Lloyd (1993) says:

> There is good reason to believe, therefore, that the British economy would be stronger if its engine room were occupied by a larger number of mid sized companies, of the kind that have given the German and Japanese economies such strength.

Lloyd bases his assertion on examining the largest 500 enterprises in Europe, finding the United Kingdom to have three times the number which might be expected, taking account of GDP and GDP per head. From this he infers that the UK deficiency is in the middle-sized enterprises.

Figure 2.1 demonstrates, however, that the size structure of enterprises in the United Kingdom and (pre-unification) Germany is in fact closer than between any other two large countries in the European Community. The United Kingdom does not appear to have a smaller proportion of its employment in middle-sized businesses – those with between 100 and 500 workers – than most other EC countries. The only area of notable difference is that, in 1988, the United Kingdom had a higher proportion of its employment than Germany in enterprises with less than ten workers. As we have seen from Table 2.5, the 1980s saw a sharp increase in the proportion of micro-enterprises in the United Kingdom. It seems likely that, if anything, the creation of the 'enterprise culture' in the 1980s served to move the UK economy away from, rather than closer to, the size structure of the German economy.

This point is recognised by Levy (1993) in his review of small and medium-sized manufacturing enterprises in Europe, Japan and the United States. He says:

> There is not a great deal of difference between the German and UK industrial profiles in terms of the distribution of manufacturing employees between small, medium and large firms. This would appear to conflict with the recorded wisdom that Germany has a more powerful Mittelstand of small and medium manufacturing enterprises.

Europe and the United States

A broad comparison of the size structure of enterprise units in Europe and the United States is presented in Table 2.7. All data presented are for 1988, with the data in the upper half of the table showing the per cent of *all-sector* employment in the United States, the United Kingdom and the European Community by enterprise size classes. The lower half of the table shows data for the manufacturing sector alone.

It is the case both for all-sector employment and for manufacturing that a much higher proportion of employment in the United States is in large enterprises than is the case either for the European Community or for the United Kingdom. In the United States, 49 per cent of all employment is in enterprises having more than 500 workers. This is two-thirds higher than the

Table 2.7 Employment by enterprise classes, 1988

	<100 *%*	*100–499* *%*	*500+* *%*	*Total* *%*
All sectors				
USA	37	14	49	100.0
UK	47	18	35	100.0
EC-12	55	16	29	100.0
Manufacturing				
USA	20	15	65	100.0
UK	24	15	61	100.0
EC-12	42	20	38	100.0

Sources: EC data taken from ENSR (1993)
US data from: *The State of Small Business* (1991)

average for the EC. The interesting point is that the difference between the EC and the United States lies not in the relative importance of middle-sized firms – those with between 100 and 500 workers – since these provide about 15 per cent of jobs in both economies. The difference is that the EC has much more employment in small firms – with less than 100 workers – than the United States.

Turning now to the manufacturing data in the lower half of the table, it can be seen that EC and US manufacturing enterprises tend, on average, to be larger than those for the economy as a whole. In the United States, 65 per cent of US manufacturing employment is in enterprises with more than 500 workers, compared with 49 per cent for the respective economies as a whole. Similarly, 38 per cent of EC manufacturing employment is in large enterprises, compared with 29 per cent for the economy as a whole. The finding is even more clearly illustrated for the United Kingdom.

Comparing the size structure of manufacturing enterprises in the United States with those in the EC confirms the findings for the economy as a whole. The United States has two-thirds more of its employment in large enterprises than the EC. In manufacturing, there is a bigger discrepancy between the EC and the United States in the importance of middle-sized enterprises than is the case for the economy as a whole. The table shows that in the EC, 20 per cent of manufacturing employment is in enterprises with between 100 and 500 workers, compared with only 15 per cent in the United States. Nevertheless, the key difference between the United States and the EC is in the importance of small and large enterprises. The former provided 20 per cent of manufacturing jobs in 1988 in the United States, compared with 42 per cent in the EC. Given that small business is popularly viewed as the bed-rock of the US economy, this may be regarded by some as a surprising result.

Finally, a comparison between the United Kingdom and both the EC and United States shows the distribution of manufacturing employment according to enterprise size in the United Kingdom is closer to that of the United States than to the EC. Indeed, the UK and US size distributions could be considered as virtually identical. It is the EC-12 combined that look very different from the United Kingdom/United States distributions.

CHANGES IN THE IMPORTANCE OF SMALL FIRMS OVER TIME

This section documents the striking changes in the size structure of employment units in the United Kingdom which have taken place over the past eighty years. It then compares UK developments with those occurring elsewhere.

Given our earlier reservations about the quality and coverage of UK data on smaller firms in the economy as a whole, it is clearly only appropriate to construct time series data for the manufacturing sector and for the self-employed where more consistent and reliable data exists. The information

Figure 2.2 The importance of small firms in the United Kingdom

presented in Figure 2.2 provides a long-term historical perspective on the relative importance of small firms in the United Kingdom. Two indices of the relative importance of small firms are shown:

- the relative importance of small manufacturing enterprises as a proportion of the total number of enterprises in manufacturing in the United Kingdom;
- the importance of self-employed workers, expressed as a percentage of the UK labour force.

The basic historical patterns of these two indicators are similar, subject to the proviso that both data series suffer major discontinuities – the manufacturing data containing no information between 1935 and 1958, and the self-employment data having no information between 1921 and 1951.

Both data sets show a broadly similar U-shaped pattern over time. Thus small firms in the United Kingdom appeared to have been relatively more important in the early and late years of this century, and to have had their lowest levels of importance during the 1960s.

Despite the major discontinuity in the enterprise manufacturing data set between 1935 and 1958, establishment-based analysis for 1948, 1951 and 1954 shown in Stanworth and Gray (1991) suggests that small establishments constituted a declining proportion of total establishments in each of those years. Since, particularly at the small scale, there is a broad similarity of patterns for enterprises and establishments, there is reason to believe that, had enterprise data been available, it would have exhibited the downward pattern shown in the dotted line in Figure 2.2.

The 'low point' of importance of small firms appears to have been the decade of the 1960s. At that time small manufacturing enterprises with less than 200 workers constituted about 19 per cent of all manufacturing enterprises in the United Kingdom. This proportion was about half (38.4 per cent) that which had existed in the 1935 survey, and considerably less than the 31.8 per cent which small enterprises constituted in 1990.

It is perhaps ironic that the Bolton Committee should have been established in the late 1960s to investigate the role which small firms played in the economy. On the basis of trends which it observed, the Bolton Committee concluded that: 'The small firm sector is in a state of long-term decline, both in size and in its share of economic activity' (p. 342).

The Committee explained:

> The most important question which faced us, therefore, is whether the economic climate has changed to such an extent that small firms can no longer survive and flourish in sufficient numbers as the seedbed for the industry of the future, bearing in mind that only a tiny and unidentifiable proportion of the small firm population will play this vital role.

Its answer to its own question was that:

> The small firm sector is at present, and will remain for the foreseeable future, vigorous enough to fulfil the 'seedbed' function, given a fair crack of the whip and is not therefore in need of special support. This is a finely balanced judgement which should be kept under constant review by government.
>
> (p. 344)

To a considerable degree this faith which the Bolton Committee expressed in the survival of the small enterprise sector has been seen to pay off. Although faced with clear evidence that the sector had been in decline for at least thirty years, the period following the Bolton Committee report saw a relative resurgence of small firms in Britain.

It is important to note from Figure 2.2 that this resurgence, insofar as we are able to measure it, has not been exclusively restricted to the manufacturing sector. The figure shows that numbers of self-employed individuals, who operate primarily in the non-manufacturing sectors, also showed a decline in their importance in the UK labour force from 1911 until 1965. At that time such individuals constituted only 6.5 per cent of the UK labour force. As Figure 2.2 shows, this proportion began to grow from that point onwards, but with the most striking growth being in the decade of the 1980s. By 1990 11.7 per cent of the UK labour force was self-employed, very nearly double the level of twenty-five years earlier. It was also close to the level found in 1911, and higher than that in 1921.[3]

In spite of the long-term historic plausibility of these developments, interpretation of the data on a year-to-year basis requires some caution. For example, Dunne and Hughes (1989) point out that the register of firms included in the Census of Production, which is the basis for the manufacturing time series, is subject to periodic updates. In particular, the compilation of a new register of businesses in 1984 led to an increase in the number of establishments from 107,000 to 138,000. Virtually all of these new establishments had less than twenty employees. The effect of this, of course, was to significantly increase the apparent relative importance of smaller firms, but with this merely being reflective of differences in sample construction, rather than a real change in the economy between 1983 and 1984. In practice, of course, the sample construction should reflect the population of enterprises, so it is appropriate periodically to adjust the sampling frame to reflect changes in the characteristics of the population; the problem is that this tends to lead to periodic discontinuities in the data.

Despite these statistical reservations, there can be little doubt that there has been a shift in the relative importance of small firms in the UK economy, probably since the middle of the 1960s.

It is then interesting to see whether this pattern of increased importance of small firms observed in recent decades in the United Kingdom also appears to have occurred in other developed countries. By this stage it should not come as a surprise to the reader to find that making such an assessment is very difficult, because of the problems of non-comparability of data. Each country has its own way of collecting and classifying data on enterprises, and the statistics are subject to many of the discontinuities and inconsistencies observed in the United Kingdom. It is also the case that data reliability, and comparability with current conditions, declines with the age of the data set.

A full understanding of the basis of the international comparisons of data in this area can only be obtained by being aware of these differences in data collection and analysis. The most comprehensive review of this issue is undertaken by Sengenberger, Loveman and Piore (1990). These editors review trends in small enterprises in France, Germany, Italy, Japan, the United Kingdom and the United States. They conclude:

> The most important empirical results to emerge from the country reports is that there has been a recent increase in the share of total employment in small enterprises and establishments which are defined as those with fewer than 100 employees. In general, the increase has been at the expense of large enterprises and establishments. While the magnitude of the increase varies considerably from country to country and across sectors, its significance rests primarily on the fact that it signifies the reversal of a

substantial downward trend in the employment shares of small units that had prevailed for many decades.

However, the evidence presented by Sengenberger *et al.* to support the above statements, certainly once the United Kingdom is excluded, is not wholly convincing. Table 2.8 shows data for six countries on employment shares by different sizes of enterprise for the whole economy. A variety of different years are identified, reflecting the years for which national census information is available. The most recent year for any country is 1985.

Taking the Japanese data first, the *Basic Survey of Employment Structure* data from 1959 to 1982 suggest some minor year-to-year fluctuations, but no clear and continuous pattern for small firms. For small and medium-sized enterprises, however, the *Basic Survey* data suggest a fairly continuous increase from 1959 until 1982. Turning now to the *Annual Report of the Labour Force Survey*, the data on small firms confirm the *Basic Survey* data by not suggesting any continuous pattern. If anything, the data point to a declining importance of small firms during the 1977–85 period. This pattern also appears to characterise Japanese data for small and medium enterprises.

The data for the United States, shown in the second row of the table, show no obvious pattern over time, apart from a sharp increase in the importance of both small and medium enterprises in the 1977–82 period. Prior to then, the pattern is extremely mixed.

The French data, for the three years shown, indicate that small firms have continuously increased their share in relative importance over the fourteen-year period. The table does not, however, provide any data to show whether in the years prior to 1971 small firms exhibited a declining importance and that the current period constitutes a reversal of prior trends.

The fourth row refers to Germany, but here unfortunately there are no data beyond 1970 for the economy as a whole and this therefore makes it difficult to make comparisons with other countries. The data shown, however, do suggest that during the 1907–70 period, small firms provided a decreasing share of employment in the economy as a whole.

The data for Italy suggest that between 1971 and 1981 there was a sharp increase in the relative importance of small firms, rising from providing 61.6 per cent of employment in 1971 to 69.3 per cent in 1981. A similar sharp increase occured in small and medium-sized enterprises. In the 1951–71 period, however, there appears to have been very little change in the importance of small firms.

Finally, the data on small firms in Switzerland provide no support for the Sengenberger *et al.* hypothesis. Small firms appear to have significantly increased their importance as a source of employment during the 1930s, but from 1965 to 1985 there was virtually no change in their role in the Swiss economy.

All in all, whilst there are indications in some countries of small firms

Table 2.8 Employment shares by enterprise size: time series for the total economy

Japan	*1959*	*1962*	*1965*	*1968*	*1971*	*1974*	*1977*	*1979*	*1982*	*1985*
Small[a]	46.7	43.8	43.8	45.0	45.5	46.5	48.3	49.3	48.8	
Small[b]					53.3	54.4	56.9	57.3	56.6	55.7
Small and medium[a e]	54.6	53.3	53.7	55.0	55.9	57.0	58.9	60.2	60.0	
Small and medium[b]					70.0	70.4	72.7	73.6	73.1	73.0

United States	*1958*	*1963*	*1967*	*1972*	*1977*	*1982*
Small	41.3	39.9	39.9	41.3	40.1	45.7
Small and medium	55.1	52.9	53.2	53.5	52.5	58.7

France	*1971*	*1979*	*1985*
Small	39.0	43.4	46.2
Small and medium	57.4	60.7	64.5

Germany	*1907*	*1925*	*1961*	*1970*
Small[c]	57.8	47.6	40.4	37.9
Small[d]	72.9	61.5	54.9	52.3
Small and medium[d]	72.9	61.5	54.9	52.3
Small and medium[f]	86.2	76.0	70.4	68.8

Italy	*1951*	*1961*	*1971*	*1981*
Small	60.2	63.5	61.6	69.3
Small and medium	73.0	77.1	74.4	81.5

Switzerland	*1929*	*1939*	*1955*	*1965*	*1975*	*1985*
Small[g]	54.2	60.2	52.5	45.4	46.1	46.3
Small and medium	81.2	83.4	82.0	78.9	77.4	73.4

Source: Sengenberger, Loveman and Piore (1990)

Notes: Small: fewer than 100 employees.
Small and medium: fewer than 500 employees.
[a] *Basic Survey of Employment Structure.*
[b] *Annual Report of the Labour Force Survey.*
[c] 1–49 employees.
[d] 1–199 employees.
[e] 0–299 employees.
[f] 1–999 employees.
[g] 1–50 employees, 1929–39; 1–49 employees, 1955–85.

increasing their relative importance during the 1970s and 1980s, the pattern is by no means uniform. In part, this is because the data are incomplete for several countries for either the earlier or the later years. Yet even where data are available, the hypothesis is not supported in either Japan or Switzerland. The support for the hypothesis seems based on a single data point (1981) for Italy and another (1982) for the United States. Data limitations for Germany and France prevent any clear conclusions being drawn, so that at best, in our view, the evidence presented in Table 2.8 suggests the Sengenberger hypothesis is unproven.

A similarly fuzzy pattern emerges in discussing data on enterprise size for the manufacturing sector only. This is shown in Table 2.9, which again takes the countries of Japan, the United States, France, Germany, Switzerland and Italy. The Japanese data on small manufacturing enterprises do not suggest any resurgence during the 1975–83 period. Furthermore, insofar as a comparison can be made, it appears that small enterprises in Japan were relatively more important during the 1949–55 period than at any time either previously or subsequently. This is of course the opposite to the pattern observed in the United Kingdom and that proposed by Sengenberger *et al.*

The US data for manufacturing seems to follow fairly closely that for the all sector data, suggesting that the 1967–77 period was one in which small firms were of least significance in the manufacturing sector, but with evidence of some increase between 1977 and 1982. However, no US data beyond 1982 are produced by Sengenberger *et al.*

The French data consist of only two years – 1971 and 1979 – and suggest a slight increase in importance in these two years of the small firm and small and medium-sized firms.

The German data suggest there has been some relative increase in the importance of the smaller firm and small and medium-sized firms between 1970 and 1984.

The Swiss data do not support the Sengenberger *et al.* hypothesis, but support is provided for it from Italy; again, however, this is based exclusively upon the major change observed between 1971 and 1981.

Overall, the pattern which Sengenberger *et al.* identify is only clearly illustrated in the data for the United Kingdom. Other countries, such as Italy and France, do exhibit evidence of some increase in the relative importance of small firms from the 1970s onwards, but the absence of data on a continuous basis tends to leave these conclusions open.

It will be recalled from Figure 2.1 that, in the examination of trends for the United Kingdom, two measures of the relative importance of small firms were presented. The first was the relative importance of small enterprises in manufacturing, and the second was the proportion of the total UK labour force which was self-employed. Acs, Audretsch and Evans (1991) have collected data on self-employment in twenty-three OECD countries. They plot the change in self-employment, expressed as a proportion of the labour force,

Table 2.9 Employment shares by enterprise size: time series for manufacturing

	1919	*1935*	*1949*	*1955*	*1972*[c]	*1975*[c]	*1979*[c]	*1980*[c]	*1982*[c]	*1983*[c]
Japan										
Small	45.0[a]	48.0[a]	51.0[a]	57.0[a]	43.0	45.0	49.0	49.0	47.0	47.0
Small and medium	78 .0[b]	83.0[b]	77.0[b]	85.0[b]	63.0	65.0	68.0	68.0	67.0	67.0
	1958	*1963*	*1967*	*1972*	*1977*	*1982*				
United States										
Small	20.6	19.1	16.3	16.2	16.2	17.6				
Small and medium	37.1	34.5	30.4	28.9	29.0	30.3				
	1971	*1979*								
France										
Small	26.4	28.6								
Small and medium	49.5	50.6								
	1963	*1970*	*1976*	*1977*	*1980*	*1983*	*1984*			
Germany[d]										
Small	14.0	12.5	13.1	15.9	15.4	16.0	16.2			
Small and medium	39.6	37.3	38.0	40.4	39.9	40.8	41.1			
	1965	*1985*								
Switzerland										
Small[e]	34.8	29.7								
Small and medium	71.0	69.4								
	1951	*1961*	*1971*	*1981*						
Italy[f]										
Small	50.5	53.2	50.5	55.3						
Small and medium	67.4	72.0	69.2	73.9						

Notes: [a]5–99 employees.
[b]5–999 employees.
[c]From OECD (1985), Chart 13.
[d]63–76 data are not comparable with 77–83 data due to inclusion of the *handwerk* sector only in the latter period. Also data covers enterprises with 20+ employees.
[e]1–49 employees.
[f]Excludes NACE divisions 21 and 23.

over the period 1965–87. Their graph is reproduced as Figure 2.3. This shows a clear U-shaped pattern, with self-employment rates declining from 1965 until 1977, but then rising fairly steadily for the following decade. This is precisely the type of pattern which Sengenberger *et al.* argue is taking place.

This apparently neat pattern, however, serves to mask some very different trends amongst the countries concerned. Table 2.10 shows four major types

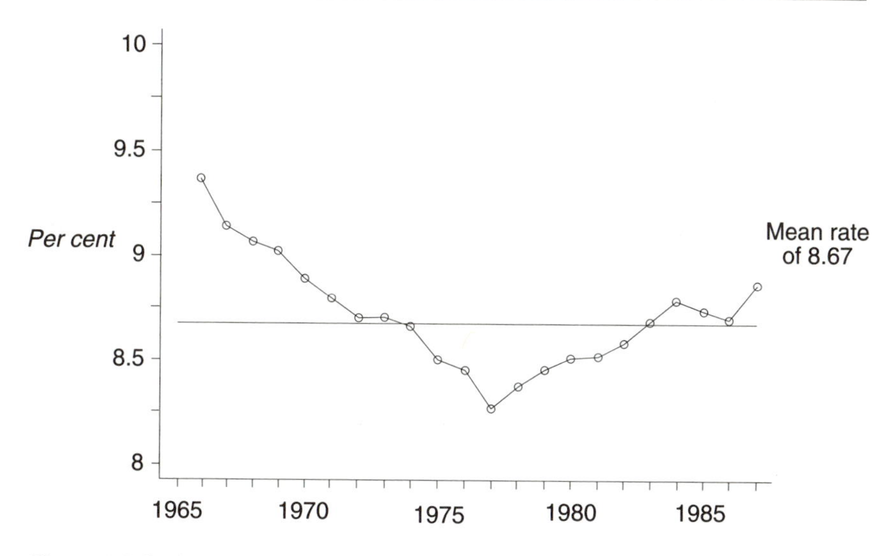

Figure 2.3 Self-employment rate in OECD countries

Table 2.10 Time series pattern of self-employment in OECD countries

U-shaped pattern	*Continual decrease*
Belgium	Austria
Canada	Denmark
Finland	France
Germany	Greece
Iceland	Luxembourg
Italy	Norway
New Zealand	
Portugal	
Spain	
Sweden	
Turkey	
USA	
Continual increase	*n-shaped pattern*
Australia	Japan
Ireland	Netherlands
UK	

Source: Acs, Audretsch and Evans (1991)

of pattern in self-employment over these years amongst OECD countries. Twelve countries follow the dominant pattern of a decline in self-employment in the early years and an increase in self-employment in later years. Virtually as many countries, however, have a different pattern; six countries exhibit a continuous decrease over time, three countries exhibit a continual increase – one of these countries being the United Kingdom – and two countries – Japan and the Netherlands exhibit an n-shaped pattern – the opposite to that observed for the bulk of the countries. Hence the country which is the best illustration of the Sengenberger *et al.* hypothesis for the manufacturing sector – the United Kingdom – actually exhibits a basically different pattern in terms of self-employment from that of the bulk of OECD countries, showing a fairly continuous rise in self-employment over twenty-two years.

Overall, this brief review of historical data suggests there is a wide variety of patterns between the countries.

- It is certainly *not* the case that all countries exhibit the same patterns as the United Kingdom – of a decreasing importance of small firms until the mid-1960s, followed by an increase in the importance of small firms from the 1970s onwards.
- There is some evidence that the change in relative importance of small firms which occurred in the United Kingdom in the 1960s predates those changes observed in other countries during later periods. For example, the relative increase in importance of small firms does seem to occur rather later in the United States and in Italy than in the United Kingdom.
- The increased importance of self-employment from about 1975 onwards in the OECD in general is also significantly later than that observed in the United Kingdom.
- It would be extremely unwise, on the basis of currently available data, to infer that all countries are exhibiting a resurgence of small and medium enterprises. The fact that such a pattern is clearly observable in the United Kingdom from the late 1960s onwards does not necessarily mean that the same pattern is to be repeated somewhat later in other countries.

WHY THESE CHANGES?

The above sections demonstrated that the 1980s saw an increase, in most developed countries, in the proportion of the workforce classified as self-employed. There is rather more ambiguity about whether, for developed countries as a whole, smaller enterprises provided an increasing share of total employment. In the United Kingdom it is the case that small firms became relatively more important, but for other countries the evidence is mixed.

This section will outline some reasons which may account for the rise in relative importance of small firms. Given that this rise is most apparent in the United Kingdom, many of the explanations will be UK-based. However, where there are instances of explanations being particularly relevant to other developed countries, these will be included as appropriate.

To assist this explanation, Table 2.11 provides an overview of the reasons. For descriptive purposes it distinguishes between explanations which are

Table 2.11 Reasons given for the re-emergence of small-scale enterprise

Supply	*Demand*
Technological changes • New products • New industries	*Structural changes* • Demand for services
Fragmentation/cost advantages • Subcontracting • Japanisation • Buy-outs	*Uncertainty of demand*
Labour force/unemployment • Demography • Unemployment • Education	*Macroeconomic conditions* • Unemployment
Government • Privatisation/deregulation • Welfare/benefits/taxes • Enterprise culture • Attitudes to risk	*Economic development* • Services • Agriculture • 'Niches' • Flexible specialisation
Prices • Energy prices	

influenced by supply-side factors and those which are influenced by demand-side factors. Nevertheless, whilst the table categorises explanations in this way, it should not be assumed that the explanations are mutually exclusive. The value of the table is in its presentation of a categorisation which then provides a structure to the subsequent discussion. This is not to suggest either that only a simple explanation or a single type of explanation is appropriate. The table also illustrates that the majority of the explanations relate to supply-side, rather than demand-side factors.

Turning now to the first supply-side element in Table 2.11, a number of authors have emphasised the importance of technological change as a key factor explaining the re-emergence of small-scale enterprises. Taking the longer-term view, it is argued that advanced economies are now entering the fifth Kondratieff cycle. In these 'long cycles', which average approximately fifty years, the early years are characterised by new technologies being developed and diffused by smaller enterprises. It is during that time that small firms become relatively more important in the economy because of their rapid rates of growth associated with the development of the new technology. Only once the cycle becomes more mature do larger enterprises begin to assert their 'control' over the economy. At this time some of the new firms established in the early stage of the cycle have become large, and existing large firms will have acquired many of the small firms having access to the new technology.

During this phase of the cycle, therefore, large firms become relatively more important.

The last comparable early stage of a cycle was during the late 1920s and early 1930s, a period which saw a huge upsurge in what are now referred to as consumer durables, such as electrical goods, motor cars, chemical and pharmaceutical products. It is argued today that, whilst the fourth Kondratieff cycle was based upon mass production and electricity, the fifth cycle is based upon information. What is being seen today is the upsurge in new and small firms whose presence is based upon the 'new' commodity of information. Explanations of this type, of course, suggest that the shift towards small-scale enterprises is merely temporary until larger enterprises once again reassert their control (Freeman 1983).

One of the most striking illustrations of this trend is the major growth in numbers of firms in the business and information services sector. This development is discussed by Wood, Bryson and Keeble (1993) and Keeble, Bryson and Wood (1992a,b). They show that between 1985 and 1989 the computer services sector exhibited the largest growth in the total stock of firms of any VAT four-digit trade code. They also show that computer services had the highest rate of growth in total stock of firms, with the exception of the medical and health services sector, where the number of firms was tiny in 1985.

The developments shown in Table 2.11 may also be considered as demand-led. In particular, the huge development of the business service sector observed by Keeble *et al.* may be considered as part of a fundamental change in the role of services in the economy. Not only are existing enterprises increasing their demand for externally provided business services, but consumers are also shifting their preference towards services, at least partly at the expense of manufactured goods. Thus it is argued that, since services are more likely to be provided by smaller-scale enterprises, the modern economy is more likely to be characterised by smaller-scale enterprises than was the case in the past. But, as Campbell and Daly (1992) point out, this can only constitute a partial explanation for the trends in the UK economy in Figure 2.2. This is because in the United Kingdom the changing patterns of self-employment and the size structure of manufacturing enterprises broadly parallel one another, even though the vast bulk of self-employed workers are in the services sector rather than the manufacturing sector. In the United Kingdom, therefore, it seems unlikely that a shift in demand from manufactured goods to services has been the sole influence in the changing size structure of enterprises. Nevertheless the increasing importance of the service sector in advanced economies is clearly one influence upon the relative increase in the importance of small firms.

Under the broad heading of technological change, Table 2.11 also makes reference to the possible role which new industries play in influencing the size structure of enterprises. We have already observed above that the early stages of the Kondratieff cycle are characterised by new industries being created, often by new independent firms. This clearly happened in the United Kingdom in the 1980s: for example the medical laser industry came into being during that period, and classically was established and developed by wholly new firms (Shearman and Burrell 1988). Yet new industries alone cannot be an adequate explanation of changing overall size structure, since the number of wholly new industries is very small and their overall impact on the size structure of enterprises in the economy is tiny.

The second major group of supply-side explanations for the re-emergence of small-scale enterprises relate to questions of cost advantages and fragmentation. The theoretical framework for this type of analysis was provided initially by Coase (1937) and more recently developed by Williamson (1985). At their most simplistic, the Williamson-Coase arguments are that activities will be undertaken within the firm when the perceived costs of these are lower than obtaining the same input from the external market-place. The limits to vertical integration and scale economies are therefore determined by these two relative prices (Lyons 1992).

Lyons argues that the Williamson-Coase hypotheses imply that inputs which require a specific production technology are more likely to be produced 'in house', whereas those exhibiting substantial scale/scope economies are more likely to be purchased in the market-place. This is because the more specific the asset, the more likely it is that the purchasing firm may be exploited by its subcontractor. Conversely, the purchasing firm is more likely to purchase externally where there are scale economies, since it can share in these. In his empirical work Lyons finds support for both these hypotheses. Over time, therefore, shifts in asset specificity or scale economies, by influencing the make-or-buy decision, could influence the size distribution of units in the economy.

Lyons (1991a,b), in a review of the development of UK subcontracting, finds, using the Census of Production, that there was little evidence of increase between 1974 and 1981. Subcontracting, however, had grown by 25 per cent by 1989. This is broadly in line with his own survey data which suggests that, whilst the growth is uneven, significantly more firms have increased than decreased their subcontracting.

Writing from a more overtly political perspective, Shutt and Whittington (1986) observe what they see as the fragmentation strategies of large firms. They distinguish three types of fragmentation:

i Decentralisation of production in which large plants are broken up but retained under the same ownership, by hiving off into smaller plants or by creating new subsidiary companies.
ii A detachment where large firms cease directly to own units but retain revenue links with them i.e., licensing or franchising.

iii Disintegration of production and innovation: large firms cease to own units of production or innovation but retain control through market power (especially in the case of vertical integration), or, latently, through the power to re-purchase the units.

Shutt and Whittington present interesting evidence to support their categorisations. In some senses their observation of developments reflect both supply and demand-side influences. The central influence seems to be that of uncertainty in the market-place as identified in item 2 of the demand-side of Table 2.11. Stemming from that uncertainty, Shutt and Whittington argue that, to retain control over the labour process, business owners respond in the three ways noted above. Whilst this may be an effective explanation for changes in the early years of the 1980s, it has to be incomplete, since the trend towards small-scale units continued throughout much of the 1980s – the latter half of which decade was one of considerable prosperity.

A simpler explanation of developments in the United Kingdom is that the relative increase in the importance of small-scale enterprises in the manufacturing sector in fact reflects the poor performance of large firms, rather than the good performance of the small. This argument is presented in Storey and Johnson (1987). They show that the relative importance of small firms in the United Kingdom as a source of manufacturing employment stems primarily from the declining importance of large firms. During the 1971–82 period, manufacturing employment in firms with under 100 employees remained broadly constant, but contracted sharply for enterprises with 500 or more employees. Thus the relative increase in the importance of small firms reflects the relatively poor performance of large firms in terms of job-shedding.

Evidence to support this is provided by Johnson (1989), who shows that a significant influence on employment 'creation' in the small establishment sector in manufacturing, defined as establishments with less than 200 employees, has arisen as a result of the contraction of establishments which formerly had more than 200 employees. Taking the 1975–83 period, Johnson shows that the share of employment in small enterprises rose from 28.9 per cent to 36.2 per cent of manufacturing employment. Whilst the key influences on employment change are the birth and death of establishments, he shows that in the 1979–83 period in particular, there were more than 150,000 jobs in 1983 in small establishments which in 1979 had been large establishments. This compares with less than 50,000 jobs which were in establishments classified as small in 1979 but which had grown to be large by 1983. The Johnson data suggest that at least some of the 'job creation' in small firms was attributable to the decline of large firms in the UK economy. For most purposes, 'establishment' may be treated as the equivalent of 'firm'. This decline may reflect poor productivity levels of such enterprises. However, the validity even of this statement is open to question, since the 1980s saw growth of manufacturing productivity in the United Kingdom – primarily in large firms – being higher than in all of its formal competitors.[4]

The third group of explanations shown in Table 2.11 relate to labour force and labour market-based explanations. Both Meager (1992b) and Campbell and Daly (1992) demonstrate that the self-employed have a number of characteristics which distinguish them from employees. Meager (1992b), in an analysis of the self-employed in Germany and the United Kingdom, points to a number of these. For example, he shows that whilst men are more than twice as likely as women to be self-employed, the key feature of the 1980s was a particularly fast growth in female self-employment. He also shows the self-employed are significantly more likely to be older than the employed population. In the United Kingdom, although there is no evidence that the self-employed male is more likely to have high educational qualifications, this is not the case for females, for whom those with degrees or equivalent are virtually twice as likely as those without qualifications to be self-employed.

Demographic changes in society and the labour force mean that females are becoming a higher proportion of the labour force, that the labour force itself is getting older, divorce and separation are becoming more common, and educational attainments are rising. The impact upon aggregate self-employment levels of these demographic changes is mixed. For example, since females are less likely to be self-employed than males, a changing gender composition of the workforce is likely to lead to lower aggregate rates of self-employment. On the other hand, the ageing of the workforce is, on balance, likely to lead to higher self-employment. The impact of divorce/separation upon self-employment patterns has yet to emerge clearly from research.

Whilst Table 2.11 discusses labour market demographic influences, it also raises the question of the role of unemployment in influencing the increased importance of small firms. Unemployment appears as both a demand-side and supply-side influence and, *a priori*, it is possible to present arguments which suggest that increases in unemployment will be associated with either lower or higher rates of new firm formation, self-employment and relative importance of small firms. This matter will be discussed in more detail in Chapter 3.

Unemployment reduces the opportunity cost of entering self-employment, in the sense of an individual being more prepared to accept the uncertainty of self-employment when there is a low likelihood of obtaining paid employment. On the other hand, unemployment may also be associated with low levels of aggregate demand in the economy. In these circumstances the business which the entrepreneur establishes is perhaps less likely to be successful or to survive than in conditions of more buoyant demand. This may deter, rather than encourage, individuals to start a business. It is not possible, *a priori*, to determine which of these two influences will be the greater.

A fourth set of factors influencing the supply of entrepreneurs relate to the role played by government. Table 2.11 examines four dimensions of this role.

The first is the growth of privatisation and deregulation which has occurred in many developed economies, particularly in the United Kingdom. Here, services previously provided by government, such as gas, water, electricity, telecommunications, etc., have been placed in the private sector. Furthermore, a number of services originally undertaken by the public sector – particularly by local authorities – such as refuse collection and cleaning, are now supplied by private sector companies. Competition has been encouraged by the removal of regulations and, as we discuss in Chapter 8, the government has been very active in attempting to eliminate the 'red tape' associated with operating a small business. Privatisation and 'contracting out' are likely to have led to some increase in the total number of businesses in the economy. Research on this by Abbott (1993) however, suggests that the impact on small firms of these changes has been relatively modest, since state organisations appear to prefer to deal with a single large contractor than a myriad of small organisations.

A second group of factors influenced by government are those relating to the welfare and taxation system. As Meager (1992b) observes, much of the pressure to reduce rates of personal taxation in the United Kingdom came from government's belief that individuals were likely to work harder if they worked for themselves and were able to retain a higher proportion of their income after taxation. Blau (1987), however, suggests that individuals are more likely to choose self-employment at a time of high rates of personal taxation, on the grounds that only this employment status will yield them the opportunity for minimising their tax bill through tax avoidance (and possibly evasion). This is particularly true for high income earners, who might be the most likely to establish successful businesses. Furthermore, as we shall show later in Chapter 8, Rees and Shah (1993) find that amongst the UK self-employed there is no evidence that these individuals worked longer hours, once account is taken of demographic differences, during regimes of low taxation. Again, if anything, the reverse is the case.

Meager's (1992b) evidence suggests that the nature of the state welfare system can influence self-employment. He shows, in a study of self-employment trends between 1973 and 1989 in the United Kingdom, Germany, France and Denmark, that only in the latter country was there no rise in self-employment after 1979. He links this to Denmark having the highest payment levels to individuals who are unemployed, so raising the 'reservation income' level which they require from self-employment.

A third component, certainly of the UK government strategy, has been the attempt to create an 'enterprise culture' (Burrows 1991, Storey and Strange 1992, Ritchie 1990). A key component of this has been to encourage groups of individuals to seek self-employment as a way of 'creating their own job'. The main group upon whom this has focused has been the unemployed, and schemes such as the Enterprise Allowance in the United Kingdom and *Überbrückunsgeld* in Germany have been introduced. Other illustrations of this type of initiative in the United Kingdom have been schemes to encourage enterprise in schools, and the Graduate Employment Programme (GEP), which is designed to make graduates more aware of self-employment as a career. All these schemes are intended to provide positive encouragement to individuals to at least consider the option of becoming self-employed.

Finally, governments may act in a more subtle way to encourage self-employment. For example they may act to change what they consider to be the stigma of business failure, so that owners of failed businesses are not so stigmatised by the experience that this stops them ever again becoming self-employed or a business owner. Changes in the Companies Act legislation in the United Kingdom during the 1980s reflect such changes in attitude.

The fourth element on the demand side of Table 2.11 includes four dimensions under the category of economic development. The first, which has already been alluded to above, concerns the movement over a long period of time away from agriculture – where self-employment rates are extremely high, through manufacturing – where self-employment rates are relatively low, to services – where self-employment rates are higher at least than those in manufacturing. In this sense the economic development explanation is highly compatible with the data shown for the United Kingdom in Figure 2.2. Loufti (1992) shows this very clearly. Table 2.12, taken from her work, shows that low-income economies have more than five times the proportion of self-employed in the labour force than upper high-income economies. The second column of the table shows that these differences in self-employment

Table 2.12 Proportion of the self-employed in the global labour force by per capita income categories (circa 1987; per cent)

	Self-employed in the labour force	*Self-employed in agricultural employment*	*Self-employed in non-agricultural employment*
Low-income economies (GDP/capita under $500)	48	58	37
Lower middle-income economies (GDP/capita $500–$2,000)	29	44	25
Upper middle-income economies (GDP/capita $2,000–$6,000)	23	47	18
Lower high-income economies (GDP/capita $6,000–$12,000)	14	55	13
Upper high-income economies (GDP/capita over $12,000)	9	43	6

Source: Loufti (1992)

in the agricultural sector alone do not vary as sharply as might be expected. In the lowest income economies, 58 per cent of employment in agriculture is in the form of self-employment, compared with 43 per cent in the upper high-income economies, hence the major differences in self-employment between countries occur in the non-agricultural sector, where there is a greater than six-fold discrepancy between the highest and the lowest. Nevertheless, it is the case, as Meager (1992b) shows, that self-employment rates, both for males and females, are significantly higher in the service sector than in manufacturing. In the United Kingdom, however, the highest rates of self-employment are found in agriculture and in construction.

The third element in the economic development category refers to 'niches'. In many senses this idea is very persuasive, because it was one of only two 'favourable' factors in the economy identified by the Bolton Committee in 1971 which was operating in favour of small firms at that time. Bolton argued that as societies become richer, individuals spend a higher proportion of their income on specialised or 'one-off' services or products, and conversely a lower proportion of their income upon 'standardised' products. Bolton also argued that 'one-off' products and services were, because of the absence of scale economies in their provision, more likely to be provided by small firms. In essence, Bolton argued that the structure of demand changed as income levels rose, and that this change was to the advantage of small firms.

This argument is at the heart of the 'flexible specialisation' hypothesis, most coherently expressed by Piore and Sabel (1984). Flexible specialisation, however, contains both demand and supply-side elements.

Other than the United Kingdom, the country where there has been the most rapid shift in the relative importance of small firms is Italy, the North East Central region of which is seen by Piore and Sabel as the epitome of flexible specialisation. This area comprises a myriad of small independent enterprises producing high-quality specialised products, particularly in the textiles, ceramics and footwear industries. For much of the 1980s Italy was the only OECD country to increase its world market share of exports in textiles. This was because of the high quality and design of Italian textiles. Piore and Sabel believed they had identified a new industrial form, in which small independent enterprises which specialised in a particular product combined with one another to become highly competitive. They saw this form of organisation as the successor to 'Fordism' in which large enterprises, using a Taylorist philosophy, reaped scale economies for production of standardised products. By contrast, flexible specialisation provided an 'ideal' combination of small independent firms combining flexibly whilst specialising in particular products or services.

This development excited researchers for a number of years but, despite much searching, there appear to be very few instances, outside North East Central Italy, where flexible specialisation could be seen to have made a major impact. Indeed, the Italians themselves have very great difficulty in learning the lessons of flexible specialisation and applying them to other regions of Italy – most notably the *Mezzagiorno* or the South. As the 1980s progressed, it also became clear that the North East Central area of Italy had begun to suffer from the same economic problems which affected textile-producing areas elsewhere in Europe (Forlai 1991). Interest in the concept of flexible specialisation therefore declined.

Table 2.11 has attempted to summarise some of the reasons given by researchers for the recent emergence of small-scale enterprise. The difficulty with reaching a conclusion as to which of these influences is the most important is that the evidence presented tends to be somewhat piecemeal. In some cases the evidence in support of particular hypotheses looks flawed, and in these cases the hypotheses can be easily dismissed, More frequently, however, where evidence is cited it tends to be from a single country or for a particular time period, and in almost no instances is there an attempt to hold other influences constant. It is therefore difficult, from the qualitative evidence presented so far, to reach a judgement as to the key factors which have led to the fairly clear rise in self-employment observed for many (but not all) OECD countries, or for the relative increase in importance of small scale manufacturing enterprises in the United Kingdom. This requires genuinely comparative studies over periods of time, over several countries, and it is to the results of these studies that we now turn. The problem is that the analysis is restricted to examining changes in the proportion of workers classified as self-employed. Data limitations prohibit a comparable analysis of changes in the relative share of small enterprises.

THE QUANTITATIVE STUDIES OF CHANGING IMPORTANCE OF SELF-EMPLOYMENT

This section reviews six major empirical studies which have analysed the factors influencing changes in the proportion of the workforce classified as self-employed in developed countries in recent years. A comprehensive review of these developments is also provided by OECD (1992). The six studies share the common theme that they use multiple regression analysis to explain changes in self-employment in a variety of different countries over a long time period. Each attempts to explain the changing importance of self-employment in terms of the explanations outlined in Table 2.11.

These explanations are the basis of the nine variables shown as the rows of Table 2.13. The studies are shown as the columns of the table and the table shows whether the researchers found a positive or negative relationship between the variables and the changes in importance of self-employment. Although each study uses multiple regression analysis, not all researchers include all nine variables and so blanks occur where the variable is not included. Where the variable is included but no relationship is observed, this is also shown. Where the relationship is present but very weak, the sign is shown in parenthesis and where positive and negative findings emerge from differently specified equations, both symbols are shown.

Part of the interest of the table lies in the different ways in which researchers have attempted to operationalise and measure the factors identified in the previous section. For example, the role of technological change is identified in two out of the six studies, but is measured in very different ways. For example Acs, Audretsch and Evans (1991) measure technological change as the proportion of total manufacturing employment which is in four industries which are classified as being high technology. Blau (1987), however, uses a 'Total Factor Productivity' (TFP) index as his means of measuring technological change. Table 2.13 demonstrates that, in both instances, technological change measures are positively associated

Table 2.13 Factors influencing changes in the proportion of the labour force classified as self-employed

	Studies					
	1	*2*	*3*	*4*	*5*	*6*
FACTORS						
1 Technological change		+				+
2 Fragmentation/cost changes						
3 Demography – gender		–				x
– age						x
4 Unemployment rate	+	+	+	+	+	
5 Government – schemes			(+)	+	+	
– taxes						–/+
– benefits				–	–	
6 Economic development		–				
7 Left-wing government					–	
8 Attitudes to risk		+				
9 Time trend	+/–		+	–		

Studies:
1 Bögenhold and Staber (1991)
2 Acs, Audretsch and Evans (1991)
3 Johnson, Lindley and Boulakis (1988)
4 Meager (1992a)
5 Bögenhold and Staber (1992)
6 Blau (1987)

Key:
+ Positive relationship
– Negative relationship
x No relationship observed
( ) Weak relationship

with increased self-employment, as predicted.

None of the empirical studies in Table 2.13 directly include measures of fragmentation or cost changes. Given our earlier discussion of this matter this is surprising, since the make-or-buy decisions of large firms would be expected to influence changes in self-employment.

Only two studies explicitly include demographic change as an influence upon self-employment. The Acs *et al.* study shows that increases in the proportion of the labour force which is female are associated with lower rates of self-employment. This is because, although female rates of self-employment have been rising faster than male rates, in absolute terms they still remain below that of males. The Blau study on self-employment in the United States included an age variable, but failed to find any evidence that it exerted an influence upon self-employment rates.

The most powerful influence, which is consistently identified in five out of the six studies, is the role of unemployment in encouraging self-employment. It is unquestionably the case that increases in unemployment, other things being equal, are associated in time series studies with increased self-employment rates.

The fifth group of influences relates to the role of government. This role is subdivided into three: the role of specific government schemes designed to channel the unemployed into self-employment – referred to as schemes; secondly, the role of the taxation environment in providing incentives; and thirdly, the role which state benefits for the unemployed and others exert on the self-employment decision. Both the Meager (1992a) study of self-employment in United Kingdom, France, Germany and Denmark, and the Bögenhold and Staber studies point to a positive role for government schemes, whereas the Johnson *et al.* study of the United Kingdom alone is only able to identify a weak impact of the Enterprise Allowance Scheme.

The role of the taxation environment is examined by Blau who finds that self-employment rates rise when taxation rates for high income groups rise. This he attributes to the self-employed having greater opportunity for tax evasion and tax avoidance and the fact that the incentive for such evasion/avoidance increases with income. More perplexing, however, is his finding that self-employment rates fall when tax rates rise for low income groups.

One of the most interesting findings of both Meager and of Bögenhold and Staber (1992) is that the level of state payments to the unemployed exerts a negative influence upon rates of self-employment. Countries which make relatively generous payments to the unemployed have lower rates of self-employment. This, as argued earlier, is because the state payments raise the 'reservation income' level for the unemployed, who then do not need to seek the uncertain income from self-employment. Bögenhold and Staber (1992) demonstrate this clearly by showing that Denmark and Sweden, which have the most generous forms of unemployment assistance, also have the lowest rates of self-employment. Conversely the United States, which has the least generous system of the countries compared, has very much higher rates of self-employment.

The sixth factor identified is that of economic development, but this seems to have been ignored in most of the empirical studies. Only Acs *et al.* include it directly, using the measure of GNP per head of population. They find that countries with high GNP per head, other things being equal, have lower rates of self-employment than those with lower rates of GNP per head, thus supporting the hypothesis outlined by Loufti (1992).

Although it was not explicitly discussed in the previous section, Bögenhold and Staber (1992) make a powerful case that self-employment is also likely to be strongly encouraged by right-wing governments, such as the Conservative Government's attempts during the 1980s to create an 'enterprise culture' in the United Kingdom. Such developments would be likely to be discouraged by left-wing governments on the grounds, to be discussed in Chapter 6, that the jobs created are of poor quality and the small firm owner is much more likely to seek to exploit his or her workforce. The problem with testing this hypothesis is that the extent to which a government is either left or right-wing is unlikely to be independent of the other characteristics of government which are incorporated within factor five. For example, it is unlikely that right-wing governments will have high rates of taxation, or pay high rates of state benefit to the unemployed. Equally, it is unlikely that left-wing governments will utilise schemes to encourage the unemployed to start their own businesses. Nevertheless, Bögenhold and Staber do include this variable and find, not surprisingly, that countries with left-wing governments are less likely to have high rates of self-employment.

The eighth factor identified is that of attitude to risk. Here, it is argued by Acs *et al.* that a significant characteristic of countries is the prevalent attitude to risk. They argue that avoidance of uncertainty is a national characteristic in some countries, yet much less obvious in others. They argue that countries with a high risk-avoidance characteristic are likely to have low rates of self-employment, and this also appears to be supported from their empirical evidence.

Finally, the ninth factor identified in the table merely attempts to take account of imperfect model specifications in time series analysis. It is not to be viewed as significant in its own right.

Overall, the multiple regression empirical studies point to generally strong support for the hypothesis and explanations provided in pp. 34–43. They strongly support the view that increases in unemployment are associated with increased levels of self-employment. They also suggest that governments can accelerate that development by the establishment of schemes to encourage the unemployed to become self-employed and by cutting unemployment benefit. Most interesting, perhaps, is the finding that increases in the proportion of the workforce classified as self-employed run contrary to long-term economic development.

CONCLUSION

The main conclusion of this chapter is that small enterprises, virtually no matter how they are defined, constitute at least 95 per cent of enterprises in the European Community. The average employment size for firms in the European Community varies from three employees in Greece to ten employees in the Netherlands. Despite their huge importance, and the relevance that politicians now give to the small firm sector in terms of economic development, the message seems to have been virtually ignored by financial and economic commentators.

Of course, the importance of the small firm sector depends upon the definition of 'small' which is used. The chapter concludes that both the economic and statistical definitions employed by the Bolton Committee in 1971 are no longer relevant. Bolton employed a hotchpotch of different definitions of a small firm, according to the sector in which it operated, thus making international comparisons and comparisons over time virtually impossible. Even in the manufacturing sector, where Bolton used an upper limit definition of 200 employees, this was clearly incompatible with its economic definition that a small firm should be owned and managed by the same individuals. Finally, productivity improvements since 1971 mean that output per employee has virtually doubled. For all these reasons the European Community definitions of a small enterprise as one having less than 100 employees, and of a micro-enterprise as one having less than ten employees, seem much more appropriate to current economic conditions.

Whilst broadly acceptable and consistent definitions are needed for international and time series comparisons, small firm researchers are not restricted by these parameters. The heterogeneity of the small firm sector means it is often necessary for these definitions to be modified according to the particular sectoral, geographic or other contexts in which the small firm is being examined. We applaud researchers' use of 'grounded' definitions, in which those in the industry are asked to identify what they regard as being a small firm. That definition is then used as the basis for 'smallness'.

Despite the importance which politicians currently place upon the small firm sector as a source of economic development, only rough estimates can be made of the total number of small firms in the United Kingdom. That there were estimated to be almost three million small businesses in the United Kingdom in 1989 is as much a testimony to the ingenuity of the researchers who produced the figure, as to the coverage and quality of the data. The consistent theme which emerges throughout this volume is that, if politicians are interested in the contribution which the small firm sector makes to economic development, the data and information collected about that sector have to be improved. Unfortunately, the reverse trend seems to be in operation, with politicians being more influenced by pressure from small business lobby groups arguing that their members are over-burdened with paperwork, and need to be relieved of the responsibility of completing any additional forms. We shall return in Chapter 8 to the need to resolve these conflicts.

Probably the most extensively documented finding relating to small firms in the United Kingdom has been that their share of manufacturing employment and output has been rising since the end of the 1960s. This follows at least forty years during which it was large firms which increased their share of employment and output in manufacturing. It is also the case that the proportion of the UK labour force classified as being self-employed was at its lowest point during the 1960s and has increased since, with particularly rapid increases during the 1980s. The chapter also reports that whilst the evidence on the manufacturing sector is more patchy, similar trends in the growth in self-employment, albeit less stark, are observed for a number of European countries.

Our conclusion is that there are a number of common influences at work which explain these changes. Probably the most important of these are technological change, demography, unemployment and the role of government policies.

Much of the increase in self-employment observed in the United Kingdom during the 1980s can probably be attributed to a combination of increasing unemployment, a lowering of the real level of unemployment benefit, government schemes such as the Enterprise Allowance, the fact that the United Kingdom had a significantly lower level of self-employment than most other comparable countries, and to technological changes associated with the increasing role of information in the economy.

What seems less likely is that the growth in self-employment is related to lower rates of personal taxation – indeed the opposite is probably the case, or that in the long term this increase in self-employment will continue. If Acs, Audretsch and Evans are to be believed, other things being equal, economic development is associated with lower levels of self-employment rather than higher. The extent to which there is likely to be an increase in self-employment depends upon the relative strengths of the various factors within this basket of influences. Clearly, however, a government less committed to the enterprise culture and which abolished schemes such as the Enterprise Allowance, which lowered unemployment, and which raised the benefits received by the unemployed, would be likely to lead to a sharp deceleration of the rate of increase in self-employment. We are not able to estimate what the effect of this would be on the performance of the UK economy.

To obtain a clearer view on this it is necessary not simply to examine the changes in the total number of firms in the economy at any one point in time. It has to be recognised that, particularly for smaller firms, their contribution to economic activity depends upon the quantity that are born (births) and the quantity that die (deaths). Equally, if not more important is the quality of the small firms – the best indicator of which is observing which firms grow. The births, deaths and growth of small firms are therefore the topics covered in the next three chapters.

Chapter 3

The birth of firms

INTRODUCTION

There were approximately 1.7 million businesses registered for VAT in the United Kingdom in 1990. More than 95 per cent had a turnover of less than two million pounds and therefore can be regarded as small. The total number of businesses in the economy at any one time is referred to as the 'stock' of businesses; over time, this stock changes as a result of new firms being created (births) and firms ceasing to trade (deaths).

This chapter provides an understanding of the factors which influence the birth of firms. Chapter 4 will provide a comparable analysis of the factors which influence the death of firms – particularly smaller firms.

The birth and death of firms occurs on a huge scale. In the United Kingdom each year nearly 14 per cent of all businesses have registered for VAT during the previous twelve months; they constituted a gross addition to the stock of UK businesses of approximately 235,000 in 1990. Each year there are almost as many firms deregistering for VAT (185,000 in 1990). Hence, in 1990 the *net* contribution to stock, i.e. births minus deaths, was only 50,000 (Daly 1991).

This chapter will begin by presenting data on the quantitative significance of births. It will examine the extent to which birth rates have changed over time; it will make comparisons between countries and it will examine differences in birth rates between different industries and different geographical areas.

Unfortunately, this immediately returns us to the statistical difficulties discussed in Chapter 2. The most important of these is that for no developed country is there a comprehensive list of all enterprises in the economy. As was noted in Chapter 2, even the VAT-based statistics on births and deaths of businesses in the United Kingdom are incomplete. Bannock and Partners (1989) estimated that less than two-thirds of UK businesses are registered for VAT. The United Kingdom reflects the general pattern that, whilst there is generally excellent coverage of larger firms within an economy, neither government statistical services nor taxation authorities find it cost-effective to maintain records on all firms.

It is the case that the longer an enterprise has been in business, the higher is the probability of it appearing in some official records. Yet if we are interested in births of firms, these firms by definition are new, and also both very small and likely to have a short lifespan. For all these reasons they are the least likely to appear in public records. The next section therefore presents data on birth rates, but these must be accompanied with a health warning to readers that they are in no sense comprehensive.

This chapter then goes on (pp. 60–7) to examine a range of theories about why new firms are established, and the reasons why such firms are deemed to be important. In particular, a distinction is made between the perspective adopted by economists and those of other disciplines. Broadly we argue that economists do not have a direct interest in new firms *per se*; instead, their interest is in the extent to which new firms influence the pricing and output decisions of incumbent firms in an industry. This theoretical background is used to explain (pp. 67–71) the observed spatial variations in new firm formation rates which exist, not only in the United Kingdom, but in many other developed countries.

The theory is also drawn upon (pp. 71–5) to explain temporal variations in firm formation rates, primarily in the United Kingdom. It also shows that the results of a study of cooperative formation rates in Mediterranean countries by Bartlett (1993b) shows a broadly similar pattern, suggesting that the theory is sufficiently robust to accommodate different types of business enterprise.

This chapter concludes by emphasising the importance of new firms to the stock of small firms and the considerable variations which are observed over time, space and sector.

BIRTHS DATA

As Chapter 2 shows, there are no comprehensive statistics which identify all the firms in an economy. The greatest deficiency in this respect is likely to be amongst the smallest size of firm and the youngest firms. Since the bulk of young firms are likely to be small, information on young firms is particularly sparse.

This section examines data on new firms and demonstrates the existence of huge variations in rates of formation, according to sector, over time and over space. The text will highlight the extent of these variations and seek reasons for them.

In the United Kingdom we have already seen that there is a wide range of data sets available for the business population. These include data on businesses registered for value added tax (VAT), the Census of Production, Labour Force Survey, Incorporated Businesses, as well as private sector data bases such as Dun and Bradstreet. None of these data sources are comprehensive. It is estimated by the Small Business Research Trust (1992) that only 56 per cent of UK business enterprises are registered for VAT. In 1989, Daly and McCann (1992) estimated there were three million businesses in the United Kingdom. Of these, only 19 per cent were incorporated companies.

The Census of Production, as its name implies, only covers the production sector. Although it is *not* a perfect comparison, production firms in the VAT data constituted approximately 160,000 in 1990 out of a total of 1.7 million businesses registered for VAT. Hence production sector firms constitute less than 10 per cent of UK business enterprises.

Data on self-employment in the United Kingdom are derived from the Labour Force Survey (LFS). From this it is possible to identify those individuals whose employment status has changed to that of self-employment within the last year, and these could also be used as a measure of the number of new firms or 'births'. However, the LFS enables people to classify themselves. It means that individuals whose 'employers', for example, in the construction and hotel sectors, require them to be self-employed are included when in only the loosest sense could they be classified as being a business owner. On the other hand a company director is not classified as self-employed, but as an employee. In short, self-employment as defined in the LFS does not always correspond to business ownership, and changes in the status of an individual do not necessarily correspond to a business birth.

Although each of the data sets referred to above has its limitations in terms of coverage, it is relatively easy to identify the birth of a firm. For example, in the VAT data a 'birth' can be regarded as a business which is newly registered for the payment of value added tax. Similarly, newly incorporated businesses can be identified as those which are registered for the first time in the most recent year.

However, both these are administrative decisions which do not necessarily correspond to a decision to start trading for the first time, and it is often more problematic to define *when* a firm started – when it got its first order, when its lease began, when it took on its first employee, when the owner started in the business on a full-time basis (Mason 1983). On these grounds a business may have been trading for some time prior to registering for VAT if its turnover (sales figure) is less than the registration threshold (£45,000 in 1994). Similarly, many businesses operate either as sole proprietorships or partnerships, sometimes for many years, prior to choosing to become limited companies. However, that change in legal status is a new registration and therefore is regarded as a 'birth'. Conversely a number of newly registered limited companies never trade (Scott 1982a).

In only the broadest sense, therefore, can the number of businesses which are newly registered for VAT, or the number of new incorporated businesses, be regarded as an indicator of the number of new business starts in any particular year.

A second problem associated with interpretation of data on births of firms is that the focus of interest differs between different disciplines. To understand this, we must make the key distinction between the terms 'enterprise' and 'establishment'. In most cases, particularly for small firms, these are synonymous. However, the distinction is that 'enterprise' can be considered as the ownership term broadly equivalent to the word 'firm', whereas 'establishment' can be considered to be the productive unit or factory. Thus a single enterprise may have several establishments in different locations.

This distinction between 'enterprise' and 'establishment' has particular importance for economists looking at the question of entry. As we shall show later, economists generally regard entry as additions to the productive stock by the creation of new establishments, even where there has been no increase in the number of firms or enterprises. Take, as an example, the case of an industry in which there are currently three enterprises: Enterprise A has one establishment, Enterprise B has one establishment and Enterprise C has three establishments. In total there are five establishments or factories, and three enterprises. If Enterprise B decides to open another factory or establishment, this would increase the number of establishments in the industry to six. The economist considers this to be identical to the case in which a new firm, to be called Enterprise D, enters the industry with one establishment. In both cases the total number of establishments is therefore six, but in one case it has occurred through an increase in the number of enterprises to four, whereas in the other it has occurred through an increase in the number of establishments to six with the number of enterprises remaining at three.

These distinctions are reflected in the data which are used. Economists have tended to make the greatest use of Census of Production data which, although focusing exclusively on the manufacturing and related sectors, makes a clear distinction between enterprise and establishment.

We now present data on new firms or enterprises, recalling that this will be different from data on new establishments. A clear distinction is made between sectoral variations, spatial variations and temporal variations in new firms.

Sectoral variations

Data on industry births, both in the United Kingdom and in the United States, normally relate to new establishments, rather than to new firms. It is these data which have been used by economists to measure inter-sectoral variations in entry rates. Our purpose is to illustrate the existence, between sectors, of huge differences in the numbers of both new entrants and new firms.

Table 3.1 shows data for the United States between 1978 and 1980 and is part of a much larger table of data on more than 400 industry sectors. The value of the table is that it makes a direct comparison between entry and new firm formation at a sectoral level. The first column shows the total number of jobs created in entrants – defined as new establishments to the sector – with these ranging from 152,000 in the radio and TV communications equipment sector to only sixteen in electrotyping and stereotyping. The sectors chosen

Table 3.1 Industry births, the small firm birth share, and net entry compared between high- and low-birth industries: United States 1978–80

Industry	*Employment in entrants*	*Small firm entrants' share*	*Net entry 1978–80*	*(Rank)*
Radio and TV communication equipment	152,524	0.1220	90	(47)
Miscellaneous plastic products	149,065	0.4672	687	(4)
Motor vehicle parts and accessories	120,334	0.1260	235	(17)
Electronic computing equipment	118,833	0.1964	224	(21)
Electronic components	92,107	0.3312	284	(12)
Machinery, except electrical	77,612	0.7501	1,904	(2)
Primary lead	210	0.1154	–3	(311)
Chewing and smoking tobacco	142	0.3067	–5	(234)
Millinery	112	0.8803	–24	(404)
Space propulsion units and parts	100	0.5856	–4	(317)
Chewing gum	90	1.0000	0	(277)
Electrotyping and stereotyping	16	1.0000	–12	(370)

Source: Acs and Audretsch (1989)

are the six with the highest number of births, shown in the top half of the table, and the six sectors with the lowest number of births, shown in the lower half of the table.

The second column shows there is a wide variation in the proportion of new entrants which are new firms. Thus only 12.2 per cent of employment in entrants in the radio and TV communications sector was in new firms. This compares with 100 per cent of employment in new firms in the chewing gum and electrotyping and stereotyping sectors. The third column of the table shows net entry – defined as the number of new entrants (establishments) minus the number of exits (establishments) between 1978 and 1980. The final column shows the ranking of the sectors according to the net entry criterion.

Overall, Table 3.1 demonstrates only a modest association between the measure of net entry and the measure of employment in births. It emphasises that wide sectoral variations exist in the number of new firms entering an industry, the employment in those new firms, and the proportion of all entrants which are new firms. This suggests that different explanations are needed to understand the factors which influence the number of entrants, the number of entrants which are new firms, and the impact which those new firms have upon incumbent firms in the industry.

Spatial variations

There is also evidence of a wide variation in the rates of new firm formation across space. These are reflected in both inter-country differences and differences within the same country on a regional or local basis. New firm formation rates are normally defined in two ways: the first is the number of new firms established in a given period, normalised by the working population; the second is the number of new firms, normalised by the number of existing firms. As will be demonstrated later in this chapter, these measures are not identical, in the sense of leading to comparable rankings of geographical areas in terms of firm formation rates.

Table 3.2 shows that, within the European Community, there are wide variations between countries in the numbers of new firms established in 1989, expressed as a proportion of the working population.

In 1989 the highest rate of new firm formation in Europe, other than that for Denmark, which appears somewhat anomalous, was in the United Kingdom, and the lowest rate was in the Netherlands. From the data it would appear that firm formation rates in the United Kingdom are almost five times as high as in the Netherlands. The ranking of the countries, however, does not appear to relate to other obvious economic variables. For example, it might have been expected that the less developed economies would exhibit

Table 3.2 Start-ups as a percentage of the active labour force, 1989

Country	*Percentage*
Denmark	(5.4) *
United Kingdom	1.59
Luxembourg	1.46
Ireland	1.25
Italy	1.20
Germany	1.13
France	1.12
Spain	0.64
Belgium	0.62
Portugal	0.34
The Netherlands	0.33
Greece	n.a.
EC	0.97

Source: Van der Horst (1992)
Note: * Data in respect of Denmark are not fully comparable with other countries due to the large number of start-ups for fiscal reasons and a special category of female entrepreneurship.

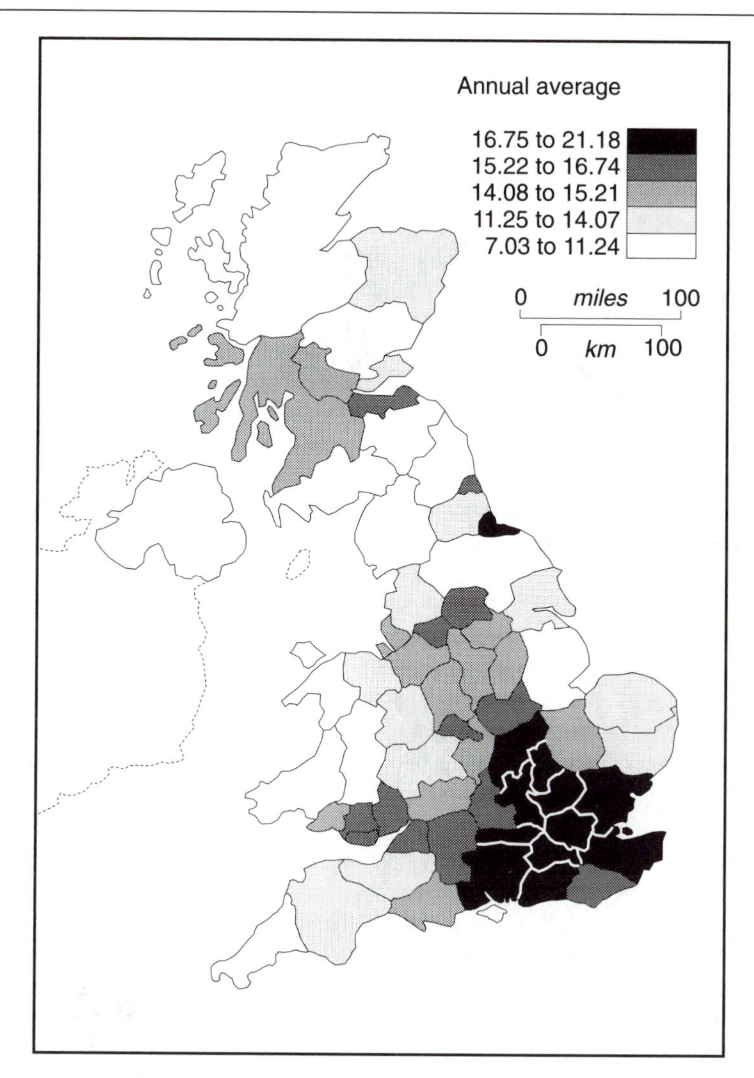

Figure 3.1 New firm formation rates in the total economy, 1980–90 (business stock-based)
Source: Keeble, Walker and Robson (1993)

different patterns from those of the more mature developed economies, but this is not the case. It is also not obviously related to GDP growth over the period, or to unemployment.

There are also wide variations in the rate of new firm formation within the same country. Using the definition of new firm formation as being a business which is newly registered for value added tax, Figure 3.1, taken from Keeble, Walker and Robson (1993), shows that new firm formation rates in the total

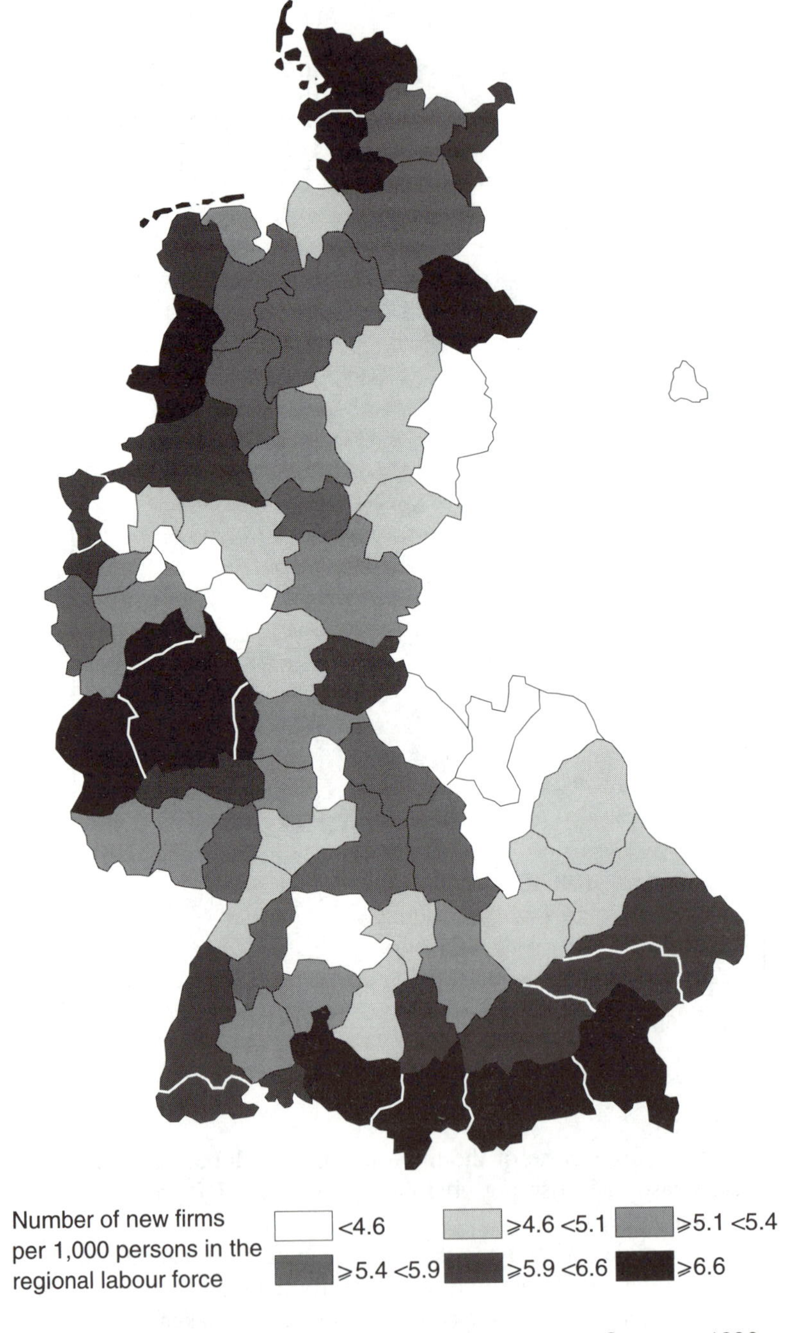

Figure 3.2 Spatial variations in new firm formation in West Germany, 1986
Source: Fritsch (1992)

economy between 1980 and 1990 varied widely in the United Kingdom. The rates of formation were virtually three times higher in some areas than in others. There was a strong clustering of high rates of new firm formation in London and in the bordering counties of south-east England. Only the county of Cleveland in north-east England had a rate of new firm formation comparable to that of counties in south-east England.

In this case, with the exception of Cleveland, there appears to be a pattern which suggests higher rates of new firm formation in areas of relative prosperity which have service-based economies. However, the fact that an area such as Cleveland, which has an economy heavily based on manufacturing and high levels of unemployment, also has high rates of new firm formation suggests there may also be other explanations (Storey and Strange 1992).

Figure 3.2 shows spatial variations in new firm formation rates within the former West Germany. Fritsch (1992), using social insurance statistics, shows that the birth rate of new firms in 1986 varied markedly, but again there appears to be evidence of a spatial pattern, with the higher rates being in the areas around the northern, western and southern borders. Relatively lower rates were found in the east.

Temporal variations

Major short-term and long-term variations in firm formation rates occur over time. For example, Figures 3.3(a) and (b), taken from Keeble, Walker and Robson (1993) show the number of new businesses in the United Kingdom which registered for VAT during each quarter between 1980 and 1991. Figure 3.3(a) shows the stock of businesses expressed as a proportion of the labour force, whereas in Figure 3.3(b) new registrations are expressed as a proportion of the labour force.

There is a similarity and contrast in the figures. The similarity is that they both exhibit an upward trend over the decade, but the difference is that the pattern is much smoother in Figure 3.3(a) than in 3.3(b).

Examination of Figure 3.3(a) shows that the most rapid period of growth was 1981–2, which was a period of extreme recession in the United Kingdom, and in 1988–9 which was the last year of the upswing of the economy.

The relatively smooth pattern in the change in the stock of businesses is not reflected in the series of new registrations (births) in Figure 3.3(b). This shows considerable fluctuations on a quarter-by-quarter basis and implies that there are offsetting fluctuations in the deregistrations (deaths) data in order to produce the smooth pattern of Figure 3.3(a).

Unfortunately, interpretation of these data is made more complex by the fact that there is a minimum threshold of sales turnover which firms must reach before they are legally required to register for VAT.[1] The problem arises that the monetary value of this threshold is generally changed annually. In most years, but not all, it is simply changed in line with inflation, but its

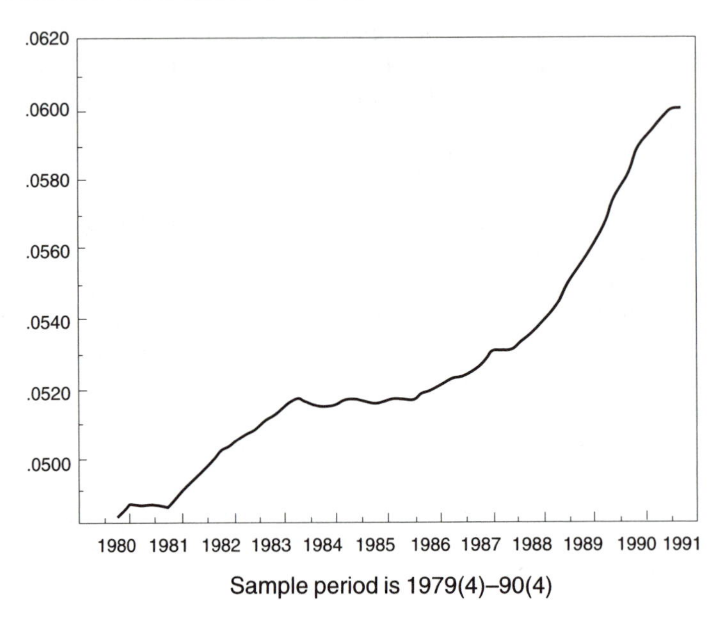

Figure 3.3(a) Ratio of the stock of VAT-registered businesses to the labour force
Source: Keeble, Walker and Robson (1993)

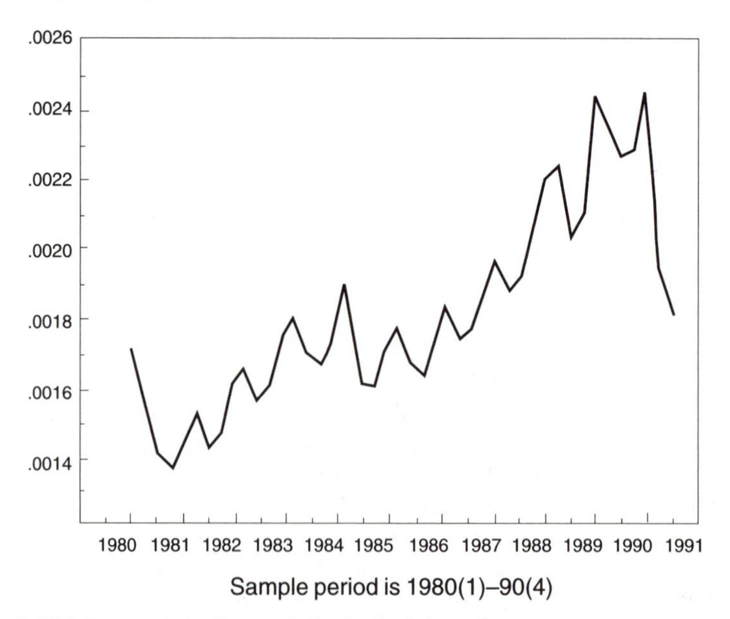

Figure 3.3(b) New registrations relative to the labour force
Source: Keeble, Walker and Robson (1993)

modification explains why there is a sharp drop in registration rates in the quarters during which the threshold rises. Finally, it should be pointed out that the sharp drop in 1981 almost certainly reflects the effects of an industrial dispute in which civil servants withdrew their labour, rather than a 'real' effect. The sharp drop in 1991 almost certainly reflects the 37.8 per cent increase in the VAT threshold (Freedman and Godwin 1994), which was virtually ten times the prevailing rate of inflation at the time. A secondary influence may have been the recessionary conditions in that year.

VAT-based data are available from 1973 onwards, but it is only from 1980 that consistent annual data according to size and sector are available. To examine longer-term changes it is necessary to consult other sources.

Data on company incorporations are available for more than seventy years, even though, as we noted previously, limited companies constituted less than 20 per cent of businesses in the United Kingdom in 1990.

Figure 3.4 Company incorporations, 1945–89

Figure 3.4 shows the pattern of company registrations in Great Britain in the post-war period. It shows that immediately after the war there was a sharp jump in the number of companies registered, but this peaked by 1948 and fell back each year until 1952. From that year onwards it rose consistently until 1964, when again it fell for a four-year period. In 1968 it began to rise again, peaking in 1973 then falling sharply in 1974 but rising in virtually all subsequent years.

THE THEORY OF NEW FIRM BIRTHS

Until now this chapter has presented data on the births of firms and shown that, despite reservations about the quality of the data, the birth of firms does vary over time, space and sector. This section briefly synthesises some explanations which have been provided for these variations.

A crude distinction is made between the work of industrial economists and that of labour market economists. The former can be considered to be the more 'traditional', in the sense of conducting analysis within the Structure-Conduct-Performance (SCP) paradigm, which assumes the structure of the industry influences the conduct of the firms, which in turn influences their performance (Clarke 1985). On the other hand, labour market economists examine new firm formation as a decision exercised by the individual in the context of the labour market. In making that decision the individual is influenced by a variety of factors, such as work experience, motivation, personality, family environment, societal 'norms', status, etc. These influences have also been the prime focus of explanations for entrepreneurship provided by non-economists.

The industrial economist's approach

The prime focus of the industrial economist's attention is upon the pricing and output decisions of firms already in an industry, rather than upon new firms entering that industry. The vocabulary of economists also makes use of the term 'entrants', rather than 'new firms'.

Both these points are illustrated by Mueller (1992). He argues that an entrant is defined as a firm which manufactures a product in a given four-digit industry in a year, but did not manufacture it in the preceding year. He points out that there are five main categories of entrant:

- a newly constituted firm;
- an existing firm that builds a new plant in the industry;
- an existing firm that buys a plant already in the industry;
- an existing firm that alters the product mix in the existing plant;
- a foreign-owned firm which enters in one of the above ways, as opposed to a domestic firm.

From the above it is clear that entry by a newly constituted firm, although generally the most frequent form of entry, is not necessarily of dominant importance. Indeed it is possible to argue that economists are less interested in entry by the newly constituted firm, because of its lower impact on incumbent firms, than other types of entrants.

As Mueller puts it: 'The leading firms in most industries stand calmly in the centre, as if in the eye of a tornado, while myriad smaller challengers whirl in and out along the periphery.'

The equation below sets down the basic economist's empirical model of entry, derived primarily from Orr (1974), with the predicted causations shown in parenthesis.

$$E = f(\pi, BE, GR, C)$$

where E = entry, π = profits (+), BE = entry barriers (–), GR = growth (+) and C = concentration (–).

Entry into the ith industry is assumed to take place following a rise in the expected post-entry profitability of entrants to that industry. Entry is deterred by barriers such as the existence of scale economies, product differentiation, restricted access to unique inputs, etc. Entry is assumed to be positively related to the growth of the industry. Finally, highly concentrated industries are assumed to exist where there is an opportunity for collusion between existing incumbent firms to minimise the possibility of entry. Entry is therefore expected to be low when industrial concentration is high.

If our interest is in explaining the formation of new firms, as opposed to entrants, then, as Acs and Audretsch (1989) point out, there is little reason to assume that small firm entry is an exact replica of large firm entry. Indeed Acs and Audretsch show that small firm entry, which is primarily by new firms, does differ in one major respect. They show that the incidence of small-firm births is *lower* in highly concentrated industries, whereas that of large-firm births appears to be *greater*. This suggests that large firms have a relative advantage in entering concentrated markets. They also show that those industries in which innovation plays an important role are more accessible to large than to small firms.

A labour market approach

Historically, the study of entry of firms has been the province of industrial economists. Where the topic has been studied at all, the subject of self-employment tends to have been the province of labour economists and, until recently, there has been little overlap between these two groups. Even the terminology of the two groups differs, with industrial economics using the term 'entry', whereas labour market economists use the term new 'self-employment' (de Wit 1993).

Even though the move into self-employment is probably the single most important source of new firm formation (and hence the major numerical influence upon entry rates), there has been little attempt to link the two approaches. This reflects the assumption of entry theorists that there is a queue of entrants outside industry, just waiting for price to persistently exceed long-run average costs.

Labour market economists have become increasingly dissatisfied with this assumption. They have begun to ask the question: 'What happens if we reject the assumption of a continuous supply of entrants?' Simply by posing this question, economists begin to address issues which have been a central focus of the study of entrepreneurship by other disciplines. For example, case studies of leading entrepreneurs (Rassan 1988) have often pointed to certain characteristics which appear to distinguish these individuals from the rest of the population. Such individuals have powerful personalities, may have failed in business before, have considerable personal drive, have a family background in business, are more likely to come from certain ethnic or cultural minorities, and are not 'team-players'.

These are characteristics with which the economist is neither familiar nor even comfortable. They suggest that various groups in society differ in their willingness to supply themselves as entrepreneurs, but this is in keeping with the economist's recognition of differences between individuals. The area of distinction is that, in general, the economist is not interested in *which* individual becomes an entrepreneur, *why* they do so, or even from which group the individual comes. Instead, the economist is interested in the question of what change in relative prices is necessary to induce *how many* individuals to make that shift. Only if each 'group' has a separate 'price', does this variable begin to interest the economist.

The difference between the industrial economist's approach to firm formation and that of other groups therefore reflects the different questions which the two groups are trying to answer. The industrial economist is asking, 'Into which sectors, and under what circumstances, will entry take place?' The industrial economist is therefore not interested in the total number of entrants in the economy as a whole, but only in their sectoral distribution and the impact which that entry has upon prices. A supply of entrants is assumed to be given. Other groups, including labour market economists, are interested in the total number of new firms. In this sense the supply of entrepreneurs and the factors which influence this are of central importance.

The labour market economist interested in new firm formation derives intellectual inspiration from the work of Knight (1921). Knight argued that an individual could exercise choice in terms of being in one of three states: unemployment, paid employment or self-employment. Furthermore, he argued that changes in the relative prices of these three states would induce some individuals to move from one state to another. Thus an individual who loses a job has to consider income levels associated with seeking new paid employment, becoming self-employed, or remaining unemployed. Two illustrations show the power of this simple insight. First, if the individual loses a job when unemployment is high, that person will be more likely to be pessimistic about obtaining alternative paid employment. This means they would be more likely to consider either self-employment or unemployment. Second, a reduction in the income associated with being unemployed would encourage movements into both self-employment and paid employment.

Whilst the Knight framework is useful for the derivation of hypotheses, it does not explicitly take into account the fact that some groups of individuals may be more likely to choose one of the three states (paid employment, self-employment or unemployment) than others. Labour market economists are interested in the question of occupational choice. In this sense the choice of a self-employed occupation can be considered to be little different from the choice of any other occupation.

This section identifies three main influences upon this decision:

- personality;
- human capital;
- ethnic origin.

Personality characteristics are examined by both Blanchflower and Oswald (1990) and by Blanchflower and Meyer (1991). They argue that one factor influencing the probability of an individual starting a business is entrepreneurial vision, as reflected in the personality of the entrepreneur at a young age. Blanchflower and Oswald show that individuals who currently are self-employed were (as children) less likely than average to be unforthcoming and more likely than average to show hostility to other children.

These characteristics clearly relate to the personality of the individual – a topic central to the interests of economic psychologists such as Chell, Haworth and Brearley (1991). According to these authors, entrepreneurs are alert to business opportunities, are proactive rather than reactive, innovative and easily bored. Indeed, the quest by psychologists to identify a group of personality traits which are capable of predicting entrepreneurial behaviour patterns has gone on for many years. Early work by McClelland (1961) pointed to entrepreneurs' need for achievement, which was more intense than that of other groups in society. Others such as Kets de Vries (1977) have pointed to entrepreneurs often having an unhappy family background, leading to their inability to accept authority or to work closely with others. This would appear to be the psychological basis for the 'hostility' and 'unforthcoming' variables of Blanchflower and Oswald.

Whilst personality is clearly not independent of family circumstances, Stanworth *et al.* (1989) have placed particular emphasis on the inter-generational entrepreneur. In a survey of more than 600 respondents, they showed that between 30 per cent and 47 per cent of individuals either considering, about to start, or in business, had a father who had also been in business. This is significantly higher than the 20 per cent of employees generally as reported by Curran and Burrows (1988a). They argue that the cultural inheritance of entrepreneurship does indeed move within families.

To these variables we also need to add factors which economists would normally include within the category of 'human capital'. For example, Pickles and O'Farrell (1987) argue that the educational attainment of entrepreneurs in the Republic of Ireland is higher than that of the Irish population in general. They do, however, point out that individuals with the highest levels of educational attainment are rather less likely to enter business. US empirical work presents rather more consistent evidence that, *ceteris paribus*, educational attainment levels are positively associated with a move into self-employment/new business formation. Evans and Leighton (1990) show that, for both unemployed and employed workers, the probability of entry into self-employment increases with education. Bates (1991) also finds the education variable to be positive in his study of white and non-white entrepreneurs. Finally, Townroe and Mallalieu (1993) demonstrate that founders of businesses in rural areas in the United Kingdom are generally more likely to have higher educational qualifications that those founders of businesses in urban areas.

The other human capital characteristics which an individual brings to entrepreneurship relate to work experience. Here it has been shown by several studies of manufacturing firm founders, such as those by Cross (1981) or Gudgin, Brunskill and Fothergill (1979) that an individual formerly employed in a small firm with less than ten workers was between seven and twelve times more likely to become an entrepreneur than an individual employed in a firm with 500 or more employees.

More recent research by Keeble, Bryson and Wood (1992a) of founders of business service firms, however, indicates precisely the opposite results. They show that individuals previously working in large firms are significantly more likely to establish their own firm in the same sector than individuals previously working in a small firm. This serves to emphasise the point made consistently by Curran, Blackburn and Woods (1991) that generalisations about the small firm sector can be hazardous and that, at a minimum, a sharp distinction has to be made between the service and the manufacturing sectors. For example the differences may reflect the greater niche market possibilities in services, or the greater level of customer/client contact amongst large service sector firms than is the case for manufacturing firms – an illustration of the role of economies of scope rather than scale.

Finally, amongst the human capital variables, individuals' managerial experience is generally thought to provide a positive incentive to encouraging the individual to become an entrepreneur (Bates 1990).

The third factor which has been argued to influence the choice between self-employment and paid employment is that of ethnic origin. There is a long tradition throughout history of immigrants to a country entering into

Table 3.3 Factors influencing self-employment

Factors	*Evans and Leighton (US)*	*Dolton and Makepeace (UK)*	*Blanchflower and Oswald (UK)*	*Blanchflower and Meyer (Australia)*
Married	+	x	o	x
Divorced	+	o	o	o
Education	+	x	x	+
Children	x	x	x	o
Unemployed	+	x	+	o
Previous wage	–	x	o	o
Experience	x	o	o	+
Age	x	+	x	x
Ethnic	x	x	x	x
Sex	x	+	x	x
Social class	o	+	o	o
School type	o	+	o	o
Region/urban	x	o	x	+
Inheritance/ liquidity	+	o	+	o
Personality	o	o	+	o
Manager	o	o	x	x
Family in business	o	o	x	o

Key:
+ Variable is statistically positively significant in the study
– Variable is statistically negatively significant in the study
x Variable included in the equation, but not shown to be significant
o Variable not included in the equation

business. In the United Kingdom, examples of this include the seventeenth century Huguenots fleeing from religious persecution in France and the Low Countries and becoming merchants in Britain, as well as the Jewish immigrants of the 1930s (Loebl 1978). More recently it is reflected in the high self-employment rates of the Indian, Pakistani and Bangladeshi communities in the United Kingdom. Jones, McEvoy and Barrett (1993) show that 22 per cent of the economically active population in this ethnic group are self-employed, compared with only 12 per cent of the white population. However, it is not uniformly the case that in-migrants have a higher propensity to become self-employed. Jones *et al.* (1993) show that only 7 per cent of the West Indian/Guyanese population in the United Kingdom were self-employed in 1987–9, at a time when 12 per cent of the white population was self-employed. Nevertheless there does seem to be evidence that some in-migrants are much more likely than the resident population to be self-employed. Support for this hypothesis is also provided by Keeble, Tyler, Broom and Lewis (1992) in a study of business in the countryside, which shows that founders of rural businesses are much more likely to have been in-migrants than are the founders of urban businesses.

Table 3.3 attempts to synthesise the results from four multivariate analyses which have examined the factors influencing self-employment. Of the four studies, two are for the United Kingdom, one for the United States and one for Australia. Our purpose in putting these results together is not to suggest that the four studies are identical: for example, the Dolton and Makepeace (1990) study focuses upon graduates, whereas the Blanchflower and Oswald study contains individuals with a much greater range of levels of educational attainment. Instead, the table illustrates the attempts which have been made to explain differences between the self-employed and the employed, and the movement of individuals between these two groups.

The table indicates whether the variables were shown to be statistically significant in influencing movement into self-employment, and also whether the variable was included in the equation but was not shown to be significant, or was not included in the equation.

Several conclusions may be drawn from this table. The first is that although all four studies are addressing a broadly similar issue, there must be some risk of omitted variable bias, since none appeared to include all variables, or even all variables which had been shown to be significant in other studies. Only four variables appear in all the studies – ethnic, sex, age and education – and only three variables appear with a significant coefficient in more than one of the studies. Thus unemployment appears to be positively associated with higher levels of self-employment in two studies, as does higher levels of education and being in receipt of some form of inheritance, enabling a liquidity constraint to be overcome.

Table 3.3 does not provide strong support for the impact of family and cultural influences on the self-employment decision. Perhaps most surprisingly, in none of the four studies does the ethnic variable appear significant, despite evidence from other studies, which have used univariate analysis, suggesting marked differences (Curran and Burrows 1988c, Meager 1991). It is also the case that family circumstances, with the exception of the Evans and Leighton study in the United States, also appear to exert only a modest influence. Finally, whether the individual has been a manager in their prior job does not appear to be significant in either of the two equations in which it is included.

Overall, there are clear differences in the characteristics of those individuals prepared to offer themselves for self-employment, as opposed to working as employees. This section has examined these influences and concludes that higher education and unemployment are both positively associated with self-employment. However the variety of testing procedures used, differences in the data sets, and genuine differences between countries mean that the pattern observed is fuzzy.

EXPLAINING SPATIAL VARIATIONS IN RATES OF NEW FIRM FORMATION

Earlier in this chapter we saw that, in both the United States and the United Kingdom, there were wide variations in the rates at which new firms were founded. The current author has previously argued (Storey 1982a), before comprehensive data were available, that new firm formation rates were likely to vary over space in a predictable pattern. Over the last decade, data on the formation rates over space have become available in several countries, and this section reviews the observed patterns. For the United Kingdom the major works are those by Keeble, Walker and Robson (1993), Ashcroft, Love and Malloy (1991) and Westhead and Moyes (1992).

The factors used to explain spatial variations in new firm birth rates are closely related to, and in some instances are derived from, the industrial and labour market economist's approaches discussed in the section above. This section draws heavily upon Reynolds and Maki's (1991) analyses of the United States, broadly comparable to studies which have been conducted in Europe (Reynolds and Storey 1993).

The factors are shown in Table 3.4. Eight basic types of factor are identified. Factor 1 relates to population and characteristics, factor 2 to unemployment, factor 3 to wealth, factor 4 to qualifications and occupations, factor 5 to the characteristics of the enterprises in the area, factor 6 to housing, factor 7 to local government and factor 8 to policy. The precise variables chosen to measure these factors do vary somewhat. Factor 1 comprises three variables: the first is the proportion of population in the region between the ages of twenty-five and forty-four, on the grounds that this is the age group which is most likely to start businesses. The second variable is the extent to which the population of the area has grown, or a measurement of the extent of in-migration. The third variable relates to the density of employment in the area: here the variable measures the extent to which there are differences between urban areas with dense populations and rural areas with sparse populations.

The second factor is that of unemployment. As noted earlier, there are two conflicting hypotheses designed to explain variations in new firm formation.

Table 3.4 Factors influencing spatial variations in new firm formation

Factor Variables		*Countries*									
		France		*Germany*		*Sweden*		*UK*		*US*	
		Pop	*Stk*	*Pop*	*Stk*	*Pop*	*Stk*	*Pop*	*Stk*	*Pop*	*Stk*
1	Population 25–44 years	–	x	x	x	o	o	o	o	x	x
	In-migration/growth	+	+	x	+	+	+	+	+	+	+
	Density/urban	+	+	x	x	+	(+)	+	+	x	x
2	Unemployment level	+	+	x	+	+	x	x	x	+	+
	Change in unemployment	x	x	+	+	–	–	x	x	x	x
3	Wealth	x	x	o	o	o	o	x	x	o	o
	GDP growth	o	o	x	x	x	+	(+)	+	+	+
4	Qualifications	x	–	o	o	x	x	x	x	–	–
	% managers	x	+	x	(+)	o	o	+	x	+	+
5	Firm size	+	+	+	+	+	(–)	+	–	+	x
	Specialisation index	+	x	x	x	o	o	o	o	x	+
6	Owner-occupied housing	–	–	x	x	x	–	x	x	x	x
	House prices	o	o	o	o	o	o	+	+	+	+
	Land prices	o	o	x	x	o	o	o	o	o	o
	Secondary housing	+	x	o	o	o	o	o	o	o	o
7	Socialist voters	x	x	o	o	x	x	–	+	o	o
	Local govt expenditure	o	o	x	x	o	o	x	x	–	–
8	Policy	o	o	o	o	x	x	x	x	o	o
	n	96	96	74	74	80	80	64	64	382	382
	$\bar{R}^2$	[0.84]	[0.87]	0.80	0.69	0.45	0.60	0.80	0.77	0.59	0.53

Source: Reynolds and Storey (1993)
Notes:
Col. 1 for each country is births/active population
Col. 2 for each country is births/stock of firms
Key:
+ Variable is significant at 5% level, positively associated
– Variable is significant at 5% level, negatively associated
( ) Variable is significant only at 10 per cent level
x Variable is not significant
o Variable is not included
[ ] Indicates unadjusted R^2

The first is that if unemployment is high, then more individuals would be prepared to offer themselves for self-employment, because of the shortage of alternative job opportunities. On these grounds high rates of, or increases in, unemployment would lead to higher rates of new firm formation. Yet, high rates of unemployment also reflect a lack of buoyancy in the economy, perhaps a lack of 'enterprise' in the population, and therefore a shortage of demand. On these grounds areas of high unemployment would be expected to have low rates of new firm formation (Storey 1982a).

The third factor shown in Table 3.4 is that of wealth. Here it is to be expected that wealthier areas would have higher rates of new firm formation. This reflects two separate influences. The first is that wealthy areas are more likely to have higher disposable income, leading to greater demand for income elastic services provided by small firms. The second is that this higher disposable income enables founders to raise capital more easily, at lower cost, to enable them to start a new firm.

The fourth factor relates to the occupational and educational characteristics of the workforce of an area. Here again, conflicting hypotheses may be presented. The first is that areas with a high proportion of the workforce having both high educational qualifications and with managerial experience will be more likely to have higher rates of new firm formation. This is because such areas are more likely to be wealthy. The converse is that such areas are also likely to have a greater opportunity for individuals obtaining employment within large firms, without having to take the risk of becoming an entrepreneur themselves.

The fifth factor relates to the firm size/specialisation issues. Here it is argued that geographical areas dominated by small firms are more likely to have higher rates of new firm formation, on the grounds that individuals working in small firms see their natural career progression as to become, one day, an entrepreneur themselves. This also relates to the structure of industry, where the entry barriers to starting a small firm may be much lower. This specialisation index argues, primarily from the experiences of Italy (Garofoli 1994), that areas which are wholly dependent upon a single industry are more likely to have higher rates of new firm formation.

Factor six in Table 3.4 relates to housing. This is a particularly important issue since, for many entrepreneurs, access to capital to start a business is crucial. Housing is potentially the prime source of this capital. It is hypothesised that areas having a high proportion of owner-occupied housing, and which have relatively high prices of housing, are more likely to have individuals with access to capital to start their own businesses and hence are likely to have higher rates of new firm formation (Black, De Meza and Jefferies 1992).

Factor seven relates to the nature of government in the area. Here it is hypothesised that where government expenditure is large, this will create additional demand and so lead to higher rates of new firm formation (Birley and Westhead 1992). The political complexion of the government could also influence business formation rates, but the direction of this impact is unclear. For example, it could be argued that left-wing local/regional governments are more likely to spend money and hence create demand in the locality. Yet to finance this, such governments may have to have high tax rates, which could depress demand; it could also be argued that socialist administrations are unlikely to be found in areas where the small business ethic is prominent.

The final factor is public policy. Numerous national and central government initiatives to stimulate birth and growth of small firms have been implemented during the last decade or so. It might therefore be expected that regions which have been most in receipt of these policies would have higher rates of new firm formation than other areas.[2]

Table 3.4 examines these hypotheses for five countries – Sweden, France, the United Kingdom, Germany and the United States. For each of these countries, two definitions of birth rate are employed. The first examines the birth rates of new firms over a period of time, dividing that by the active population, or employed population in the area. This is shown as the first of the two columns for each country. It is called the 'population' index for short. The second measure of birth rates is the number of births of new firms, normalised by the existing stock of businesses. It is called the 'stock' measure for short.

These two measures are far from identical. Thus a region with relatively few firms but which, for some reason, experiences a significant increase in the number of new businesses, will be seen to have a high formation rate according to the stock index, even though it may still have relatively low rates of formation according to the population index. There has been some debate upon the relative merits of these two indices. Garofoli (1994) probably expresses the majority view in stating that the population index is preferred to the stock index. The reasons for this are twofold. First, new business founders emerge from the population as a whole, rather than the existing stock of firms. Thus business founders may be previously unemployed, be new to the workforce, or be returners to work. The population index therefore captures this group rather better. The second reason is that the same number of new firms being formed will lead to apparently much higher rates of formation in geographical areas which are dominated by large firms than in areas which are dominated by small firms. Even so, there is some merit in presenting data according to both indices of births, so that differences can be identified.

Table 3.4 shows there are differences between the various countries in the extent to which the particular variables 'explain' regional variations in firm birth rates. Nevertheless, it is also clear that it is possible to explain much of the variation across regions in new firm formation rates in the various countries. The adjusted R^2 values range from 45 per cent to 87 per cent, averaging about 75 per cent.

The overall thrust of the table is to suggest that the (prior) growth of population in an area is a significant and consistent positive inducement to new firm formation rates. It is also the case, in three out of the five countries, that formation rates are higher in urban than in rural areas.

Unemployment and changes in unemployment appear to have a broadly positive impact upon new firm formation, except in Sweden where changes in unemployment have a negative impact and in the United Kingdom where there is no impact.

It is also clear that geographical areas having a high proportion of their employment in small firms are more likely to have higher rates of new firm formation.

The impact of the other variables is rather more mixed, with virtually none of the public policy measures in factors 7 and 8 having any identifiable impact.

The results shown in Table 3.4 refer to an examination of firms in all economic sectors, but some differences emerge when the analysis is conducted for the manufacturing sector alone. The first is that the explanatory power of the models for the manufacturing sector is generally lower than for the 'all sector' models. Secondly, manufacturing formation rates are less influenced by population-related factors and more influenced by the size structure of existing firms. This is to be expected, since population-related factors will directly influence the demand for services, which are the prime element in the 'all sector' equations. The finding that areas with many small manufacturing firms have high rates of new manufacturing firm formation is well established (Fothergill and Gudgin 1982, Storey 1982a).

EXPLAINING TEMPORAL VARIATIONS IN RATES OF NEW FIRM FORMATION

Figures 3.3 and 3.4 showed that over time there were wide variations in the rates of new firm formation. Figure 3.3 showed data for the businesses registered for value added tax between 1980 and 1990, and Figure 3.4 showed data for company incorporations.

This section will provide a brief overview of the UK-based studies which have attempted to explain these temporal variations in new firm formations. It will draw heavily upon the review by Storey (1991) but will also include the more recent study by Keeble, Walker and Robson (1993), the conclusions of which appear to conflict significantly with the earlier studies.

The review by Storey (1991) is primarily concerned with the role of unemployment in encouraging new firm formation. Again, two hypotheses are proposed: the 'pull' and the 'push' hypotheses. The 'push' hypothesis suggests that unemployed individuals are more likely to start firms because of a lack of alternative employment opportunities. The converse 'pull' hypothesis suggests that new firm formation is higher when aggregate demand in the economy is higher, because business founders are attracted by market opportunities.

To test these hypotheses it is necessary to hold a number of other influences constant. These influences are shown in Table 3.5 in a total of eight groups. The first is unemployment (or unemployment divided by vacancies) itself.

The first of the set of 'control' variables are measures of public policy such as the Enterprise Allowance Scheme (EAS), set up in 1981, under which unemployed individuals received a payment of £40 per week for twelve months if they started a business. A full discussion of the impact of EAS is given in Chapter 8, where it is shown that the prime purpose of the scheme is to encourage the unemployed to become self-employed. A second policy influence was Selective Employment Tax which, between 1966 and 1973, was levied on employed workers and businesses in much of the service sector, with the exception of the self-employed. It may therefore have discouraged the formation of limited companies and encouraged businesses to opt for a partnership or self-proprietorship legal form. A third possible public policy impact is taxation. As discussed earlier in this chapter, a 'push'/'pull' argument may be put forward. Blau (1987) suggests that increases in the rate of personal taxation could provide an incentive for individuals to set up in business for themselves, on the grounds that self-employment provides a greater opportunity for income concealment than other forms of employment. The converse argument is that lowering the rates of taxation will provide an incentive for those already in business to legitimise their activities. A fall in the rate of taxation would therefore apparently lead to an increase in the number of legitimate businesses. The final public policy impact is upon the way in which statistics are collected and the changes in definitions which occur over time. These also have to be taken into account.

The third major group of factors influencing firm formation rates is profitability. Here it is argued that new firm formation will be higher when income from self-employment is higher, or when share prices are higher, on the grounds that this will attract individuals to start businesses.

The fourth group refers to interest rates and, *a priori*, it is to be expected that when real interest rates are high, access to capital will be restricted and new firm formation rates will be lower. Higher interest rates are, of course, an additional cost to the business and would therefore be expected to lead to lower profits.

The fifth influence is consumer expenditure. Here it is to be expected that new firm formation will be higher when consumer expenditure is high, reflecting the fact that the highest number of new firms, certainly in the United Kingdom, are in consumer services and increases in demand would be expected to provide a stimulus to formation.

The sixth variable is personal savings. As noted in the section above, personal savings have consistently been shown to be the prime source of financing of new businesses. These personal savings may take the form of directly realisable savings, or collateral against which the new firm founder may borrow from a financial institution; most particularly this relates to housing collateral.

Finally, the economy may be undergoing key structural changes which favour the formation of new businesses. For example, developed economies have seen a shift in structure away from both primary and manufacturing, and towards the service sector. During the 1980s there was also evidence of movement within the service sector in the United Kingdom away from personal services and towards business and financial services (Batstone 1989). These trends, on balance, are likely to favour new firm formation, since the minimum efficient scale of operations in business services, and in the service sector in general, is likely to be lower than in manufacturing.[3]

Unfortunately, conducting adequate time series analysis is hampered by serious data limitations. A long series of data are available for company incorporations but, as we have seen earlier, these constitute only a small proportion of UK businesses. It would be very unwise to assume that the factors which explain new company incorporation are identical to those which explain the birth of firms in the United Kingdom more generally, for two reasons. The first is that Scott (1982b) shows that 23 per cent of Scottish companies newly registered in 1969 never provided any evidence of trading activity, and the bulk are assumed never to have traded. The second is that a number of new companies are businesses which have been trading previously in an alternative legal form – as a sole proprietorship or partnership – possibly for some years.

More extensive data on self-employment which was examined by Johnson, Lindley and Boulakis (1988) and by Robson and Shah (1989) still provide relatively few data points, since the data are collected only on an annual basis. Value added tax (VAT) data has only recently been provided on a quarterly basis, and it is this which is used by Keeble, Walker and Robson (1993) for their analyses. Although it is estimated that only about two-thirds of UK businesses are registered for VAT, the data set does constitute the most comprehensive time series data available.

Table 3.5 shows that seven studies have used time series analysis with a view to examining the relationship between unemployment and new firm formation. We shall concentrate upon the more recent and econometrically robust work of Robson (1991), Hudson (1987a), Johnson, Lindley and Boulakis (1988), Robson and Shah (1989) and Keeble, Walker and Robson (1993). The studies by Hudson and by Robson use data on company incorporations, whereas that by Keeble *et al.* used VAT data; the remaining studies use data on self-employment.

With the exception of the Keeble *et al.* study, the time series analysis suggests that increases in unemployment are associated with increases in the rates of new firm formation. Keeble *et al.* are the exception, perhaps because they examine only the decade of the 1980s when, apart from the very early years and the final year, unemployment was falling at a time when new firm

Table 3.5 Time series studies of new firm formation in the United Kingdom

Concept	*Variable used*	*Studies*	*Signif.*	*Sign*
1 Labour market	Unemployment, or U/V	Robson	Yes	+
		Hudson	Yes	+
		Binks and Jennings	Yes	+
		Hamilton	Yes	+
		Johnson *et al.*	Yes	+
		Robson and Shah	Yes	+
		Keeble *et al.*	Yes	–
2 Public policy	Selective Employment Tax	Johnson *et al.*	Yes	(+)
		Robson	Yes	(+)
		Hudson	Yes	+
	Enterprise Allowance Scheme	Johnson *et al.*	Yes	+
		Robson	No	o
	Data changes	Johnson *et al.*	Yes	+/–
		Robson	Yes	+/–
		Hudson	Yes	+/–
		Keeble *et al.*	Yes	+/–
	Taxation	Robson	Yes	+/–
		Keeble *et al.*	Yes	–
3 Profitability	Income from self-employment	Robson	Yes	+
		Robson and Shah	Yes	+
	Share prices	Robson	Yes	+
4 Interest rates	Real interest rate	Hudson	No	o
		Robson and Shah	Yes	–
		Robson	No	o
		Keeble *et al.*	Yes	(–)
5 Consumer expenditure	Real disposable income	Hudson	Yes	+
		Keeble *et al.*	Yes	+
6 Personal savings	Sum of real savings	Hudson	No	o
	Real liquid assets from the personal sector	Robson	No	o
		Robson and Shah	Yes	+
	Real net housing wealth	Keeble *et al.*	Yes	+
7 Cyclical indicator	Ratio of GDP to GDP trend	Johnson *et al.*	Yes	+
8 Structural indicator	IER structural indicator	Johnson *et al.*	Yes	+/–

Key:
o Not applicable
() Weak significance
+ Variable is positively significant
– Variable is negatively significant

formation rates were rising. The other studies use a significantly longer real-time period, even though they may have fewer data points.[4]

As far as public policy is concerned, the results suggest that Selective Employment Tax had a positive impact upon new firm formation, but that a less clear impact is identifiable for the Enterprise Allowance Scheme. On the contentious issue of personal taxation there appears to be some support provided by Keeble *et al.* that a lowering of the average rate of income taxation induces an increase in the rate of new firm formation. In this sense the results contrast with those of Blau (1987) for the United States who found a positive relationship between marginal tax rates and self-employment.

Items 3 and 5 in Table 3.5 suggest the time series studies consistently point to a marked 'pull' effect, with formation rates of firms being higher in times of high income from self-employment and in times of high disposable incomes. This appears to be a quite consistent pattern from all the studies, and also supports the results obtained from the regional studies discussed in the previous section.

The findings on interest rates are also broadly compatible with *a priori* theorising. They suggest that firm formation rates will be high when real interest rates are relatively low, on the grounds that the interest rates will reflect ease of access to finance for business start-ups. This also parallels the findings referred to earlier which suggest that firm formation rates are higher when access to liquid assets is easier or when housing wealth is greater. It also parallels the findings from the spatial studies.

Finally, the cyclical and structural indicators do indicate a long-term shift in favour of higher rates of new firm formation.

Overall, the time series studies yield a fair degree of consistency on the factors which influence new firm formation in the United Kingdom. With the exception of the recent study by Keeble, Walker and Robson, unemployment appears to be positively associated with new firm formation, as does the general level of economic activity in the economy, together with access to finance. Real interest rates, on the other hand, appear to be negatively related to formation rates.

Bartlett (1993a) has undertaken a similar analysis to explain temporal variations in the formation of cooperative enterprises in Italy, Spain and Portugal. For Italy he finds the formation rate is positively associated with the rate of employment growth, suggesting better economic conditions are associated with higher rates of cooperative formation. However, for Spain, Bartlett finds that the birth rate of cooperatives is inversely associated with growth in GDP. He suggests that the formation of cooperatives in Spain is a defensive reaction by workers likely to experience unemployment.

CONCLUSIONS

This chapter, and Chapter 2, in some senses, address broadly similar issues. In Chapter 2 we ended by attempting to examine why, in several countries, in the 1980s, there had clearly been a rise in self-employment and possibly a relative increase in the economic role played by smaller firms. One index of this was the increase in the stock of firms in the economy – that is, the number of births exceeded the number of deaths.

This chapter has focused more narrowly on the factors influencing the birth rate of firms. Perhaps the single most important point which emerges from the chapter is the huge importance of new firms to the stock of businesses in an economy. As noted at the start of the chapter, nearly 14 per cent of all businesses registered for VAT in the United Kingdom in 1990 were new registrations during the previous twelve months. Given that only two-thirds of businesses are registered for VAT, and that those which are unregistered are likely to be younger than those which are registered, it suggests that the 14 per cent figure is likely to be, if anything, a significant under-estimate of the importance of very young firms in the stock of businesses.

The second key point is that the formation rates of new firms vary markedly from one sector to another, from one time period to another, and from one country or region to another. For example, Daly (1991) shows that during the 1980–90 period, registration rates for VAT varied from 3.5 per cent for new firms in agriculture (which was clearly a special case), to 12.9 per cent for motor trades, but was as high as 20.2 per cent for the miscellaneous service sector. Wide temporal variations were also observed with, for example, formation rates of new companies in the United Kingdom being very high during the 1980s, but comparatively low during the late 1960s and early 1970s.

Thirdly, in the United Kingdom during the 1980s, whilst rates of formation were very high by historical standards, rates of formation were three times higher in some counties than in others. This threefold variation across regions is also observed in countries as diverse as the United States and Germany.

Much of the chapter has been concerned with providing a theoretical framework for explaining these variations. The purpose is to use this theoretical framework to explain both the spatial and temporal variations in new firm formation.

The central conclusions from this work are that the existing sectoral composition of enterprises is a key factor, as industrial economists have stressed, in influencing new firm formation. However, it is emphasised that the focus of work by industrial economists has been primarily to explain entry into an industry, rather than new firm formation *per se*. Thus, whilst expected profitability and the presence of entry barriers are important for all types of entrants, a distinction has to be clearly made between the formation of new independent business units and the entry of existing businesses into different sectors.

The time series and spatial analysis confirms that profitability, perhaps as measured by the level of aggregate demand in the economy, is a key positive influence upon new firm formation. This is particularly true for new businesses in consumer services. It also confirms that access to capital and the real interest rate charged on that capital are important explanatory variables.

Two matters, however, remain unresolved. The first is the extent to which new firm founders are 'pushed' into entrepreneurship through a lack of alternative employment opportunities, and the extent to which they are 'pulled' by market opportunities. Probably the fairest conclusion is that both influences are at work and that their relative impact will vary sectorally, spatially and temporally. Even so, on balance, it would appear that the weight of evidence is that unemployment generally exerts a positive influence upon new firm formation.

The second unresolved issue relates to the impact of public policy upon new firm formation. At a casual level it is very tempting to infer that UK government policy was effective during the 1980s in increasing the rate of new firm formation. However, the studies reviewed in this chapter suggest that explicit public policies to encourage new firm formation have had a relatively marginal impact. Instead, the influences have been the structural changes which the United Kingdom commonly has experienced, the high level of aggregate demand in the economy and the access to capital, perhaps induced by changes in the housing market. We return again to these matters in Chapter 8.

These items do not constitute the core of a programme to stimulate enterprise. Nevertheless they clearly do have an impact upon the rates of new firm formation. The central policy question, however, which we will address in Chapter 9, is the extent to which it is an appropriate objective of policy, even assuming it to be achievable, to increase the rate of new firm formation.

Chapter 4

The death of small firms

INTRODUCTION

The fundamental characteristic, other than size *per se*, which distinguishes small firms from large is their higher probability of ceasing to trade. Ganguly (1985) shows that, in the United Kingdom in the 1980s, firms with an annual sales turnover of less than £13,000 in 1980 were six times more likely to deregister for VAT than firms with a turnover in excess of £2m. In the United States, Dunne, Roberts and Samuelson (1989) show that, for manufacturing plants, those with between five and nineteen employees had an exit rate which was 104.7 per cent higher than that for plants with more than 250 employees.

Although most empirical studies have consistently shown that smaller firms have higher failure rates than larger firms, it is essential to understand the terminology used in the legal framework to regulate business, in order to understand the true significance of these findings. For those businesses which cease and leave behind them unpaid creditors, the legal framework is necessary to ensure that such creditors are not exploited. The statistics provided by governments, and by private organisations, reflect that legal framework. Hence understanding the coverage and implications of these statistics requires some knowledge of how and why they were collected.

Whilst the death of firms can often cause anguish and hardship to the owner of the business, and to any unpaid creditors, it does provide a mechanism which can lead to allocative improvement within the economy, with resources being shifted from low returns to higher returns. Furthermore, business failure information provides guidance to those contemplating starting a business. It gives clear signals that entry into industry *a* is risky or, at least, more risky than entry into industry *b*. In both these senses, business failure is seen to exercise a valuable function in a market economy. A third economic role for business failure is to provide experience for those involved; thus there are a number of apocryphal stories of individuals who ultimately became very successful business owners but who had failed in business before – some of them several times. The implication from the 'popular' articles which highlight the careers of these individuals is that it was somehow by failing

Table 4.1 Business failure: some terms

Individual	*Firm*		*Plant*
	Limited companies	*Unincorporated businesses*	
Bankruptcy			
Exit			Exit
Insolvencies	Insolvencies		
	Liquidations		
	Failure	Failure	
	Death	Death	
	Deregister	Deregister	
	Cease to trade	Cease to trade	
	Closure	Closure	Closure

that they ultimately learned the secrets of a successful business.

The above paragraphs have already used a number of the confusing range of terms to describe the demise of firms; these include 'death', 'ceasing to trade', 'deregister', 'exit', and 'failure'. This chapter will use not only these terms, but also 'bankruptcy', 'liquidation' and 'insolvency', and so it is very important, at this early stage, to be clear about their meaning.

Table 4.1 is designed to explain some of these terms, but the reader should be aware that use of the particular terms is specific to the United Kingdom. Other countries may use exactly the same word, but its meaning may differ. The classic example is that of 'bankruptcy' which, as will be shown, has a different meaning in the United States from that in the United Kingdom.

Table 4.1 makes a clear distinction between individuals, plants (or establishments) and firms (or enterprises), so that only the terms which are relevant to each are shown under the column heading.

The first column shows the terms associated with an individual. It shows that in the United Kingdom the term 'bankruptcy' applies *only* to an individual who is declared bankrupt in a court of law. Such an individual is unable to repay debts in full and, until he or she is able to and is formally 'discharged' by the Court, is unable to obtain new credit or conduct business activity. The vast bulk of cases of bankruptcy are associated with business debt, but it is the individual who is declared bankrupt. An individual who is self-employed may, however, choose no longer to be self-employed and, in that sense, exits from self-employment. Only a tiny proportion of these will do so for reasons of bankruptcy. The majority will do so because they become an employee, retire, or choose to become unemployed. Thus the term 'exit' may also be applied to an individual, and is *not* synonymous with bankruptcy.

The only term which links the individual and the firm is 'insolvencies'. Official statistics on insolvencies are produced, and these combine personal bankruptcies with liquidations of limited companies. As shown in Table 4.1, only limited companies are formally liquidated, in the sense of a liquidator being appointed under the Companies Acts to sell the assets of the business and distribute the proceeds to creditors according to the priorities laid down in the Acts. From a statistical viewpoint, total insolvencies are defined as all liquidations of limited companies plus all personal bankruptcies.

Moving now to the right-hand side of the table, this shows that a business may continue even after it has shut one of its establishments or plants. Plant closure is defined as 'exit' and is, of course, the opposite of the term 'entry', discussed extensively in Chapter 3. 'Exit' therefore reflects reductions in the capacity of the industry, but not necessarily changes in the number of enterprises, except where the plant exiting is a single-plant enterprise. Plant 'closure' is a synonym for 'exit'.

The bulk of the terms in Table 4.1 apply to firms and are shown in the two central columns. Most, but not all, apply both to limited companies and to unincorporated businesses. The most clear-cut of them is 'deregister', in which a firm's registration for VAT is cancelled. The remaining four terms, 'death', 'failure', 'cease to trade' and 'closure' should be considered as synonymous.

The term 'failure' is often considered to have a pejorative connotation, implying either that the business should never have been started in the first place, or that the person who ran the business was not competent to do so, or that the business left behind significant unpaid debt. In fact none of these connotations need apply, and the reader can choose any of the four terms to apply to a business which has ceased to trade. In many senses the term 'failure' is used solely because of ease and recognition.

The structure of the remainder of this chapter is broadly similar to that for Chapter 3 on births. It begins with a review of the existing data sets on deaths/ failures of businesses, primarily within the context of the United Kingdom. Given the different definitions, their implications for estimation of *rates* of business failure are assessed.

The chapter reviews theoretical work (pp. 89–91) designed to improve our understanding of the factors which influence business failure, examining the influences upon failure rates over time, why small firms might be expected to have higher rates of failure than large firms, the factors which influence the decisions of multi-plant firms to close individual plants, and the influence upon the form of failure.

There is also a review (pp. 91–105) of the empirical studies of business failure. This makes a distinction between those which have examined why business failures are higher in certain years than in others, and those which investigate why they vary spatially and sectorally. However, the main thrust of the empirical studies relates to how failure rates vary according to type of business. For example, we examine the extent to which failure rates vary according to whether or not the business is in receipt of support from the state, and we compare current business failure rates with those which have been documented for the United Kingdom in the nineteenth century. We also make a comparison of business failure rates in general with those of certain types of business; for example, we compare the failure rates of franchises with those of the small business population as a whole; we compare the failure rates of firms according to their legal form. We also examine the differences between the failure rates of cooperative businesses, compared with those of small firms more generally.

The chapter then moves away from discussing the failure rates of businesses in aggregate to ask why it is that certain businesses fail, whereas others continue in business. Here we review briefly a substantial literature – much of it, however, relating to large firms – which attempts to distinguish between the characteristics of those firms which fail and those which survive. The relevance of this literature is that it can provide important insights for providers of finance such as banks or creditors, to enable them to identify the firms 'at risk'. Given that it is small firms which have the higher rates of failure, it might be thought surprising that the majority of research in the area has concentrated upon larger firms.[1] In recent years, however, there has been a significant upsurge in interest in predicting small firm failure.

This question is also examined (pp. 105–9) from an alternative perspective. Instead of focusing upon the firms which die, a number of studies are reviewed which look at the characteristics of firms which survive over a period of time. The issue is examined of whether there are clearly observable characteristics, either in terms of sector, age, markets or strategy which the business employs that influences its probability of survival.

Finally, this chapter provides a synthesis of these developments and some concluding statements.

DATA

Business deaths over time

This section draws heavily upon an unpublished paper, 'Business Failure Statistics', by Michael Daly (1992) of the UK Employment Department.

It might seem a simple question to ask 'How many firms go out of business each year?', but the simple answer is that we do not know. In some senses this is not surprising since, as was pointed out in Chapters 2 and 3, we do not even know the total number of firms in the economy. Therefore it cannot be surprising that we do not know the number that go out of business.

This may come as a surprise to casual readers of the financial press, in which highly publicised numbers are quoted which purport to relate to firms going out of business. It certainly is the case that such data are presented on the number of individual bankruptcies, on the number of company liquidations and also on businesses deregistering from VAT. Unfortunately, none of these indices relates to all businesses in the economy, and since limited companies constitute only about 19 per cent of UK businesses,[2] data on them alone must be particularly suspect.

This imperfect coverage would be less of a problem if the indices or measures of business failure all pointed in broadly the same direction at any one time. Unfortunately, as Figure 4.1 shows, this is far from being the case. Figure 4.1 takes five indices of business failure: compulsory liquidations, all companies no longer on the Companies Register, VAT deregistrations, exits from self-employment and individual bankruptcies.[3] Where appropriate, the numbers 'at risk' are normalised, so that compulsory liquidations data provide absolute numbers and these are normalised by the stock of companies in the base year to provide a *rate* of business failure. VAT deregistrations data are also normalised by the stock of businesses registered for VAT in the base year. Exits from self-employment are normalised by the total number of individuals who are self-employed. Unfortunately it is not possible to normalise the data on individual bankruptcies since it is not possible to determine the numbers 'at risk'.

The first point to note from Figure 4.1 is that whilst the data on companies is continuous from 1966 onwards, that on individual bankruptcies does not usefully begin until 1977, that on VAT deregistrations does not begin until 1980, and that on exits from self-employment until 1984. The data on individual bankruptcies and on companies are presented as a continuous time series but the reader is warned that there have been a considerable number of legislative changes over the quarter century for which data are presented. This has influenced the ways in which the statistics are collected, and so comparability over time declines, as the data becomes more historical.

The pattern for the 1980s, when most of the data sets are operational and should be broadly comparable, does vary markedly from one data set to another. Probably the most extreme differences are reflected in the VAT deregistration data, compared with the other data sets. The VAT data show that, whilst there has been a steady increase in the absolute numbers of deregistrations, when this is normalised by the stock of businesses, the deregistration rate remained at 11 per cent for ten out of twelve years. The only exception was a fall to 9 per cent in 1981, when the figures were almost certainly influenced by a civil servants' dispute, and a rise to 12 per cent in the severe recession of 1991.

This can be contrasted with data on the rate of compulsory liquidations of companies during the same period. Here the rate rose from 3.9 per cent of all

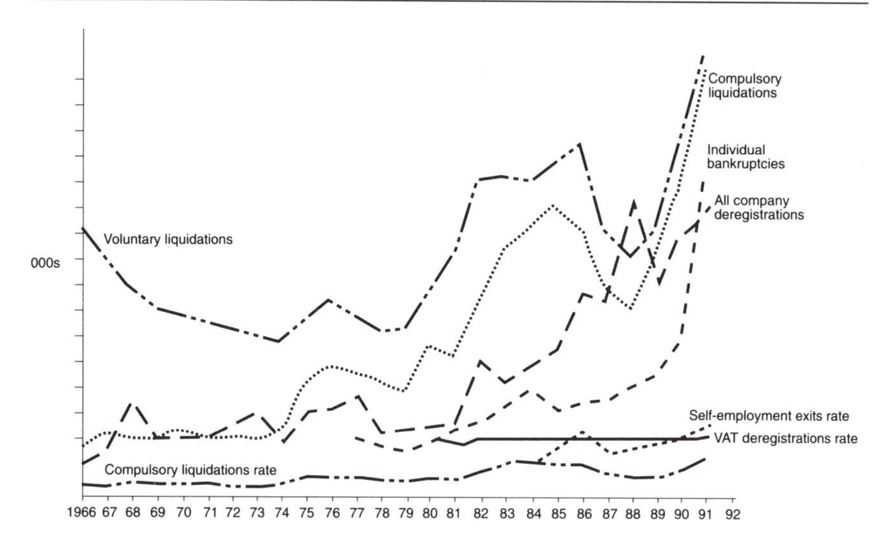

Figure 4.1 Trends in UK business deaths data, 1966–92

limited companies in 1980 being compulsorily liquidated in that year to 6.1 per cent in 1985. It then fell in each successive year until 1988, when only 3.5 per cent of the stock of companies in England and Wales were compulsorily liquidated. It then rose in each successive year, to reach 7.4 per cent of the stock in 1991. This pattern appears to correspond broadly to the business cycle in the United Kingdom, with the early 1980s being years of high and rising unemployment, whereas the middle to late 1980s were years of boom, followed by a further recession starting in 1989.

An alternative corporate measure is to take all companies which deregistered, rather than only those which were compulsorily liquidated. When normalised by the stock of companies, this shows little cyclical fluctuation, rising fairly continuously throughout the 1980s , with falls only in 1983, 1987 and 1989.

The rate of increase of exits from self-employment data show little change between 1985 and 1989 but do indicate, along with several of the other data sets, a rise in exits in 1989. This is particularly characteristic of the data on individual bankruptcies, where unfortunately only absolute numbers can be provided. This shows that the number of individuals declared bankrupt rose almost threefold between 1989 and 1991.

Turning now to the earlier period of 1966 to 1980, we again emphasise the need for caution over interpretation, due to definitional changes and the observed characteristic of Companies House undertaking periodic ‘purges’ of files to eliminate dead companies. Unfortunately these purges have often taken place during ‘quiet’ years, so that those removed from the register in year *t* may possibly have ceased to trade in year *t*-2. Nevertheless, the two indices of company deaths suggest the company liquidations data is much more stable over time than the 'all deregistrations' data. The rate of company liquidations appears to have been quite stable between 1966 and 1973; it then rose sharply until 1976, when it again entered a period of stability until 1979. There were stronger year-to-year fluctuations in the rate of company deregistrations. The pattern of voluntary liquidations over the 1966–79 period shows a fairly significant overall fall, compared with the general rise in the number of compulsory liquidations.

The above demonstrates that it is only compulsory liquidations which, over a long period of time, appear clearly related to macroeconomic conditions within the economy. The alternative measures of business death exhibit very different patterns over time. This emphasises two key points: the first is the need for agreement on precisely what constitutes a business 'death' or 'failure'. The second is the need for a better understanding of how the data are collected. Only then can we identify the most appropriate data set for the definition of business 'death' or 'failure' which we require.

The data sets

This subsection provides more detail on the data sets which describe and quantify firms going out of business in the United Kingdom.

VAT data

As noted in Chapters 2 and 3, all trading businesses with turnover in excess of a specified sales figure (£45,000 from December 1993) are required to register for VAT. It is often assumed that those firms which deregister are the firms which fail or die. However, this is not the case, as Daly shows in his 1987 article in *British Business*. There he identifies four groups of reasons why firms deregister for VAT. Of these, only one is unambiguously where the trader goes out of the business; the other reasons include the takeover of the business by another firm, changes in legal status, or where the trader falls below the VAT exemption limit.

Table 4.2 takes the data for 1987 and shows that for all businesses registered for VAT, only 58 per cent of those which deregistered did so because the trader went out of business. Of the remaining reasons, acquisition was clearly the most important, with 21 per cent of all deregistered businesses being acquired by other firms. Changes in legal status constituted 11 per cent of deregistrations, and 9 per cent were caused by the trader falling below the exemption limit or for other relatively minor reasons.

The significance of Table 4.2 is heightened, because the reasons for deregistration varied quite sharply between sectors. For example, only 6 per cent of construction businesses deregistered for VAT because of acquisition,

Table 4.2 Types of deregistration for VAT in 1987

	All sectors		*Production*		*Catering*		*Construction*		*Retail*	
	No.	*(%)*	*No.*	*(%)*	*No.*	*(%)*	*No.*	*(%)*	*No.*	*(%)*
Reason										
1 Trader goes out of business	96,945	(58)	11,227	(68)	6,780	(34)	14,739	(64)	17,441	(49)
2 Trader goes out of business; buyer already registered	36,344	(21)	2,322	(14)	10,270	(52)	1,261	(6)	13,382	(37)
3 Trader changes legal identity	18,188	(11)	1,194	(7)	1,281	(6)	4,656	(20)	2,518	(7)
4 Trader falls below exemption limit or other minor reasons	14,672	(9)	1,821	(11)	1,511	(8)	2,215	(10)	2,309	(6)
Total	166,149	(100)	16,654	(100)	19,842	(100)	22,871	(100)	35,650	(100)

Source: Daly (1987: pp. 28–9)

compared with 52 per cent of businesses in the catering sector and 37 per cent of businesses in retailing. One explanation for this is that a key component of businesses in both catering and retail is property, which gives the business value to a potential purchaser. On the other hand, 20 per cent of construction businesses deregistered for VAT because of changes in legal identity, compared with only 6 per cent of those in catering. It is therefore clear that the catering sector, in which only approximately one-third of businesses deregistered for VAT in 1987 because the trader went out of business, is very different from the general pattern of business deregistrations. Nevertheless, the central point of the table is that only some 58 per cent of businesses deregistering for VAT do so for the sole reason that the trader goes out of business.[4]

The second problem associated with VAT deregistrations data is that only about 60 per cent of firms in the United Kingdom are registered for VAT. Hence although 203,000 businesses were deregistered for VAT in 1991, for this to reflect fully the total number of UK businesses, it clearly has to be scaled up by more than 50 per cent. This would suggest that the more appropriate number is in excess of 300,000 in that year, although again this would have to be deflated proportionately to take into account the fact that not all deregistrations reflect the trader going out of business.

Data on the deregistration of UK companies

Figure 4.1 highlighted the fact that a long time series data set existed for UK companies. It was also shown that the data on compulsory liquidations of companies appeared to differ somewhat from that of numbers of companies removed from the register. In using data on limited companies, two central problem emerge. The first is that the time series itself is unreliable because of changes over time in the definitions used and the way in which the data are collected. The second is that, whilst the VAT data on businesses is certainly not comprehensive, it is very clear that less than one-fifth of all businesses in the United Kingdom registered for VAT are limited companies.

Table 4.3 shows that, in both 1980 and 1990, 30 per cent of businesses *registered for VAT* were limited companies, whereas 42 per cent were sole proprietorships and 28 per cent partnerships. It also shows that these ratios remained essentially unchanged throughout the 1980s. The table makes several very important points: in 1990 there were 490,000 companies registered for VAT, whereas the data from Companies House indicated that, in that year, the total number of companies registered was 1,115,000. Since it is likely that the vast bulk of companies that are actually trading are registered for VAT, this suggests that approximately half of the companies registered at Companies House at any one time are not in fact trading. This figure is even higher than the 28 per cent estimate made by Scott (1982a) referred to in Chapter 3. This is a particularly relevant point when we are attempting to measure the *rate* of firms going out of business, since the 'true' stock of trading companies is likely to be closer to 500,000 than to 1.15 million.[5]

Table 4.3 makes it clear that less than one-fifth of businesses registered for VAT are limited companies. It also suggests that only about half of the companies formally registered at Companies House are actually trading at any point in time. It is this insight which helps to explain, at least in part, the substantially different temporal pattern highlighted in Figure 4.1 of compulsory liquidations compared with all companies removed from the register.

Table 4.3 Deregistrations for VAT by form of organisation, 1980–90

	Stock in 1980		*Stock in 1990*		*Total deregistrations 1980–90*	*Annual deregistration rate*
	('000)	*%*	*('000)*	*%*	*('000)*	
Companies	378	(30)	490	(30)	525	11.0
Sole proprietorships	525	(42)	706	(43)	773	12.1
Partnerships	347	(28)	434	(27)	417	9.7
Total	1,250	(100)	1,630	(100)	1,715	11.1

Source: Daly (1991)

Limited companies in the United Kingdom are legally required, under the Companies Acts, to submit information relating to their activities, such as the names and addresses of their directors, the sector in which their business trades, together with accounts data including a balance sheet. Smaller companies are now allowed to submit modified accounts, where the amount of information required is substantially less than was the case prior to 1980. Not all companies, however, comply with these requirements by submitting timely accounts, and so Companies House makes its own efforts to determine whether or not a particular company is trading. Unfortunately the efforts which Companies House has made to track companies which have not submitted data, and to strike them off under Section 353 of the Companies Act and its successor legislation, have varied quite markedly from year to year. As noted earlier, Companies House has undertaken periodic purges to track down such companies, and this is reflected in the curious year-to-year variations in the number of firms removed from the data set. It would therefore be very unwise to assume that the number of companies removed from the register in one year necessarily reflected the numbers that ceased trading in that year. The periodic purges also mean that figures relating to the stock of companies trading at one point in time are also suspect, so that calculations of failure rates in individual years are subject to error.

Hence although, for example, in 1991 only 8,368 companies were compulsorily liquidated, compared with 113,000 which were removed from the register, the compulsory liquidations data may more closely reflect macroeconomic events. The problem, however, is that in the UK economy the 8,368 compulsory liquidations is a mere fraction of the total number of firms which went out of business in that year.

Individual bankruptcies

Figure 4.1 showed that the number of individuals declared bankrupt rose fairly continuously from 1977 until 1989. In that year 9,365 individuals were declared bankrupt, but by 1991 this had risen to 25,640. It is suggested by Daly (1992) that the bulk, although not all, of individual bankruptcies are related to business debts which the individual is unable to pay. For this reason the term 'individual bankruptcy' gets closest to the concept of entrepreneurial failure. These individuals are barred from being in business as company directors until their debts are repaid in full and they are formally discharged by a court of law. Such individuals are socially stigmatised so that, for example, until recently they were not even allowed to own a motor vehicle.

However, the interpretation of even these figures presents problems, since changes in the recent legislation have been designed, in part, to reduce the stigma associated with bankruptcy. For example, car ownership is now allowed and bankrupts can be discharged more easily than was the case in the past. It is suggested that at least part of the reason for the increase in the numbers of individuals declared bankrupt in recent years is that the associated stigma is now less than in the past.

Nevertheless the key point is that whilst there may be up to 300,000 businesses which cease to trade or 'fail' in any one year, only 25,000 individuals 'fail' in the sense of being declared personally bankrupt. On these figures alone, it could be argued that 'business failure' is twelve times more likely than 'entrepreneurial failure' (Storey 1990b).

Exits from self-employment

Since 1984 the Labour Force Survey (LFS) has asked about individuals entering and exiting from self-employment. Those people exiting could be deemed to be owners of businesses which have ceased to trade. According to Figure 4.1, the numbers of individuals in this category far exceed any other estimate of businesses which cease to trade. For example, in 1991 487,000 individuals claimed to have exited from self-employment, constituting 15 per cent of the total number of individuals categorised as being self-employed.

This number is broadly compatible with the finding that 203,000 businesses deregistered for VAT since, given that two-thirds of UK businesses are registered, this probably equates to around 300,000 businesses in total. Assuming that each business which ceases to trade has 1.5 self-employed individuals, then this is close to the figure generated by the LFS. Even so, the LFS figure is higher than might be expected from other sources, since a number of individuals owning a business which has ceased to trade will enter some other form of self-employment, rather than exiting completely, and because only just over half of VAT deregistrations are due to the business ceasing to trade.

A second aspect in which LFS results differ from the VAT-based data is that the former appear to be more influenced by the nature of the business cycle. Thus exits from self-employment appear to have been at a level of about 9 per cent (with the exception of 1986) between 1985 and 1989, but then rose sharply to reach 15 per cent in the recessionary conditions of 1991. As noted earlier, the VAT statistics indicate almost no variation in business deregistrations throughout the 1980s.

Overall

The central conclusion to be drawn from this very brief review of data on firms which go out of business is that each source measures different items. The data on limited companies refer to only one type of legal entity, the data on VAT include not only traders which go out of business but also those who change their legal form or are taken over, whilst the data on self-employment refer to individuals rather than businesses. The purpose then must be to identify a data set which is appropriate to the particular definitions which we choose to employ about firm death or failure.

SOME THEORETICAL ISSUES

The subject of business failures and deaths has interested a number of disciplines of researchers. Even so, theoretical developments in this area have been less sophisticated than those on the start-up of businesses and even their subsequent growth.

Keasey and Watson (1991) say:

> It is not too much of an exaggeration to state that the overwhelming majority of empirical work on failure prediction has produced 'garbage can' models; that is, the model's development has been data driven rather than theory led.

The economist's basic assumption is that, in the long run, firms which are loss-makers will exit the industry, whereas profit-makers are assumed to continue in business. In the short run, however, those loss-makers which are able to cover variable costs and make a contribution to fixed costs, may also survive.

The more sophisticated theoretical work has set out to provide an explanation of occurrences which are not easily explained by simple theory. For example, not all loss-making firms cease to trade; it also appears to be the case that the firms which make the biggest losses do not necessarily exit first; profitable firms may also exit the market.

The work by Reid (1991) and by Baden-Fuller (1989) draws heavily upon the work by Bulow and Shoven (1978). This argued that the decision on whether or not to close the firm depended on the relative net costs of continuance versus immediate closure. Baden-Fuller expresses it in the following form:

$$\pi < rC - C'$$

where π = present value of anticipated profit in the coming period, C = residual value of the plant if scrapped now, r = rate of interest, and C' = present value of anticipated capital gain in scrap value from deferring the closure.

One contribution by Bulow and Shoven (1978) was to show that the continue-versus-liquidate decision depended upon the relationship between the owners of the business, their bank and other creditors. It also depended upon the legal framework which gave priority to these creditors. Bulow and Shoven also showed that the maturity structure ownership of the firm's debt influenced the decision of the parties, so that a longer-term debt structure and a relatively high proportion of cash or liquid assets were more likely to lead to continued operation than to liquidation.

Subsequent theoretical work, such as that by Reynolds (1988), is concerned with the question of *which* firms will exit an industry in the event of declining demand. He shows that in an industry composed exclusively of single-plant firms with identical costs, there is no way of determining which firms will exit first in the event of a decline in demand. However, if the industry is composed of enterprises with multiple plants, then Reynolds shows that large firms will begin to close plants before their smaller rivals, so long as plant cost differences between the two types of firm are small. The large firm closes plants because by doing so this provides larger revenue increases for the firm's remaining plants.

This is a similar result to that generated by Ghemawat and Nalebuff (1985), except that their work suggested that it was large firms which would quit a declining industry first, whereas Reynolds' work suggests that large firms will be likely to remain within the industry, but be more likely to close plants.

The theoretical and empirical significance of this is examined by Baden-Fuller (1989), who finds some support for the Reynolds theory. Taking data from the United Kingdom steel castings industry, he shows that firms which operate in other businesses seem, all things being equal, more likely to close a plant. This is because such firms have significant managerial resources which may be redeployed into plants in different sectors where a higher return may be obtained.

A very different economic model designed to provide an understanding of business failure has been put forward by Jovanovic (1982). This is not concerned with the formal legal structure of the businesses, but with the characteristics of the individuals who operate them. Jovanovic assumes that both the individuals themselves and financial institutions such as the banks are ignorant, before that individual starts a business, of whether or not the business will be successful. It is only by being an entrepreneur that the individual is able to obtain information on success, and the same applies to the bank. As a result of this information, both bank and entrepreneur modify their behaviour through time. Individuals who revise their ability estimates upwards tend to expand, whereas those who revise them downwards tend to contract or go out of business completely. The value of the Jovanovic model is that it provides some explanation of why younger firms have lower rates of survival than older firms. This is because the learning process of the entrepreneur takes place over a period of time, rather than immediately, so that younger firms, having less precise estimates of their true abilities, and having less time in which to learn, are more likely to be put out of business by external shocks.

As noted at the start of this section, finance theorists have contributed relatively little to our understanding of *why* it is that firms cease to trade. It probably is still true to say that financial analysts continue today to use the Beaver (1966) analogy of a firm as a tank of liquidity, into which there are flows and returns from the activities of the firm. Beaver's central proposition was that the larger the size of this reservoir, the smaller was the probability of failure. The problem with this analogy, however, as Keasey and Watson point out, is that 'this amounts to little more than asserting that firms fail when they run out of money'. The Beaver analogy is unable to point towards underlying causes of failure, although the use of financial ratios can provide useful symptoms of impending failure.

In her review of the factors which influence small business failure, Berryman (1983) places a much greater emphasis upon the managerial and personal characteristics of the business owner than is the case either with economists or financial analysts. She argues that small entrepreneurial firms generally reflect the personalities of the entrepreneurs who created them. She draws upon the work of Argenti (1976), who observes that a key defect of companies is an autocratic chief executive who is unwilling to take advice. Berryman also notes that empirical studies have suggested that those individuals most likely to fail in business have limited formal education, who resist advice from qualified sources, who undertake relatively little reading, and who are inflexible to change and reluctant to innovate.

Managerial theorists also see business failure as one 'outcome' from a crisis (Hall 1991). Churchill and Lewis (1983) and Scott and Bruce (1987) see the firm as making a transition through different stages of growth, from a small entrepreneurial flexible start-up to a sophisticated devolved and managed large organisation. They see the firm as making a series of transitions from one stage to another, with these transitions frequently being induced by an external shock event. Scott and Bruce, in particular, see the failure to make that transition in the event of the external shock as leading to a business failure.

Despite contributions from different disciplines, the theoretical framework for an understanding of business failure is poorly specified. As yet, there is no satisfactory way of integrating the emphasis upon the personal qualities of the individuals, their managerial styles and the ultimate performance of the small firm.

A REVIEW OF FAILURE RATES

The above sections have shown that there are many definitions of business failure. Watson and Everitt (1993) identify four different definitions:

- discontinuance for any reason;
- ceasing to trade and creditor loss;
- sale to prevent further losses;
- failing to make a go of it.

These constitute a wide range of definitions. For example, 'discontinuance for any reason' will encompass, as failures, those businesses which do not continue in their current form. These include, for example, businesses which are sold because of the illness or retirement of the owner, even though the business may have been perfectly viable.

At the other extreme is the second definition, which regards as 'failures' only those businesses in which there is a loss to the creditors. This is an equally unrealistic definition, since business failure would generally include businesses which are obtaining an inadequate return on the human and financial capital employed. This does not necessarily imply that they are trading at a loss or that, upon closure, there will be a loss to the creditors.

Using data from the retail sector, Watson and Everitt calculate that 52 per cent of their sample businesses could be deemed to have failed, using the criterion of discontinuance for any reason, compared with only 6 per cent which would be classified as failures using the loss to the creditors definition.

Acknowledging these problems of definition, this section identifies eleven factors which influence the probability of failure of a business. They are, of course, not necessarily independent of one another. These are:

- size;
- age;
- ownership;
- sector;
- past performance;
- macroeconomic conditions;
- people/management;
- location;
- businesses in receipt of state subsidies;
- firm type;
- 'and it was ever so'.

The remainder of this section will examine the evidence on failure/survival rates of businesses according to these dimensions. In essence we will be comparing these failure rates with those of more 'typical' small businesses.

Size

As we have noted continuously, business failure rates, almost however they are defined, are inversely related to firm size. The empirical evidence on this is virtually unanimous. For example Dunne, Roberts and Samuelson (1989) in their study of US manufacturing plants showed that the average failure rate for plants with between five and nineteen employees was 104.7 per cent higher than for plants with more than 250 employees. Gallagher and Stewart (1985) found that a firm employing less than twenty people was 78 per cent more likely to fail over the next decade than one employing more than 1,000. Deregistration rates for UK firms registered for VAT are six times higher for the smallest firms than for the largest (Ganguly 1985). For UK non-financial companies, Dunne and Hughes (1992) found that non-survivors over the 1980–5 period constituted 27 per cent of those with net assets of less than £1m., compared with 14 per cent of those with net assets exceeding £64m.

Age

Dunne, Roberts and Samuelson (1989) incorporated an age variable into their equation to estimate plant failure rates. They found that, holding size and ownership constant, increasing age was associated with lower failure rates. They also found that this effect was identifiable not simply for young firms, such as those less than five years old, but was also present amongst those between six and ten years old and for the third group between eleven and fifteen years old.

For the United Kingdom, Daly (1987) showed that deregistration for VAT is clearly related to business age. His data, reproduced as Figure 4.2, show that half-yearly deregistration rates are at their peak in the second and third years of the life of a business. At that time the *annual* deregistration rate is equivalent to almost 20 per cent; it then falls away, to reach perhaps 7 per cent once the business is ten years old.

In his study of compulsory liquidations of UK companies between 1978 and 1981, Hudson (1987b) also finds clear evidence that insolvency is much more characteristic of young firms. He found that, of those which become insolvent, 61 per cent did so between two and nine years after formation and that there was a peak between two and five years of age.

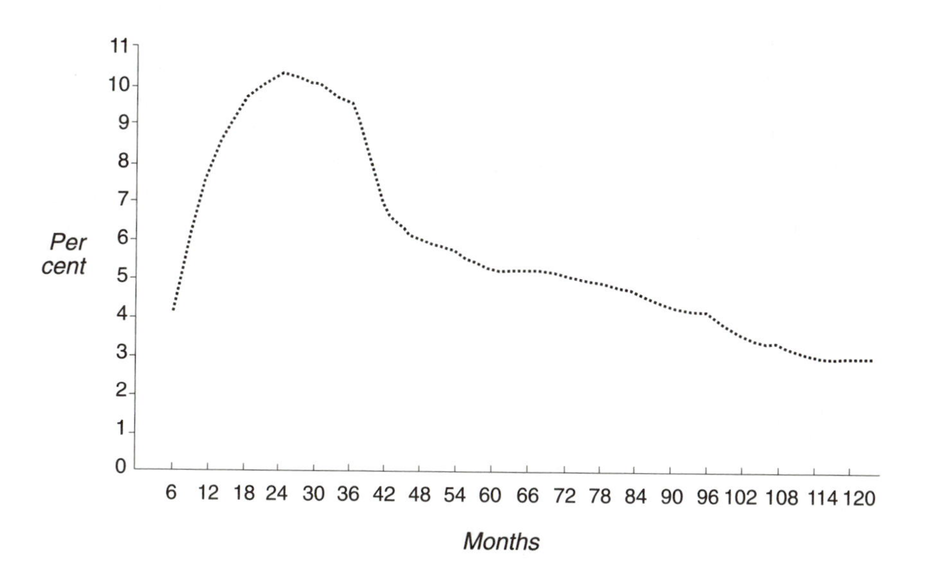

Figure 4.2 Half-year VAT deregistration data by age
Source: Daly (1987)

Ownership

Aggregate studies demonstrate that, *ceteris paribus*, small firms have higher failure rates than large firms. However, as we noted earlier, there have been theoretical and empirical studies showing that the introduction of ownership can reverse this finding. Ghemawat and Nalebuff (1985) argue that, where demand is declining, it is the largest firms which are likely to leave first and the smallest firms which are most likely to hang on, thus possibly reversing the results of the empirical studies reviewed above. Reynolds (1988) also argues that, where firms have the same number of plants, in an industry experiencing decline, the high-cost plants will close before lower-cost plants. He also argues that firms which operate more than one plant begin closures before the single-plant firms. This is because the larger firm gains more from a plant closure, as this provides a larger revenue increase for the firm's remaining plants. Alternatively, the large firm may more easily be able to redeploy its managers into other markets which are not in decline, than the single plant firm which may be more committed to a particular sector.

The empirical study by Baden-Fuller (1989) suggests that whilst profitability does influence exit decisions, the least profitable firms do not consistently exit from the industry first. It is firms which also operate in other business sectors that are most likely to exit. Baden-Fuller, however, finds little support for the Ghemawat and Nalebuff hypothesis that it is the largest firms which quit first. In his study, all four of the largest firms in the industry remained active and were not major closers of plants, illustrating the importance of ownership, as well as size, as factors influencing plant survival.

The work of Schary (1991) suggests that the form of exit – bankruptcy, voluntary liquidation or merger – may also be influenced by the ownership of the firm. However, taking data from the declining US cotton industry during the period 1924–40, she also finds no support for the Ghemawat and Nalebuff hypothesis that it is the largest firms which exit first. Her work points in the same direction as that of Baden-Fuller, in finding little association between exit and profitability.

Sector

Failure rates of businesses do vary from one sector to another but, given the attention which economists pay to industry sector, the differences are relatively modest. The range of business failure rates between sectors does not vary as markedly for smaller firms as it does in some of the other dimensions discussed above. For example, the annual average VAT deregistration rates between 1980 and 1990, excluding agriculture, varied from 9.2 per cent for firms in the finance sector to 13.3 per cent for firms in the retail sector.[6] Gallagher and Stewart (1985) found a broadly similar pattern: taking firms with between twenty and forty-nine workers in 1982, they found the lowest

Table 4.4 New firm survival in the United States, 1976–86

Industry	*% firms surviving*
Agriculture, forestry and fishing	43.1
Mining	39.1
Construction	35.3
Manufacturing	46.9
Transportation, communications, utilities	39.7
Wholesale trade	44.3
Retail trade	38.4
Services	40.9
Finance, insurance and real estate	38.6
All industries	39.8

Source: Phillips and Kirchhoff (1989b)

dissolution rate to be 3.87 per cent, for firms in miscellaneous services, with the highest being 5.48 per cent, for firms in the manufacturing sector. Perhaps the most striking illustration of the lack of sectoral differences in firm dissolution rates is shown by Phillips and Kirchhoff (1989a) in their study of new firms in the United States between 1976 and 1986. Their results, reproduced as Table 4.4, show a striking similarity of survival rates of new businesses according to sector. Taking the all-industry average as 39.8 per cent, Phillips and Kirchhoff show that the range varied only from 35.3 per cent, for firms in the construction sector, to 46.9 per cent, for firms in the manufacturing sector. In one important sense the results differ from those provided by Gallagher and Stewart for the United Kingdom, where the highest failure rates are in the manufacturing sector.[7] Nevertheless the central point is that, whilst there are differences in failure rates between sectors, the range of variation is much less than for several other dimensions.

This finding is also reflected in some of the multivariate studies of business failure/survival. For example, Kalleberg and Leicht (1991), in a study of 411 small US firms in computer sales and software, food and drink and health industries found that there were no overall differences in business failure rates, once company and owner operator characteristics were taken into account. Storey *et al.* (1987), in their attempt to produce a predictive model for small firm failure in the United Kingdom, also found that the sectoral variable added no significant explanatory power.

Past performance

Of the recent research on new business survival, the major contribution has undoubtedly been made by Phillips and Kirchhoff (1989a). As noted above, their paper identifies only relatively modest sectoral differences in new firm failure rates, and points to the key influence on survival of young firms being

Table 4.5 Six-year survival rates of firms classified by beginning employment size and number of jobs created: born 1976–8 surviving to 1984–6

	Percentage surviving in 1984–6				
Number of employees at birth (all industries)	*Zero growth*	*Low growth*	*Medium growth*	*High growth*	*All classes*
1 to 4	26.0	65.0	75.6	77.2	37.2
5 to 499	34.1	72.4	75.3	79.2	49.2
Under 500 (all small firms)	27.5	66.3	75.5	78.4	39.8

Source: Phillips and Kirchhoff (1989a)

that of growth. Table 4.5 shows that, of firms born between 1976 and 1978, 39.8 per cent survived after six years. This is slightly lower than the UK VAT statistics.

The real interest of Table 4.5, however, is the striking difference in the survival rates according to whether or not the firm increases employment. Only 26 per cent of firms, which when they started to trade had four or less employees and which did not increase in level of employment, survived for the six-year period. However, if firms in the group increased their number of workers, then their survival rates increased – to 65 per cent if they increased the number of workers by four or less (low growth), to 75.6 per cent if they increased their number of workers by between five and nine (medium growth), and to 77.2 per cent if they increased the number of workers by ten or more (high growth).

The second key finding of Table 4.5 is that those firms which start larger, on average, have higher survival rates. Thus 37 per cent of firms which began with less than five workers survived for a six-year period, compared with 49 per cent of new firms which began with five or more workers. However, these differences in initial size have only a modest impact upon whether or not the firm survives, compared with whether or not employment increased within the firm in its early years of life.

Thirdly, Table 4.5 also shows that, whilst it is the case that the high-growth new firms have a higher probability of survival than the low-growth new firms, these differences are relatively marginal. The central distinction is related less to the rate of growth, and more to whether or not the new firm grows at all. In other words, the results show that the key to survival for new firms is to achieve growth; the rate of that growth is of secondary importance.

Macroeconomic conditions

A number of recent studies have attempted to relate macroeconomic conditions to business failure in small firms. For example, Desai and Montes

(1982) relate the number of business bankruptcies to the growth of the nominal money stock and the level of nominal interest rates. Hudson (1986) finds, somewhat surprisingly, that higher interest rates are associated with fewer company liquidations.

Simmons (1989) takes the number of personal bankruptcies in a sector, normalised by the total number of self-employed in that sector, and attempts to explain changes in this variable by a combination of demand and supply-side changes specific to the industry, together with national interest rate changes. He concludes that failures are associated with unfavourable cost shocks, but that interest rates are not a major influence. He draws a distinction between large and small firms, suggesting that small businesses may not be subject to credit market squeezes of the kind experienced by larger firms. Instead he argues that industries dominated by small firms can increase their output prices at a rate faster than increases in interest rates.

This, however, seems a somewhat unlikely conclusion. Keeble, Walker and Robson (1993) suggest the Simmons result probably reflects his inability to find an appropriate deflator for cost changes in the industries he surveys. As Keeble, Walker and Robson note, in one industry where an appropriate deflator is available – the construction industry – higher interest rates are associated with higher rates of business failure.

This is confirmed in the analysis by Hudson and Cuthbertson (1992). In their analysis of personal bankruptcies over the period 1971–86, they find the key positive influences to be increases in unemployment and interest rates. They also find that administrative influences, such as changes in the minimum amount of debt which needs to be incurred before bankruptcy can be petitioned, also is a major influence. The final factors are changes in the number of self-employed workers and in credit availability. All these seem intuitively plausible influences, even though the dependent variable (personal bankruptcies) is an amalgam of both personal and business elements and ideally it would be better to estimate them independently.

Other studies in the United States and the United Kingdom have suggested that macroeconomic conditions do not exert a major influence upon small business failure rates. For example, in the United States, Lane and Schary (1990), Phillips and Kirchhoff (1988) and Birch and McCracken (1981) suggest that temporal variations in small business failure rates are more strongly related to the ages of the firms than to macroeconomic conditions. Lane and Schary find that a high failure rate in year t reflects a relatively high number of business starts in years t-2 and t-3, rather than current macroeconomic conditions such as interest rates, changes in GNP, corporate profits, or changes in prior investment and unemployment.

The lack of a clear relationship between macroeconomic conditions and VAT deregistration rates has also been observed in the United Kingdom. As was pointed out earlier, Daly (1987) showed that failure rates by age of firm did not appear to vary on a year-by-year basis. Furthermore Daly (1991) shows that the overall rate of deregistrations for all businesses constituted 11 per cent of the stock in all the years between 1980 and 1990, with the exception of 1981 when, as noted earlier, an industrial dispute by civil servants almost certainly affected the figures.

Hudson and Cuthbertson (1990), however, show that rates of compulsory liquidation of UK companies between 1972 and 1988 are related to changes in unit labour costs, GDP and interest rate changes. They also find that the age distribution of new firms is a powerful influence. This finding is echoed by Keeble, Walker and Robson (1993), who also point to the central importance of a lagged business births variable.

Overall, the results suggest that macroeconomic conditions do seem to influence some definitions of failure – such as compulsory liquidations and bankruptcies – more than others, such as VAT deregistrations. However, the variable which best explains the number of firm deaths in year t seems to be the number of new firms started in year t-2 or t-3.

People/management

Chapter 3 identified a number of personal characteristics of individuals which were hypothesised to be related to their likelihood of becoming a business owner. This section examines the extent to which these personal characteristics influence their probability of surviving in business, having once started.

For ease of presentation these individual characteristics are placed into four categories: work history, family background, personal characteristics and education. It should not be assumed, however, that these are 'independent' categories in the sense that they are, statistically, uncorrelated.

Amongst the relevant work history characteristics which might be thought to influence the likelihood of an individual staying in business are prior business ownership, prior managerial experience, experience of unemployment, experience of working in a large firm, work experience in the same sector, and training.

For example, prior business ownership may make owners more aware of the problems of ownership; they will have had the opportunity to learn the lessons of previous mistakes, so that prior ownership would be associated with survival. Prior managerial experience could also positively influence survival, since those individuals will have experience of the management of others (Townroe and Mallalieu 1993).

Experience of unemployment could be thought to influence business survival in either a positive or a negative direction. It could provide a stimulus to the individual, in the sense of making them more determined that the business did not fail, through fear of returning to a state of unemployment (MacDonald and Coffield 1991). This may be reflected in a willingness to work for less money than that provided for the unemployed through benefits, through a determination to avoid the stigma of unemployment. On the other hand, having been unemployed may reflect a lack of skills on the part of the individual, and this lack of skills may ultimately result in higher rates of business failure.

Other work history characteristics may be thought to influence small business survival rates: large firm work experience and work experience in the same sector. The latter would be expected to be positively associated with survival, since the individual can be expected to have a better understanding of 'norms' and 'accepted practices' in the sector than someone totally new. The impact of prior experience working for a larger firm is less clear; on the one hand it could be argued to provide, particularly for managers, a wider breadth of experience, but this may have been gained in a rather more 'cosseted' and 'narrow' environment than the hurly-burly of being the owner-manager of a small business.

Amongst the personal characteristics of an individual which might influence business survival can also be included the age of the individual, their gender and their ethnic background.

The relationship between age and small business survival is often argued to be of an inverted U-shape. The age groups least likely to survive are those who are very young and who lack both experience and capital, and the old, who lack energy and motivation, many of whom see the business as a hobby. The middle-aged, however, avoid both of these extremes (Cressy 1992).

A priori it is unclear what impact, if any, gender is likely to have upon small business survival. With respect to ethnic background, the common preconception (Jones, McEvoy and Barrett 1992) is that Asian businesses in particular are likely to have higher survival rates than white-owned firms. This reflects the greater use of family networks for financial support, a reluctance to seek salaried work through fear of racial prejudice, and perhaps a clearer awareness of the business skills which are needed to succeed.

Finally, two other characteristics which have been examined include educational attainment of the individual and whether or not they came from a family with a history of business ownership. Both these would be expected to be associated with higher rates of business survival. Thus, high educational attainment signals a high level of skills which may be drawn upon to avoid business failure. Similarly, family history of involvement with business can provide access to capital and also confidential business advice, which could be crucial in avoiding failure (Stanworth *et al.* 1989).

There are very few studies which have managed to incorporate more than a few of these personal characteristics of the founder into a study of small business survival, alongside the other influences upon business failure identified in this chapter. Notable partial exceptions to this include the study by Kalleberg and Leicht (1991), which shows that prior self-employment experience for men is associated with a higher likelihood of going out of business. However, it shows that there are no clear gender differences between survivors and non-survivors. The number of years of prior experience of the founder in the industry is not an influence on survival and neither is their age when they began the business.

A study by Bates (1990) is concerned with examining the human capital factors which influence exits from self-employment in the United States. Whilst the study specified a relatively limited range of human capital characteristics – it includes only education levels, family business ownership experience, management experience of the owners and their age – the findings suggest that higher levels of education are associated with higher survival rates once in business. The other elements of human capital included by Bates do not seem to have a major influence on the survival of businesses.

The study by Cressy (1992), which examined 2,000 new businesses which survived for four years, also found the personal characteristics of founders to be a relatively unimportant influence on survival rates. The only two characteristics which appeared to influence survival were the age of the proprietor and whether they had qualifications, even though employment status, gender, prior business ownership and managerial experience were all included within the equations.

Overall, these findings suggest that whilst there is considerable speculation on the impact of the personal characteristics of an individual which influence whether or not they survive in business, it is difficult to draw clear patterns from the results so far. Similar conclusions are appropriate for the psychological testing literature, which is also at an early stage of development in this area (Chell, Haworth and Brearley 1991).

Location

Two major UK studies have examined the factors influencing the spatial variation of business deaths. In the United Kingdom, spatial analysis of business deaths is restricted to deregistrations from VAT, since no data are published on the corporate sector in this respect.

Westhead and Birley (1993b) examine VAT deregistrations between 1987 and 1990, whereas Keeble, Walker and Robson (1993) examine deregistrations over the longer period 1980 to 1990; the latter also conduct a subsequent analysis for two separate five-year time periods.

Figure 4.3 shows that all of England's major urban areas (London, Birmingham, Manchester, Liverpool, Cardiff, Newcastle and Cleveland) have high rates of deregistration, whereas the rural counties have comparatively low rates. This finding is also highlighted by Westhead and Birley.

The second finding of both groups of researchers is that geographical areas with high rates of new firm formation are also those which have the highest death rates. As pointed out earlier, researchers generally attribute this to high formation rates leading to a higher proportion of the stock of firms which are very young and hence most vulnerable to failure. However, Binks and Jennings (1986) argue that the direction of the causation in observing

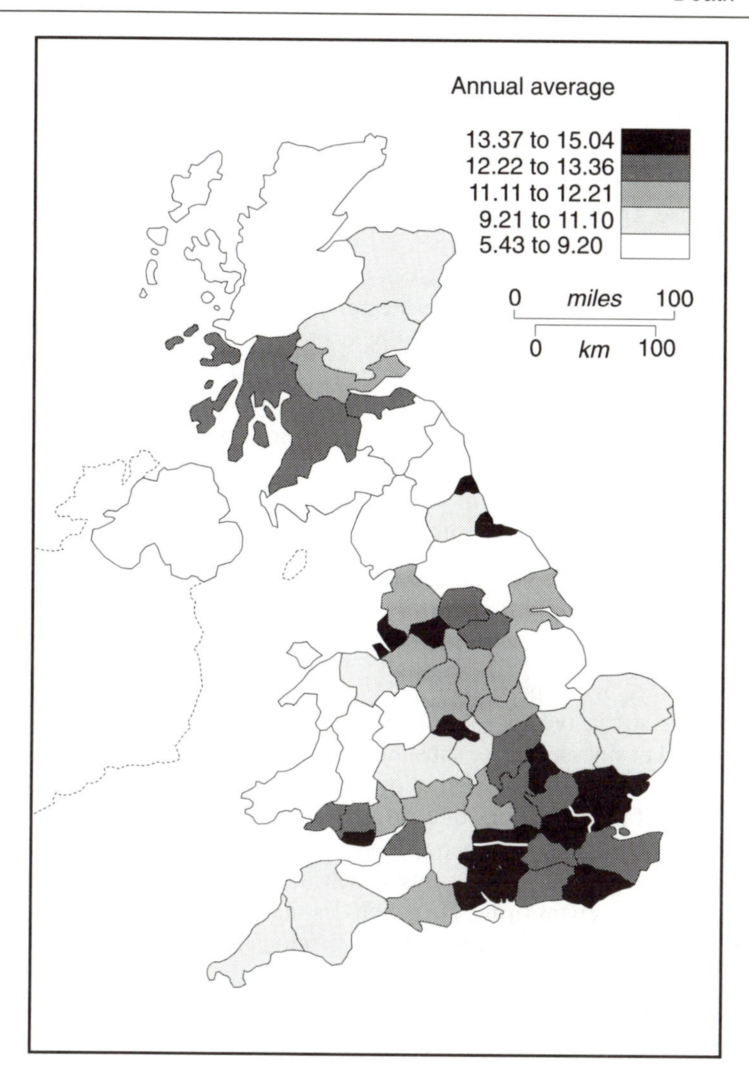

Figure 4.3 Firm closure rates in the total economy, 1980–90
Source: Keeble, Walker and Robson (1993)

correlation between births and deaths is not obvious. This is because the death of (primarily large) firms in an area can lead to additional market opportunities and to easier access to second-hand equipment for new firms. Hence it may be the deaths which 'cause' the births, rather than vice versa. Whilst it is likely that labour-shedding leads to increases in new firm formation, it seems less likely, however, that a high *number* of firm deaths will lead to a high *number* of firm births.

The third finding identified by Keeble *et al.* is that areas which have an

Enterprise Agency providing loans, grants and business advice are likely, other things being equal, to have lower rates of business failures than areas without such support services. They find this result plausible on the grounds that the Small Business Research Centre (1992) found it was the newer and more rapidly growing firms which were most likely to utilise the support of an Enterprise Agency. The reservation must be expressed, however, that the prime focus of Enterprise Agencies for much of the 1980s was not on supporting the existing businesses, but rather in stimulating the formation of new businesses. In this sense the result can be deemed slightly surprising, and the Enterprise Agency variable may be a proxy for some other influences, such as the general commitment of the area to encouragement of enterprise.

Since it is only the Agencies with access to finance, rather than all Enterprise Agencies, this suggests that it is their provision of finance, rather than their provision of information, which is the key influence on failure rates. We return to this question of the relative effectiveness of public provision of information and finance upon small firms in Chapter 8.

Businesses in receipt of state subsidies

A full discussion of the role of Enterprise Agencies is reserved for Chapter 8. Nevertheless, it is appropriate here to examine evidence about whether small businesses in receipt of a state subsidy have lower failure rates than unsubsidised businesses. State subsidies can be in the form of loans or grants, or even in the form of subsidised information. Smallbone (1988, 1990), in an examination of the operations of a single Enterprise Agency, concluded there was little evidence that the Agency made a significant contribution either to stimulating the growth of the firms which it supported, or to lowering the failure rates of its client firms. He concludes that the businesses which failed did so because their owners lacked the motivation and/or ability needed to run a successful business. In this sense there was little that any Agency could do. Even so, of the twelve businesses which did fail, and which Smallbone followed up, in only one case did the Enterprise Agency become involved in trying to save the business.

Perhaps not surprisingly, in a study for Business in the Community, Enterprise Dynamics (1987) comes to a somewhat different conclusion, but, as is shown in Chapter 8, the study exhibits methodological shortcomings.

A second publicly supported scheme to stimulate enterprises was the Enterprise Allowance Scheme (EAS), which is also discussed in detail in Chapter 8. Participants in this scheme had to be between sixteen and sixty-four years old, have been unemployed for eight weeks, and have £1,000 to invest in their new business. Those wishing to start under this scheme were provided with £40 per week in compensation for lost state benefits for a maximum of one year. In his examination of the impact of the Enterprise Allowance Scheme, Gray (1990) shows that 43 per cent of EAS businesses fail within three years – a considerably higher rate of failure than that for VAT-registered firms, reported by Daly (1987) as being about 35 per cent. Yet, again, it is unwise to make direct comparisons, since the characteristics of individuals participating in EAS differed from UK small business owners generally. For example, EAS entrants may have less 'human capital' than other groups, and so could be expected to have lower survival rates.

Firm type

This section examines three different types of small business: franchises, limited companies, and cooperatives.

A follow-up study by Power (1993) of franchises originally contacted in 1987/88 was conducted in 1992. Four to five years later it was found that about 30 per cent had disappeared. This is a somewhat lower rate than might be expected through a direct comparison with VAT deregistration data. It is also slightly lower than implied by the follow-up studies of small firms conducted by Jones (1991) or by Woods, Blackburn and Curran (1993). The latter found a 35 per cent non-survival rate over the three years 1990–3 – a valid comparison of years in which there was a severe recession.

This may suggest that the franchisee obtains a genuine 'added value' from purchasing a franchise, even taking account of the costs. The study by Power also provides further insights into the factors associated with survival/non-survival amongst franchisees. In these respects the results are similar to those for small business owners in general, with a failure to achieve high levels of sales turnover and the employment of others a key factor. Franchisees, therefore, in this respect, confirm the Phillips and Kirchhoff (1989a) findings.

We have already observed that, using the VAT deregistration definition, deregistration rates for the 1980 to 1990 period were 11 per cent for limited companies, 12.1 per cent for sole proprietorships and 9.7 per cent for partnerships. This suggests that differences in legal form exert a slight, but not major influence in explaining the failure rates of smaller firms. However, this appears to contrast with the work by National Economic Research Associates (1990) in their evaluation of the Loan Guarantee Scheme. They present, as an annexe to their chapter 11, an equation which attempts to explain the default rate on the small firms Loan Guarantee Scheme, related to the characteristics of the firm and its owner. They found that the two most important characteristics of the defaulting firms were their limited company status, and the absence of personal assets being pledged by the borrower.[8] These results suggest that limited companies are a more risky form of business venture than either self-proprietorships or partnerships.[9]

Thomas and Cornforth (1989) attempted to estimate the survival of cooperative businesses, comparing them with other types of small businesses.

Table 4.6 Businesses with different types of support

Types of business support	*Proportion surviving three years*
All VAT-registered businesses (1974–84)	64
Worker cooperatives (starts 1975–83)	66
Worker cooperatives (starts 1982–3)	56
Enterprise Allowance Scheme (starts from 1983)	53

Source: Thomas and Cornforth (1989)

The results of their analysis are shown in Table 4.6 and suggest that cooperatives formed between 1975 and 1983 had a similar survival rate to VAT-registered businesses in general. However, those formed in the 1982/3 period appear to have had rather lower rates of survival, more comparable to businesses started under the Enterprise Allowance Scheme.

'And it was ever so'

It might be assumed, given the long history of many of Britain's family businesses, that in the nineteenth century business failure rates were very much lower than they are today. Nenadic (1993) writes: '19th century literature, be it fiction or fact, made extensive use of the business owning family as the exemplar of British respectability.'

In reality, it appears that little has changed in terms of business failures in more than 100 years. Nenadic examined business in Edinburgh between 1861 and 1891: she finds that 55 per cent of male-owned firms and 59 per cent of female-owned firms had a life span of three years or less. Indeed, in sectors such as the book and paper trades, she found that only 5 per cent of businesses survived for more than ten years. This is significantly lower than the rate of VAT deregistrations today, in which about 30 per cent of businesses would be expected to survive for a decade.

Not only does Nenadic rebut the view that it is the long-established family firm which was the norm for business in the nineteenth century, but she also draws other interesting business parallels with today. She points to business ownership of a multitude of enterprises being in the hands of a single individual. Thus John Dobbie, an Edinburgh entrepreneur, over a period of twenty years operated nine separate businesses simultaneously. These included four hotels, two restaurants and three grain dealing firms. He also appears to have had an involvement as an insurance agent.

It seems that, although some businesses survive for long periods of time, the norm is, and probably always has been, that the bulk survive for only short periods. This fact therefore raises one key question, discussed in the next section.

WHY DO SOME SMALL BUSINESSES FAIL?

The above section demonstrates that small business failure rates vary according to the characteristics of the business and of those who own it. They demonstrate that failure is endemic to the small firm sector. In this section we shall examine some of the evidence presented as to *why* it is that *some* small businesses fail.

Perhaps the most obvious, if not the most unbiased, source of information on the causes of business failure is the opinions of the owners of businesses which have failed. Brough (1970), in his early study of the causes of failure of companies which were compulsorily wound-up in 1965, contrasted the opinions of directors of the failed business with those of the Official Receiver. He showed that, whilst the Official Receiver regarded mismanagement as the overwhelming cause of business failure, directors of companies tended to point to insufficient working capital, insufficient capital overall, and to bad debts. Brough also showed that business owners were much more likely than the Official Receiver to highlight causes of business failure which were beyond their control – such as bad weather, ill health, etc.

Hall and Young (1991) and Hall (1992) repeated this exercise for 1,064 involuntary liquidations in 1973, 1978 and 1983. The arithmetic mean number of years' trading for the insolvents was 6.9, and the median was 4.

Hall did not find the same difference between the views of business failure expressed by the owners as opposed to those of the Official Receiver which Brough had found. He found, as did Brough twenty years previously, that owners still tended to point to shortages of working capital as the prime cause for business failure. The change appears to be that this view is now more likely to be shared by the Official Receiver, who also pointed to under-capitalisation as the single most important source of failure. In his 1992 work Hall examines whether there is evidence that the owners' perceptions of the reasons for failure varies with the age of the firm. He concludes:

> It would appear that the owners of young firms were more likely to suffer from inadequate funding, poor products and inefficient marketing. As their companies aged, however, they were more likely to be buffeted by strategic and environmental shocks for which they did not have the managerial skills to respond.

WHICH SMALL BUSINESSES FAIL AND WHICH ONES WILL SURVIVE?

The central problem with business failure is that in some cases financial institutions, the businesses themselves, and/or their trade creditors can incur significant financial loss.

For this reason, each of these three groups has an interest not only in the *number* of businesses which fail, but also in the question of *which* ones fail. This is particularly relevant to an institution providing finance, such as a bank, which needs to know about the firms within its portfolio which are 'at risk'.

There is a long history of research into the identification of businesses which are deemed to be at risk of failure. It has derived its intellectual inspiration from the contribution of Altman and colleagues (Altman 1968 and Altman *et al.* 1981). They took conventional financial ratios measuring liquidity, profitability, gearing, etc. and identified the most appropriate combination which best distinguished failed from non-failed businesses.[10] It was then possible to use this combination of ratios, appropriately weighted, to produce a so-called 'ZETA score' which would provide an indicator of the extent to which an individual business was at risk of failure. Altman's ZETA score could then be calculated and applied to existing businesses to predict impending failure.

Although innovative at the time, and much copied subsequently, this type of work is open to several major criticisms. First is the absence of any clear theoretical criteria for the inclusion or non-inclusion of particular ratios. The inclusion of ratios is based exclusively upon their predictive power, rather than upon *a priori* theorising. The second criticism is that the models do not provide an explanation of business failure, but rather identify symptoms of poor performance and offer little insight into what actions should be undertaken to overcome these problems. The third criticism is that the analysis is based exclusively upon financial ratios, whereas there might well be other items which can better predict failure, such as sector, ownership, entrepreneurial background, firm's age, etc., but which are not included. The fourth criticism is that the methodology used and models derived have been primarily applied from the large firm, rather than from the small firm sector.

Keasey and Watson (1991, 1993) in their review of the small firm failure prediction literature demonstrate that there has been some attempt by researchers to overcome these problems. In their own work Keasey and Watson (1987) examine a number of qualitative indicators of impending small business failure such as average submission lag (the length of time it takes limited companies to submit their accounts to Companies House), the number of directors, the presence of bank secured loans and prior year audit qualifications. These variables, in combination with financial ratios, add significantly greater predictive power to the use of financial ratios alone. Keasey and Watson justify the inclusion of the submission lag variable on the grounds that failing firms will be reluctant to make public information which clearly demonstrates their vulnerability. Similarly, the presence of audit qualifications is a signal that the accountants are unhappy with the accounts, and this is also likely to be related positively to impending failure. They also find that small companies with fewer directors are more likely to fail, as are those where the assets of the business are secured with a bank loan.

The converse of the questions addressed in the failure prediction literature is to ask about factors which influence the survival of businesses. Reid (1991) examined, between 1985 and 1988, the progress of seventy-three small firms in Scotland. He found that fifty-four were still in business in 1988 and was interested in those factors which distinguished the survivors from the non-survivors. He also combined both financial ratios and a number of other, more qualitative, indices such as the competitive nature of the market in which the firm operated, its size in terms of employees, age, whether or not it advertised, the size of its product range and its use of external debt. Reid concluded that, *ceteris paribus*, the greater the product range and the lower the levels of external borrowing, the higher the chances of the firm staying in business. The number of product groups which the firm has may also be considered as a proxy for the size of its customer base. Dependence upon a narrow range of customers, or dependence upon a single customer or small number of customers, is clearly a major element affecting survival and non-survival. Despite this being a consistently identified element characteristic of small firms, in *The State of British Enterprise*, the Small Business Research Centre (1992) shows that this continues to be characteristic of UK smaller firms.

Table 4.7, taken from *The State of British Enterprise*, shows that 55.4 per cent of micro-businesses, those with less than ten workers, sell at least half of their output to their five largest customers. This compares with only 30 per cent of firms with between 200 and 499 workers. Since we also know that larger firms have significantly higher survival rates, it is very tempting to infer that a diversified customer base is a key ingredient to survival. It is also interesting to note that *The State of British Enterprise* suggests that, in this regard, little has changed over the last twenty years or so. For example, in 1991, one firm in three in the Cambridge sample relied on one customer for 25 per cent or more of its sales, this being virtually identical to the findings of the 1971 Bolton report.

The criticisms of the exclusive reliance upon financial ratios, the importance of particular market-place conditions and the role of the owners and managers of the business in influencing survival point to the need for careful case studies of surviving and non-surviving small businesses. An example of this type of work is that conducted by Smallbone, North and Leigh (1992),

Table 4.7 Concentration of sales by firm size

% of sales to five largest customers	*<10%*	*10%–24%*	*25%–49%*	*50%–100%*
<10 workers	5.5	13.4	25.7	55.4
10–99 workers	8.4	18.9	27.3	45.5
100–199 workers	9.5	33.5	23.5	33.5
200–499 workers	9.5	31.0	29.2	30.4

Source: *The State of British Enterprise* (1992): Table 2.6, p. 18

Leigh, North and Smallbone (1991) and North, Leigh and Smallbone (1992). These researchers examined 293 independently owned manufacturing firms employing less than 100 workers in 1979; these firms were tracked between 1979 and 1990. They found that 169 or 58 per cent survived for the period, and in 1990 the researchers were able to interview 126 of the survivors. This constituted a contact rate of 74 per cent.

In many respects the North *et al.* (1992) examination of the characteristics of survivors as opposed to non-survivors summarises well the findings in this chapter. This shows that survivors are older and larger than non-survivors; the presence of sectoral differences is also shown. Most interesting, motivation differences are shown, with failure rates being lowest amongst those expressing a desire, in 1979, to grow, and rates being highest amongst those expressing a desire to contract.

However, it is the examination of the adjustments which the surviving firms made over a long period of time that is the real contribution of this research.

Smallbone *et al.* (1992) identified five broad types of adjustment:

- product and market adjustments;
- production process adjustments;
- employment and labour process adjustments;
- ownership and organisational adjustments;
- locational adjustments.

The basic hypothesis to be tested was that the firms which had been most active in making adjustments were the most successful in terms of employment change and survival. The research clearly confirmed the hypothesis. The researchers' second key finding was that, of the five adjustment areas identified, management development of markets was essential for most firms for both survival and growth, but 'achieving real growth' required active market development in terms of both the identification of new market opportunities and increasing the breadth of the customer base.

This research also drew an interesting distinction, pointing out that survival was possible with relatively conservative market strategies, but that managing the product profile was apparently necessary for both survival and growth, in the sense that firms with very different performances all made significant adjustments to the range or mix of their products. It was also the case that it was the declining firms which undertook the fewest steps to improve competitiveness, and that, where these were taken, they tended to focus more upon reducing costs, rather than upon other dimensions of competitiveness, such as quality improvement.

It is interesting to note that the researchers identified 'internal organisational adjustment' as the second most common type of adjustment characterising surviving firms. Of particular interest here is that the high-performing firms were most likely to point to organisational changes which had enabled top managers to free themselves from operational decisions and to delegate responsibilities more extensively.

The Leigh, North and Smallbone research, however, does point to rather greater sectoral differences in both survival and growth than has been the case for most of the other research reviewed here. For example, they found that 88 per cent of the firms in the printing sector had survived throughout the period, compared with only 24 per cent of the firms in clothing and 35 per cent of firms in the toys and games sector.

CONCLUSIONS

This chapter has attempted to provide an overview of the quantitative significance of the death of small firms and, notwithstanding the variety of confusing technical terms associated with this, an understanding of the factors which underlie it.

The central point of the chapter has been to emphasise that the death of firms is particularly characteristic of the small business sector. No policy can be formulated for small firms without a central understanding of the importance of business failure. Although not all small firms fail, certain 'types' are more likely to fail than others.

The broad pattern which emerges is that the young are more likely to fail than the old, the very small are more likely to fail than their larger counterparts, and that, for young firms, probably the most powerful influence on their survival is whether or not they grow within a short period after start-up.

More complex relationships are observed when account is taken of sector and ownership: here the impact of sector is considerably less than might have been expected, but the impact of ownership on plant closures is difficult to predict.

The chapter also shows that whilst the characteristics of an individual entrepreneur – such as age, gender, work experience, educational qualifications, family background, etc. – are frequently hypothesised to influence business performance, these do not, other than education, appear to be consistently verified in major empirical studies. This does suggest some support for the Jovanovic notion that neither the individuals themselves, nor other bodies, have a clear understanding of whether or not a particular individual will succeed in business. It is only by being in business, and observing performance, that these matters become clarified.

For a small firm particularly, the analogy of the rowing boat on a rough sea is particularly apposite. The ability to keep the boat afloat, in the event of unpredictable external shocks, is not something which can be easily predicted from examination of the individual's personal characteristics. Once in business, however, the research reviewed here suggests the crucial role which product and market adjustments need to play to ensure survival. A continuous theme is the importance of achieving a diversified customer base and the introduction and development of new products. As Smallbone *et al.* make clear, adjustment is associated with survival.

APPENDIX: UK business failure statistics

	Deregis-trations from VAT		Exits from self-empl't		Individual bankrupt-cies *	Compulsory liqui-dations *		Voluntary liquidations *			Dereg rates	All co deregs * †	Receiver-ships (Grant Thor'n)	Bad debts (trade in-demnity)	Dissolved & volun-tary wind up †	Struck off †	On register 1 Jan E & W ††	Notes
	No.	%	No.	%	Number	No.	%	C	M	T	%	No.	No.	No.	No.	No.	No.	
1966					4,062	934	1.9	2,322	8,190	10,512	2.0	10,881			4,712	6,166	489,588	
1967					4,386	1,230	2.5	2,235	4,908	7,143	3.5	17,068			6,129	10,937	487,547	
1968					4,298	1,108	2.4	2,109	6,108	8,217	7.8	36,088			6,349	29,731	458,025	
1969					4,772	1,181	2.5	2,376	4,940	7,316	5.0	24,568			6,563	17,999	477,223	
1970					5,087	1,269	2.6	2,420	4,579	6,999	4.6	22,746			6,085	16,585	480,945	
1971					4,793	1,166	2.4	2,340	4,450	6,790	4.2	21,092			6,136	14,939	489,273	*Change here to stock
1972					4,337	1,150	2.1	1,913	4,680	6,593	4.9	27,068			7,137	19,918	551,456	
1973					3,917	1,080	1.9	1,495	4,297	5,792	5.6	32,861			7,266	25,586	576,594	
1974					5,718	1,395	2.3	2,325	3,746	6,071	3.5	21,604			5,786	15,807	608,607	
1975					7,271	2,287	3.6	3,111	3,917	7,028	5.2	32,941			6,075	26,858	627,657	
1976					7,207	2,511	3.9	3,428	4,173	7,601	5.3	34,057			6,769	27,247	638,511	
1977					4,485	2,425	3.7	3,406	3,650	7,056	5.9	39,036			7,423	31,598	658,686	
1978					3,902	2,265	3.4	2,821	3,615	6,436	3.6	24,190			7,343	16,839	673,020	
1979					3,500	2,064	2.9	2,473	4,030	6,503	3.4	23,919	805		6,581	17,330	709,899	
1980	142	11			4,038	2,935	3.9	3,955	3,970	7,925	3.5	25,909	1,349	2,255	5,340	20,558	749,377	
1981	120	9			5,151	2,771	3.5	5,825	3,638	9,463	3.5	28,285	1,560	2,611	6,062	22,217	789,865	
1982	145	11			5,700	3,745	4.5	8,322	3,908	12,230	6.3	52,015	2,190	3,624	5,809	46,200	830,727	
1983	145	11			7,032	4,807	5.6	8,599	3,808	12,407	5.0	43,023	2,082	3,921	8,900	34,114	862,001	
1984	152	11	180	7	8,229	5,260	5.8	8,461	3,772	12,233	5.6	51,146	1,803	3,924	8,802	42,331	910,765	
1985	163	11	257	9	6,778	5,761	6.1	9,137	3,946	13,083	6.0	57,566	1,781	3,808	10,011	47,540	952,912	
1986	165	11	305	11	7,155	5,204	5.3	9,201	4,525	13,726	8.0	78,958	1,771	3,398	9,480	69,476	981.7	(Transitional 15 months)
1987	169	11	235	8	7,427	4,116	4.1	7,323	3,001	10,324	7.4	75.0	1,325	2,451	10.7	64.3	1,015.4	
1988	172	11	297	9	8,507	3,667	3.5	5,760	3,460	9,220	10.7	114.7	1,217	2,146	11.7	103.0	1,061.3	
1989	176	11	314	9	9,365	4,020	3.7	6,436	3,966	10,402	7.5	81.6	1,720	2,590	12.6	69.0	1,076.0	
1990	184	11	422	12	13,987	5,977	5.4	9,074	4,092	13,166	9.0	99.8	5,047	4,581	11.3	88.6	1,115.0	
1991	203	12	487	15	25,640	8,368	7.4	13,459	3,719	17,178	10.0	113.8	8,134	7,807	10.9	102.9	1,125.1	

Key: C = Creditors; M = Members; T = Total

Notes: * The statistics are collected by Department of Trade and Industry from a variety of sources. Since 1966 there have been many changes in legislation and methods of collection. Hence they should *not* be seen as a consistent time series data set.

†Changes to '000s in 1987 ††Changes to '000s in 1986

Chapter 5

The growth of small firms

INTRODUCTION

Whilst Chapters 3 and 4 discussed the birth and death respectively of small firms, this chapter focuses upon small businesses which survive. Its particular interest is in pointing to the major diversity in the performance of surviving small firms, emphasising that the small business sector cannot be considered a homogeneous group. There is a high proportion of firms which are likely to cease to trade in the short term. There are also firms which today are small, but are moving rapidly towards becoming medium sized. Even so, the numerically dominant group of small businesses are those which are small today and, even if they survive, are always likely to remain small-scale operations.

This chapter examines in more detail that tiny proportion of small-firms which plan to and achieve rapid growth in employment. This group of firms is of interest for a number of reasons. The first is that they are the major direct providers of new employment opportunities within the small firm sector, even though they constitute only a small proportion of all small firms. Hence they must be of interest to public policy makers whose task is to maximise the creation of employment opportunities for all. Secondly, fast-growing small firms are of interest to providers of finance, whether in the form of loan or equity capital since, if they can be identified, they constitute suitable clients because they are likely to purchase a wide range of financial services. Thirdly, fast-growth firms are of interest to those providing advisory services – such as accountants, management consultants, etc. because they are much more likely to be seeking a wide range of advisory services than is the case for firms experiencing only modest growth or no growth at all.

Our prime focus is upon businesses which grow rapidly, but it is recognised that many small business owners may be owners of more than a single business. Concentration upon the single business may therefore be an underestimate of the contribution to the economy since, as Storey *et al.* (1987) show, virtually 80 per cent of the directors of fast-growth firms owned other businesses, compared with a figure of only 30 per cent in the case of directors of other firms. 'Portfolio' owners are therefore of key importance.

The chapter begins with an attempt to quantify the significance of rapidly growing businesses within the small firm sector, showing that only 4 per cent of those businesses which start today will, in ten years time, provide 50 per cent of employment in the surviving firms.

The chapter then shows (pp. 119–21) that, even in times of buoyant macroeconomic conditions, less than half of the small firms in the United Kingdom see the growth of their firm, in terms of employment, as an objective.

There then follows (pp. 121–5) an attempt to construct a more satisfactory theoretical framework than exists currently to describe these different types of small firm. It is argued that there are three key influences upon the growth rate of a small independent firm: the background and access to resources of the entrepreneur(s), the firm itself, and the strategic decisions taken by the firm once it is trading. Each of these three influences – or components – comprises a number of elements which can be examined both separately and in combination with other elements, to determine impact upon firm performance. This is the basis of the empirical material reviewed on pp. 125–54.

Some firms which wish to grow are constrained by barriers, and these are explored on pp. 154–6. The material is then synthesised in a study of mature small firms on pp. 156–8. The conclusions are then presented.

It is, however, appropriate to begin by recognising the limitations of the chapter. It is concerned with the individual small firms which grow rapidly in terms of employment. The evidence of Storey *et al.* (1987) and of North and Smallbone (1993) is that this is strongly correlated with sales growth. Growth in employment is less clearly related to growth in profitability, which in turn can only be considered as a weak proxy for efficiency. Despite its limitations, therefore, the chapter chooses to regard direct employment creation as a key policy objective.

THE SIGNIFICANCE OF GROWTH BUSINESSES

The significance of the direct contribution made to employment levels by rapidly growing small firms can be easily demonstrated. It has, for example, been frequently asserted by the current author that, 'out of every 100 small firms, the fastest growing four firms will create half the jobs in the group over a decade' (Storey *et al.* 1987).

The justification for this belief is shown in Tables 5.1 and 5.2. Table 5.1 takes data on employment in surviving openings of wholly new manufacturing firms in northern England.[1] The firms could have been established at any time between 1965 and 1978. The data show employment in those firms only in the final year – i.e. 1978. Of the 774 firms identified and surviving until 1978, 55.4 per cent had less than ten workers, and only 1 per cent had more

Table 5.1 Employment in surviving openings of wholly new manufacturing firms in northern England, 1965–78.

Employment size in 1978	*Number of firms*	*Percentage of survivors*	*Total employ-ment*	*Arithmetic mean employment*	*Percentage of total employment in each size group*
1–9	429	55.4	1,862	4.3	15.7
10–24	217	28.1	3,297	15.2	27.8
25–49	81	10.5	2,693	33.2	22.7
50–99	39	5.0	2,629	67.4	22.2
100 +	8	1.0	1,376	172.0	11.6
Total	774	100.0	11,587	14.9	100.0

Source: Storey (1985)

than 100 workers. Aggregate employment in the firms was 11,587. However, it is the distribution of the employment according to the size of firm which is of central interest. The table shows that only 6 per cent of the surviving new firms had employment in excess of fifty workers, but these firms contributed 33.8 per cent of total employment.

We now turn to Table 5.2. This table makes the assumption that, if 100 firms are formed in year *t*, in year *t* + 10 only forty will survive.[2] It then makes the second assumption that their employment is distributed, according to size of firm, in the same way as the firms in Table 5.1. Hence the forty surviving firms would be expected to have a total employment of 702 workers, as shown in the third column of the table. The fourth column of the table shows the employment in the largest four firms at the end of the time period and this can be seen to be 347 workers or, as shown in the fifth column, 49.4 per cent of the employment in surviving firms.

Table 5.2 Estimated employment in surviving small manufacturing firms

Employment size after ten years of survivors	*Number of survivors after ten years*	*Arithmetic mean employment*	*Total employ-ment*	*Employment in 4% of firms*	*'4% firms'' employment contribution*
1–9	22	4.3	95	0	
10–24	11	15.2	167	0	
25–49	4	33.2	133	40	5.7
50–99	2	67.4	135	135	19.2
100 +	1	172.0	172	172	24.5
Total	40	14.9	702	347	49.4%

On this basis, over a decade, 4 per cent of those businesses which start would be expected to create 50 per cent of employment generated. Several criticisms of these calculations could be made. The first is that the data on which they are based are rather old, ending in 1978. It is therefore appropriate to search for alternative data sources to verify whether or not there have been any changes in recent years. A useful alternative is a study of new independent manufacturing businesses surviving to 1986 in Northern Ireland (NIERC 1988). This examined the size distribution of survivors in 1986 and found that 9.5 per cent of surviving firms created 43 per cent of employment. If the survivors then are assumed to have constituted 40 per cent of the initial population, then it can be seen that 3.8 per cent of new firms in Northern Ireland yielded 43 per cent of employment. This is fairly close to the results derived in Table 5.2.

Two further criticisms may be made of the analysis in Table 5.2. The first is that it refers only to manufacturing firms, rather than to a representative sample of small firms in all sectors. A second criticism is that it refers to new firms established over a period of time, rather than taking a 'representative' sample of firms at any one point in time and tracking them.

The problem is that taking a group of new firms means that it is not possible, by definition, to obtain figures for declines in employment, since the new firm is assumed to start with zero employment and, if it ceases, it will also provide zero employment. In this sense, the examination of new firms only means the employment effects are apparently greater than where a cohort of firms is tracked over time, where declines in employment are possible, either amongst surviving firms or those which cease to trade.

Tracking exercises have been undertaken, but it is more difficult to analyse their findings. Nevertheless, the small firms first surveyed in Rajan and Pearson (1986) have been subject to two follow-up surveys, one reported in Johnson (1989, 1991) and the second by Jones (1991).

The difficulties in making such a comparison are reflected in Table 5.3, which tracks 298 small firms trading in six locations in the United Kingdom in 1985. The sample is designed to be representative of VAT-registered businesses in terms of both their sectoral and geographical composition in that year. A full sample description is given in Rajan and Pearson (1986) and in Johnson (1989). The firms were reinterviewed both in 1988 and in 1991.

Table 5.3 shows that in 1985, employment in the 298 firms was 1,932 workers. However, by 1991 total employment had fallen by 860 jobs to 1,072 in 130 firms. Hence there had been an exit/closure of 168 firms over the six-year period. This suggests a higher 'failure' rate than would be expected from the VAT deregistrations data. Some of this may reflect the difficulties which researchers have in tracking established businesses which either change their names or move location. Even so, it suggests that the 'death' rate from VAT statistics discussed in Chapter 4 is, despite its limitations, broadly reflective of changes in the small business population in general.

Table 5.3 Employment change 1985–91 in UK small firms

	1985		*1991*		*Change*	
	No.	*Emp.*	*No.*	*Emp.*	*No.*	*Emp.*
All firms	298	1,932	130	1072	–168	–860
Surviving firms	130	994	130	1072	0	+ 78
Continuous growing firms	24	127	24	225	0	+ 98

Source: Jones (1991)

A net overall decline in employment in the cohort makes it difficult to assess of the contribution to employment change of particular groups of firms. The researcher is therefore required to examine, not job creation overall, but any job creation within firms which survive over this six-year period. Row two of Table 5.3 shows that, amongst the surviving 130 firms, there was an increase in employment, by seventy-eight jobs, over the period. Row three examines the contribution of firms defined as 'continuous growers'. These are firms which had more employment in 1988 than in 1985, and also more employment in 1991 than in 1988, i.e. they grew in both time periods. These twenty-four firms, as row three shows, created in aggregate ninety-eight jobs – more than the total for surviving firms as a whole.

The table makes it clear that it is not possible to provide a simple measure of the contribution of a small number of firms to job creation, where firms can both increase and decrease their employment. Even so, the table is able to demonstrate that twenty-four firms out of the original 298 (8 per cent) are the *only* source of net job creation in the sample as a whole.

Similar findings emerged from the study by Smallbone, Leigh and North (1993) and from Woods, Blackburn and Curran (1993). Smallbone *et al.* show that over the 1979–90 period, employment in a sample of 306 small UK manufacturing firms rose from 6,312 to 7,471. However, within the group of survivors there were major differences in employment change. In essence, Smallbone *et al.* demonstrated that 1,709 jobs were created in seventy (23 per cent) of the firms, whereas the remaining firms in the sample – 236 (77 per cent) – showed a net total of 550 jobs. Later in the chapter (pp. 156–8) we shall examine the characteristics of these firms as outlined by Smallbone *et al.*

Woods, Blackburn and Curran (1993) examine employment change in 350 service sector enterprises between 1990 and 1993. They find 35 per cent of firms had ceased to trade over those three years, but that out of the 204 surviving firms which provided data there had been a net gain of 266 jobs. The interesting point, however, is that *one* of these firms contributed in excess of one hundred jobs alone, and that employment growth over the period only took place in one-fifth of the surviving firms.

This type of evidence constitutes the basis for the classification used in Storey (1993), which makes a distinction between 'failures', 'trundlers' and 'flyers'. Table 5.3 demonstrates that there is a clear distinction between the three groups: the businesses which cease to trade, of which there are 168 in this sample, are the 'failures'; the 'trundlers' are those which survive but do not add significantly to job creation – of which there are 106 in this sample. The 'flyers' are growing firms, of which there are only twenty-four. The point which clearly emerges is that although the 'flyers' are massively outnumbered by both the 'failures' and the 'trundlers', they are the only group which consistently contributes to net job creation.

This categorisation is verified elsewhere, most notably by Gallagher and Miller (1991). They compare the performance of 2,600 new firms which were started between 1980 and 1982 in Scotland, with 20,000 which started in south-east England during the same period. Employment is then examined in 1987. Gallagher and Miller's conclusion is that:

> It is the high flying firms which create the jobs. In both regions, the difference between flyers and sinkers in terms of job creation was considerable. In the South East, while the flyers made up only 18% of all firms, they nevertheless accounted for 92% of the jobs created.... The Scottish flyers, although they accounted for only 11% of the firms in this study, accounted for 68% of the jobs created.

Yet Gallagher and Miller conclude, somewhat curiously: 'Thus it is a modest (but not tiny) proportion of all firms which make the most significant contribution to job generation and growth.'

It is slightly frustrating that Gallagher and Miller do not present their findings in a way which enables the reader to determine, for example, what proportion of firms provide 50 per cent of the jobs, to facilitate comparison with other studies. Nevertheless, given the skewed distribution of employment created by new firms, it seems highly likely that somewhere around half of the employment creation in both south-east England and in Scotland over this five to seven-year period was generated by around 4 per cent of the firms. In this sense the Gallagher and Miller findings are entirely in line with those described above, and it is for this reason that it *does* seem possible to say from their evidence that half of the job creation in smaller firms is generated by a 'tiny' proportion (i.e. 4 per cent) of firms.

Readers of Daly, Campbell, Robson and Gallagher (1991), may therefore be slightly surprised when they read that 'Overall job growth (between 1987 and 1989) was due to the contributions of a large number of firms and was *not* concentrated in a few cases of very rapid expansion.'

Gallagher, using the same data base, appears to draw rather different conclusions in the two articles. Yet the apparent difference is easily explained. It reflects the different time periods over which the two analyses were conducted. It will be recalled that the statement that 4 per cent of firms create

50 per cent of the jobs refers to one decade. During that period of time it is to be expected that between 30 per cent and 40 per cent of the new/small firms would survive. The Gallagher and Miller (1991) study identifies the major impact which a small proportion of firms make to employment creation, since it examines changes over a five to seven-year period. On the other hand, Daly *et al.* (1991) examine changes only over a two-year period, from 1987 to 1989. Such a short period means the impact of deaths is much less; it also does not allow for the full growth of surviving firms to be achieved and is also probably related to the low persistence of growth over long periods (Dunne and Hughes 1992). Hence the shorter the period, the more correct it is to say that the contributions to job creation are more widely spread. The longer the period, the more concentrated is employment creation in a small number of firms.

The question therefore arises as to what is the appropriate period for examining employment change in smaller firms. It is our assertion that it is about one decade. This period has two advantages and one disadvantage. The first advantage is that it takes *at least* one full decade for new firms to have any significant impact upon aggregate employment levels in a locality. For example the NIERC (1988) study estimated that new indigenous manufacturing firms formed in Northern Ireland between 1973 and 1986 provided 16.5 per cent of manufacturing employment in 1986. The study also shows that equivalent figures for studies conducted in the Republic of Ireland and for Leicestershire were 14.5 per cent and 14.7 per cent respectively. Whilst these are important sources of new job creation in these localities, it is clear that the process takes at least a decade to achieve and that to select a shorter period for analysis would be to under-estimate this contribution. The second advantage is that it is only after a long period, such as a decade, that all of the 'failures', which make only a transitory contribution to direct job creation, are eliminated. For these reasons it does seem that the appropriate period over which to assess the contribution of growing small firms is one decade. The major disadvantage of choosing such a time period is that growth into a large enterprise normally takes more than a decade from start-up, and to cut off at one decade means that interesting constraints on long-term growth are not addressed. The practical problems of conducting research on this topic are, however, immense and almost certainly explain why the decade cut-off is frequently employed. The lack of persistence of growth over long periods of time means there is a major gap in our knowledge of this important subject.

Taking account of these reservations, the results for the United Kingdom do not seem to be substantially different from those obtained by Reynolds and Miller (1988), in their study of new firms in Minnesota in the United States. Reynolds and Miller examined new firms in Minnesota established between 1979 and 1984. They found that by 1986 these firms were responsible for between 6 per cent and 14 per cent of jobs in the state. The United States new firms on balance appear to have been slightly larger that the UK samples referred to above, with 4 per cent of the survivors having fifty or more employees after a two to seven-year history. Nevertheless, the pattern in which employment growth was concentrated in relatively few firms emerges clearly. Reynolds and Miller showed that 9 per cent of surviving new firms provided in excess of 50 per cent of employment in the sample. If account is then taken of sample attrition over the period due to death of firms, and the assumption is made that approximately half of the firms which started survive to the end of the period, then similar patterns to those in the UK studies emerge, suggesting that approximately 4 per cent of firms create approximately half the new jobs.

Overall, then, it is clear that the small firm population is not homogeneous. Although crude, the distinction between 'failures', 'trundlers' and 'flyers' is designed to be analytically helpful.

As shown in the next section, the 'failures' and the 'trundlers' vastly outnumber the 'flyers', but the long-term contribution of the flyers in terms of job creation substantially exceeds that of the two other groups. It is for this reason that we need to have a much better understanding of the factors which influence and determine the characteristics of the flyers. This is not a search for the 'Holy Grail' which will enable perfect prediction of the flyer. Indeed, the general pervasiveness of log normal distributions in social science could easily be consistent with random shocks leading to some fast-growth firms, but without any consistent factors 'explaining' their growth.

THE WISH TO GROW

For many business owners, as Curran (1986) points out, growth of their business is not an objective. These are the 'trundlers'. For them, whatever state assistance is available, and whatever the nature of the market-place into which they sell, they do not see taking on additional employees as an objective. The extent of this is illustrated in Tables 5.4(a) and (b).

Table 5.4(a) examines the growth aspirations of UK micro-firms in 1987, which was virtually the 'high point' of trading conditions in the United Kingdom in the 1980s. The table shows a very clear association between the absolute size of the firm and its aspirations for growth. Looking at the right-hand side of the table, it can be seen that 68 per cent of firms with two or less employees propose no growth, compared with only 23 per cent of those with between twenty-five and forty-nine employees. Turning to the left-hand side of Table 5.4(a), it can be seen that 60 per cent of all firms which do not propose to grow have two or less employees.

Overall, Hakim reports the results of the aspirations for growth of 747,970 firms. Of these, 55 per cent had no plans for growth, at a time when macroeconomic conditions in the United Kingdom were certainly at their most favourable for at least a decade. When she looked further into this matter, Hakim found that the typical no-growth firms were unincorporated businesses that were home-based and which employed only one or two

Table 5.4(a) Growth aspirations – micro-firms

No. of people employed, including owner-managers	*No-growth firms*	*Slow-growth firms*	*Fast-growth firms*	*No-growth firms*	*Slow-growth firms*	*Fast-growth firms*
0–2	60	38	26	68	27	6
3–4	15	22	21	47	42	11
5–9	15	20	19	47	48	11
10–24	8	15	25	37	42	21
25–49	2	6	9	23	55	22

Source: Hakim (1989)

Table 5.4(b) Growth aspirations – smaller firms

Growth objective	*Micro*	*Small*	*Medium*	*Large*
Stay same size	13.2	10.4	9.8	6.3
Grow smaller	2.7	1.7	2.2	1.7
Grow moderately	65.7	64.3	55.2	63.6
Grow substantially	17.0	22.9	32.2	27.8

Source: Cambridge Small Business Research Centre (1992)

people, including the owner-manager. Conversely she found the faster-growth firms were much more likely to be limited companies.

It is the aspirations of this type of business which are reported in Table 5.4(b). This reports the growth aspirations of primarily limited companies in manufacturing and business services at the onset of the recession. It also demonstrates that it is the micro-enterprise which is more likely to report that its objective is either to stay the same or to get smaller.

Turning now to the proportions of small firms which are seeking to grow, the Hakim study found that in June 1987 15 per cent of independent small firms overall were 'actively looking for significant expansion'. The Cambridge study reports that in 1991 22.5 per cent of small firms in manufacturing and business services saw their objective as being to grow substantially, with 64 per cent seeking moderate growth.

The proportion of small firms stating that they are seeking growth is very much higher than the proportion of firms which appear to achieve growth, as reported in Table 5.3. There may be several reasons for this. The first is that some firms which do not seek growth are reluctant to admit this to outsiders, and so this leads to an over-estimation of the proportion of 'growers'. The second is that the definitions of 'growth' may differ between those asked, in advance, by researchers, compared with the actual measures used *ex post*. The third reason may be that whilst the firm seeks to achieve growth it is, in some senses, constrained from achieving that growth. These 'barriers' will be discussed later (pp. 156–8).

The final reason why small firms may eschew growth is that they feel it is risky. They may feel that faster growth leads to a higher risk of failure – and for them it might. In aggregate, however, this is not the case. The US data of Phillips and Kirchhoff (1989), referred to in Chapter 3, showed this. Reynolds (1993) also clearly shows that survival and growth are positively correlated.

TOWARDS A THEORETICAL FRAMEWORK

Given the significance of employment created in rapidly growing small firms, it is surprising that theoretical and empirical understanding of the characteristics of these firms remains somewhat sketchy. In part, this is because the small firm which makes the transition from small to large fundamentally changes in character. As Penrose (1959) points out:

> The differences in the administrative structure of the very small and the very large firms are so great that in many ways it is hard to see that the two species are of the same genus. . . . We cannot define a caterpillar and then use the same definition for a butterfly.

The metamorphosis which lies at the heart of this Penrose quotation has encouraged some analysts to consider the changes in a firm which are associated with growth. These changes are presented in the form of stage models. An illustration of these models is provided in Table 5.5, which is taken from Scott and Bruce (1987), who infer that the small firm moves from Inception (Stage 1) through to Maturity, the fifth stage. At each of the stages it is assumed that the role which top management plays, the management style

Table 5.5 Management role and style in the five stages of small business growth

Stage	*Top management role*	*Management style*	*Organisation structure*
1: Inception	Direct supervision	Entrepreneurial, individualistic	Unstructured
2: Survival	Supervised supervision	Entrepreneurial, administrative	Simple
3: Growth	Delegation/ co-ordination	Entrepreneurial, co-ordinate	Functional, centralised
4: Expansion	Decentralisation	Professional, administrative	Functional, decentralised
5: Maturity	Decentralisation	Watchdog	Decentralised functional/product

Source: Scott and Bruce (1987)

and the organisation of structure change, so that the butterfly at Stage 5 genuinely is fundamentally different from the caterpillar at Stage 1.

There are, however, four limitations of these stage models.

- The first is that, although it is implied in the table, not all firms begin at Stage 1 and move to Stage 5. This is because, as we have seen in Chapter 4, a significant proportion of small businesses cease to trade fairly early in their lifetime, so never progress beyond either Stage 1 or 2.
- The second problem is that, in practice, the firm may well have a management style which is more or less advanced than the stage, for example, of its organisational structure. The management roles do not move in parallel, as assumed in the table.
- Thirdly, firms may achieve a particular stage, most notably Survival, and never have any intention of moving beyond that stage. Hence not all firms move from Stage 1 to Stage 5, even if they continue to exist.
- Fourthly, stage theorists such as Scott and Bruce or Churchill and Lewis (1983) assume that the movements from one stage to another are 'triggered' by a point of crisis. To our knowledge this has essentially remained an untested – and possibly untestable – hypothesis.

For these reasons we remain unpersuaded of the value of stage models. This is partly because the models describe, rather than predict. It is also because the vast bulk of firms make no clear transition and, if they do, the transition is often in only one of three dimensions identified. Instead, we see rather more merit in considering the growing small firm by a categorisation combining three components. These are:

- the starting resources of the entrepreneur(s);
- the firm;
- strategy.

Table 5.6 shows that each component can be considered as a variety of different elements. Furthermore, as Figure 5.1 demonstrates, the three components may be considered as overlapping or intersecting circles. They cannot be considered as wholly independent influences.

The purpose of Figure 5.1 is to demonstrate that the three components – the entrepreneur, the firm and strategy – *all* need to combine appropriately in order that the firm achieve rapid growth. Figure 5.1 shows that it is only in the shaded area, where all three circles intersect, that the combination is appropriate. It is also clear that the shaded area constitutes only a small proportion of the area of each of the individual circles or components. Less rapidly growing, no-growth or failing firms may have some appropriate characteristics in the entrepreneur, firm or strategy areas, but it is only where all three combine that the fast-growth firm is found.

Each component provides a distinctive contribution to our understanding

Table 5.6 Factors influencing growth in small firms

The entrepreneur/resources	*The firm*	*Strategy*
1 Motivation	1 Age	1 Workforce training
2 Unemployment	2 Sector	2 Management training
3 Education	3 Legal form	3 External equity
4 Management experience	4 Location	4 Technological sophistication
5 Number of founders	5 Size	5 Market positioning
6 Prior self-employment	6 Ownership	6 Market adjustments
7 Family history		7 Planning
8 Social marginality		8 New products
9 Functional skills		9 Management recruitment
10 Training		10 State support
11 Age		11 Customer concentration
12 Prior business failure		12 Competition
13 Prior sector experience		13 Information and advice
14 Prior firm size experience		14 Exporting
15 Gender		

of the growth of small firms, but it is possible to consider the components as comprising a set of separate elements. Table 5.6 identifies fifteen elements within the entrepreneur/resources component. These refer to the characteristics of the individual or individuals who provide the prime managerial resources of the small business. The entrepreneur(s) and their access to resources can be identified *prior to* the business being established. In principle, each element could be measured or assessed prior to starting the business, although some elements are more difficult to measure than others. For example, measuring motivation or social marginality might pose more

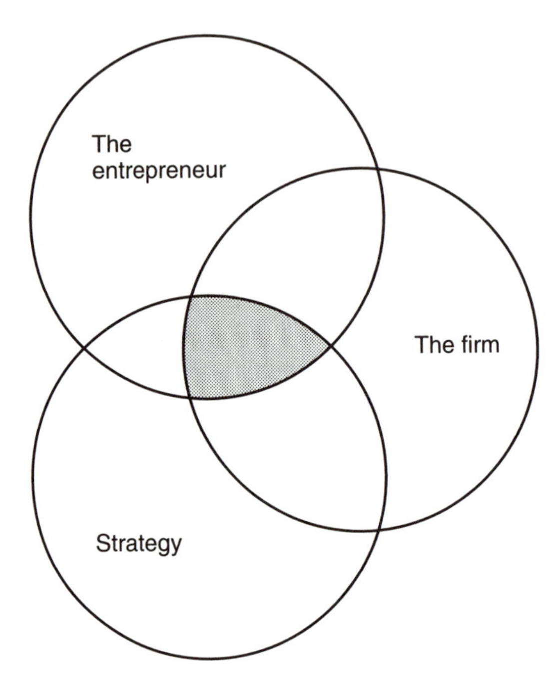

Figure 5.1 Growth in small firms

problems than specifying gender, number of founders or their ages. Nevertheless, the integrating, or common, characteristic of the entrepreneur/resources component is that all elements can be identified prior to business start-up and they relate exclusively to the entrepreneur and his/her access to resources, *not* to the business which is established.

The characteristics of the business itself, when it begins, are shown in component 2 – the firm. The six elements identified in Table 5.6 reflect decisions made by the entrepreneur upon starting in business, such as the choice of legal form, the location, or the sector in which the business is to operate. They are not, however, operational decisions which are made once the business starts, since these would be included within the strategy component, although clearly it is possible to change location or legal form once the business has begun to trade. The second 'common' characteristic of firm elements is that they are factors which are generally held constant in examining the growth performance implications of entrepreneurial characteristics.

It is perhaps the elements within the third factor – strategy – that are of prime interest. To some extent 'strategy' in this context can be considered as asking the question – given the characteristics of the entrepreneur(s) and the firm – what managerial actions, once the firm has started, are likely to be associated with more rapid rates of growth? Table 5.6 lists fourteen elements which have been considered by researchers as dimensions of strategy which could influence small firm growth.

THE EMPIRICAL EVIDENCE

This section reviews a number of empirical studies which relate elements within the entrepreneur, firm and strategy components to the growth of the firm. It will focus exclusively upon studies which have used quantitative analysis. The focus is upon those studies using multivariate analysis, in the sense of incorporating more than a single factor in examining its relationship to small firm growth. This is because the relationships are often complex, requiring more than one element to be held constant. Unfortunately there are relatively few such studies, and so it is also necessary to draw upon the results of univariate studies. The studies are primarily taken from the United Kingdom and the United States.

There are a number of problems in using this approach, because the vast bulk of studies have been conducted independently of each other. Frequently they address issues of specific interest to the researcher, but do so in a way which makes comparability with other studies difficult.

The first major problem relates to the definition of growth. Where possible, the results presented in the tables relate to studies where the criterion for growth is actual employment change over a period of time. In others, a *rate* of employment growth is used as a measure. Four studies, however, deviate significantly from employment criteria. The first is by Hakim (1989), which simply distinguished between those businesses which were seeking growth and those which were not. The study by Kalleberg and Leicht (1991) was also not concerned with employment growth, but with the growth in business earnings of the owner of the firm, as well as survival/non-survival. Finally, the Reynolds (1993) study examined firms between two and six years old which had compound sales growth in excess of 100 per cent and annual sales of more than $5m. Barkham was also concerned with changes in sales.

The second problem of comparability is that the periods of time over which growth occurred vary markedly from one study to another. For example, Woo *et al.* (1989) examined growth in US new businesses founded in 1984 and surveyed in both 1985 and 1987. Change in employment was therefore recorded over a two-year period. This can be contrasted with the criterion used by Wynarczyk *et al.* (1993), which selected as fast-growing businesses those which reached the UK Unlisted Securities Market (USM) within ten years of starting up as an independent operation. These firms were then 'matched' with less rapidly growing firms of a similar age, in similar locations and trades, and with similar ownership. The period over which growth is measured is considerably longer in the case of the Wynarczyk *et al.* study, than for that of Woo *et al.*

A third problem of comparability is that the sample sizes analysed also vary considerably. For example the Reynolds and Miller (1988) study conducted interviews with 1,119 new firm owners, whereas the study by Storey, Watson and Wynarczyk (1987) examined only twenty fast-growth firms and twenty 'matched' firms.

Fourthly it is always important to be aware of the risk that samples of small businesses may not be 'representative' of the population. Curran, Blackburn and Woods (1991) demonstrate that, even within services, there are major sectoral differences. Keeble, Bryson and Wood (1992a) show that the characteristics of founders of business services firms differ markedly from those of the founders of manufacturing firms. A keen recognition of sector-specific findings is therefore important.

Two further problems are that business conditions and the characteristics of new firms may well be different in the United States from the United Kingdom. For this reason, 'pooling' of research results from the two countries could be misleading. Finally, employment growth in a small business is likely to be more difficult during poor trading conditions; different skills may be required to bring about growth in times of recession, compared with boom. Since the studies cover a variety of macroeconomic conditions, it is quite possible that for this reason they will yield different results.

All of the above criticisms clearly have validity. Nevertheless, our purpose is to investigate whether, despite the varieties of research methods, definitions, time periods, etc., general patterns emerge. If they do, this would suggest that there are some generalisable lessons to be learnt.

The entrepreneur and access to resources

This subsection will examine the relationship between the characteristics of the entrepreneur and his/her access to resources – which can in principle be identified prior to the start of business – and the ultimate success of the business in terms of its growth.

Table 5.7 takes the evidence from eighteen studies and the fifteen characteristics of the entrepreneur set out in Table 5.6, and examines whether these elements are shown to be related to the growth of the firm.

Probably the most striking feature of the table is the number of gaps or blanks. This reflects studies in which, as far as we can determine, the researchers did not include the particular element in their efforts to 'explain' growth in the small firm. It suggests that, although fifteen factors which relate the characteristics of the entrepreneur to the growth of the firm can be identified, most quantitative research only identifies between three and seven. There must therefore be an *a priori* risk of specification error through omitted variable bias in models, given that the proportion of variance explained is generally rather low.

Table 5.7 The entrepreneur

	Barkham (1992)	Hakim (1989)	Woo *et al.* (1989)	Kinsella *et al.* (1993)	Johnson (1991)	Storey, Watson and Wynarczyk	Jones (1991)	Macrae (1991)	Wynarczyk *et al.* (1993)	Storey (1982a)	Storey (1994)	Dunkelberg *et al.* (1987)	Dunkelberg and Cooper (1982)	Kalleberg and Leicht (1991)	Solem and Steiner (1989)	Reynolds and Miller (1988)	Westhead and Birley (1993a)	Reynolds (1993)
1 Motivation	+			+	+	+			x			x					x	
2 Unemployment push				x	x				–	–	–					x	x	–
3 Education	x		x	+	+	+	+	+	x	x	(+)	x	+	x	x	x	x	+
4 Management experience	+		x	x		+		+			x	–	+		x		x	
5 Number of founders	+		+	+		(+)						+					x	+
6 Prior self-employment				x		x					x	–		x		x	x	
7 Family history																	x	
8 Social marginality (ethnic)			–								+	x					x	
9 Functional skills							+		+									
10 Training			x				x		x									
11 Age				(+)		x		x	x		(+)		–	–	x	x	x	+
(Age)^2				(–)		x		x	x		–				x	x	x	–
12 Prior business failure																		
13 Prior sector experience						x	–				+	–		x	x	x	x	–
14 Prior firm size experience			x	x		x						x	–				+	
15 Gender		x	x	x	x	x	–	x	x		x	x		x		x	x	+

Key:
\+ Positive relationship between the element and growth of the firm
– Negative relationship between the element and growth of the firm
() Relationship present in a univariate context, but weak in a multivariate context
x Element not shown to be significant in influencing growth

We now turn to an examination of the relationship of each element to small firm growth.

Motivation

This variable attempts to categorise why the business was established and to relate that to whether or not the business grows. At its most simplistic, a crude distinction is made between positive and negative motivations, the hypothesis being that those individuals beginning with a positive motivation are more likely to establish a business which subsequently grows than those with negative motivations. Illustrations of positive motivations include the perception of a market opportunity for a product or service and the desire to make more money. Negative motives include dissatisfaction with an existing employer and/or the threat of, or actual, unemployment. Also included here would be founders who seek to establish a 'lifestyle' business, designed solely to provide a satisfactory level of income to the business owner.

Table 5.7 shows that four out of the seven studies which included indicators of this variable found a relationship between the growth of the firm and the existence of a positive motivation on the part of the entrepreneur when the business began. The exceptions to this are the Westhead and Birley and Wynarczyk *et al.* studies, which were unable to find a direct impact. The Dunkelberg *et al.* study also found no relationship between the reasons the entrepreneur gave for leaving their previous employment and whether or not their newly established firms grew in employment.

Unemployment push

A second aspect of motivation, and one which has been the subject of attention for a number of researchers, is whether those businesses established by unemployed individuals are likely to grow any less rapidly than businesses established by employed workers. The reason why this may be the case is that, on balance, the unemployed, and even the unemployed who start their own business, have lower levels of skills (human capital) than individuals who are employed. They may also have lower aspirations for business growth than the individual who moves out of employment to become an entrepreneur.

The evidence from row 2 of the table is that for the eight studies which have examined this element, four found no impact and four found the predicted negative impact. Overall, this suggests that if the founder is unemployed prior to starting a business, that firm is unlikely to grow as rapidly as where the founder is employed.

Education

Two conflicting hypotheses can be put forward with regard to the role of the education level of the entrepreneur in influencing business growth. It could be argued that education provides a basis for the intellectual development which the entrepreneur requires to be in business successfully, and that higher levels of education provide the individual with greater confidence in dealing with customers and bankers. In short, education is a key constituent of the human capital needed for business success. The educated individual also has higher earning expectations than less educated individuals so is less likely to become an entrepreneur unless he or she expects earnings will at least equal those which could be obtained in alternative employment. Since earnings from business ownership are likely to be broadly related to firm size, this implies that educated individuals are more likely than less educated individuals to form businesses which grow larger.

The converse argument is that business ownership is not an intellectual activity. Instead, entrepreneurship is an opportunity for the less academically successful to earn high incomes. It may even be that individuals with the highest academic attainment are likely to be insufficiently challenged by many of the mundane tasks associated with business ownership.

It can be seen from row 3 that the education level of the entrepreneur is analysed in seventeen out of the eighteen studies. In nine studies there is no identifiable impact upon employment growth, but in eight there is some form of positive relationship. This provides fairly consistent support for the view that educated entrepreneurs are more likely to establish faster-growing firms.

It is, of course, appropriate to point out that the measure used of educational attainment varies from one study to another. In some instances a distinction is made only between graduates and non-graduates, whereas in others the distinction is made only between individuals with formal academic qualifications and those without. It is also the case that the nature and grading of educational qualifications varies from one country to another. Even so, the generally positive results obtained suggest the existence of a broad relationship between firm growth and the educational background of the entrepreneur.

Management experience

Here it is hypothesised that entrepreneurs with some managerial experience – normally in their previous job – are likely to form firms which grow faster than individuals without such experience. It is argued that a key role which the entrepreneur plays, other than in the smallest of firms, is in organising the work of others. Prior experience of this task is likely to supplement the expertise of the entrepreneur and enable business objectives to be more easily achieved. Existing managers are also likely to command a higher salary than non-managers. Hence the manager is likely to have a higher 'reservation wage' than the non-manager and will become an entrepreneur only if he/she expects that wage to be met. Since entrepreneurial income is generally related to firm size, the higher the 'reservation wage', the larger the expected size of the firm needs to be.

Row 4 of the table provides some support for these hypotheses. Four studies indicate a positive relationship, six demonstrate no impact, and one demonstrates a negative relationship. Dunkelberg *et al.*, the authors of the latter study, confessed to being somewhat surprised by this finding.

Our overall conclusion is that prior managerial experience is positively associated with new firm growth.

Number of founders

A business may be established either by one individual who owns the whole of the business, or it may be established by groups of individuals, each of whom has part ownership. Since the management of a business requires a range of skills, it is hypothesised that businesses owned by more than a single individual are more likely to grow than businesses owned by a single person.

Row 5 of Table 5.7 shows that seven studies have formally tested this theory. Five out of the seven indicate support for the hypothesis, whilst one indicated that the relationship was broadly but not consistently positive. Although the studies by Barkham and by Reynolds use sales/profitability measures rather than employment growth, the results are robust since sales and employment are correlated.

The generally positive findings suggest that businesses begun by more than one individual are more likely to grow than single person-owned firms. It is certainly a variable which should be included more consistently in studies attempting to explain the growth of smaller firms. The preliminary evidence suggests it is an important aspect of fast growth.

Prior self-employment

It was argued above that prior managerial experience was likely to be associated with more rapid growth of the small firm. Similar arguments may be advanced for prior self-employment experience. Thus, individuals who have previously owned a business will have gained valuable experience in the management of a smaller enterprise. It is hypothesised that this experience enables them to overcome more easily the problems which are experienced when the business grows.

The converse hypothesis is that those individuals who have previously been self-employed are likely to have been unsuccessful as a business owner. Even though their business may not have failed, in the sense of leaving behind debtors, former owners may well have drawn the lesson from their previous experience that growth was not an appropriate objective. Furthermore, the fact that they have been in business before, and are no longer running that business, may reflect a lack of managerial ability. Whether or not they have learnt from their previous mistakes is an open question.

Row 6 of Table 5.7 shows that seven studies have explicitly examined this question. Six were not able to identify any impact upon firm growth of whether or not the firm founder had previously been self-employed. The negative sign we have imputed to the Dunkelberg *et al.* (1987) is our interpretation rather than theirs. Unfortunately these authors did not ask a specific question about prior self-employment, but they did show that those individuals who had managed or owned a business previously were significantly more likely to have firms which declined in employment than those which rose in employment. They also show that 17 per cent of firms which declined were owned by people who previously had their own business, compared with only 12 per cent of individuals currently owning a growing firm.

The evidence suggests that prior business experience does not seem to be a factor which influences the growth of the firm. It may well be that the two conflicting hypotheses identified above effectively cancel each other out.

An alternative explanation is that many of those with prior self-employment experience are 'opportunists'. These are 'portfolio' business owners who frequently change their portfolio of businesses in response to perceived market opportunities. None of their businesses may exhibit rapid growth, but the portfolio itself could grow markedly. Curran, Blackburn and Woods (1991) found a considerable number of such 'opportunists' in the leisure sector – video hire and health businesses such as keep-fit studios and sports clubs.

Family history

Stanworth *et al.* (1989), Bannock (1981) and Leach (1991) have all emphasised the importance of family businesses. The emphasis by Leach is upon businesses which are owned by a single family, and also upon problems associated with transferring the ownership of that business from one generation to the next. This is a slightly different issue from that addressed by both Bannock and by Stanworth *et al.*, who suggest that individuals whose parents were either self-employed or business owners are significantly more likely to become business owners themselves than a random sample of the population. It might also be hypothesised that these individuals would be more likely to be successful in the sense of owning faster-growing firms, for several reasons. If their family is in business then they can call upon managerial expertise to help them overcome business problems; they may also have easier access to finance to establish the business or to overcome short-term financing problems than other individuals. For these reasons it might be expected that a positive relationship would exist between individuals whose families were in business, and who started up on their own, and the success of that business.

Row 7 of Table 5.7, however, shows that only one of the seventeen studies tested this hypothesis, and this did not isolate an impact. Given the frequency with which it is popularly asserted that this relationship exists, the lack of empirical testing for it is extremely unfortunate.

Social marginality

This concept is most clearly associated with the work of Stanworth and Curran (1976). They define social marginality to be where there is a perceived incongruity between the individual's personal attributes – physical characteristics, intellectual make-up, social behaviour patterns – and the role(s) he/she holds in society. They argue that classic examples are Jews, who have developed business skills and a culture at least partly in response to the discrimination which they have experienced in society. Other illustrations include talented individuals who are overlooked by their employers because of their unorthodox attitudes and personal idiosyncrasies, or cases where an individual's career has been abruptly terminated for reasons beyond their control. It is hypothesised that individuals may respond to this social marginality by a determination to demonstrate their skills and expertise, and that growing a successful business constitutes one way of effectively 'thumbing their nose at society'.

Testing the more sophisticated versions of this hypothesis is difficult. Nevertheless, it is possible to examine whether in-migrants to an area, or minority races, form businesses which grow more rapidly than those of the native population.

Row 8 of Table 5.7 shows that four studies have examined this question, but the results are mixed. The Woo *et al.* study suggests that businesses established by minority races in the United States grow less rapidly than businesses established by the majority population. On the other hand, the Storey (1994) study shows that businesses established by in-migrants to Cleveland – only a small proportion of whom are from minority races – establish businesses which grow more rapidly than those established by native Clevelanders. Finally, neither the Dunkelberg *et al.* (1987) nor the Westhead and Birley (1993a) studies identified an impact.

The most likely explanation for this conflicting evidence is the lack of sophistication in the testing of the hypotheses. Separate evidence on this topic produced by Jones, McEvoy and Barrett (1993) suggests there are marked differences in the types and growth rates of businesses established in the United Kingdom by those from Asian and Afro-Caribbean backgrounds. The latter are significantly smaller and have experienced much lower growth rates than Asian-owned businesses, which appear to perform at least as well as white-owned businesses in the researchers' sample.

The social marginality theory is therefore difficult to test and, even where testing is undertaken – particularly related to racial groups – the findings are not consistent. It suggests that testing needs to become more sophisticated than has been the case to date.

Functional skills

Whilst managerial experience and prior business ownership have already been discussed, the particular functional skills of the business owner can be hypothesised to influence the growth of the firm. For example, individuals with a background in marketing may be more conscious of the need to expand sales and grow the business, than individuals with a background in finance, who may be more cautious. Clearly the management of a small business does require a range of skills, which will include marketing, production, personnel, research and development and finance, as well as general managerial skills. The question is whether the presence or absence of such skills at start-up hampers the growth of the firm.

The functional skills which the owners of small businesses bring to their firm are examined in two studies. Both indicate that individuals with backgrounds in marketing are likely to form businesses which experience more rapid growth than businesses founded by individuals with other functional skills.

Training

In a number of countries, individuals who are considering establishing their own firm can undertake training in business management. Townroe and Mallalieu (1993), in their study of rural entrepreneurs in the United Kingdom, found that one quarter of business owners had attended some sort of training course in connection with the setting up of their business. The authors recognised that this was an unusually high proportion of respondents, which they attributed at least in part to the high educational attainment levels of rural entrepreneurs in the United Kingdom. In a subsequent analysis they attempted to examine the characteristics of individuals who attended a training course, and found that the probability of attendance was higher both for younger entrepreneurs and for female entrepreneurs. They did not, however, examine whether the attendance at the training course was a factor which influenced the growth of the firm.

This issue is examined in only three of the studies enumerated in Table 5.7, all three of which show no identifiable relationship between training and business growth. This matter is considered in more detail in Chapter 8.

Age of founder

Two hypotheses may be presented to explain the impact of the age of the founder when the business is formed upon whether or not the business grows. The first is that only younger entrepreneurs will have the energy and the commitment to work the long hours which generally are necessary for a business to be successful. It is argued that the older entrepreneur is not only likely to lack the physical energy for such hard work but also, if they are getting close to retirement, may have much more modest objectives or ambitions for the growth of the business.

The converse argument is that whilst younger entrepreneurs may have more energy, they lack credibility, as well as business experience, in the market-place and are more likely to be financially constrained. For these reasons older entrepreneurs are more likely to have growing businesses.

A third hypothesis combines the two: it suggests the middle-aged entrepreneur is likely to have the experience, the credibility, the energy and access to resources, and so is most likely to own a growing business. Both the younger and the older entrepreneurs are least likely, for the reasons given above.

To test these hypotheses, row 11 of Table 5.7 specifies two variables – age and $(\text{age})^2$. The latter formulation enables us to test whether the relationship between entrepreneurs' age is linear, or of a quadratic form, of the type compatible with the third hypothesis. Unfortunately not all researchers specify the quadratic form, and the lack of a relationship, using only a linear model, does not preclude the possibility that such a relationship may exist using the quadratic form.

Three studies observe a quadratic form, whilst two observe a negative relationship, suggesting that younger entrepreneurs are most likely to own rapidly growing businesses. The six remaining studies fail to observe any clear relationship between age of the entrepreneur when the business is formed and the subsequent performance of the business. However, none of these studies specified a quadratic form for the age variable as compatible with the third hypothesis.

Overall, there looks to be some support for the view that the age of the entrepreneur when the business is established is an influence on the growth rate of that business.

Prior business failure

One 'fact' which is periodically asserted in business magazines is that highly successful entrepreneurs are individuals who have previously failed in business. It is also asserted that the experience of business failure constitutes a learning process for that individual, providing an incentive similar to that of social marginality discussed above. Indeed, the changes in the legal system which attempt to remove the stigma of personal bankruptcy imply that, at least in the United Kingdom, individuals who have failed in business and become bankrupt have been too strongly discouraged from starting again. This is contrasted with the United States, where it is asserted that the stigma of business failure is much less and so individuals are much more prepared to start again in business and ultimately develop rapidly growing firms.

Given the frequency with which this assertion is made, it is curious that none of the studies identified here, four of which cover the United States, actually test this proposition. The nearest to this are the tests for prior business ownership or self-employment, where no impact was identified, apart from one study in the United States which identified a negative influence.

Overall, the impact of prior business failure clearly needs to be formally incorporated into studies to determine whether or not it influences the growth of the firm. However, given the outcome of the prior self-employment, it seems extremely unlikely that it would exert a positive impact. It seems as likely, if not more likely, that individuals who have failed in business before are perhaps, because of their lack of managerial skills, more likely to have lower growth rate businesses.

Prior sector experience

Two contrasting hypotheses may be presented here. The first is that individuals who previously have worked in the same sector in which they establish their business will have developed their expertise and experience about the acceptable norms and practices in that sector, and it is only once those are understood and implemented that significant business growth can be achieved. The converse argument is that for a business to grow, it needs to provide a product or service which is different, in some respects, from that which the market-place already provides. To do that requires producing something different or novel, and this is less likely amongst entrepreneurs who have too readily accepted the 'norms' of the sector. Instead, it is the individual coming fresh to the market who is more likely to bring innovative business ideas, to do things differently from other firms and thus to achieve growth. Such an individual may not necessarily bring ideas which are totally new, but transfer them from other sectors.

Nine studies examine the relationship between business growth and whether the founder has experience in the sector prior to the business being formed. The picture is mixed. Five studies do not identify an impact, three indicate that prior sectoral experience is associated with slower-growing firms, and one suggests that prior sector experience is associated with faster-growing firms. In part this again probably reflects 'measurement' problems, since questions are asked both about *whether* the individual has sectoral experience and the *duration* of that experience. If there is a pattern it suggests that, as shown by Reynolds (1993), those with long experience in a sector are less likely to found rapid-growth firms.

The empirical evidence therefore is far from conclusive on this topic and would suggest that both hypotheses have some merit.

Prior firm size experience

Here again, two conflicting hypotheses may be presented. The first is that individuals who formerly worked in a large firm are more likely to found a firm of their own which grows rapidly. This is because their managerial skills are more appropriate to those of a larger firm. Furthermore, since they were formerly employed in a large firm and, in general, large firms pay higher wages than small firms, they would expect their firm to grow to a sufficient size to yield them a level of income which was comparable to that which they formerly earned. The converse argument is that individuals who leave a large firm in order to establish their own business often do so because they dislike the characteristics of large firms – such as their formality, bureaucracy and lack of flexibility. Such individuals then are unlikely to wish to establish a business which replicates these characteristics.

In many senses these arguments are very similar to, and closely integrated with, the motivation which an individual has in establishing a business in the first place. Nevertheless, they suggest conflicting expectations of the impact which prior firm size has upon the growth rate of the entrepreneur's business.

The evidence from empirical studies shown in row 14 of Table 5.7 reflects this conflict. Four studies are unable to identify a relationship between the size of firm for whom the entrepreneur previously worked and the growth of the business which the entrepreneur establishes. The two remaining studies point in different directions, one suggesting that entrepreneurs from a large firm background are more likely to found firms which grow slowly, and the other suggesting the reverse.

Gender

There has been a considerable literature in recent years on the characteristics of female entrepreneurs (Carter and Cannon 1989, Allen and Truman 1993). Much has focused upon the real or imagined problems which female entrepreneurs experience in the market-place. These include commitments to children and to the family which prevent them from working the number of hours which may be necessary in order to develop a rapidly growing business, the lack of credibility with financial institutions in taking the business seriously, a lack of personal confidence in business matters by some females, and the concentration of female-owned businesses in sectors where female employment is concentrated, but which seems to provide few opportunities for rapid business growth – illustrations include hairdressing, textiles, retailing, etc. Nevertheless, the publicity given to 'role models' of females who have been extremely successful in business is argued to provide an important incentive to females, demonstrating that business success can be achieved.

Row 15 of the table shows that fourteen studies examine whether the gender of the entrepreneur was a factor in influencing the growth of the firm. In all but two cases, gender was not shown to be significant. In one case where the gender variable was significant, the study suggested that it was females who were more likely to be owning rapidly growing firms than males. This was reversed in the other. The overall conclusion must be that the gender of the entrepreneur is not a key influence upon subsequent business performance.

Overall

Taken as a whole, Table 5.7 suggests that, although fifteen elements of the background of the entrepreneur have been identified and examined in a number of studies, the impact which this background has upon the subsequent performance of the firm looks to be relatively limited. Of course, if all fifteen elements were simultaneously included within a single study, then a more accurate assessment could be made of their relative impact. This, however, has not been undertaken and so we are forced to conclude, albeit on the basis of incomplete information, that some variables appear to be more significant than others.

Of the fifteen elements, the motivation for establishing the business appears to be of some importance, with individuals who are 'pushed', possibly through unemployment, into establishing businesses being less likely to found a rapidly growing firm than those attracted by a market opportunity. The evidence also suggests that individuals with higher levels of education are more likely to found rapidly growing firms, as are those with some prior managerial experience. More rapidly growing firms are more likely to be founded by groups, rather than single individuals. Finally, middle-aged owners are most likely to found rapidly growing firms.

Even so, it would mislead the reader to suggest that these patterns are strong. The table demonstrates that what the entrepreneur has done prior to establishing the business exerts only a modest influence upon the success of the business. Prior to start-up, the identikit picture of the entrepreneur whose business is likely to grow is extremely fuzzy.

The firm

This subsection highlights the impact upon performance of the component which includes elements relating to the firm itself. Table 5.6 included six such elements; they can be considered as being in two groups. The first are those elements which reflect decisions made by the owner of the business at the

Table 5.8 The firm

	Cambridge Small Business Research Centre (1992)	Dunne and Hughes (1992)[a]	Westhead and Birley (1993a)	Barkham (1992)	Variyam and Kraybill (1992)	Storey (1994)	Hakim (1989)	Kalleberg and Leicht (1991)[b]	Jones (1991)	Dunne, Roberts and Samuelson (1989)	Johnson (1989)	Reynolds and Miller (1988)	Macrae (1991)	Storey *et al.* (1987)
1 Age	–	–			–	+	–	x	–	(–)				–
2 Sector/markets	+	+	+	x	+	+	x	+	+			+	x	x
3 Legal form						+	+	+			+	+		
4 Location	+						+		+		+			
5 Size	–	–			–		+	+	–	–	+			–
6 Ownership	x				+					+				

Notes:
[a] Dunne and Hughes measure growth in terms of net assets.
[b] Kalleberg and Leicht measure growth in terms of business earnings

Key:
+ Positive relationship between the element and growth of the firm
– Negative relationship between the element and growth of the firm
() Relationship present in a univariate context, but weak in a multivariate context
x Element not shown to be significant in influencing growth

time at which the business is started. These include the sector in which the business is to begin trading, its legal form, its ownership pattern and its location. These decisions are observable immediately the business starts to trade. They are different from the entrepreneur/resources, which are identifiable *before* the business starts.

The other two elements included within the 'firm' component are size and age. These are included because they refer explicitly to the characteristics of the firm and are not related to either the background of the entrepreneur or the strategy employed by the entrepreneur once he or she is in business. They are frequently included by researchers as 'control' variables.

We shall now examine the empirical evidence relating to the impact of these firm-specific characteristics upon business performance. Studies of small firms in both the United States and the United Kingdom are reviewed. Some of the studies included here differ from those reviewed in the previous section, since relatively few incorporate both information on the background of the entrepreneur and a complete enumeration of elements in the firm component.[3]

Table 5.8 identifies fourteen separate studies which have examined the performance of small firms and which have explicitly included firm characteristics. The table does not set out to constitute a comprehensive review of such studies, but merely to be illustrative of the overall pattern of results which researchers have derived. In selecting the studies the object has again been to favour those which have used employment growth as a measure of performance within a multivariate framework, and also to include as many of the same studies as were included in Table 5.7. This enables the reader to see the extent to which it is elements within the entrepreneur/resources or the firm-specific components which are most influential in explaining performance. Each of the firm-specific elements is discussed in turn.

Firm age

The table illustrates that there is an almost unanimous finding in both the United Kingdom and the United States that younger firms grow more rapidly than older firms. The only exceptions appear to be the cases examined by Kalleberg and Leicht, where no relationship was obtained, and the study by Storey (1994) which obtained the alternative sign. The latter is probably because this study examined only very young firms; such a sample composition means it contains a large number of young firms which are not expanding and, if Phillips and Kirchhoff (1989a) are correct, are likely to die quickly. On the other hand, the sample will contain some slightly older firms which have experienced some growth.

The general pattern, therefore, is clearly that young firms are more likely to achieve significant growth than older firms; this reflects the need for a new business to grow quickly to achieve minimum efficient scale (MES). The fact that, once this is achieved, businesses subsequently grow less rapidly can be explained either by the lack of motivation of the individuals to continue to grow the business once they have achieved a satisfactory level of income from the firm (Watson 1990), or by low MES, particularly in service sector businesses, or by the diseconomies which emerge from the need to employ and manage others.

Sector

The second element within the table relates to the sector or market in which the firm operates. The table records whether or not researchers found there were significant differences between the sector in which the firm trades and its growth rate. Here the + sign indicates clear sectoral patterns and so the only other possible symbol is ×, which indicates the sectoral variables were insignificant.

In the bulk of the studies there are significant differences between sectors in terms of the typical growth rates of firms. The level of disaggregation data in the studies, however, does vary markedly. For example, the Cambridge Small Business Research Centre (1992) study makes a distinction between manufacturing and business service firms. On the other hand, the Dunne and Hughes (1992) study of limited companies examines sectoral composition for nineteen industries.

Legal form

United Kingdom studies consistently point to more rapid growth being experienced by limited companies than by either sole proprietorships or partnerships. Hakim finds the same result when firms are questioned not about their *actual* growth, but about their *plans* for growth. Kalleberg and Leicht (1991) and Reynolds and Miller (1988) find similar results for the United States.

The choice of legal form, particularly the choice of incorporated status for small businesses in the United Kingdom, has been examined in detail by Freedman and Godwin (1992, 1994). Their conclusion from surveys of entrepreneurs and business advisers is that the prime benefit of corporate status is limited liability, followed by apparent increased credibility which the business has with both its customers and its bank. Even so, Freedman and Godwin do not believe that the provision of limited liability status to micro-enterprises is necessarily appropriate, since it can be 'undermined' by the need for the entrepreneur to provide personal guarantees for bank loans, and secondly by the costs of incorporation – most notably that of the statutory audit. Nevertheless, the empirical studies suggest that, other things being equal, limited companies generally are associated with more rapid rates of employment growth than either sole proprietorships or partnerships.

It will be noted that we have assumed that the decision to opt for limited company status is made when the business begins trading, but this is not necessarily the case. Freedman and Godwin report that 40 per cent of limited companies in their sample started as either a sole proprietorship or a partnership and then moved to limited company status at a later stage. In this case any association between limited company status and growth could be considered to be reversed, with the change in legal status being the result of growth, rather than an aspiration or motivation to achieve growth. The empirical studies have generally categorised firms according to current legal status, rather than initial legal status when the business began. In these cases we cannot reject the hypothesis that current legal status is a consequence rather than a cause of growth.

It will also be recalled that Chapter 4 suggested that limited companies had a higher failure rate than either sole proprietorships or partnerships. Hence it would be unwise to assume that the incorporated form is necessarily conducive to good management.

Location

Table 5.8 also suggests that the location of the small business is a factor which influences its performance. This is to be expected, since the bulk of sales of small firms are to highly localised markets. For example, Curran, Blackburn and Woods (1991) showed that for small service sector firms in six UK labour markets, three-quarters sold 75 per cent or more of their services within their own locality. The buoyancy of these local markets therefore must be a key determinant of the sales patterns and performance of new businesses, particularly given the dominance of service sector enterprises amongst the small business population (Kingston Centre 1992).

The Cambridge Small Business Research Centre (1993) study of both manufacturing and business service sector firms suggests that some quite marked differences exist according to location. They show that, whilst median employment growth rates do not differ between firms located in the north or the south of the United Kingdom, there is evidence that firms in rural areas experience more rapid growth rates than those in the conurbations. Other work, however, most notably Keeble, Tyler, *et al.* (1992), and Keeble (1993) suggests that, whilst on balance rural firms may grow more rapidly than their urban counterparts, firms in remote rural areas in the United Kingdom grow less rapidly than those in the more accessible rural areas. North and Smallbone (1993) find that although employment growth is more rapid in rural SMEs, there is less evidence of difference in terms of sales growth.

Finally, it has to be emphasised that these results are UK-specific. The US work by Reynolds (1993) finds more rapid growth firms in the urban than in the rural areas – but this almost certainly reflects the difference in definition between urban and rural in the two countries (Curran and Storey 1993).

It would be misleading to suggest that there is total unanimity amongst researchers that urban/rural differences exist. Blackburn and Curran (1993), in their study of UK labour markets, do not find striking spatial differences in performance between small firms in the service sector, and they suggest that sectoral differences are probably a more powerful influence on performance than location.

Overall, whilst location may be less important than some other firm-specific variables identified in Table 5.8, the general consensus is that location does play a role, with firms located in urban and remote rural areas of the United Kingdom being likely to grow least rapidly. Conversely, firms in accessible rural areas appear most likely to exhibit employment growth.

Firm size

Row 5 of Table 5.8 shows the impact of firm size upon performance. The general pattern is that smaller firms grow more rapidly, with six of the studies showing a negative sign. The reasons for this are closely allied with the reasons why young firms grow more rapidly – the achievement of minimum efficient scale (MES) being the most relevant.

It is also interesting to look at the three studies which suggest an opposite finding. The first is by Hakim (1989) of independent establishments in the United Kingdom with up to fifty workers. Of the 750,000 establishments, 366,000 have either one or two employees. As reported in the section on 'the wish to grow' (pp. 119–21), Hakim found 68 per cent of these establishments were not seeking any employment growth, compared with only 23 per cent of establishments in the 25–49 employee range. However, there are two problems with the Hakim analysis: the first is that her survey classifies establishments according to their *intention* to grow, rather than *actual* growth rates, which are used in almost all the other studies. The second re-emphasises that, amongst the tiniest enterprises, growth is not seen to be an objective. It appears to be the case that growth becomes an objective in smaller firms only amongst those with ten or more employees.

An insightful finding on this issue is provided by the Cambridge Small Business Research Centre (1992) survey of manufacturing and business service sector firms. This showed that those firms which had grown quickly in the past were much more likely to seek substantial growth in the future as an objective than is the case for firms which had not grown rapidly in the past. Thus 33 per cent of fast-growth companies expected to grow substantially in the future, compared with 21 per cent of companies that had experienced medium growth, and 13 per cent of those which had experienced stability or decline. This, however, seems to contrast with the findings of Dunne and Hughes (1992), who find little evidence that growth is 'persistent' over time.

We are less clear about the reasons for the positive signs in Table 5.8 for the analyses by Kalleberg and Leicht (1991) and by Johnson (1989). Perhaps the fact that the Kalleberg and Leicht study measures growth in terms of business earnings rather than employment may be a factor.

Overall, the fairly consistent pattern which emerges is that small firms grow faster than large. Even so, the significant number of exceptions to this finding emphasise the point that this is not a wholly consistent pattern.

Ownership

Row 6 of the table shows the impact which the ownership variable has upon the performance of the firm. In the bulk of the studies in Table 5.8 ownership is not specifically taken into account, since the firms are generally independent, or even single-plant independent enterprises. One exception to this is the Cambridge Small Business Research Centre study, which specifically addresses the question of changes in ownership through acquisition and merger. The study shows that historic growth rates do not appear to be a major influence in determining whether or not a firm is a target for acquisition. It also shows the frequency of acquisition activity amongst small firms, with 20 per cent of firms in the sample having acquired at least one firm in the last five years. Amongst the firms with between 200 and 500 workers, virtually half had acquired another firm in that time. This serves to illustrate again the fact that growth amongst small firm owners occurs organically, through acquisition and through individuals starting and developing other businesses, to become 'portfolio' owners.

In the United States, Variyam and Kraybill (1992) and Dunne, Roberts and Samuelson (1989) find that smaller firms which are part of larger multi-plant firms have significantly higher growth rates than single establishment firms. Dunne *et al.* show that, for single-plant firms, growth rates decline with increasing size, but for multi-plant firms growth rates increase with size.

Overall

The results in Table 5.8 relating to firm-specific characteristics are generally more consistent and definitive than those relating to the background and resources of the entrepreneur. The pattern which emerges is that younger firms grow more rapidly and that there are sectoral differences. Legal form also appears to have an influence on growth, with limited companies having faster growth than either sole traders or partnerships. The direction of causation in this relationship is, however, somewhat unclear.

The evidence also suggests that there are differences in small firm growth rates according to where the firm is located, with those located in accessible rural areas in the United Kingdom having higher employment growth rates than those located either in urban areas or in inaccessible rural areas.

Probably the most complex results relate to the impact of firm size. Here it is clear that the smallest firms are the least likely to grow. Nevertheless, it also seems to be the case that few firms, once they have achieved MES, continue to seek further growth. In the United Kingdom the growth group appears to be those with between two and twenty employees.

Strategy

For the purposes of this subsection, strategy is defined to be the actions which are taken by the small business owner once in business. Fourteen elements are identified which can be considered to be elements of business strategy. The extent to which these are characteristic of a fast-growth small firm, primarily where the criterion for growth is an increase in employment, is examined below.

Table 5.9 Strategy

	Woo *et al.* (1989)	Dunkelberg *et al.* (1987)	Macrae (1991)	Cambridge Small Business Research Centre (1992)	Kinsella *et al.* (1993)	Solem and Steiner (1989)	Wynarczyk *et al.* (1993)	Storey *et al.* (1989)	Kalleberg and Leicht (1991)	Westhead and Birley (1993a)	Birley and Westhead (1990)	Siegel *et al.* (1993)
1 Workforce training				x	x		x	(+)				
2 Management training			+		(+)		x				+	
3 External equity				+	(+)	+		(+)				
4 Technological sophistication				+		+		x	x			+
5 Market positioning			+			+		(+)	x	x	+	+
6 Market adjustments												
7 Planning	+				(+)							
8 New product introduction	+	+			x	+	+	(+)	x		x	
9 Management recruitment			+				+	(+)				+
10 State support				(+)	(+)			(+)		x	x	
11 Customer concentration					x			x		–		
12 Competition			x						x	x	x	
13 Information advice		+		+	x			(+)		x		
14 Exporting				x	(+)			(+)		x		

Key:
+ Positive relationship between the element and growth of the firm
– Negative relationship between the element and growth of the firm
() Relationship present in a univariate context, but weak in a multivariate context
x Element not shown to be significant in influencing growth

Workforce training

Atkinson and Meager (1994) demonstrate that the likelihood of firms undertaking training for their workforce appears to increase with the size of the firm. This is because the small firm employer, aware of the high risk of failure, is reluctant to make a long-term investment in workforce training. The second reason is that external training, in particular, focuses upon deepening the skill base, whereas small firms require greater flexibility from their labour, rather than deeper specific skills. The third reason is that labour turnover in smaller firms is generally greater than in larger firms, and so the value of training from the employer's perspective is reduced. For these reasons the strategy of small firms is to 'poach' trained labour and then to 'mould' it according to their requirements.

It might be expected that growing small firms would behave differently. For example, growing firms might be more likely to perceive the skill base of their enterprise to be one of its comparative advantages and so might be expected actively to encourage workforce training to a greater extent than slow-growth or no-growth firms. Judging by the evidence in row 1 of Table 5.9, there appears to be little evidence for this. Of the four studies reviewed, three were unable to identify an impact of workforce training and only one indicated it to be positively associated with growing businesses. However, even in that case, since the growing businesses were consistently larger than other firms in the study, it suggests that workforce training is associated with greater size, rather than necessarily growth.

Management training

Casson (1982) elaborated, from a theoretical perspective, the skills and competencies needed for successful entrepreneurship. In essence, he saw the central skill of the entrepreneur as being forecasting and decision making under conditions of uncertainty – these conditions being highly context-specific in terms of changes over time, between sectors, etc. It might therefore be expected that these competencies can be formally taught to entrepreneurs and that those in receipt of this training would perform better in business than untrained individuals. Here we are referring to management training, once the business has started, rather than management training received by the individual in a prior job.

The evidence provided in the four studies which examine this question in Table 5.9 might at first sight seem to provide some support for this hypothesis. However, whilst the Kinsella *et al.* (1993) study in the Republic of Ireland and Northern Ireland shows firms providing management training to constitute 73 per cent of fast growth firms, as compared with 40 per cent of match firms, the study examines this only on a univariate basis. In the Irish context it is also likely to be associated with state support, which Kinsella *et al.* demonstrate to be associated with faster-growth firms. Furthermore, since the fast-growth firms are currently much larger than the match firms, there is again a problem over whether it is a 'growth' effect or a 'size' effect. Similar comments apply to the Macrae study.

It must therefore remain an open question as to whether there is an identifiable impact of the provision of management training to entrepreneurs currently in business, which ultimately leads their businesses to grow more rapidly than would have been the case without such training. This matter is further discussed in Chapter 8.

External equity

The sources used for financing a business are likely to be an influence upon its growth (Hall 1989). The small firm owner can finance the growth of a business in a number of ways, but one fundamental decision by the entrepreneur is whether or not to allow external finance to be provided by outsiders in return for part ownership of the business. Many small business owners are strongly opposed to sharing ownership, either with financial institutions or with other individuals, and so use short-term debt financing. This may constitute a constraint upon the growth of the business.

Row 3 of Table 5.9 shows that in all of the studies of fast-growth businesses, those which indicated that either they had shared, or were willing to share, equity were more likely to grow or to have grown than the businesses which indicated a reluctance to share equity. Here again, however, some care is needed in interpreting the findings, since the positive association between external equity and growth may simply reflect the fact that the only businesses which would be of interest to an external owner are those which have shown, or which show the potential for, growth. Nevertheless it is clearly the case that growth can be constrained by an unwillingness to share equity.

As we will discuss further in Chapter 7, this is a very important finding. It emphasises that if encouragement to growing businesses is to be given, it is vital to persuade entrepreneurs of the benefits of sharing equity either with a financial institution or with a business angel.

Technological sophistication

Phillips and Kirchhoff (1989b) show that in the United States, high technology small firms are likely to grow more rapidly, other things being equal, than small firms in more conventional sectors. It may also be the case that more technologically sophisticated businesses, even in conventional sectors, are likely to grow more rapidly than those with lower levels of technical sophistication.

The central problem with testing this hypothesis is the definition used for 'technological sophistication'. This question is tractable in the high technology sectors, where conventional measurements of technological sophistication include the frequency of patenting, expenditure on research and development, or employment of qualified scientists and engineers (QSEs) (Monck *et al.* 1988). For firms outside the high technology sectors, where these considerations are not relevant, there is a measurement problem in this area.

Measures used by the five researchers identified in row 4 of Table 5.9 do differ quite markedly. For example, the Cambridge Small Business Research Centre study asks respondents about any major innovations introduced during the last five years in products or services. It finds that 72 per cent of fast-growth firms have introduced such innovations, compared with only 50 per cent amongst stable or declining firms. Solem and Steiner, on the other hand, simply ask about whether the company has changed its technology. Kalleberg and Leicht identify six types of innovations which the firm could have made and produce a 'scoring system' based upon their responses. In their case, one of the measures was the introduction of new products, which we will specifically consider as item 8.

Three out of the five studies which include some measure of technological sophistication indicate that it is positively associated with more rapid growth of the firm. In some senses this variable may be collectively considered as an indicator of business excellence, which was seen by Peters and Waterman (1982) in the large firm context, as the key to business success.

Market positioning

One element which emerges from a review of the factors influencing small business success strategies by Wingham and Kelmar (1992) is the role of what we call 'market positioning'. Alternative terminology includes 'niches' (Bradburd and Ross 1989) or 'interstices' (Penrose 1959). All three argue that, whilst there may be differences between the growth rates of firms according to the sector in which they operate, this has less impact upon the performance of the small firm than the buoyancy or otherwise of the highly specific market-place in which it competes. For example, two small firms in mechanical engineering may be affected by very different market-places; one may be selling the bulk of its output to a large firm which is expanding rapidly and may be a specialist producer with few, if any, competitors. The second firm may be a 'jobbing' engineering firm producing a range of products, but not having any clear comparative advantage over numerous rivals.

Market positioning is a complex concept which is not easy to measure or categorise. It is probably for this reason that researchers have used a number of indices of the market positioning of smaller businesses. For example, the Macrae (1991) study sees market positioning as a wide-ranging concept which includes other items within Table 5.9. Within market position, Macrae finds that fast-growth firms are more likely to be entering export markets, to place more importance on the actions of their competitors and the actions of big business, and to have more suppliers. Solem and Steiner (1989) show that faster-growing firms have distinct product properties, even at the sectoral level. This is certainly a dimension of market positioning. The impression which emerges from the Storey *et al.* (1989) survey of fast-growth and match firms is that even though the two groups were matched in terms of sector, they rarely competed directly against each other. The fast-growth firm was much more likely to see its comparative advantage in terms of the quality of the product which it offered or the service which it provided, whereas the match firm was more likely to see its comparative advantage in terms of price. Hence, whilst there were no sectoral differences, the two groups of firms generally competed in different positions in the market place.

Row 5 of Table 5.9 shows that despite the plausibility of these arguments, neither the Kalleberg and Leicht (1991) nor the Westhead and Birley (1993a) studies were able to identify such a distinction. Nevertheless, the general thrust of research results in this area suggest that market positioning is a key ingredient of growth amongst smaller firms, but that the dimensions of this positioning need further investigation.

Market adjustments

The achievement of growth by a small firm over a period of time requires, as a minimum condition, that the firm survives. It may have to survive crises relating to changing customer composition, changing regulations, changing technology, etc. It is argued by Smallbone *et al.* (Smallbone, Leigh and North 1993, Smallbone, North and Leigh 1993a) that the ability to make these adjustments in response to these crises is central to growth: indeed, they argue that it is the more rapidly growing firms which are more likely to have made adjustments in a variety of different dimensions, than the slower-growing firms.

Unfortunately, as Table 5.9 shows, this is not an issue which has been included explicitly within the multivariate studies reviewed here. Nevertheless, it does seem plausible to argue that growing firms have to make successful adjustments. It is for this reason that the work of Smallbone *et al.* provides the basis for the overall picture of growth in small firms, presented later (pp. 156–8) in this chapter.

Planning

The use of 'formal' strategic planning is defined in terms of the plans of an organisation being written down, relatively long planning horizons being chosen, and objectives and goals being specified. Associated with this is the information necessary to monitor the extent to which these plans materialise and the opportunity to review the reasons, if any, why the plans and the outcome differ.

Although they are not shown in Table 5.9, there have been a number of studies which have attempted to link the existence of formal planning procedures within small firms to performance. Probably the best known is by Robinson and Pearce (1983, 1984), who are unable to show that formalised planning leads to, or is associated with, better small firm performance.

This is reflected in the results of Table 5.9 which shows that only two of the studies specifically examined the impact of planning upon the performance of small firms. The Woo *et al.* (1989) study found that those firms which claimed to spend a higher proportion of their time in planning activities were those which experienced the more rapid growth. However, the Kinsella *et al.* (1993) study, which examines in detail the question of small firm planning, makes a distinction between small firms which had a written business plan at start-up, and those which introduced one later on. It concluded that 93 per cent of the fast-growth firms in the study had a written business plan, compared with only 70 per cent of match firms, but that fewer differences existed between the two groups at start-up. Even so, both these figures are very much higher than those obtained by Nayak and Greenfield (1994) in their study of financial control in micro-businesses. These authors, whose study is discussed in more detail in Chapter 7, demonstrate that business planning is almost wholly absent from the UK micro-business sector; many such firms indeed appear to keep few financial records of their business, and so would not be in any position to monitor plans, even if they had them.

Formal planning procedures and their monitoring appears to be more characteristic of larger businesses. It may also be the case that faster-growing firms are more likely to be devising and implementing formal planning procedures. The evidence is less clear as to whether this is a factor which encourages growth, or whether it is merely associated with a movement towards greater size and formality.

New product introductions

We have already observed in rows 4 and 5 of Table 5.9 that innovation and the identification of a particular niche were key strategies associated with more rapid growth in small firms. Associated with this is the specific question of new product introductions. Although this is an indicator of innovation, it is a topic which researchers have considered independently. The problem here is that of distinguishing between genuine innovation – in the sense of the product being one which is wholly new – and more mundane forms of innovation, such as adding a product which is new to the firm's product range, but which is well known in the market-place itself.

Row 8 of the table shows that eight studies have specifically examined this question, with five suggesting that the more rapidly growing firms are more likely to have made new product introductions. The remaining three studies do not find this to impact upon firm performance.

The results from rows 4, 5 and 8 suggest that these three elements are central strategic issues for the growing small firm.

Management recruitment

The stage models illustrated in Table 5.5 are effective in pointing to the need for managerial styles and roles to change as the firm expands. At the heart of this, for the small firm, is that growth leads to increased complexity of decision making for the business owner; it means the individual is required to delegate these functions to others. As Casson (1982) points out:

> As the business grows, the complexity of decision making may be such that the entrepreneur is obliged to delegate. If the business is growing fast then it may be necessary to allow delegates considerable discretion. New opportunities may be missed unless quick decisions are made, and this strongly favours decentralised decision making by delegates who possess significant autonomy.

The problem for the entrepreneur or business owner is that the success of delegation depends upon the owner's ability to identify and motivate managers. Despite the centrality of this issue, it is curious that it has received relatively little attention among small firm researchers who have undertaken quantitative analysis. In part, this may be because one aspect of the 'conceptual' definition of a small firm used by the Bolton Committee (1971) was that a small firm was owned and managed by the same individual or group of individuals. In practice, once firms exceed between ten and twenty workers, they begin to employ individuals to act as managers or supervisors of the work of others, but who are not owners of the business.

The issue is to determine whether the characteristics of this group of non-owning managers influences the subsequent growth of the firm. For example, does the choice of the disciplinary or functional specialisms of the individuals employed lead to more rapid growth? Do the backgrounds of these managers influence the growth of the firm. Are fast-growing firms more likely to recruit managers from inside or outside their own organisation?

The pattern which emerges is that the nature of non-owning manager recruitment is a factor which is associated with small-firm growth. The Wynarczyk *et al.* (1993) study concludes that fast-growing firms are more likely to recruit managers externally, and are more likely to recruit from larger firms. It is also shown that the recruitment of senior financial expertise tends to take place only well after the business has started.

State support

Chapter 8 examines this issue in greater depth. Governments in many developed countries have introduced legislation to assist the small business sector, for three reasons: the first is because of the numerical dominance of smaller firms in most developed economies; the second is because the small-firm sector is thought to be a dynamo of growth, thirdly, governments have intervened for reasons of assumed market failure.

For current purposes, it is appropriate to investigate whether the provision of state support is associated with, or even causes, small firms to grow more rapidly. State support can come in a number of forms: it could be as loans at subsidised rates of interest, it could be the provision of free or subsidised information and advice, or it could be ensuring that small firms obtain shares of government contracts.

Four studies in Table 5.9 explicitly examine this question. Westhead and Birley (1993a) and Birley and Westhead (1990) are unable to identify an impact of state support upon firm performance in the form of awareness of incentives or industry-related grants. In part, this may be because these grants tend to be provided to smaller firms in the less prosperous areas, where small firm performance is generally weaker. Storey *et al.* (1987) and Kinsella *et al.* (1993) observe an impact of state assistance, with more rapidly growing small firms being more likely to be in receipt of assistance in the form of either finance or information than the slower-growing firms. The advantage which the Storey *et al.* (1987) study has is that it covers only a single geographical area where assistance is available, and so it is able to compare utilisation of a common 'pool' of assistance between fast-growth and other small firms; its disadvantage is that only forty cases are examined in a univariate framework. Finally, the Cambridge Small Business Research Centre (1992) study finds that utilisation of government advisory services is higher amongst faster-growing firms.

In a multivariate framework it has yet to be demonstrated that the provision of all forms of state support to small businesses encourages small firms to grow more rapidly. The most positive findings are those produced by Kinsella *et al.* for Northern Ireland and the Republic of Ireland where, particularly in the latter, selective state support has a longer history. For the United Kingdom as a whole, results are uncertain, although as Chapter 8 shows there is evidence that grants can be effective.

Customer concentration

The Bolton Committee Report (1971) identified a key characteristic of small firms to be their high dependence upon either a single customer or a small number of customers. More than twenty years later, the Cambridge Small Business Research Centre (1992) study produced similar results, with one in three of all small firms in their sample relying on one customer for 25 per cent or more of sales. The Cambridge study did not present any data which related customer dependence to firm growth, other than pointing out that customer dependence seemed to decline with increasing firm size.

A priori it is not clear whether dependence upon a single customer is, or is not, likely to be associated with the more rapid growth of a small firm. Clearly, this will depend upon the requirements of the customer and how these change. It is apparent, however, that heavy dependence upon a single customer is extremely risky, since changes in the fortunes of that customer impact directly upon their suppliers. Switching costs may also be high. On the other hand, these high risks, from the point of view of the small firm, may be offset by the high returns associated with supplying a customer which is experiencing rapid growth.

Row 11 of Table 5.9 shows three studies examined customer concentration and its relationship to small firm performance, with two finding no observable impact. Indeed Westhead and Birley (1993a) show that the most rapidly growing firms were those which had the lowest levels of customer concentration, hence the negative sign.

Empirical results do not therefore provide any support for the view that more rapidly growing small firms have a narrow customer base. This suggests that, not only is such a strategy clearly risky, but it also does not yield high returns to the firm.

Competition

Covin and Slevin (1989) argue that the nature of the market-place into which the firm sells is a key influence upon potential growth. They make the distinction between hostile and benign environments and suggest that successful surviving firms in hostile or highly competitive environments are those which illustrate organisational flexibility and a willingness to undertake risky projects. However, in the more benign environment, the successful firms are those which place a greater emphasis upon formality and rules within the organisation.

Obtaining an objective index or measure of competition within the market-place is difficult – as is even classifying environments between those which are benign and those which are hostile. Empirically, the studies which have used a measure of competition have tended to focus upon the number of direct competitors to the firm. In many senses this is also unsatisfactory since, although it is compatible with the concept of perfect competition, it is not clear that competition is linearly related to the number of firms serving that market-place. It could also be considered as being inversely related to market positioning, one characteristic of which was associated with rapid-growth firms: the ability to provide a product or service which essentially differentiated them from the competition. The purposes of market positioning can therefore be effectively to eliminate competition.

Finally, it has been shown by Storey *et al.* (1987) that the low-growth firms seem to have the poorest understanding of their competitors. Hence subjective estimates on the part of firms of the nature of the competition which they experience may tell the researcher as much about the firm's own understanding of their market-place as anything else.

It is perhaps for these reasons that row 12 of Table 5.8 is not able to identify any clear impact between subjective estimates on the nature of competition in the market place and the performance of the firm.

Information and advice

In the discussion above about the role of state support to small firms, and any impact which this had on the growth of small firms, one aspect of this was seen to be the provision of, possibly subsidised, advice. This section extends that analysis by examining not only state-subsidised assistance, but also the much more frequent use of sources of information or advice provided by the private sector – most notably by lawyers, accountants, banks, consultants, etc.

The central question is whether these services are any more likely to be utilised by rapidly growing small firms, than by other types of small firm.

Of the five studies which explicitly examine this question, three indicated that it was the more rapidly growing firms which were more likely to utilise information and advice services provided by the private sector, than other types of small firm. Dunkelberg *et al.* (1987) show that accountants were much more likely to have provided growth firms with information and assistance which proved to be important, than was the case for firms in decline. The Cambridge Small Business Research Centre (1992) study showed that 69 per cent of fast-growth firms had sought taxation and financial management advice, compared with only 59 per cent of stable or declining firms. The fast-growth firms were also rather more likely to have sought advice in the areas of business strategy, personnel and recruitment matters, public relations and advertising. However, they appeared no more likely to have sought advice in product design, market research, new technology or computer services.

The two studies which are not able to relate small firm growth to the use of external information and advice services are those by Kinsella *et al.* (1993) and by Westhead and Birley (1993a). In the case of the Kinsella *et al.* study this may be because almost all the firms, irrespective of growth rates, claimed to have sought external advice.

Overall, the evidence points to more rapidly growing firms being more likely to have sought and used information and advice provided by accountants, bankers, consultants, etc. It is, however, more difficult to infer that the provision of this advice *caused* the growth of the firm.

Exporting

Most small firms do not export. Curran, Blackburn and Woods (1991), in their study of small firms in the service sector, found that only 0.7 per cent of firms had 75 per cent or more of their services going to export markets. However, the Kinsella *et al.* (1993) study reports the opinion of the rather high proportion of firms which export in both Northern Ireland and the Republic of Ireland, that export markets constitute virtually the only opportunity for growth for firms of their size and type. In some senses the ability to sell into the export market can be seen as a more objective measure of the quality of the product or service provided. It can be considered 'objective' in the sense of being less likely to be influenced by local arrangements, and can be seen by analysts as reflecting a willingness to enter what are naturally more competitive market-places, but with a view to achieving sales growth.

Two of the four studies which incorporate this issue indicate that firms which are more likely to export are also more likely to be growing. An exception to this is the Cambridge Small Business Research Centre (1992) study, which demonstrates the limitations of the univariate framework. It showed that the fast-growth firms were less likely to export than the medium-growth firms. However, it also showed that large firms were more likely to export than smaller firms. As noted earlier, large firms are likely to grow more slowly than smaller firms, so it is difficult to disentangle these influences.

Overall

Of the fourteen elements identified in Table 5.9 there are four elements, or groups of elements, which stand out as important. The first is element 3, which indicates that growing firms are much more likely to have owners who share equity with external individuals or organisations. This demonstrates that the willingness to share equity is central to the achievement of growth.

The second fairly consistent finding is that rapidly growing firms have often made a conscious decision on market positioning – element 5. They have chosen to occupy particular niches or segments where they can exploit any quality advantage which they have. Very often this quality advantage is reflected in greater technological sophistication and a willingness to introduce new products.

Thirdly, the introduction of new products – element 8 – is important in the balance of cases.

Finally, the ability of the small business to grow must be influenced by the willingness of the owners to devolve decisions to non-owning managers – element 9. The selection, motivation and retention of these individuals in the creation of a strong managerial team is likely to be important, but our research-based understanding of this issue remains weak.

BARRIERS TO GROWTH

An alternative perspective to addressing the question of growth in small firms is adopted in the so-called 'barriers to growth' literature. This assumes that a proportion of small firms wish to grow, but are prevented from so doing by 'barriers'. In their initial study, *Barriers to Growth in Small Firms*, Barber, Metcalfe and Porteous (1989) summarised the literature on this topic under three headings: Management and Motivation, The Sources, and Market Opportunities and Structure.

One issue which emerged was the extent to which the fundamental barriers were internal to the firm – such as a lack of motivation – as opposed to being external to the firm – such as 'shortages' of finance, government controls, lack of skilled labour, etc.

Barriers to growth in high technology businesses were examined by the Advisory Council of Science and Technology (1990), which concluded that external barriers were present which restricted the growth of some firms. In particular they focused upon the extent to which the availability of finance restricted the growth of this type of firm.

However, a study for the Department of Trade and Industry by Aston Business School (1991) 'demonstrated that small firms in Great Britain currently faced few difficulties in raising finance for their innovation and investment proposals in the private sector'.

The most recent authoritative work on this topic has been undertaken in the Cambridge Small Business Research Centre (1992) survey. Table 5.10, taken from the Cambridge document, reports the responses of 1,933 businesses which were asked to rank eleven possible constraints and their ability to meet their business objectives. The results report a mean ranking, where zero indicates that the factor is completely unimportant and nine indicates that it is highly important. Hence the higher the 'score', the more important is the constraint. The table makes a distinction between the results for all firms in the survey, shown in the first column, and between stable/declining firms, shown in column two, and fast-growth firms, shown in column three.

The two most important perceived constraints for all firms in the sample relate to matters of finance. This is then followed in importance by the level of aggregate demand in the economy and the nature of competition within the market-place. All of these may be considered factors which are 'external' to the firm. Of somewhat lower significance are factors relating to employment, such as managerial skills, and skilled labour. Technological problems are of very modest importance and the availability of premises is mentioned by very few.

Comparing the results from columns two and three shows that firms' rates of growth over the past three years have some, but not a major, impact upon the ranking of their constraints. Not surprisingly, stable/declining firms are more likely to point to slow growth in market demand as a constraint upon meeting their business objectives, whereas, for fast-growing firms, the two key constraints are those relating to finance and then those relating to internal and employment matters, such as access to marketing and sales skills or management skills.

The overall pattern which emerges is that for fast-growth small

Table 5.10 Constraints on ability to meet business objectives

	Mean rank*				
Constraints	*All*	*Stable/ declining*	*Rank*	*Fast growth*	*Rank*
Availability and cost of finance for expansion	4.95	4.60	4	5.17	1
Availability and cost of overdraft facilities	4.90	4.69	2	5.16	2
Overall growth of market demand	4.67	5.08	1	4.24	5
Increasing competition	4.33	4.64	3	4.03	6
Marketing and sales skills	4.12	3.96	5	4.43	3
Management skills	3.85	3.38	6	4.29	4
Skilled labour	3.42	2.99	7	3.58	7
Acquisition of new technology	2.32	2.09	8	2.42	9
Difficulties in implementing new technology	2.16	1.94	9	2.34	10
Availability of appropriate premises or site	2.09	1.56	11	2.53	8
Access to overseas markets	1.89	1.84	10	1.85	11
Total responses (no.)	1,933	500		401	

Source: Cambridge Small Business Research Centre (1992)
Note:
* These are means of ranked data. 0 indicates that the factor is completely unimportant and 9 indicates that it is highly important.

businesses the key constraints upon growth are related to matters of finance, employment and markets. These topics are examined, in detail, in Chapters 6 and 7.

MATURE SMALL FIRMS

We now draw together these diverse threads by focusing upon a study by David Smallbone, David North and Roger Leigh (1992) on the characteristics and strategies of a group of high-growth, but mature, SMEs in the United Kingdom. Their maturity enables us to relate this to the stage models outlined earlier in Table 5.4, and it enables us to focus upon strategy variables and barriers to growth.

The prime data set used by Smallbone, North and Leigh is 293 manufacturing firms located in the London area, which the researchers first interviewed in 1979 and 1981. These firms were then contacted again in 1990 to examine the changes which they had experienced over that time. Two other samples of firms are drawn by the authors: the first are firms in the outer metropolitan areas of Hertfordshire and Essex, and the second are a group of manufacturing firms in UK rural areas. Although these firms in the outer metropolitan and rural areas were not interviewed in 1979 or 1981, they were asked in 1990 about their employment in these years. The purpose was to construct a sample of mature small manufacturing firms located in urban, outer metropolitan and rural areas, which operated in broadly similar sectors. The research then investigated the factors associated with more rapid employment growth, amongst the surviving mature firms.

The researchers identified a group of 'high-growth firms' – those which had more than doubled their turnover in real terms between 1979 and 1990, had a turnover in 1990 in excess of £500,000 and had been consistently profitable over the years 1987–90. Of the firms in the sample, 23 per cent satisfied these criteria.

The purpose of the Smallbone *et al.* research was to determine the respects in which these firms differed from other mature small firms in the sample. They conclude, with hindsight, that the fast-growth firms can be seen to have had different strategies both in relationship to their product and market development, their management of production and their internal organisation structure.

The researchers were struck by the frequency with which fast-growth firms built upon an established product base primarily by identifying new markets for existing products for existing customers. This involved the identification and movement into an important and profitable market niche, and underlines the importance of market positioning, which we identify in Table 5.9. The researchers also confirmed a second finding from that table, which is that the nature of competition in the market-place, whilst of some importance, is not a central influence upon the growth rate of the individual small firm.

Whilst the researchers did not confirm that the development of new markets is necessarily associated with a geographical market extension, their findings did suggest that fast-growth firms are significantly more likely to export than is the case for the remaining firms in the sample.

They also point out that fast-growth firms were more likely to have products or services which were in some way innovative than is the case in the sample as a whole. However, the importance of innovation in this respect seems to differ more markedly between sectors than between fast growth and other types of small firm.

In examining organisational change in their sample, Smallbone *et al.* also highlight that the high-growth firms are distinguished by the fact that senior individuals – normally the major equity shareholders – had implemented organisational changes which created more time, enabling them to manage the business. This concept is closely allied to the question of management recruitment, identified in Table 5.9.

Overall, the Smallbone *et al.* research encapsulates many of the issues which have already been highlighted in the chapter, although their discussion tends to be focused more heavily upon market and employment rather than finance-based issues.

CONCLUSIONS

This chapter has reviewed research on fast-growth small firms. It finds that rapidly growing firms constitute a tiny proportion of the small firm population but, over a ten-year period, they make a major contribution to job creation.

Most firms, even in 'ideal' macroeconomic circumstances, do not wish to grow in employment. However, the firms which exhibit low or negative growth have significantly higher death rates than the fast-growth firms.

There are three main factors which influence the growth of the firm – the background/resources of the entrepreneur(s), the nature of the firm itself, and the strategic decisions taken by the owner-managers in the firm. The three components need to combine appropriately for growth to be achieved. This means it is very difficult to identify whether or not a firm will be a success, at start-up.

The elements which appear to be associated with growth in the entrepreneur/resources factor are: motivation, education, having more than a single owner and having business owners in middle age. Amongst the firm-related elements, smaller and younger firms grow quicker, as do limited companies. There are also sectoral and locational differences. Finally, amongst the strategy variables, a willingness to share ownership, the ability to identify niches, the introduction of new products and the ability to create teams of managers are generally related to growth.

Constraints upon growth apply to less than half the small business population. These external constraints can be broadly categorised as relating to finance, labour market issues and markets. The nature of these constraints varies according to macroeconomic circumstances with, for example, labour market and skill-related issues being of greater importance in times of 'boom', whereas in recessionary times, finance constraints and a lack of demand appear to be rather more important. The role of finance, labour market issues and government are the three key issues which constitute the basis of the next three chapters.

If employment creation is an objective of government, then fast-growing SMEs deserve more attention than they currently receive. Our ability to predict, at start-up, those businesses which will exhibit rapid growth, however, remains limited, but once the business is in operation, forecasting improves somewhat.

In the longer term – say more than a decade – few businesses exhibit consistent fast growth. It is the failure of UK small enterprises to grow into large enterprises that may be at the heart of the country's long-term poor economic performance.

Chapter 6

Employment

INTRODUCTION

When a steelworks closes, or – more topically – a large defence industry contractor shuts, it is the small firm sector which is seen as the source of new employment opportunities for the redundant workforce. Former unskilled employees become self-employed taxi drivers, window cleaners and small garage employees. Draughtsmen, precision engineering fitters and computer specialists become self-employed in their own trades. Where major job shedding takes place, the small firm sector is seen to be the way in which the local economy can create its own employment by 'pulling itself up by its own boot-straps'.

This view of the small firm sector as a major source of job creation has emerged only in the last ten to fifteen years, for reasons which were discussed extensively in Chapter 2. At the time of the Bolton Committee (1971), the focus given to employment issues was very modest indeed. Although there were nineteen chapters in the Bolton Report, none were given over exclusively to considerations of employment.

Today, any consideration of the small firm sector which overlooked employment issues would be like *Hamlet* without the prince. In the United Kingdom this change in perception can be dated to approximately 1978–9, although, as Chapter 2 shows, the real change in the structure of the UK economy was occurring as the Bolton Committee was sitting at the start of the 1970s. By 1978 the thirteenth report from the Expenditure Committee (*People and Work, Prospects for Jobs and Training*) argued that 'If each small business could take on one more employee the unemployment problem would be solved.'

At the time, the Committee estimated that there were 1.3 million small businesses in Britain and that 1.3 million people were unemployed, and in this sense their arithmetic was faultless.

The year 1979 brought two key developments. The first was the election of a Conservative government under the leadership of Margaret Thatcher, committed to a policy of stimulating 'enterprise'. Central to that policy was a strong focus upon the small firms sector. The second development was the publication and wide coverage given to the results generated by David Birch in the United States, which were widely interpreted as showing that two-thirds of the increase in employment in the United States between 1969 and 1976 had been in firms with less than twenty workers. This provided the *raison d'être* for Mrs Thatcher's new administration to highlight the benefits of a vibrant and flexible small firm sector as a way of both creating new jobs and reducing unemployment.

Throughout the 1980s there continued to be a lively debate about the precise contribution of smaller firms to job creation – that debate is reviewed in the following section of this chapter. Employment, and its impact upon unemployment, is not, however, solely about the numbers of jobs which are created. To ensure that employment creation ultimately leads to reductions in unemployment, the characteristics of the jobs which are created need to correspond broadly to those which are capable of being filled by the unemployed. The characteristics of the small firm workforce, and how these individuals differ from those working in larger firms, are discussed on pp. 173–9. There is then an examination of the quality of jobs which are created in smaller firms (pp. 179–96).

Finally in this chapter, the logical process is reversed, and the question is asked, not what can the small firm sector do for the labour market, but what does the labour market do for smaller firms? Here we review the research which examines how small firms interact with the labour market, and the extent to which their requirements are adequately served.

THE QUANTITY OF JOBS IN SMALLER FIRMS

One side-effect of the revolution in information technology during the 1970s was the creation of computerised files of information on individual enterprises and establishments. Using these files it became possible to compare, over time, changes in the employment and financial characteristics of businesses and enterprises.

In the United States, credit rating companies such as Dun and Bradstreet began to assemble huge quantities of data about businesses, in order to assess credit-worthiness. One element of this was employment data. The first person to exploit the use of such data for analysis of employment change was David Birch. His original paper in 1979 proved to be hugely influential, since it manipulated existing data files on changes in employment in more than 5.6 million establishments in virtually all sectors of the US economy. Birch was widely interpreted as showing that two-thirds of new jobs in the United States between 1969 and 1976 were in firms with less than twenty workers. His work was cited extensively in the United Kingdom to justify the benefits which could be obtained by the creation of a more enterprising society, such as that which the newly elected Margaret Thatcher was setting out to achieve. The

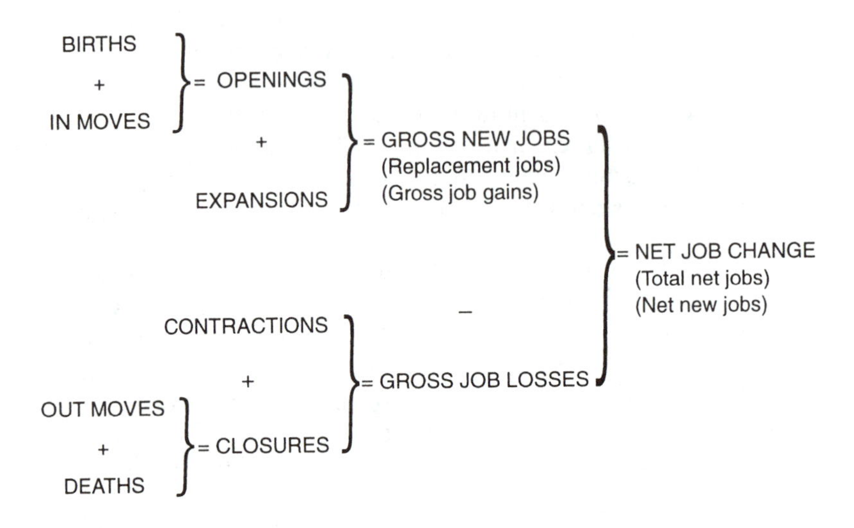

Figure 6.1 The job generation process
Source: Storey (1980)
Note: Terms in parenthesis are synonyms

inference was clear: that small firms could be a massively important source of job creation, provided an appropriate environment for them was created.

Any report as influential, on both sides of the Atlantic, as that by Birch will inevitably be the subject of intense scrutiny. This section will provide some commentary on that scrutiny.

The chief methodological contribution of Birch was the specification of the so-called 'components of job generation'. These are shown in Figure 6.1, which is best understood by reading the 'wrong' way, from right to left. The right-hand side of the figure shows that net job change, which can be either positive or negative, is the outcome of the jobs which are created in an economy (gross new jobs) and the jobs which are lost (gross job losses).

Moving towards the left-hand side of the figure it can be seen that gross new jobs are defined to comprise the jobs created through increases in employment in existing firms/establishments (expansions) and the jobs in new establishments/enterprises (births). Conversely, gross job losses are defined as employment in firms/establishments which continue in business but which contract their employment (contractions) and in those which close (closures). Finally, a subdivision, which will not be used here, is that openings and closures can be disaggregated, as shown in Figure 6.1.

Given this terminology, Birch was able to quantify the magnitude of each of these components over time. He was also able to quantify the extent to which smaller or larger establishments/firms contributed either to net job change or to its constituent parts.

There have been five significant areas of criticism of Birch's work:

- The first relates to the use of net job change as a measure of employment change. It is argued that the measure is inappropriate, particularly where the contributions of differing size of firms are being quantified, on the grounds that it can be either a positive or a negative number. For example, Birch showed that, for the US manufacturing sector, net job change was negative between 1969 and 1976, primarily because of the significant shedding of jobs in large manufacturing firms. It is suggested that a measure of employment change such as gross new jobs is more appropriate.
- A second criticism relates to confusion over whether Birch's data referred to enterprises or establishments. It is clear that the original data from the Dun and Bradstreet files referred to both enterprises and establishments, but unfortunately the sum of all employment in individual establishments did not equal total employment in all enterprises. This meant that different figures were obtained, depending upon the measure used. More recently, the US Small Business Administration has, however, sought to rectify these data deficiencies, and enterprise data, rather than establishment data, are now the basis for analysis.
- A third criticism was levelled by Armington and Odle (1982). They took the same data set on which Birch had conducted his analysis, and found themselves unable to replicate his results. The reasons for this are numerous and are explored in detail by Storey and Johnson (1987). In essence, they stem from the fact that the Dun and Bradstreet data base, whilst it is huge, is nevertheless incomplete. For this reason assumptions have to be made by the researchers about firms which are not in the data base, if a full scaling-up to cover the whole US economy is to be undertaken. Quite simply, the assumptions made by Armington and Odle differed from those made by Birch. However, the impact of these different assumptions could not be described as marginal. Under the Birch assumptions, firms with less then 100 workers were estimated to provide 70 per cent of net job change in the United States, whereas under Armington and Odle's assumptions small firms with less than 100 workers provided 39 per cent in the 1978–80 period. Here again, work has now been conducted by the US Small Business Administration to reach a more informed judgement about firms excluded from the data base.
- A fourth problem with the Birch analysis was that the data provided by Dun and Bradstreet was insufficiently 'clean' for the analytical purposes to which they were put. For example, firms/establishments frequently remained on the data base after they had ceased to trade. Secondly, the firms which entered the data base were unlikely to be a random sample

of US establishments, and were more likely to be those experiencing some growth. This is because Dun and Bradstreet, as a credit rating agency, would be significantly more likely to require information on this type of business. Again, work to overcome these data deficiencies has been undertaken by the US Small Business Administration.

- A fifth criticism relates not so much to the establishment/enterprise data itself but to the inferences which can be made from the observation that smaller firms provide a disproportionately high percentage of net job change. This criticism is most clearly associated with the work of Brown, Hamilton and Medoff (1990), and will be discussed later in this chapter.

The work which the Small Business Administration in the United States has undertaken on the Dun and Bradstreet files means it is now possible with some confidence to provide a picture of job creation in the United States between 1976 and 1988, according to size of firm. Fortunately, in virtually all years, all firm sizes had positive net job change and thus can be said to have made a positive contribution to employment creation.

The outcome is shown in Table 6.1, which takes a succession of two-year periods and identifies the contribution to net job change made by different sizes of firm. It shows that small firms, in most two-year periods, have been the major contributor to employment creation. Even so, this contribution varies sharply, according to macroeconomic conditions. For example, during the recessionary period 1980–2 it was small firms, most notably those with less than twenty workers, which provided almost all jobs in the US economy (97.9 per cent). On the other hand, during the periods of prosperity, such as that between 1986 and 1988, the large-firm sector was a more important

Table 6.1 Share of net job change by firm size, 1976–88

	Total, all sizes ('000s)	*Share of jobs by employment size of firm (per cent)*		
Period of observation		*<20*	*20–499*	*500+*
1986–8	6,169	24.1	20.8	55.1
1984–6	4,611	35.5	16.8	47.7
1982–4	4,318	48.8	27.9	23.3
1980–2	1,542	97.9	–2.4	4.5
1978–80	5,777	26.3	18.8	54.9
1976–8	6,062	38.2	34.5	27.3
Weighted average, 1976–88		37.1	22.5	41.4
Employment share, 1976–88		19.4	30.6	50.0
Index: growth/share	–	1.91	1.36	0.83

Source: US Small Business Administration, Office of Advocacy, Small Business Data Base, 1976–86, 1984–8 USELM files, version 8.

source of job creation (55.1 per cent).

Taking the period 1976–88 as a whole, the US Small Business Administration estimates that small firms provided about 37 per cent of net employment change. This is a substantially lower figure than the 'headline' figure of Birch; almost certainly it reflects the much more careful analysis which the Administration was able to conduct over a number of years. In summary, therefore, over this period, firms with less than twenty workers provided 19.4 per cent of total employment in the United States but about 37 per cent of new jobs. It is on these grounds that it is argued that small firms provide a disproportionate share of new jobs.

The second key point of Table 6.1 is that the periods when the rate of new job change was higher – such as 1978–80 and 1986–8 – were the periods when rates of job creation were highest amongst large firms. Conversely, during the 1980–2 period, it was large firms which performed worse and small firms which performed better.

In essence, the US results suggest that the fluctuations in the economy reflect changes in large firms, whereas small firms are consistent creators of employment, irrespective of macroeconomic conditions.

In the United Kingdom, the Dun and Bradstreet data bases have been analysed by Colin Gallagher and colleagues (Gallagher, Daly and Thomason 1990, Daly, Campbell, Robson and Gallagher 1991). Since they have chosen to follow the methodology used initially by Birch, and subsequently by the Small Business Administration, this enables some broad comparisons between the United States and the United Kingdom to be undertaken.

Data available for the United Kingdom for the 1987–9 period are reproduced as Table 6.2, enabling comparisons to be made with the United States. The first row of the table shows net job change, disaggregated by size of firm. It shows that during the 1987–9 period, 54 per cent of the increase in employment was in firms with less than twenty workers. The second row of the table shows these firms provided only 32 per cent of the base year employment in 1987. This suggests the UK results are broadly similar to those of the United States reported in Table 6.1, indicating that smaller firms provided a disproportionate share of new job creation. This is shown in row three of the table, where the index is above unity for small firms, but below unity for larger firms. For example, the index for firms with less than twenty employees is 1.69 for UK firms. It will be recalled from Table 6.1 that the comparable index was 1.91 for US small firms.

Turning now to the components of employment change in the form of gross job gains and gross job losses, the lower half of Table 6.2 shows that, at least for these two years, the distribution of the components was virtually identical. Firms with less than twenty workers provided both 54 per cent of gross job gains and 54 per cent of gross job losses. However, when we examine these components in more detail, we find there are striking differences according to firm size. For example, as shown in the top row of this section, 85 per cent

Table 6.2 Components of job generation by firm size in the United Kingdom, 1987–9 ('000 jobs)

	Total	*Employment size of firm*			
	All sizes	*<20*	*20–99*	*100–499*	*500+*
Net job change	1,127	+614	+161	+123	+231
(per cent)	(100)	(54)	(14)	(11)	(20)
Employment in base year (1987)	14,633	4,741	2,468	1,966	5,468
(per cent)	(100)	(32)	(17)	(13)	(37)
Index: growth/share	–	1.69	0.82	0.85	0.54
Employment change because of:					
Births	802	681	84	31	7
(per cent)	(100)	(85)	(10)	(4)	(1)
Expansions	1,831	751	338	283	459
(per cent)	(100)	(41)	(18)	(15)	(25)
Deaths	955	641	162	91	61
(per cent)	(100)	(67)	(17)	(10)	(6)
Contractions	550	177	99	100	174
(per cent)	(100)	(32)	(18)	(18)	(32)
Gross job gains	2,633	1,432	422	314	466
(per cent)	(100)	(54)	(16)	(12)	(18)
Gross job losses	1,506	818	261	191	235
(per cent)	(100)	(54)	(17)	(13)	(16)

Source: Daly, Campbell, Robson and Gallagher (1991)
Note: This table contains rounding errors.

of employment in births of firms in the United Kingdom was in firms with less than twenty workers. Conversely, only 1 per cent was in births of firms with 500 or more employees. On the other hand, 41 per cent of the jobs created through expansions were in firms with less than twenty workers and 25 per cent were in firms with 500 or more workers. Thus employment creation in births was almost exclusively in firms with less than twenty workers, whereas jobs created through the expansion of firms were much more evenly distributed.

Similarly, an examination of the components of gross job losses indicates that 67 per cent of employment lost through the closure of firms was in those with less than twenty workers, and only 6 per cent in firms with 500 and more workers. Employment loss through the contraction of firms, however, was much more characteristic of large firms. Thus 32 per cent of job losses through contractions were in firms with 500 or more workers.

Rather than concentrating on absolute numbers of jobs, the reader may find it easier to see job generation expressed in terms of ratios, rather than in

Table 6.3 Job generation in the United States and the United Kingdom: key ratios

Ratio		United Kingdom 1985–7	United Kingdom 1987–9	United States 1988–90
1 Net job change / Base year employment	(per cent)	1.8	7.7	2.9
2 Gross job gains / Base year employment	(per cent)	18.4	18.0	25.1
3 Gross job loss / Base year employment	(per cent)	16.6	10.3	22.2
4 Births: expansions	ratio	4:6	3:7	6:4
5 Deaths: contractions	ratio	6.4	6:4	7:3

absolute terms. This facilitates comparisons both over periods of time and between countries.

Table 6.3 compares job creation in the United States and in the United Kingdom over a two-year period. In many senses this is the best comparison which can be made: the time period observed is the same – two years – the calendar years overlap and in these cases we may assume that the macroeconomic conditions in the two countries were broadly similar.

Row 1 of Table 6.3 shows that net job change expressed as a proportion of base year employment differed sharply in the United Kingdom for the two periods. During the 1985–7 period it was only 1.8 per cent, compared with 7.7 per cent in the 1987–9 period.

However, when we examine gross job gains in the United Kingdom, we see these were very similar in both periods, at about 18 per cent. Hence the difference in net job change over the two periods reflects the higher gross job losses in the earlier period.

The period of job creation boom between 1987 and 1989 therefore reflects lower rates of job-shedding (gross job losses), rather than increases in the rate of new job creation (gross job gains).

The contrast with the United States is that both gross job gains and gross job losses in the United Kingdom constitute a smaller proportion of base year employment than in the United States. During the 1988–90 period, gross job gains in the United States constituted 25 per cent of base year employment, compared with only 18 per cent in the United Kingdom. Equally, gross job losses in the United States were also substantially higher than in the United Kingdom. This provides some support for the notion that the US economy exhibits a higher degree of 'churning' than is the case in the United Kingdom.

The final two rows of Table 6.3 also illustrate that the structure of both gross job gains and gross job losses was different in the United Kingdom from in the United States. Examining first the structure of gross job gains in the

United Kingdom, it can be seen that, during both periods, significantly more jobs were created in the expansion of firms than in firm births, this being particularly the case during the boom of the 1987–9 period, when more than twice as many jobs were created in the expansion of firms as in the birth of new firms. The reverse was the case in the United States; here, significantly more jobs are created in the birth of new firms than in the expansion of existing firms.

Finally, row 5 of the table shows that in the United Kingdom, during both periods, approximately 60 per cent of gross job losses were through the deaths of firms, compared with 40 per cent through the contractions of existing businesses. In the United States the deaths of firms appear to be a more important source of gross job losses than is the case in the United Kingdom.

Overall, Table 6.3 makes several significant points. The first is that in comparing a period of rapid net job change in the United Kingdom with one in which there is only modest increase in employment, the key influence appears to be not the rate of new job creation, but rather a fall in the rate of gross job loss. Secondly, in comparison to the United States, the United Kingdom shows lower rates of 'churning', with all components of employment change being of lower magnitude than in the United States. Thirdly, in comparing the United States with the United Kingdom, job change in the former is more strongly influenced by contributions made by births and deaths, whereas in the United Kingdom change is more influenced by expansions and contractions.

So far, the analysis has not formally examined the contribution of different sizes of firm to job generation. Table 6.4 provides an analysis of three firm size groups, which provide the bulk of job generation in the United States and the United Kingdom. The omitted firm size group is firms with between 100 and 500 employees.

The first row of Table 6.4 demonstrates that, in general, in both countries for the range of time periods, rates of job creation in firms with less than twenty workers were high, and were low in firms with more than 500 workers.

Rows 2 and 3 of the table examine the contribution of different sizes of firms to gross job gains, in the form of either births or expansions. There are some striking differences between these two components, both between countries and between the components themselves.

In the United Kingdom, firms with less than twenty workers created between 78 per cent (1985–7) and 85 per cent of total new employment from births. In the United States these smaller firms created only 38 per cent of total new employment. By striking contrast, in the United States, firms employing over 500 workers created 33 per cent of total new employment from births, compared with a figure of only 1 or 2 per cent in the United Kingdom.

The contribution of large firms (with more than 500 workers) in the United States to expansions in employment is also considerably greater than in the

Table 6.4 Job generation in the United States and the United Kingdom: key ratios by firm size

		United Kingdom						*United States*		
		1985–7 Firm size			*1987–9 Firm size*			*1988–90 Firm size*		
		*<20**	*20–100*	*>500*	*<20*	*20–100*	*>500*	*<20*	*20–100*	*>500*
1 Net job change / Base year employment in size band	per cent	+8.3	+0.1	+4.9	+13.0	+6.5	+4.2	+18.3	+0.6	–1.3
2 Employment in births / Total employment in births	per cent	78	16	2	85	10	1	38	17	33
3 Employment in expansions / Total employment in expansions	per cent	31	20	32	41	18	25	25	18	43
4 Employment in closures / Total employment in closures	per cent	60	22	7	67	17	6	20	21	44
5 Employment in contractions / Total employment in contractions	per cent	16	17	50	32	18	32	12	21	45
6 Gross job gains / Total employment in gains	per cent	49	18	20	54	16	18	33	18	37
7 Gross job losses / Total employment in losses	per cent	43	20	24	54	17	16	17	21	45

Note: *In this study, only firms with between five and nineteen employees are included.

United Kingdom. Thus 43 per cent of jobs created in expansions in the United States were in firms with more than 500 workers, compared with between 25 and 32 per cent in the United Kingdom. The absence of large births in the United Kingdom data is almost certainly the reason for the relatively small share of new jobs in births in the United Kingdom, compared with the United States, which was observed in Table 6.3.

Taking now the components of gross job losses in the two economies, rows 4 and 5 of the table show there are some marked differences in the structure of job losses by firm size between the two countries. In the United States, 44 per cent of employment losses through closures were in firms with 500 or more workers, compared with a figure of only 6 or 7 per cent in the United Kingdom. Conversely, in the United Kingdom the prime source of employment loss through closures was in firms with less than twenty workers.

The overall conclusion which emerges from Table 6.4 is the very different role which large firms appear to play in job generation in the United States and in the United Kingdom. In particular, large firms seem to play a much bigger role in employment in both births and closures in the United States than they play in the United Kingdom. This is rather curious, given the emphasis placed on the small firm in terms of job creation in the United States.

A question mark must therefore hang over whether the two data sets are fully comparable. Given the substantial resources that the US Small Business Administration has devoted to producing a longitudinal data set chronicling the contribution of smaller firms to job creation, it seems likely that their data set will be cleaner and more comprehensive than anything which exists in the United Kingdom. If, therefore, we wish to examine changes over a period of time, it is probably more appropriate to use the US data, whilst recognising that its applicability to the United Kingdom is imperfect. The remaining two tables in this section, therefore, will examine job generation in the United States over the four-year period between 1984 and 1988, and the two-year period between 1988 and 1990.

The top row of Table 6.5 shows that, according to the measure of net job

Table 6.5 Job generation in the United States, 1984–8 and 1988–90: key ratios

			1984–8	*1988–90*
1	Net job change / Base year employment	per cent	12.9	2.9
2	Gross job gains / Base year employment	per cent	46.7	25.1
3	Gross job losses / Base year employment	per cent	33.7	22.2
4	Births: expansions	ratio	7:3	6:4
5	Deaths: contractions	ratio	8:2	7:3

Table 6.6 Job generation in the United States, 1984–8 and 1988–90: key ratios by firm size

		1984–8 Firm size			*1988–90 Firm size*		
		<20	*20–100*	*>500*	*<20*	*20–100*	*>500*
1 Net job change / Base year employment in size band	per cent	+19.1	+8.8	+13.7	+18.3	+0.6	−1.3
2 Employment in births / Total employment in births	per cent	20	13	53	38	17	33
3 Employment in expansions / Total employment in expansions	per cent	29	21	36	25	18	43
4 Employment in closures / Total employment in closures	per cent	23	16	46	20	21	44
5 Employment in contractions / Total employment in contractions	per cent	15	18	51	12	21	45
6 Gross job gains / Total employment in gains	per cent	23	15	48	33	18	37
7 Gross job losses / Total employment in losses	per cent	21	17	47	17	21	45

change, and recognising the differences in the two periods, the years 1984–8 saw a rate of annual net job change of about twice that for the 1988 to 1990 period. The data also suggest that during the more rapid growth period, gross job gains were not significantly higher on an annual basis than during the lower-growth period. Crudely, job gains over the four-year period 1984 to 1988 were about 11½ per cent annually, compared with just over 12 per cent in the 1988–90 period. The difference occurs in the gross job losses, which were only just over 8 per cent annually during the 1984–8 period, compared with about 11 per cent during the later period.

This again suggests that periods of high net job change are characterised more by low gross job loss than by high gross job gains. Rows 4 and 5 of the table show the overall contribution of births and expansions, together with deaths and contractions. The data are presented here, but there is a problem in interpreting the implications of this, since the duration of the two periods differs. In essence, the longer the period examined, the greater is likely to be the contribution of births and deaths, and this is reflected in the table. We cannot therefore be certain whether this reflects a real difference in the periods or – as is more likely – only reflects the way of calculating contributions of these components.[1]

Table 6.6 examines the contribution of different sizes of firms through job generation in the United States over the four-year period 1984–8 and the two-year period 1988–90. In interpreting these figures it has to be remembered that the earlier period was one in which the rate of net job change was significantly higher than in the later period. This is particularly important in interpreting row 1 of the table.

Comparing the contributions of different firm sizes over the two periods, two important findings emerge. The first is that during both time periods firms with less than twenty workers made a larger proportionate contribution to net job change than any of the larger size groups. The second, equally important, finding is that whilst the rate of net job change of firms with less than twenty workers varied very little over the two time periods, the contribution of large firms varied considerably. Thus firms with more than 500 workers were a major source of new job creation in the 1984–8 period, but were a source of net job loss during the 1988–90 period. This suggests support for the findings of Mills and Schuman (1985) that small firms' contribution to job creation does not seem to vary markedly with the trade cycle. The converse of this is that it is not the performance of small firms which influences aggregate job creation in the United States, but rather the performance of the large firm sector.

It should be noted that this is precisely the opposite to the statement made by the UK Chancellor of the Exchequer in his Budget speech on 16 March 1993, in which he said: 'Small firms play a crucial role in our economy. Small businesses do not follow the economy – they lead it. That has been demonstrated time and time again.' Furthermore, the evidence for the United Kingdom generally supports the US findings, with periods of employment growth coinciding with when the large firm sector exhibits rapid employment growth, and the slowest growth occurring when the large firm sector declines.[2]

Returning now to the final two rows of Table 6.6 and examining gross job gains and gross job losses for the United States according to firm size, it can be seen that the large firm sector plays a significantly larger role in gross job gains during the more prosperous 1984–8 period, than during the less prosperous 1988–90 period. Its role in gross job losses, however, and those of other sizes of firms do not appear to be markedly different between the two periods.

If we now examine the components of gross job gains and gross job losses, a fairly predictable pattern emerges. There appears to be little evidence that firms of different sizes have markedly different impacts on job change from contractions or expansions. The striking difference is in the contribution which large firms make to employment through births, with large firms with more than 500 workers providing 53 per cent of employment in births during the 1984–8 period, compared with only 33 per cent in the 1988–90 period.

Overall, four main conclusions emerge from studies of the quantity of jobs created by smaller firms:

- The first is that, as originally demonstrated by David Birch, small firms in the United States make a disproportionately large contribution to net job creation in the economy. The same result is seen to hold for the United Kingdom.
- The second key finding, however, is that this contribution is nowhere near as high as originally estimated by Birch. Probably the best estimate is the most recent figure produced by the US Small Business Administration, which suggests that over the 1976–88 period, firms with less than twenty workers provided 37 per cent of net employment creation, at a time when they provided 19 per cent of employment.
- The third finding is that there are differences in the pattern of employment creation according to firm size in the United States and the United Kingdom. It is certainly possible that these reflect different definitions in the data but, interpreted at face value, they suggest a more rapid rate of 'churning' in the United States – in the sense that both gross job losses and gross job gains during a period of time are higher in the United States than in the United Kingdom.
- The fourth point stems from these differences. The periods in which rates of net job change are highest are those in which large firms make a significant contribution. It appears that small firms make a more consistent contribution to job creation, irrespective of the trade cycle, whereas large firms make weak or negative contributions when net job change is negative or low, but make a major contribution when net job change is high. Over short periods such as two years, in the United Kingdom, the major influence on net job change appears to be the rates at which jobs are being lost in the economy. Net job change in the United Kingdom appears to be influenced much less by the rate at which jobs are being created, since this does not seem to vary markedly over time.

TYPES OF JOB

The previous section drew on findings which suggest that, in the United Kingdom, small firms in the 1980s were a significant source of new employment opportunities. Whilst they have not been as important as some of the more evangelical statements made by politicians would suggest, the small firm sector is now seen as a more important source of employment than was the case ten or twenty years ago.

However, as part of the 'wider picture' which Brown, Hamilton and Medoff (1990) refer to, it is necessary to examine the *quality* of these jobs in smaller firms, as well as their *quantity*. This is very much easier in the United States than in the United Kingdom. As part of its efforts to reduce the 'burdens on business', the small-firm sector in the United Kingdom has been deliberately exempted from a wide range of information-collection responsibilities. We therefore remain poorly informed, on the basis of official

Table 6.7 Wage and salary workers in the United States, 1979–88

	Employment size of firm *1–24* *Per cent of total workforce*	*500+* *Per cent of total workforce*
Age 16–24		
1979	29.7	21.8
1988	22.8	17.0
Age 65 and over		
1979	4.1	0.5
1988	3.9	1.0
Women		
1979	43.2	36.3
1988	44.8	43.5
Less than four years of high school		
1979	26.4	17.6
1988	18.6	13.9
Part-time workers		
1979	33.3	16.7
1988	31.1	12.5
Previously self-employed		
1979	10.8	0.4
1988	14.3	0.8
Unemployed in prior year		
1979	13.7	9.1
1988	12.8	7.6

Source: US Small Business Administration (1991) *The State of Small Business: A Report of the President*, Tables 11 and 12, pp. 36 and 38.

statistics, about what type of individuals are occupying these newly created jobs. Instead of comprehensive official censuses, UK information relies on *ad hoc* surveys, where there is no compulsion on the part of small firm owners to participate. The same is not true in the United States, where a clear picture emerges about the types of worker most likely to occupy jobs in the smaller firm sector. Table 6.7 presents data for both 1979 and 1988, and identifies characteristics of workers where there are major differences between those employed in small firms, defined as those with less than twenty-five workers, and those working in large firms, defined as those with 500 or more employees.

An examination of the age structure of employees shows that small firms in the United States are very much more likely to employ young workers – defined as those between sixteen and twenty-four years of age – and more likely to employ older workers – defined as those aged sixty-five or over. It is large firms which are most likely to employ 'prime age' workers. Nevertheless, it is interesting to note that over the 1979 to 1988 period, small firms have become somewhat less dependent upon very young and very old workers.

In the United States in 1979, 43 per cent of the workforce in firms with less than twenty-five workers was female, compared with only 36 per cent of the workforce of large firms. Over the following nine years, however, there is evidence of convergence between the figures for the two sizes of firm, so that by 1988 about 44 per cent of the workforce of both sizes of firm was female.

The small firm workforce in the United States is much more likely to have less than four years of high school education than those working in larger firms. Small firms are also very much more likely to be employing on a part-time basis and its workforce is much more likely to have been unemployed in the prior year. Interestingly, the biggest difference between small and large firms is that the workforce in the smaller size of firm is more than twenty times as likely to have been previously self-employed as the workforce in larger firms.

We now turn to the evidence for the United Kingdom, repeating that nothing comparable to the comprehensive United States data is available. Nevertheless, the *ad hoc* work which has been conducted broadly supports the US findings, subject to the proviso that there are wide sectoral variations within the smaller firm category.

The most direct comparison for the United Kingdom is data derived from the Labour Force Survey, which examines worker characteristics according to workplace (not firm) size. This has been analysed by Hughes (1989) in a government document and is reproduced as Table 6.8. It confirms the broad results of the US data, suggesting that young male workers constitute 28 per cent of the labour force in workplaces with less than twenty-five workers, compared with 21 per cent for the sample of workers as a whole. There is no evidence from this survey that this finding applies to females, although there is a suggestion that small workplaces were more likely to have a higher proportion of their workforce composed of females above the normal retirement age of sixty. The table also provides support for the US data that employees in small workplaces are less likely to have degrees and more likely to have no qualifications.

It is important to recognise that these findings do *not* relate to firm size.

Table 6.8 Employees of business owners in the United Kingdom, 1987

		Small workplaces (<25 employees)		*All employees*	
		Males	*Females*	*Males*	*Females*
Age: 16–24 years	per cent	28	22	21	23
60+ years	per cent	7	5	6	4
Per cent degree		7	4	12	6
Per cent no qualification		28	37	26	34

Source: Hughes (1989). Data derived from Labour Force Survey (1987)

Nevertheless, there is a strong overlap, and so it is not surprising that similar results are obtained by independent researchers. Curran and Stanworth (1979), in their study of manufacturing firms, found that small firms generally contained an above-average share of younger workers. These workers were preferred by small-firm owners on the grounds that they were not only cheaper but also more flexible.

There is also evidence to support the United States findings that it is the smaller firms who are likely to employ a higher proportion of their labour force in a part-time capacity. An examination of employment structure in manufacturing plants by Storey and Johnson (1987) showed that 22.4 per cent of the labour force of plants with less than four workers was part-time, compared with only 3.7 per cent of the labour force in plants with more than 100 workers. That analysis, however, does not provide any evidence that, amongst full-time workers, the proportion of females is greater in the smaller plants.

These issues are also addressed by Scott *et al.* (1989) in their study of management and industrial relations in small firms. They examined 397 firms in four sectors: traditional manufacturing, traditional services, high-technology manufacturing and high-technology services. They also found that the proportion of full-time employees rises according to the size of the establishment, but they find no clear pattern relating the size of the establishment to the proportion of employees who are female.

Scott *et al.* also highlight the significance of non-employee workers in UK small firms. Table 6.9 shows there is a wide range of non-employee workers associated with small firms, such as homeworkers, outworkers, freelances, etc. The number and types of work vary markedly from one sector to another, with the high technology services and manufacturing firms being the most extensive users of this type of worker. On the other hand, the traditional service sectors – haulage firms, taxis, hotels and catering, etc. – are the least

Table 6.9 Non-employee workers in smaller firms

	Type of industry					*Size of establishment*				
	Total %	*Trad. manu.* %	*High-tech servs* %	*High-tech manu.* %	*Trad. servs* %	*1–5* %	*6–10* %	*11–20* %	*21–50* %	*51+* %
Homeworkers	6	8	4	10	3	6	7	6	9	2
Outworkers	3	7	–	3	–	2	1	3	7	2
Freelance workers	9	9	13	14	3	10	12	9	7	2
Contract workers	12	11	18	22	3	5	10	16	13	22
Self-employed	11	12	17	8	7	9	12	15	15	–
None of these	65	60	56	49	86	73	64	57	56	76

Source: Scott *et al.* (1989)

likely to use these workers. Scott *et al.* found, overall, that one-third of firms were using non-employee workers.

Scott *et al.* also conducted detailed case studies of thirty out of the 397 firms and obtained further insights into the workers employed. They emphasise the considerable importance of family involvement and employment in the sectors they studied, with 37 per cent of their case study firms using family members, or individuals with family connections.

This issue is investigated further by Jones, McEvoy and Barrett (1993) in their study of ethnic businesses. They found that, in a survey of 403 Asian, Afro-Caribbean and white businesses in fifteen UK locations, 35 per cent of respondent firms used unpaid family labour. This was higher for the Asian and Afro-Caribbean group (41 per cent and 44 per cent respectively) than for the white group (25 per cent). Nevertheless, as Jones *et al.* point out, the use of family labour is 'a traditional and important feature of *all* small firms, one which may well have weakened amongst white firms in recent generations, but which is far from dead'.

What is clear from the Scott *et al.* case studies is that there is considerable 'informal employment' in the small firm sector. In total, virtually one-third of their case study firms were employing labour at the margins of legality. As Scott *et al.* say:

> It is highly possible that there were other cases which did not come to light during the course of our field work, because this was a subject which respondents were reluctant to talk about, especially since, in all cases, some form of evasion, usually of tax and insurance contributions, was involved. The apparent reason, in all cases, for this irregular employment was a cost cutting exercise, saving money on full – or part time employees by taking in people 'off the cards' or on a casual, cash in hand basis.

Finally we present UK data on the skill composition of employment according to firm size. In this case the data encompasses primarily limited companies and therefore can be considered as relating to enterprises rather than establishments. The data are taken from Cambridge Small Business Research Centre (1992) and are reproduced as Table 6.10. The table discloses striking differences according to firm size, with semi-skilled and unskilled manual workers constituting 44 per cent of employment in the larger firms with between 200 and 499 workers, compared with only 12 per cent of labour force in micro-firms – those with less than ten employees.

Conversely, micro-firms have a much higher proportion of their employment in clerical and administrative workers and in managerial workers; although in such firms, in practice, it can be difficult to categorise workers in this way. This is clearly illustrated by the owner who could be categorised as a managerial worker, but who also exercises clerical and administrative and probably a number of other functions in a micro-firm.

Thus far, the analysis, whilst recognising that differences do exist between

Table 6.10 The skill composition of labour in smaller firms

Skill	*All*	*Manuf.*	*Services*	*Micro*	*Small*	*Medium*	*Larger*
Semi-skilled and unskilled manual	23.5	34.0	11.7	12.2	24.3	35.4	43.9
Skilled manual	19.2	29.0	8.4	15.1	21.6	17.1	19.9
Clerical and administrative	18.9	14.3	24.1	25.4	17.0	15.6	12.7
Technicians and lower professionals	11.5	6.8	16.7	9.8	12.5	11.5	10.0
Technologists, scientists and higher professionals	12.3	3.7	21.9	15.3	11.6	12.5	6.9
Managerial	14.6	12.2	17.2	22.2	13.0	7.9	6.6
Total	100	100	100	100	100	100	100
Total respones (no.)	1,860	987	877	518	1,031	160	151

Source: Cambridge Small Business Research Centre (1992)

the service and manufacturing sector, has not focused upon these differences. According to James Curran, the United Kingdom's leading researcher in this area, failure to recognise the key service/manufacturing distinction leads to a highly imperfect understanding of employment and employment relations in small firms. In part, this is because almost two out of three jobs in the United Kingdom are now in services, and most of its three million small firms are also in the service sector.

However, the need to obtain a better understanding of the service sector arises only partly because of its numerical dominance. Two other influences need to be considered: first is the huge variety of workplace situations found within the service sector. Service employment therefore leads to different issues in employment relations. Curran (1991: 199) points out that much service employment involves routine direct contact with the customer, with production and consumption occurring simultaneously. He argues that this makes it more difficult for the employer to control output quality and employee performance than is the case in manufacturing, where inspection can be performed before the product reaches the customer. He also notes that much service sector work involves 'emotional labour', which he defines as 'The use of facial and bodily displays, with deliberate use of emotion – involving strategies, including sexual varieties, to elicit particular customer responses and satisfactions.'

In his view, this dimension of work-role performance is much more likely to be characteristic of workers in the service sector than the manufacturing sector. This in turn means that different problems arise in, from the owner's point of view, controlling the quality of output.

The overall picture which emerges is that the types of jobs and the characteristics of those who fill them do differ between small and larger firms. Despite the heterogeneity of the small firm sector, it appears to be the case that small firms are less likely to employ prime-age educated males. They are much more likely to employ part-time females, sometimes in a casual or *ad hoc* way, and occasionally at or even beyond the margins of legality.

THE QUALITY OF JOBS

So far, this chapter has discussed the quantity of jobs created by small firms, together with the characteristics of the individuals who fill these jobs. This section will examine the characteristics or 'quality' of the jobs themselves in the small-firms sector.

There is no single, comprehensive measure of job quality. For this reason we have chosen to examine seven dimensions of quality, which, collectively, are intended to provide a wide-ranging picture of the quality of jobs in the smaller firm sector. It is not implied that any of the dimensions are necessarily more important than others, nor even that these are the only measures of 'quality'. Instead, they constitute a range of measures where quantitative data according to firm size has been assembled and which, taken together, do provide a reasonable overall picture. The seven dimensions are:

- wages;
- fringe benefits;
- job satisfaction/'one big happy family';
- training;
- hours worked;
- unionisation/industrial disputes;
- health and safety.

Wages

United States data, as reviewed by Brown, Hamilton and Medoff (1990) show that workers in big companies or establishments earn over 30 per cent more in wages than their counterparts in small firms or at small workplaces. Brown *et al.* refer to this as 'the size-wage premium'.

Several explanations have been put forward for this premium, the most common of which is that larger firms are found in sectors or industries which pay higher wages. Brown *et al.* argue, however, that the size-wage premium appears fairly consistent *within* industries, as well as between industries.

The second explanation is that larger firms hire a higher 'quality' of worker and therefore have to pay a premium for that individual. Of course, this raises the question of why it is that large firms should be the prime recruiters of skilled/educated labour, but nevertheless Brown and Medoff say:

> The data from 1979 and 1983 indicate that of two workers who are the same in terms of sex, race, education experience, industry, and occupation the worker in the large firm will on average earn 10 to 13 per cent more than the worker in the small firm.

In summary, the US data imply that on a direct comparison, large firm workers earn 30 per cent more than small firm workers. Even when account is taken of worker characteristics and industry, the size-wage premium remains at between 10 and 13 per cent.

The final factor which is included to 'explain' the size-wage effect is supervision. Here, it is argued that in small firms, supervision is more immediate, direct and easier (less costly) than in large firms. Kruse (1992), however, when including a supervision component, finds that those workers who are most frequently supervised receive *lower* wages, and so did not influence the size-wage effect. These findings are not restricted to the United States. Morissette (1993) finds that, in Canada, even taking into account observable worker characteristics, industry composition effects and occupational differences, a clear wage-size premium exists. No adequate explanation for this has yet been provided.

No comparable comprehensive analyses have been conducted using official UK data. Nevertheless, the *ad hoc* work which has been conducted suggests there is every reason to believe that the US findings would be repeated.

Table 6.11 shows UK data from the 1986 New Earnings Survey, on gross full-time equivalent weekly earnings according to size of establishment. It must be emphasised again that 'establishment' can only be considered as a proxy for firm size, but even so, the results clearly demonstrate that, holding industry sector constant, gross weekly earnings for both males and females increase with increasing firm size. It suggests that the Bolton Committee (1971) assertion that differences in gross earnings of about 20 per cent between small and large firms continued from the early 1970s until at least the mid-1980s.

Table 6.11 Gross weekly earnings by size of establishment, United Kingdom, 1986

	<10 employees		*10–24 employees*		*All employees*	
£ per week	*Male*	*Female*	*Male*	*Female*	*Male*	*Female*
All industries and services	159	107	180	116	207	137
All manufacturing	178	109	187	109	208	123
All non-manufacturing	154	107	177	118	207	141

Source: Hughes (1989); data derived from New Earnings Survey (1986)

Evidence is also emerging that the size-wage effect applies to different occupational groups. Managers' salaries in smaller firms are clearly below those of managers in large firms. Harris (1991) notes an Institute of Directors and Reward Surveys report which reviewed managers salaries in 1991. It showed that the highest-paid person within a business with a £2m. turnover received an average annual salary of approximately £38,000; one with a turnover of around £10m. received a salary of £47,000 and one with a turnover of £15–20m. received a salary of approximately £54,000.

The work by Wynarczyk *et al.* (1993) on managers' salaries in smaller firms also indicates a strong firm-size effect. They identify other key influences upon managers' salaries as being the age of the individual, their qualifications, the location of the firm and whether the individual had previously held a managerial post.

Elsewhere in Europe, the EEC (1993) SME Observatory Report presents data comparing gross wages by enterprise size. The data are reproduced as Table 6.12, which again illustrates that gross wages are significantly higher in all countries (with the exception of France) in large, compared with small firms.

The major UK study on wage levels and firm size in smaller firms is that by Thompson and Wilson (1991). They collected survey data from 3,289 firms in Cornwall, Shrewsbury, Brighton, Manchester, Slough and Newport. They asked about the earnings of staff in four different occupational groups – managers and professional staff; technical, craftsman and semi-skilled staff;

Table 6.12 Comparisons of gross wages, selected countries and year indexed (base 100)

	No. of employees							
	1–9	*10–19*	*20–49*	*50–99*	*100–199*	*200–499*	*500+*	*Average*
Greece								
1986		100	<....	...141	<...	.....	...191	161
1989		100	<....	...136	<...	.....	...192	157
France								
1991		<...	...100	<...	...99	104	103	103
Ireland								
1987			100	112	120	138	163	133
1989			100	109	118	137	154	129
Italy								
1985–89	100	109	115	121	125	132	151	129
Netherlands								
1989	100	<...	.....	...117	<...	.....	...128	119
Portugal								
1988	100	<...	.....	...117	<...	...135	177	136
1991	100			121		140	173	135

Source: ENSR (1993) SME Observatory

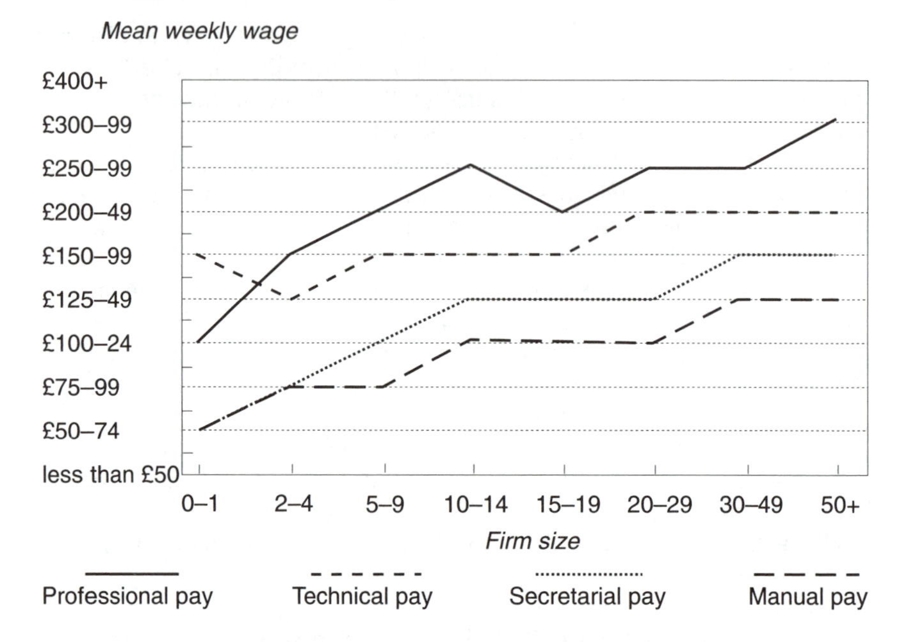

Figure 6.2 The effect of employment size on mean weekly wage levels
Source: Thompson and Wilson (1991)

clerical, administrative, secretarial and sales staff; and finally, semi-skilled and unskilled manual staff. Respondents were asked to give a figure of gross earnings, including overtime and bonuses of full-time staff. For part-time staff, respondents were asked to give the equivalent full-time earnings.

Mean weekly wages within the firms are shown in Figure 6.2, showing that wages for all groups increase with increasing firm size. Thompson and Wilson point out that this contrasts with the US data analysed by Weiss and Landau (1984), who found that the employer size-wage effect was only significant for firms employing more than 100 workers, where there was a consistent relationship between firm size and wages.

Unfortunately, Thompson and Wilson were unable to incorporate in their study all the factors which the US studies have shown influence wages. They were unable to take account of the extent to which the better quality of labour in larger firms influences higher wages. Nevertheless, it is a very significant finding that, even amongst very small firms in the United Kingdom, clear differences exist in terms of mean weekly wage levels between the very small firms and those with twenty or more employees. Thompson and Wilson attribute some of this change to 'thresholds' in firm growth. They find that paying higher wages appears to coincide with moving out of more parochial labour markets (through the employment of family and friends) to a more formal engagement with the labour market and an emphasis on seeking better-quality labour. This point is also emphasised by Atkinson and Meager (1994) and is discussed later in this chapter.

Somewhat contrasting results are derived by Curran *et al.* (1993) in their study of small firms in the service sector in Guildford, Doncaster and north-east Suffolk. They emphasised that the major differences in pay reflect the sectoral composition of small firms. Hence, in the advertising, marketing and design sector and in computer services, 63 per cent of full-time employee respondents reported gross earnings of £10,000 or more, compared with only 18 per cent of employees in the free house, wine bar and restaurant sectors. Curran *et al.* also point to striking differences according to locality, with gross annual earnings in prosperous Guildford being virtually 80 per cent higher than in less prosperous Doncaster.

An alternative approach to this question, also used by Curran *et al.* (1993), was to ask respondents in small firms in the service sector whether they felt themselves to be fairly paid for the work which they did. The interesting finding here is that it was the relatively higher paid individuals who were the most likely to indicate that they did *not* feel they were fairly paid for the work which they did: employees in advertising, marketing and design were the least likely to report that they were paid fairly, whereas those in the free house, wine bar and restaurant sectors, despite being the lowest paid, were the most likely to report that they were being paid fairly. Similar findings relate to occupational groups, with professional and managerial employees being the least likely to report that they were paid fairly and the low-paid semi- and unskilled manual worker being most likely to report that they were fairly paid.

In many senses the findings of Curran *et al.* also reflect those of Scott *et al.* (1990) and emphasise the dangers of viewing the small firm sector in this (or in any other) context as homogeneous. They point out that both workers and owner-managers in the high-technology service sector recognised their wages to be as good as, if not better, than those of other firms, including larger ones in the same industry and sector. Conversely, workers and owner-managers in small firms in the traditional service sector recognised that pay in their firm was relatively poor.

The research findings in this area suggest that large firms do indeed pay up to 30 per cent higher wages than small firms. Nevertheless, it has to be recognised that there are also wide sectoral and geographical variations which significantly influence this overall finding. It also has to be recognised that although wages may be low for certain occupational groups or in particular industries, this does not necessarily reflect either job satisfaction or dissatisfaction on the part of the workforce. The issues which continue to be unclear, however, are the reasons for this persistent difference in wages according to firm size.

Fringe benefits

In the United States, Brown, Hamilton and Medoff (1990) show that workers in small firms are significantly less likely to be in receipt of fringe benefits than workers in large firms. Their data are reproduced here as Table 6.13.

The table shows a marked difference in the proportion of the workforce in receipt of fringe benefits in large firms with more than 500 workers, compared with that of smaller firms. Given the absence in the United States of basic universal healthcare provided by the state, it can be seen that healthcare is probably the dimension in which the small firm employee is most 'exposed'. Brown *et al.* found that only 55 per cent of workers in firms with less than 500 employees had health-care provision, compared with all workers in firms with more than 500 workers. Marked differences were also found in terms of pension provision, which was provided by only 16 per cent of firms with less than 500 workers, compared with 79 per cent of those with more than 500 workers.

When these data are taken in combination with the data on wage rates, one point emerges. It is that the provision of fringe benefits cannot be seen as a substitute for lower wages, since the large firms which pay the highest wages also are more likely to provide fringe benefits. In short, the US data make it clear that, in many senses, the provision of fringe benefits is even more closely related to firm size than wages.

In the United Kingdom, again there are no comparable official data to enable such a comparison to take place. However, the study by Wynarczyk *et al.* (1993) of the managerial labour market in smaller firms found that

Table 6.13 The provision of fringe benefits to workers in the United States: percentage of large and small businesses offering various benefits, 1986

Fringe benefit	*Firms with fewer than 500 employees*	*Firms with 500 or more employees*
Vacation	58	95
Health	55	100
Sick leave	36	91
Life insurance	29	94
Pension or 401K	16	79
Bonus plan	11	29
Short-term disability	10	55
Long-term disability	9	69
Savings plan	2	29
Cafeteria-style health benefits	1	12
Vacation, sick, health, life and pension or 401K	7	75

Source: Brown, Hamilton and Medoff (1990)

managers in (generally larger) firms quoted on the Unlisted Securities Market were significantly more likely to benefit from provision of company cars, profit-sharing schemes and access to private health insurance than managers in smaller firms which operated in the same sectors.

Both Scott *et al.* and Curran *et al.* in their discussions of fringe benefits emphasise that, within small firms, there are wide sectoral variations. Scott *et al.* point to fringe benefits in the high-technology manufacturing and high-technology service sectors as being the 'norm'. On the other hand, these fringe benefits or 'perks' are almost wholly absent, or are restricted to a very few individuals, within the more traditional sectors.

Curran *et al.*'s findings on the provision of fringe benefits to employees in the UK service sector provides support for the view that these broadly increase in coverage with increases in the size of the firm. Table 6.14 shows that, with the exception of the provision of a company car, the five specified fringe benefits are more likely to be provided in firms with more than twenty employees, than for the sample as a whole. Nevertheless, they also support the findings of Scott *et al.* that there are clear sectoral differences. For example, 42 per cent of computer service firms provided at least three of the benefits specified, compared with only 4.5 per cent of firms in the free house, wine bar and restaurant sectors.

Finally, it will be noticed that Table 6.14 tabulates the employers' reported provision of fringe benefits for staff. When Curran *et al.* asked comparable questions to the employees, they found that fewer employees than employers identified the existence of such benefits. Thus only half the proportion of

Table 6.14 Percentage of employers' reporting provision of fringe benefits by size of firm

	Number of employees:				
	Less than 5	*5–9*	*10–19*	*20+*	*All*
Full pay when sick	61.7	85.2	81.8	88.9	75.3
Company car	17.6	51.9	54.5	33.3	35.8
Pension scheme	5.9	29.6	36.4	66.7	25.9
Profit-share scheme	5.9	37.0	18.2	44.4	22.2
Health insurance	5.9	22.2	18.2	55.6	18.5
Other bonus/incentive scheme	61.7	66.7	45.5	55.6	60.5
N =	34	27	11	9	81

Source: Curran *et al.* (1993)
Note: Benefits provided only for owner-manager are excluded from the table. Full pay when sick need only be offered for a limited period to be included. Profit-share schemes have been defined broadly to include any practices where some part of an employee's pay is explicitly related to the profitability of the business.

employees reported themselves as being in receipt of a company car, as compared with the reports of the employer! Nevertheless, the broad pattern, that fringe benefits provision increased with firm size, remained.

Overall, it appears that the limited research conducted in the United Kingdom on this topic broadly supports the central findings of the US analysis – that small firm employees are significantly less likely to be in receipt of fringe benefits. Nevertheless, there are wide variations by sector according to the extent to which fringe benefits are provided, and it is probably fair to say that the consequences for the UK worker not having access to these benefits are less serious than is the case for the US worker without, for example, provision of health insurance.

Job satisfaction/'one big happy family'

In its 'state of the art' report on smaller firms in 1971, there is probably no dimension in which the Bolton Committee report was so seriously in methodological error as in its very brief review of employment relations. Almost all researchers who have investigated this topic over the past twenty or more years (Goss 1991, Curran 1991, Rainnie 1989) have referred, almost with incredulity, to the following quotation from the Bolton Committee:

> In many aspects a small firm provides a better environment for the employee than is possible in most large firms. Although physical working conditions can sometimes be inferior in small firms, most people prefer to work in a small group where communication presents fewer problems: the employee in a small firm can more easily see the relation between what he is doing and the objectives and performance of the firm as a whole. Where management is more direct and flexible, working rules can be varied to suit the individual. Each employee is also likely to have a more varied role with a chance to participate in several kinds of work . . . no doubt mainly as a result . . . turnover of staff in small firms is very low and strikes and other kinds of industrial dispute are relatively infrequent. The fact that small firms offer lower earnings than larger firms suggests that the convenience of location and generally the non-material satisfaction of working in them more than outweigh any financial sacrifice involved.

Those researchers who subsequently investigated this matter have concluded that the complacent tone of the Bolton Committee reflects the absence of any research by the Committee itself on the attitudes of employees within small firms. Instead it is inferred that the Committee chose to be aware only of the opinions of employers. We have already observed in the earlier section that a rather different perspective upon employer relations can be obtained from seeking opinions from the two groups. This is most neatly illustrated by Goss (1991), who reports the following statement from a young worker in the printing industry:

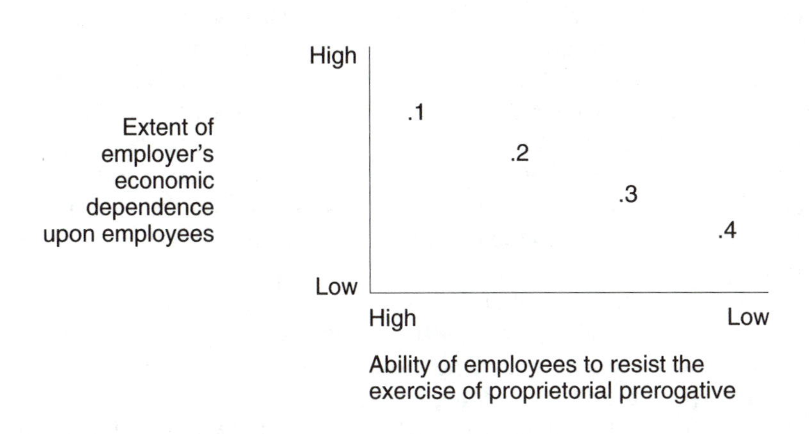

Figure 6.3 Types of employer control in small firms
Source: Goss (1991)
Key:
1 = Fraternalism
2 = Paternalism
3 = Benevolent autocracy
4 = Sweating

> 'You have got to play it by ear and be a bit careful what you say. If the boss starts going on about something, even if you don't agree, you have got to keep quiet and nod your head and pretend to agree, even if you don't. That way you don't get into an argument, you have just got to grin and bear it, humour them almost.'

In this area Goss (1991) makes a helpful contribution to our understanding of employer controls in the small firm sector. His taxonomy is shown in Figure 6.3, which identifies two dimensions along which different forms of employer control can be categorised. The first is the ability of the employees to resist the exercise of proprietorial prerogative, and may be considered as the relative strength of the employees. The other dimension is the extent to which employers depend upon their employees. Given these two dimensions, four types of employer control are specified: fraternalism, paternalism, benevolent autocracy and sweating.

Goss identifies fraternalism as the characteristic form of employee relations within small firms, illustrations of which are found in the high-technology sector, where there are relatively modest differences between boss and worker. Scott *et al.* (1990) in their examination of employer relations in the high-technology sectors where skilled workers are in considerable demand show that a tradition of team working has been established. Another illustration of fraternal employer relations occurs in the building and construction sectors where the boss works alongside the employee.

Goss's illustrations of paternalism are derived exclusively from the agricultural sector, where the employer is of significantly higher social standing than the employee, who is also dependent, often for housing, upon the goodwill of the employer. Nevertheless, a tradition seems to have been established here that the employer has a responsibility for the well-being of the employee, and exploitation, given the power imbalance, is nowadays surprisingly rare.

The third categorisation of employment relations is what Goss refers to as 'benevolent autocracy'. Curran (1991), in his critique of Goss, regards this type of employee relations as being most characteristic of smaller firms. As Goss puts it, 'Employees are neither so independent as to warrant (or be able to demand) fraternal treatment, nor so dependent as to be susceptible to crude economic coercion.'

The central feature of benevolent autocracy is that the employer tends to emphasise the closeness of the links with the employee, whilst at the same time making the employee keenly aware that his or her poor performance could endanger the livelihood of all working for the enterprise. Scott *et al.* (1990) refer to this as 'organic solidarity', although they point out that 'The obedience of individual workers may be the paradox of "submission agreements".'

The final category of employment relations in small firms is classed as sweating. Here the employee is clearly exploited, and does not have even token involvement with the management of the business. The most familiar illustrations of this are in the textile sector where, frequently, immigrant female workers work extremely long hours, for low rates of pay, often in poor working conditions.

As mentioned above, Curran's (1991) criticism of the Goss categorisation is that the vast bulk of small enterprises have a form of employment relations which could be placed in the benevolent autocracy category. The Curran *et al.* (1993) empirical work on employment relations in the service sector emphasises, however, that both employers and employees stress the high quality of social relations within their firms. Curran *et al.* point out that there appears to be very little evidence of overt employer–employee conflict in their sample of firms and, even where employers had dismissed employees, those remaining in the business felt the action was justified. Further discussions with the employees suggest that, in the relatively few cases in which a dispute had occurred, their grievances with their employer appeared to have been resolved to the satisfaction of the employee. The general impression provided by the Curran *et al.* survey is that, whilst there are differences according to sector, there appear to be few instances in which the 'submission agreement' is enforced in an overbearing manner.

It is therefore interesting to see the most recent Curran *et al.* work on employment relations in service sector businesses in the 1990s providing authoritative support for the much criticised Bolton Committee statements on this subject more than twenty years earlier. The central criticism of Bolton – that it never discussed employment relations with the employees – must remain, but the general picture of relative harmony in smaller firms which emerges from Curran's work on employers and employees in the service sector is interesting and important.[3]

Training

In their review of US research on this topic, Brown, Hamilton and Medoff (1990) conclude that 'On balance it appears that large employers provide more training. But the evidence is not overwhelming, perhaps because the most training is provided by both the very smallest and the largest firms.'

The UK evidence presented needs to distinguish between training of the workforce and training of management. Figure 6.4 is taken from the Cambridge survey of smaller firms and suggests that formal workforce training is more likely to take place in larger firms. Recalling that micro-firms are those with less than ten workers and larger firms are those with between 200 and 500 employees, Figure 6.4 shows a consistent pattern of increase with firm size. It also suggests that formal workforce training is more likely to be provided in manufacturing than service sector firms.

The most important finding, however, is that there is no evidence that it is the faster-growing firms which are most likely to provide formal workforce training, although it is the case that these are more likely to provide such training than stable/declining firms. In no sense should this result be considered surprising. As Hendry *et al.* (1991) point out, whilst growth stimulates training through an increase in numbers of employees doing the same job and the recruitment, possibly for the first time, of new specialists, it puts additional pressure on people's time. The emphasis in SMEs in periods of growth is to get the product 'out of the door', rather than to train, on the grounds that this is seen to be taking the workforce away from production activities.

Townroe and Mallalieu (1993), in their study of rural businesses, also examine training of small business owners. They express disappointment at the low levels of take-up of even modest amounts of training by those starting a business. Those most likely to attend a training course are females and younger proprietors, whereas being in business before does not influence training take-up. In essence, Townroe and Mallalieu report that entrepreneurs had no real desire for training.

When the nature of formal training provided is investigated, the Cambridge study makes it clear that larger firms are much more likely to use some form of external training than smaller firms. For example, only 25 per cent of larger

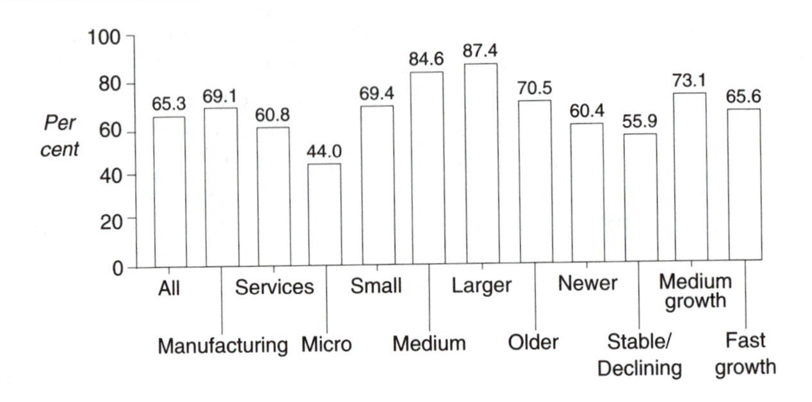

Figure 6.4 Firms providing formal training
Source: Cambridge Small Business Research Centre (1992)

firms which undertook formal workforce training relied exclusively upon insiders, compared with 51 per cent of micro-firms.

Blackburn (1990) reports similar findings in a study of 106 small electrical and electronic engineering firms in Dorset. He finds that although only 3 per cent of the total workforce of the sample were engaged in formal training, these places were provided by about one-third of the firms in the sample. These firms were, on average, three times as large as non-participants. Unlike the Cambridge study, Blackburn finds that those small firms participating in formal training schemes were those which had experienced faster recent rates of employment growth than non-participants.

Curran *et al.* (1993), examine training in small service sector firms and provide reassurance that, even amongst this unlikely group of firms, some training is undertaken. They find some form of training is provided by virtually all firms in their sample, and that more than half of employees interviewed had received some training whilst with the firm. Clearly much training was informal, but it did seem to have been provided for a range of occupational groups.

Curran *et al.* warn that the reluctance – often referred to – of small firms to train may as much reflect employees' attitudes as employers'. The conventional view of training in the small firm sector is that the employer is reluctant to invest, on the grounds that the worker is likely to be 'poached away' by competitors. Curran *et al.*, whilst not discounting this, found that small firm employees were also reluctant to participate in training, on the grounds that they did not require more training to do their jobs better.

This observation parallels the findings of Wynarczyk *et al.* (1993) in their examination of managerial salaries in smaller firms. In estimating their wage equations, the authors were unable to identify the provision of formal training, either in their current job or in their prior job, as a factor influencing current wages. If there is no demonstrable link in a small firm between an individual undertaking training and his or her earning capability, then it is not surprising that small firm employees show little enthusiasm for additional training.

In many respects, Curran *et al.*'s emphasis on the reluctance of the small firm employee to undergo training is as important in explaining the low level of training in small firms as the owner-manager's reluctance to provide it. Judging from studies of managers in UK small firms and studies of employees in the United States, we know that the worker in a small firm is most likely to have previously worked in another small firm. We also know that 'career progression' or 'internal labour markets' (Creedy and Whitfield 1988) are less likely to exist in small firms, so the worker moves between firms, rather than 'up the organisation'. From the viewpoint of the firm, however, training is often designed to ensure that the job is undertaken 'in our way', so making the worker more firm-specific in his or her skills. Since the small firm employee realises that their next job is likely to be with another (small) firm, training is not perceived as having the added value which it has to an employee in a large firm who intends to make a career with that firm. Indeed it may even be perceived to have a negative effect for the employee, by narrowing the range of skills and hence making the employee less attractive to other potential employers.

Training for both owners and employees in smaller firms is, in fact, one of the most contentious areas in small firm policy and research. Over the last decade there has been a huge growth in the training 'industry', much of it supported by extensive public funding. As we shall show in Chapter 8, there does not appear to be any thorough empirical study which demonstrates that the provision of training either by, or for, a small firm clearly leads to better performance of that firm. Equally, we are unable to point to any thorough study which demonstrates that, within the small firm sector, the individual in receipt of workplace training is more likely to be in receipt of higher earnings, or could reasonably expect to be in receipt of higher earnings in future.

Hours worked

Small business owners work considerably longer hours than the norm for full-time employees. Curran and Burrows (1988b), in their analysis of the General Household Survey 1979–84, report that over half of small business owners claimed to work more than fifty hours per week. Storey, Watson and Wynarczyk (1989), in their study of fast-growing small businesses, state that the average working week was reported to be fifty-five hours, whilst Jones *et al.* (1993) found the average to be fifty-three hours, with Asian business owners averaging sixty hours. Data on employee hours are reported in Table 6.15, which is derived from the Labour Force Survey and so refers to workplace size, rather than firm size.

Table 6.15 Employee hours by workplace size in the United Kingdom, 1987

	Workplace size			
	Small (<25 employees)		*All*	
Hours worked per week	*Males* %	*Females* %	*Males* %	*Females* %
0–19	5.7	37.5	2.8	25.0
20–40	33.8	49.6	38.0	59.4
41–50	39.9	10.0	41.6	13.0
50+	20.2	2.6	17.1	2.3
Not known	0.4	0.3	0.4	0.3
Total	100.0	100.0	100.0	100.0

Source: Hughes (1989)

The table demonstrates clear differences in working hours between employees in small workplaces compared with employees as a whole. It shows that a much higher proportion of female employees in small workplaces work part-time – less than twenty hours per week – than is the case for employees more widely. Only 5.7 per cent of male employees in small workplaces work less than twenty hours per week, but this again is much higher than the average. At the other extreme, a higher proportion of the workforce in small workplaces also work very long hours (more than fifty) than is the case overall.

The small workplace therefore provides a high proportion of employment opportunities, both for part-time workers and for those working long hours.

Unionisation/industrial disputes

Early work by Prais (1976) indicated that larger plants were significantly more likely to be involved in an industrial dispute than smaller plants. It has also been shown that large firms are much more likely to have a unionised labour force than smaller firms (Daniel and Millward 1983). These two elements have been consistently linked to suggest that the presence of trade unions is a factor influencing the proneness to strikes of plants. Hence the decrease in average plant size which has occurred over the last twenty years is desirable, in the sense that it is associated with less frequent stoppages.

Relatively little new empirical research was undertaken on this topic in the 1980s, but that which was pointed in some important new directions. Scott *et al.* (1989) showed that, even within the small firm sector, unionisation increased with firm size. Unionisation also appears to be inversely related to the proportion of female workers – which may be considered to be a proxy for part-time workers, in the establishment. However, probably the most interesting finding of Scott *et al.* is that, contrary to popular myth, the small firm owner does not appear to be as strongly opposed to trade union membership, on the part of employees, as is commonly thought. Opinions were almost equally divided amongst business owners about whether or not trade unions were beneficial to the business world.

These results are confirmed by Abbott (1993), who shows that just over 30 per cent of all employers would accept a request for trade union recognition on the part of their workforce, whereas 40 per cent of employers would resist such a request. He also reports that when employees were asked about whether they would join a trade union if the opportunity arose, only 24.4 per cent indicated positively. When asked for their reasons for this, employees emphasised their ability to influence their working environment, in the sense of being able to deal directly with the boss in the event of a grievance arising. In this sense trade unions were thought to be an unnecessary encumbrance upon this negotiation. Holding these views, however, appeared to be quite compatible with a willingness to contemplate striking. Abbott found that more than two-thirds of employees believe there were situations in which employees should go on strike, this willingness being highest amongst the group of workers (those in computer services) who were the least likely to join a trade union under any circumstances.

A somewhat more complex view is therefore beginning to emerge of industrial relations within the small firm sector. As Goss (1991) points out:

> There was the recognition that within the small firms it was all but impossible for union regulation to override the personal authority of the employer at the practical level. For the owner manager always held the trump card; the power to define workers' non-compliance as a potential contribution to uncompetitiveness, business failure and of course, job loss.

The overall picture which emerges is that in the small firm sector formal disputes are infrequent and trade union membership is low. This is likely to reflect the inappropriateness of trade unions in small workplaces, where direct discussion between employer and employee is most appropriate. This is not intended to imply that the partners to that discussion have equal power. It is clear that the boss is much more powerful than the employees, but it is equally clear that employees within smaller firms do not feel their bargaining position would be significantly enhanced by membership of trade unions as they are currently constituted. The position is well summarised by Abbott (1993), who says:

> The need for trade union representation was further eroded by the reported good relations between employees and their employers. Over 9 out of 10 employees indicated that they 'got on well' with their employer. This, coupled with the reported low level of disputes within the firm, makes the prospect of an increased union presence extremely unlikely.

Health and safety

The final dimension of job quality to be discussed relates to the likelihood of an individual being injured whilst at work. The empirical evidence in the United Kingdom points to the likelihood of major injury to workers in small establishments – those with less than fifty workers – being at least 40 per cent higher than for workers in very large establishments – those with more than 1,000 workers.

In making these statements, account has to be taken of the fact that the reporting of accidents is thought to be less comprehensive amongst smaller firms than amongst larger firms. Account has also to be taken of the fact that the data collected relate to establishment, rather than enterprise or firm size.

Given these reservations, Table 6.16 shows employee major injury rates by size of establishment in UK manufacturing industry in 1988–9. Major injuries are defined as both fatal injuries and amputations, serious fractures and other conditions requiring 24-hour hospitalisation. The Health and Safety Executive (HSE) believes that the reporting of major accidents, which is required under the Reporting of Injuries, Diseases and Dangerous Occurrences Regulations (RIDDOR) 1985, is more comprehensive than for minor accidents. The data in Table 6.16 demonstrate that accident rates are clearly inversely related to size of establishment within manufacturing.

Further analysis of the types of major injury, shown in Table 6.17, suggests there may still be significant under-reporting of these major injuries by smaller establishments/firms. The table shows striking differences between the types of accident according to the size of establishment. Over one-quarter of all major injuries in large establishments result from trips, slips and falls on the same level, compared with less than one-eighth in smaller establishments. Thomas (1991), in his review of the data, acknowledges this may in part reflect a differing risk of this type of accident in smaller establishments, but he implies that smaller establishments are less likely to diligently

Table 6.16 Employee major injury rates by size of establishment in manufacturing industry

Size of establishment	*Rates per 100,000 employees 1988–9 (p)*
1–19	163.7
20–49	161.1
50–99	156.0
100–199	139.8
200–499	135.4
500–999	135.4
1,000 +	115.1

(p) = provisional
Source: Thomas (1991)

Table 6.17 Kind of accident for major injuries to employees in manufacturing by size of establishment, 1988–9 (p)

Kind of accident	*Distribution per cent*		*Injury rate per 100,000*	
	<100 people	*100+ people*	*<100 people*	*100+ people*
Contact with machinery	29.6	16.9	52.5	22.0
Struck by moving object	13.9	12.7	24.6	16.5
Slip, trip, fall (same level)	12.0	27.2	21.3	35.5
Fall from height	16.4	15.2	26.4	19.9
Handling	6.3	8.6	10.2	11.2
Exposure to harmful substance	4.4	6.1	7.0	8.0
Walk into stationary object	3.0	5.2	2.4	6.8
All major injuries (total no.)	2,477	4,055		

(p) = provisional
Source: Thomas (1991)

report this type of accident. On the other hand, accidents involving contact with moving machinery are very much more likely to occur in smaller establishments, reflecting, in Thomas's view, 'poor training, less experienced operators, and generally less well-guarded machinery in smaller establishments'. The clear implication of Thomas's work is that 'there is some reason to believe that, because of a higher level of under-reporting by small establishments, these figures [those in Table 6.16] understate the relative risks'.

To investigate these matters further, the Health and Safety Executive asked questions of workers in the Labour Force Survey (LFS) for 1990. By asking these questions of individual workers, rather than relying on the reporting of accidents by employers, it was thought that under-reporting biases, particularly for small establishments, would be eliminated. Unfortunately the LFS does not make any distinction by establishment size beyond twenty-five workers, so it is not possible to assess injury rates over a wide range of establishment sizes. Nevertheless the strategy of asking workers directly and relating this to establishment size is a sensible approach.

The key finding from the LFS data is that, whilst the rate of fatal and serious injury is higher in smaller workplaces, the rate of less serious, three-day plus absence injuries is higher in larger workplaces. It is also interesting that the LFS finds that injuries leading to absence from work of less than three days are also higher in larger workplaces.

The provisional conclusion from the LFS data is that serious injuries are higher in smaller establishments, but that minor injuries are more likely to result in absence from work in large firms than in smaller firms, where there is a greater willingness on the part of the individual to return to work. The reason for this may be the crucial role which individual workers play in small firms, so that absence from work reflects the 'culture' within the firm. A more simple argument is that absence from work in a small firm is much more likely to lead directly to loss of pay than is the case for a large firm.

INTERACTION WITH THE LABOUR MARKET

Thus far, this chapter has appraised current research upon the role of small firms in providing jobs in the labour market. It specifically involves examining both the quantity and quality of the jobs created. But, as Atkinson and Meager (1994) point out, there is another equally important side to this relationship. Instead of asking how well does the small business serve the labour market, they ask the opposite question of how well the small business itself is served by the labour market. This section will review both the theoretical framework and the empirical results generated by Atkinson and Meager in their work on this topic.

Figure 6.5 shows the theoretical framework of Atkinson and Meager. It demonstrates that the objective is to obtain a better understanding of employment practice and experience in smaller firms, and that this is influenced by five partially independent elements. In the diagram, the five elements are assumed to exert a powerful influence, this being reflected in the large arrows, the heads of which impact upon employment practice/ experience. Nevertheless, a distinction is drawn between three characteristics – age of firm, industry/sector, and characteristics of owner/proprietor/ manager – which are assumed to be fixed for a given firm, and the two other characteristics – size of firm, and managerial approach and professionalism – which are assumed to be variable for a given firm. In the diagram, the factors which are assumed to be fixed are in the shaded area and the variables which are not fixed are shown in the unshaded area. Furthermore, the interdependencies of a number of the variables are identified by the presence of dotted arrows running from one variable to another.

Atkinson and Meager focus their attention upon the two elements which are assumed to be variable for the given firm. Their interest is on the impact of the size of firm upon the employment practice and experience but, in order to address that question adequately, they have to take account of the other four elements.

The element about which they feel the need to theorise most is the managerial approach and professionalism of the business. Here they are concerned with four thresholds which the business encounters with increasing size. These four thresholds are described as: an entry threshold – defined as the decision to take on the first worker; the delegation threshold – defined as the employment of the first manager; the formalisation threshold – defined as the movement away from *ad hoc* recruitment of labour to greater formal-isation; and a functional threshold – defined as employment for the first time

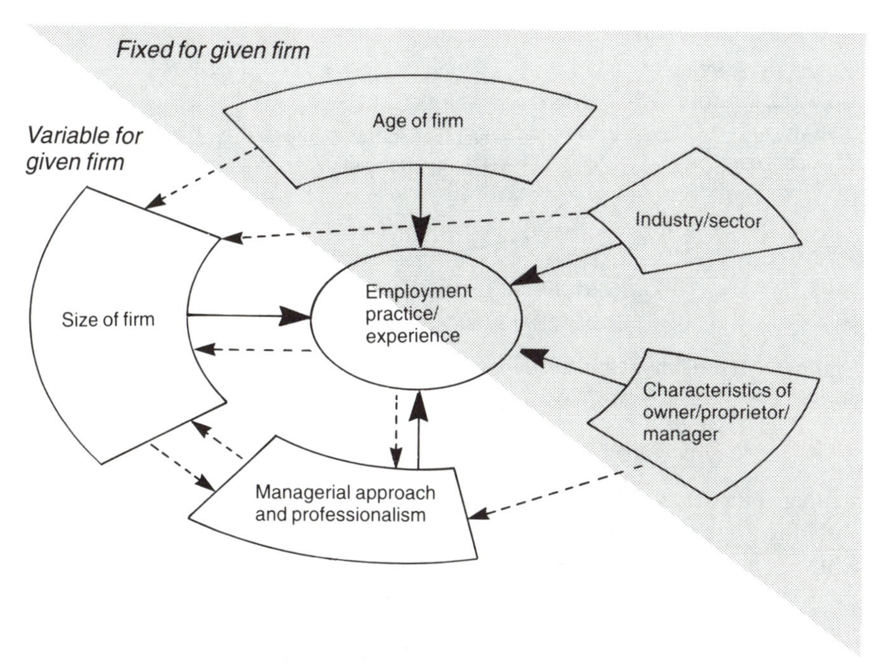

Figure 6.5 Environmental characteristics
Source: Atkinson and Meager (1994)

of a personnel or recruitment specialist.

Only the entry threshold clearly occurs at the same time in all firms. In the case of the three other thresholds, they are crossed with differing numbers of employees. Even so, crossing these thresholds is a key influence upon employment practice and experience in smaller firms.

Atkinson and Meager's empirical work is based upon a postal questionnaire administered in 1990, where responses were obtained from the same 3,289 small business analysed by Thompson and Wilson (1991), discussed earlier. Figure 6.6 shows two central findings of the survey. The first is that more than 50 per cent of businesses with between one and four workers had not recruited in the past year, but this level fell to only 5 per cent of those with between ten and fourteen workers. In essence, the continuous dark line in Figure 6.6 shows that it is only businesses which have ten workers or less which could not be considered to be active in the labour market.

Figure 6.6 also shows the responses to a question about whether they had experienced recruitment difficulties. These difficulties clearly do not exist in the smallest firms but, once the firm reaches ten or more workers, the difficulties become significant and do not diminish with increasing size, at least up until the fifty-employee mark. However Atkinson and Meager, using

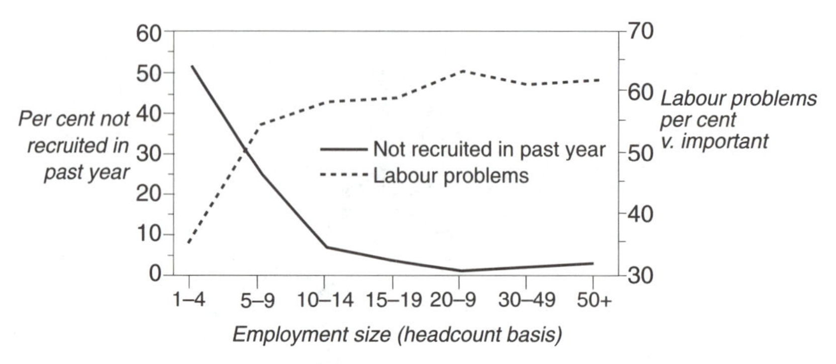

Figure 6.6 Recruitment and incidence of labour problems, by size
Source: Atkinson and Meager (1994)

another data set which has a much greater variety of different-sized firms within it, suggest that the fifty-employee size mark can be considered to be a 'peak', in the sense that labour problems then seem to be less important. In short, the firms most likely to be reporting labour market problems are those with around fifty employees. They imply that this type of firm is large enough to be active within the labour market, but too small to have structured and formal procedures which lead to appropriate labour being recruited.

Some additional light on the issue of *why* small firm owner-managers experienced recruitment problems is provided by Scott *et al.* (1990). They argue that recruitment problems emerge not only because of tight labour market conditions, but because of a search for the 'right worker'. It is the determination to avoid the 'trouble-maker', which may, in turn, reflect the dominant managerial style in small firms, which may be at the heart of recruitment difficulties.

Atkinson and Meager also compare the firms' perceptions of problems in the labour market, with those of other identified problem areas. These include administrative (legislation, official regulations, paperwork, etc.), financial (interest rates, raising finance, capital, cash flow, tax burden) and market (overall demand for business products/services, competition from other businesses). When these problem areas are identified and graphed, as in Figure 6.7, they show that it is only the labour market problems which appear to be substantially higher for the large firms than for the smaller firms. Figure 6.7 shows that financial problems are higher for all sizes of firms – supporting the findings of the Cambridge Small Business Research Centre (1992) survey. However, for businesses with more than fifty employees, difficulties with markets, finance and labour are almost equally likely to arise. It is only administrative problems which are significantly less, and no more likely to be referred to, than in the very smallest of businesses.

Firms were also asked about the factors which they regarded as important

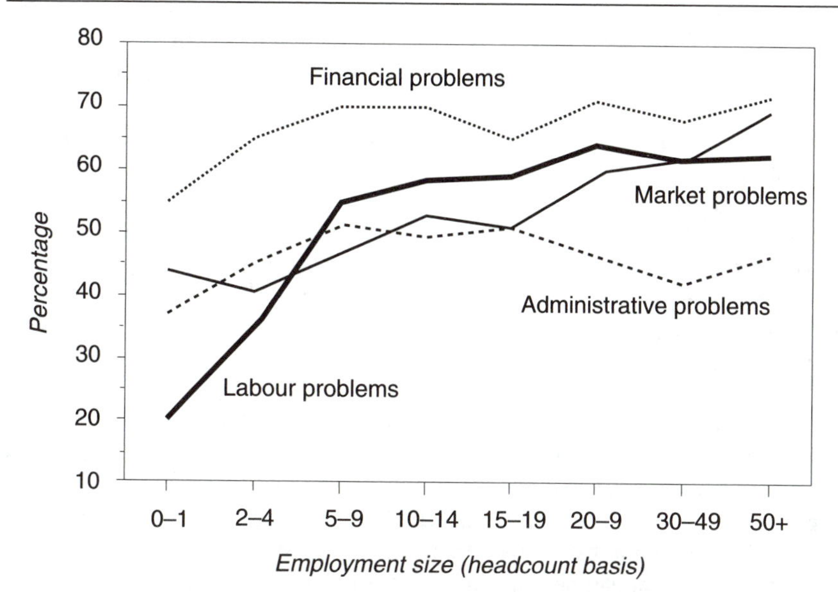

Figure 6.7 Types of problem perceived as very important, by size
Source: Atkinson and Meager (1994)

in deciding upon employment levels. Responses clearly indicated that the decision as to whether or not to take on additional workers was influenced primarily by very short-term considerations, such as current workload and current profitability. These were regarded as being very important by 69 per cent and 56 per cent of respondents respectively. It should be noted that one of the factors which the firms could have chosen was official regulations and legislation. However, this was identified as being very important by only 21.5 per cent of respondents and was ranked eleventh out of thirteen possible factors. This again supports the Cambridge Small Business Research Centre (1992) survey and earlier official government work by Clifton and Tatton-Brown (1979) indicating the low level of significance which firms attribute to such issues in making recruitment decisions. As we shall show in Chapter 8, the consistency of research evidence in this direction has, however, not been effective in persuading politicians in the United Kingdom of the low significance of this issue.

A third key finding of the Atkinson and Meager study is that recruitment methods, for virtually all groups of workers, become increasingly formalised with increases in firm size. Nevertheless, even quite substantial small businesses, such as those with more than fifty employees, continue to use word of mouth as an important tool of recruitment. Curran *et al.* (1993) find that, for smaller firms, this mode of recruitment totally dominates for all types of workers.

Jones, McEvoy and Barrett (1993) in their study of ethnic and white businesses in the United Kingdom also obtain similar results in this respect. They find, for both groups, that recruitment formality increases with firm size, with 'firms with ten or more employees standing out as more active in the formal labour market'. The ethnic dimension to this finding is that the Asian firms are more likely to rely upon personal recruitment procedures, even when the ten-employee threshold has been overcome.

Atkinson and Meager conclude that recruitment difficulties, even after excluding the non-recruiters, become more prevalent as business size increases amongst smaller firms. To test this hypothesis in a robust way, however, requires the variables identified in Figure 6.5 to be held constant. As we noted in that figure, these variables cannot be considered fully independent but, using a multivariate framework, Atkinson and Meager attempt to test this hypothesis. Their objective is to identify whether or not a particular firm experienced recruitment difficulties in the last year. To do this they take account of the industry in which the firm operates, its age, its size, its location, the tightness of the labour market in which it operates, whether or not it has a personnel manager and the extent to which it could be considered to be a low-paying firm.

The clear pattern which emerges is that it is firm size which is the dominant influence, with virtually none of the other variables explaining much of the variance.

Overall, small businesses are not well served by the labour market. There is a strong suggestion that, although businesses do cross a number of thresholds in moving from one employee to fifty or more, it is not until they are well above the latter threshold that labour market problems begin to diminish in significance. In essence, it is firms with between ten and fifty employees which are most likely to feel the labour market is not providing them with appropriate employees. In part, this is because their own circumstances are changing as they grow.

Atkinson and Meager summarise the position well:

> Our results indicate that so profound is the gap between need and capacity (i.e. between the behaviour and competencies which the small business would need to deploy to resource itself adequately from the labour market and those which it typically demonstrates) that a more or less continuous process of behavioural adjustment is able to do little more than contain the seriousness of employment problems. It is not until employment levels are well over 50 that we observe any sign of the reduced intensity of most of these problems, and even then, such a reduction appears to be a very slow business. Not only does the growing business have to run to stand still, it also has a long way to run.

CONCLUSIONS

For much of the 1980s there was a fierce debate about the extent of job creation in smaller firms. Our conclusion is that small firms in both the United States and the United Kingdom were creating jobs at a faster rate than larger firms. It is also the case that small firms are more consistent creators of jobs, in the sense of being less influenced by macroeconomic conditions.

These statements are subject to four provisos.

- First, it must be recognised that only the research at the end of the 1980s provided sufficiently 'clean' data for these statements. Much of the evangelical research prior to that time, and the politicians' statements associated with it, should be discounted on the grounds that they significantly over-estimated the contribution which small firms make to job creation.
- Secondly, even if it is the case that the small firm sector *is* a major source of new job creation, this does not automatically point to a justification for providing the sector with additional incentives. The question of whether, *at the margin*, it is appropriate to redirect resources away from large and towards small firms is not proven simply by demonstrating that small firms have in the past been significant sources of job creation.
- Thirdly, the observation that new jobs are found in small businesses does not imply that such firms can be considered to be an 'independent' motor for employment growth. Lyons and Bailey (1993) in the United Kingdom and Higham (1993) for New Zealand show that the 1980s was a period in which subcontracting increased, so that at least some of the growth in small firms arose as a direct transfer of activity from large firms. This may well have yielded efficiency gains to the economy, but again it does not constitute an unambiguous justification for a refocusing of public policy towards small firms on the grounds of job creation.[4]

  Perhaps most importantly, the fact that from an 'accounting' perspective, job creation is more likely to take place in small than in large firms, does not have direct policy implications. For example, it may be that it is the productivity gain in large firms, which indeed may be at the expense of employment, which is a source of new wealth in the economy. Additional employment, however, occurs in small firms in the service sector. In this sense the 'economic' description of employment creation differs from the implications of the job 'accounting' framework described earlier (pp. 161–73) in this chapter.
- Fourthly, the emphasis throughout the 1980s on quantifying the numbers of jobs created in smaller firms seems to have deflected the attention of researchers away from considering the quality of these jobs and the characteristics of those who fill them. The strong impression which emerges from research on this topic suggests that according to most criteria, the quality of jobs is lower in small firms than it is in large firms.

> For example, wages for the employee are lower in smaller firms, fringe benefits are less likely to be provided, training is less likely to be received and the jobs themselves are more likely to be filled by very young or old workers whose educational attainments are below average.

These disadvantages, however, have to be set again two important benefits.

- First, from the viewpoint of a government committed to reducing trade union power, is the fact that smaller firms are less likely to be unionised.
- The second, from the point of view of the employee, is that there does appear to be a considerable degree of workplace harmony in smaller firms, particularly in the service sector. Prior to the current research programme, small firm researchers argued that this apparent harmony existed because research had reported only the viewpoint of the boss. Interviews with employees conducted in the current research programme, whilst not wholly endorsing the viewpoint of the boss, do not seem to point to significant dissatisfaction on the part of the small firm workforce.

The central conclusions which emerge from examining the interaction of small firms with the labour market are that those with between ten and fifty employees are experiencing major difficulties. Although these are not quite as important as the financial problems which these firms experience, enterprises in this size band seem to be having problems in coming to terms with the increasing formality of recruitment and training which their greater size requires. Informality of relationships permeates the whole of the labour process, from recruitment to motivation through to dismissal. It is hardly surprising that such firms exhibit, and incur the cost of, high rates of labour churning.

Once a firm has more than 100 employees it seems to use more formal recruitment procedures and to obtain more satisfactory labour. The inference from this would seem to be that it is firms in the 20–100 employee range which require particular attention from the local Training and Enterprise Councils (TECs). However, to focus exclusively upon the recruitment and labour turnover problems of such groups would be to treat the symptoms and not the causes. To address the latter requires an understanding of why informal procedures exist and to encourage owners to exhibit greater formality and consistency.

Perhaps the key remaining area of uncertainty remains the question of training for employees in smaller firms. The research reviewed here has generally been unable to demonstrate a clear link between those firms which undertake training and those firms which perform better in the market-place. Furthermore, the limited evidence, so far as employees are concerned, is that those in receipt of workplace training in small firms do not either currently earn more than those not in receipt of such training, or anticipate earning more in the future. Too frequently, (Midland Bank 1993) it is assumed that training provided for smaller firms is beneficial. Indeed, a very powerful lobby of both public and private organisations have been created to promote training. Whilst it does seem to be the case at national level that training is associated with better performance, this link has not been adequately demonstrated at the level of the small firm sector. This matter is developed further in Chapter 8.

Chapter 7

Finance

INTRODUCTION

At least since 1931, when the MacMillan Committee (1931) reported, there has been continuing and vigorous discussion about the financing of smaller firms. The MacMillan Committee believed it was extremely difficult for smaller firms to obtain long-term capital in amounts of less than £200,000. This was known as the 'MacMillan Gap'.

Over the following sixty years there has been a huge number of changes in the institutional framework for financing small firms, and several learned committees (Bolton, Wilson) have examined this topic. On each occasion that the issue has been examined, the value of the 'gap' has fallen, in real terms. Nevertheless, it is still the case today that smaller firms find it difficult to obtain small sums of equity capital and feel penalised by an inability to obtain, or to obtain only at high rates of interest, loan capital.

One of the purposes of this chapter is to address the question of the extent to which small firms are penalised in their mode of financing by the existence of market failure. In principle, the chapter asks whether there should be further government involvement to eliminate imperfections in the market-place. Alternatively, are imperfections so fundamental, in the sense of stemming from financial institutions and smaller firms having different types of information – so-called information asymmetries – that no action by government could lead to improvement?

To answer these questions, the chapter relies heavily upon obtaining an understanding of the writings of theorists on this topic (Hillier and Ibrahimo 1993). In essence, theorists use a fairly common set of assumptions, providing an understanding of why it is that interest rates for small firms are higher than for large firms, why interest rates do not always reflect risk, why it is that banks seek collateral, why it is that banks do not appear to compete vigorously for each other's customers, and why banks may prefer low-risk and low-return customers to high-risk and high-return customers.

Given this theoretical underpinning, much of the chapter is concerned with providing the reader with the factual background on how small firms are financed, about their changes in profitability over time, and about their relationships with banks and venture capitalists.

It is then possible to address the central question of the chapter, which is whether there is competition in the provision of finance for smaller firms, or whether 'gaps', 'market failures' or 'credit rationing' occur.

THE THEORY OF BANK LENDING IN THE SMALL BUSINESS SECTOR

This section begins by identifying eight assumptions which underpin the bulk of theoretical writings in this area. Each assumption is then discussed in some detail and is followed in the next section by the derivation of some predictions about bank behaviour in models based on these assumptions. The eight assumptions are:

- asymmetric information;
- agency issues;
- higher objective risk in lending to small firms;
- costly monitoring;
- competing banks;
- entrepreneurs vary in ability, honesty and motivation;
- entrepreneurs gain from increased project valuation;
- banks gain only from repayment.

Asymmetric information

Central to an analysis of the financing of small businesses is the assumption that the owner of a small business has more/better information about the performance of his/her firm than the bank. Williamson (1975) argued that firms would always be better informed than 'outsiders' – or the market – since they had access to 'inside' information. However, this advantage is less helpful for larger firms, and particularly for those where the shares are publicly traded. This is because information on larger firms is collected by independent analysts and widely disseminated to a large group of potential and actual investors in the business. Such information is not so readily available for smaller firms, where 'external' investment is likely to be minimal. For this reason the small business owner is likely to be significantly better informed about the business than any outsider such as the bank.

The existence of asymmetric information, where this favours the smaller business owner, makes the bank more wary of lending to this type of firm, on the grounds of greater uncertainty. As we shall see in the next section the bank attempts to overcome these problems by looking for indications or 'signals' from the business owner, in order to reduce this uncertainty.

Although such asymmetry is an assumption made by virtually all theorists in the area, the wholly new firm or business start-up may be a type of smaller firm which contravenes this assumption. It seems quite plausible to argue, as does Jovanovic (1981), that the individual starting a business has an extremely imperfect idea of whether or not they will be successful. He argues that it is only by learning from experience that the successful, or surviving, entrepreneur is distinguished from the less successful or non-surviving.

On the other hand, the bank, or the loan officer, may have a much better idea of whether or not the new business will be successful than the entrepreneur. This is because loan officers are likely to have derived their own experience from dealing with similar customers at a similar stage of business development. They may also have benefited from bank training and decision rules which formalise bank experience in this area.

However, as the business matures, it does seem likely that the asymmetry of information will increasingly favour the small firm rather than the bank, since the business owner becomes aware of his/her abilities through experience of running the business on a daily basis. The bank's monitoring procedures are unlikely to improve at the same rate, since it will only deal periodically with the firm as one of many clients.

Agency issues

A second key assumption is that whilst the bank provides a loan, its control over the actions of the firm is only limited. The entrepreneur acts as an agent for the bank (Jensen and Meckling 1976) and the task of the principal – in this case the bank – is to ensure that its agent – in this case the entrepreneur – acts in accordance with its contractual obligations – specifically, repaying the loan plus the interest. The key issue for the principal is to ensure that a contract, which can be monitored, is drawn up which provides an incentive for the agent to satisfy the requirements of the principal. The interests of the two groups – principal and agent – are therefore not identical.

Higher objective risk in lending to small firms

Chapter 4 showed there is little doubt that, by objective measures, bank lending to smaller businesses is more risky than to otherwise comparable large firms. The bank can respond to this in three different ways:

- firstly, it may seek to reduce the risk by making loans only to firms which have a low probability of failure;
- secondly, it may seek to ensure that, even in the event of failure, it obtains some return;
- thirdly, it could increase the returns from the investment through the raising of interest rates.

In a perfect market, raising the interest rate will reduce the demand for funding, and credit rationing will not exist, in the sense that anyone wishing to obtain finance at market prices can do so. However, as we will show, banks' preferred reaction is not to raise interest rates but rather to reduce the availability of loans – i.e. to ration credit, so that even if firms are willing to pay more, they are not allowed the chance.

Costly monitoring

The agency problems discussed above, in which the interests of the entrepreneur and bank are not identical, mean that the bank has to obtain information. This occurs prior to the bank making a decision as to whether or not to make a loan, and then, after the loan is made, the bank monitors the actions of the agent to ensure they are acting in a way compatible with the contract.

Monitoring and assessment costs can be considerable if an accurate decision is to be made on the viability of the project. It is also assumed that the initial assessment costs are either invariant with the size of loan which is sought, or are a decreasing proportion of the loan size. Furthermore, the financial institution has to pass on the costs of monitoring and assessment to its clients. This applies not only to those costs which are incurred in reaching a successful decision, but also where the institution turns down proposals, having already made viability assessments.[1]

Competing banks

It is assumed the entrepreneur seeks funding from a range of competing financial institutions offering different risk/reward options. This does not necessarily mean that all financial institutions offer the same rate of interest. As we shall show below, if the bank makes a loan it will draw up a contract which could have a number of dimensions: these include instances where, although the rate of interest charged by one bank is higher, there may be offsetting advantages to firms, such as interest repayment holidays or lower charges for drawing up the contract. In addition the bank may, as a condition in the contract, penalise the firm if it borrows more than a specified sum, by charging a very much higher rate on the incremental amount.

However, the central mechanism in adjusting for risk is the provision of collateral. In this, banks may vary, as a competitive tactic, in the extent to which collateral is sought, or the value of the collateral in relation to the value of the loan. Apilado and Millington (1992) show that banks in the United States are also likely to introduce restrictive loan covenants prohibiting, for example, part purchases of other firms, or restricting firms' ability to remove money – particularly for directors' remuneration. In the United Kingdom such covenants are less frequently employed since overdrafts, which are not used in the United States, can be withdrawn immediately and without notice.

Hence, whilst theorists assume that banks compete, it cannot reasonably be assumed that competition is only in terms of price. Clearly the firm has the opportunity, at least in theory, to trade-off between price and other dimensions of the contract.

Entrepreneurs vary in ability, honesty and motivation

This is linked to the first assumption, that entrepreneurs know more about their business than the bank. Clearly if all entrepreneurs were identical, and so did not vary in ability, honesty and motivation, and the banks knew this, then no information asymmetry would exist.

However, as we argued, asymmetric information could favour either the bank or the entrepreneur. In any event there is uncertainty for the bank in judging a loan because entrepreneurs differ in their ability, honesty and motivation.

Entrepreneurs gain from increased project valuation

Entrepreneurs are assumed to have zero initial wealth, and it is also assumed that the entrepreneur has a project which, to undertake, requires a loan of K at an interest rate of i. If the project is successful it will yield H, but if it is unsuccessful it will yield zero. If the probability of success is defined as p, then the expected gain to the firm of borrowing to undertake the project is the following:

$$E(\pi)^F = p[H - (1 + i)K]$$

where $E(\pi)^F$ = expected profit of the firm.

Banks gain only from repayment

Although in practice the bank may obtain income from charges, it is assumed the bank gains only the interest from the successful loan. Where there is no use of collateral, in the event of the loan being unsuccessful the bank suffers the loss of the principal.

The net gain to the bank is the difference between the interest from the successful project, and the interest that could have been derived from investing that sum (K) in a riskless project yielding an interest rate of r.

This may be expressed as:

$$E(\pi)^B = p[K(1 + i)] - K(1 + r)$$

where $E(\pi)^B$ = expected return to the bank.

For present purposes it is assumed that the bank does not have an equity (ownership) stake in the business. In UK terminology, we are assuming that the bank is either providing an overdraft facility or a term loan, and not venture capital.

THE BANK'S RESPONSE

This section examines how theorists predict a bank will act as a lender to small firms, given the above assumptions. Four main actions are identified:

- The bank collects information and seeks 'signals' from borrowers.
- The bank draws up a contract agreement.
- The bank charges interest rates to cover risk and cost.
- The bank monitors the contract.

Information and collection of signals

The bank is interested in identifying those firms which have a lower risk of defaulting on a loan. Traditionally, banks have used personal security or collateral as a signal by the owner of commitment to a business. The purpose of collateral is to ensure, in the event of the project failing, that the bank has access to resources which can offset any losses with the project. Collateral may be in the form of either the personal resources of the entrepreneur, such as housing, or some identifiable assets of the business over which the bank asserts a prior claim over other creditors. In essence, collateral protects the bank in the event of a default.

Where the bank obtains collateral, its expected profit function becomes:

$$E(\pi)^B = p[K(1+i)] - (1-p)[C-K(1+r)]$$

From this it can be seen that in the event of the firm failing, the bank still obtains collateral to the value of C, although from this has to be subtracted the income which could have been obtained from the risk-free investment.

However, there are several problems with the use of collateral as a guarantor for loans. The first relates to the valuation of the collateral. The bank has to incur costs of valuing the collateral, since its valuation is likely to be very different (and generally much lower) than that of the firm. Perhaps the most frequently used collateral, so far as small businesses are concerned, is the owner's own house. Differences in the estimated valuation of a property between bank and entrepreneur occur because the owner is likely to value the property at current market rates. Its value to the bank, however, will be the expected selling price net of all costs of disposing of the property. Furthermore, the bank would also be expected to take a more pessimistic view of the expected selling price, since it might have to dispose of the property during poor trading conditions. It is then likely to take a 'worst case' view of the valuation. It also may be less prepared to wait for a purchaser to pay the 'market' rate, and may choose to sell through an auction, which guarantees a buyer, but at less than the 'market' price.

The result which emerges from a number of theoretical studies of the role of collateral in bank lending is that it provides an incentive for 'good' borrowers to identify themselves (e.g. Besanko and Thakor 1987, Chan and Kanatas 1985). These authors argue that, where the entrepreneur is likely to incur a significant personal loss in the event of a project or firm failure, they will be more likely to commit themselves fully to the success of the project. Given the assumption made earlier, that the entrepreneur has more information about the probability of success of the project than the bank, then the willingness of the entrepreneur to provide collateral is seen to be a positive 'signal' by the bank that the entrepreneur views the likelihood of success of the project as being high.

The role of collateral therefore is threefold:

- First, it limits the downside loss by providing an asset for the bank in the event of a project failure.
- Secondly, it provides an incentive to the entrepreneur to commit him or herself to the project.
- Thirdly, it provides a signal to the bank that the entrepreneur believes the project is likely to succeed – otherwise he or she would not commit their personal resources to it.

Berger and Udell (1990), however, argue that the theorist's view of collateral, as being associated with less risky investments (roles two and three above), does not correspond to the traditional views held by bankers. They quote the work of Morsman (1986), suggesting that it is only the *more* risky projects where collateral is sought by bankers, whereas less risky projects are not required to provide collateral. They refer to this as the 'sorting-by-observed-risk' paradigm.

Berger and Udell argue that the distinction on the role of collateral made between finance theorists and bankers in fact turns upon the assumptions made about who has access to information. Theorists such as Chan and Kanatas (1985) and Bester (1985) implicitly assume banks are not able adequately to distinguish between borrowers, since it is the latter which have more information than the bank. Berger and Udell refer to this as the 'sorting-by-private-information' paradigm. Conversely, those subscribing to the 'sorting-by-observed-risk' paradigm, assume the banks have enough information to enable them to assess the relative risks of a range of projects. It is on the basis of this information that they seek to obtain collateral from some borrowers and not from others.

Drawing up a contract

The purpose of drawing up contracts is for the bank to narrow the range of options open to the firm, to set these out and make sure both parties are aware of them. Since the firm is acting as its agent, the contract limits the scope and discretion of the firm in utilising the loan provided by the bank. The bank may specify the extent to which firms can use the money for purchasing other firms, making investment decisions and withdrawing income from the firm and transferring it to the directors. It can penalise the firm for borrowing more than the sum specified; it can even withdraw a loan facility, or ask for it to be repaid. However, the extent to which all possible options can be fully specified in a contract is limited. The bank therefore seeks some alternative mechanism in which its interests, and those of its agent, more clearly coincide.

Bank charges interest rates to cover risk and cost

In competitive markets prices are higher for 'uncertain' borrowers than for 'certain' borrowers, if only because the lender has to incur additional costs in monitoring/assessment, as well as covering the greater likelihood of bad debt. It is then to be expected that the more risky projects would be charged a higher rate of interest, and the low-risk projects a lower rate of interest.

Unfortunately, given the above assumptions, such a strategy, as demonstrated by Stiglitz and Weiss (1981), could prove counter-productive. They show that the raising of interest rates, where the bank has less information about the expected success of the project than the entrepreneur, can lead to lower returns to the bank. This happens because low-risk, but low-return, borrowers no longer find it worthwhile borrowing from the bank because of the higher interest rates. In that sense they drop out of the market-place.

On the other hand, high-risk, but high-return, borrowers stay in the market-place since, if the project fails their losses remain at zero. If their project is successful, however, then the gains accrue to them and not to the bank – other than from a marginal rise in interest repayments. Again, certain assumptions are crucial to this outcome, and they are that:

- The bank has poorer information on expected project success than the entrepreneur.
- In the event of the failure of the project the bank obtains either a zero income or an income significantly below that with a successful project.
- In the event of the success of the project the bank still only obtains repayment of the interest plus principal.

All of the above assumptions are of importance and need to be highlighted. The first is that although the bank does gain from raising its interest rates, it does not share fully in the up-side gain in the event of the success of the project. It is the entrepreneur who is the primary gainer in the event of the project being successful. The second is that, in the event of failure, the entrepreneur's loss is zero, since all funding is assumed to be provided by the bank, whereas the bank's loss is the principal plus the expected stream of interest payments. If the entrepreneur has a choice between two projects with the same expected return, but with Project A having higher variance than Project B then, in the absence of any opening equity or collateral, the rational choice of the entrepreneur is Project A.

Differences in the access to information between the bank and the entrepreneur, which lead to an unwillingness on the part of the bank to use interest rates to bring the market-place for funds into equilibrium, is referred to as 'adverse selection'. It is given this name because of the problems which the bank has in selecting, on the basis of imperfect information about risk, one project from another. The central problem which emerges because of the asymmetry of information between the parties is that the market is *not* cleared through price changes. Stiglitz and Weiss show that the rational response of banks is not to raise interest rates to reduce excess demand, but instead to ration credit in some way.[2] The consequence of this is that some borrowers may be excluded from access to credit, even though they may be prepared to pay the existing or even higher price (interest rate) for that credit. In this sense the market is seen to be imperfect and a 'gap' is identified.

The bank monitors the contract

The final act of the bank is to ensure that the terms and conditions of the contract are being met. This will involve the provision of regular reports by the firm, in a format specified by the bank. In the event of non-compliance with the contract, the bank will seek reasons for this non-compliance. Where there is a likelihood of loss to the bank, then decisions will be made on whether or not to call in the loan or to take other action.

IMPLICATIONS FOR THE MARKET-PLACE

The loan market

The previous section demonstrated that imperfect information available to the bank could result in its reluctance to use the price mechanism to allocate their loan funds. It occurs through 'adverse selection', with the bank not having enough information to identify the firms with the highest expected rates of return. It also may occur because raising the interest rates can influence the behaviour of the firm. This is referred to as 'moral hazard'. The effect here is that, in the absence of collateral, and given the nature of the repayment schedules, the firm in receipt of bank funding has an incentive to alter its behaviour to favour more risky, but higher-return, projects. This is because, if the project is successful, the firm obtains all of the gains from this success, subject to having only to pay marginally higher rates of interest. If the project is unsuccessful and the firm closes, then the bank, rather than the firm, is the loser. The argument here then is that to raise interest rates will induce firms to seek more risky and higher-return projects from which they benefit but do not lose. The converse is the case for the bank.

At the heart of the moral hazard argument is the view that, by setting a particular interest rate, the behaviour of the entrepreneur is changed. The empirical importance of the moral hazard argument will depend upon the extent to which entrepreneurs can alter the riskiness of a project, once a lending decision has been made. *A priori*, this may be likely to be of less significance than adverse selection.

Theorists argue that banks respond to both adverse selection and moral hazard by seeking collateral. Collateral provides an incentive for the entrepreneur to seek less risky projects, on the grounds that he or she incurs losses if the project fails. In principle, collateral overcomes the problems of both moral hazard and adverse selection, with the rate of interest playing its traditional role of clearing the market-place. Bester (1987) shows that no borrower will be denied credit when each can be ranked in terms of their risk. He also shows that collateral provides an incentive for borrowers to reveal their relative riskiness.

Unfortunately, not all entrepreneurs have access to collateral, and so some are excluded from the market-place. In this sense a 'gap' in the market-place exists for those viable business ventures which lack access to security to insure against downside risk. In short, collateral does not overcome moral hazard and adverse selection problems because not all individuals have equal access to it. It may also seriously disadvantage certain types of project, such as high-technology start-ups (which are perceived to be particularly risky) or capital-intensive projects where the sums to be borrowed are high.

Hence the most likely form of market imperfection is that those small firms, without access to collateral, will be unable to obtain access to funding even though their projects' returns are at least as high as those of firms with collateral. In this sense the small firm sector is deemed to experience a 'rationing' of funds, or a 'gap' because banks are reluctant to use the interest rate as a market-clearing device and cannot exact collateral where none is available.

The major theoretical contribution of De Meza and Webb (1987, 1990) has been to question the validity of this prediction. They argue that if banks are unable to discriminate effectively between good and bad projects, they are likely to make some investments in bad projects and so 'over-invest' in the market-place. In this sense, asymmetric information between banks and entrepreneurs leads to too much, rather than too little, funding being made available. It also implies that 'good' projects will be charged higher rates of interest to reflect bank losses in funding 'bad' projects.

The key difference between De Meza and Webb on the one hand and Stiglitz and Weiss on the other is that the latter assume the bank chooses between projects with the same expected values but different risk levels. From this, Stiglitz and Weiss derive their conclusion that credit rationing will occur.

De Meza and Webb, however, assume there are projects of different expected values. They argue that it is only the 'mean preserving spreads' assumption of Stiglitz and Weiss which leads to the credit-rationing result; their assumption of different mean values of projects under asymmetric information may lead to the opposite result of over-investment.

The equity market

The argument thus far has focused exclusively upon the market for bank loans, as opposed to the provision of equity. In the loan market, theorists have defined market failure to occur when feasible welfare-enhancing projects are not implemented. This might involve under- or over-investment, but the most obvious case is where finance is not made available to apparently viable small firms. Here, viability is defined to be where the expected return to the project exceeds the real costs of resources used. Stiglitz and Weiss regard the classic symptom of market failure to be credit rationing, which occurs when, amongst identical firms, some receive a loan and others do not, even though they are prepared to pay a higher interest rate. Stiglitz and Weiss see market failure as being reflected in the existence of firms which, with a given supply of credit, are unable to obtain loans at any price (interest rate), but which would obtain loans if more credit were available.

Keasey and Watson (1992) argue that loan market imperfections reflect the nature of the contracts which the bank draws up in order to overcome problems of asymmetric information. They imply that equity owners bear the business risks in return for having full ownership rights over any residual cash flows. As they are not normally entitled to such cash flows, or to exercise influence over the use and control of the firm's assets, suppliers of debt finance expect to obtain a fixed and certain return, regardless of how well or badly the firm performs.

A second, and somewhat less charitable, interpretation of the relationship between the banks and the entrepreneur is that it is those projects about which entrepreneurs are least confident are those in which they are most likely to share external ownership. Conversely, projects in which the entrepreneur is wholly confident are the least likely to be offered to the banks. In this sense, collateral and equity participation are significantly different from each other. Although both could be interpreted as providing positive signals, collateral is seen to provide the bank with a 'certain' income even in the event of a project failure, whereas equity participation enables the bank to participate in the success of a project, but without the 'safety net' of collateral.

THE FACTUAL BACKGROUND

It is now appropriate to provide the reader with a current and historical perspective upon the financing of smaller businesses in the United Kingdom.

This section provides the institutional context for the remainder of the chapter, and is divided into six main parts:

- How small firms are financed.
- Changes in the profitability of small firms.
- Financial awareness amongst small business owners.
- Small firms and their banks.
- The growth of venture capital.
- The role of the public sector.

How small firms are financed

This section draws heavily upon the work by Hughes (1992), who constructed the table reproduced as Table 7.1. The table uses the published accounts of limited companies which, as Chapter 2 shows, constituted only 18 per cent of all businesses in the United Kingdom. Even the companies regarded as small for the purposes of this table are generally very much larger than, for example, a random sample of businesses registered for VAT which, in turn, are likely to be larger than unregistered businesses.

The table demonstrates that the financial structure and profitability of large and small companies differ significantly, even where account is taken of the distinction between manufacturing and non-manufacturing. In this context 'large' companies are those ranked in the top 2,000 in terms of capital employed in the UK non-financial corporate sector, whereas 'small' companies are a one-in-three-hundred sample of the remainder of the sector, stratified by size of capital employed.

Hughes observes several differences between the two groups: he notes that small companies have a lower ratio of fixed to total assets, but that trade debt is relatively more important for small than for large firms.

Amongst the current liabilities, trade and other creditors are of greater importance for the small than the large firms. Although it is not shown in the table, small firms generally are net suppliers of trade credit, whereas larger firms are net receivers of trade credit.

Of particular relevance to this chapter is that the table shows smaller companies are much more reliant on short-term bank loans and overdrafts than large companies. Hughes summarises the position thus:

> The basic findings for the asset and liability structures of small companies are broadly similar to those of previous investigations in the 1960s and 1970s. The high reliance on short term finance provided by banks, and the relatively low proportions of assets financed by shareholders' interests are clearly long run persistent features of small business finance. The same is true of the relative importance of trade debt and trade credit and the relative unimportance of fixed assets in their balance sheet structure.

Table 7.1 The balance sheet structure, gearing and profitability of large and small UK companies in the manufacturing and non-manufacturing industries (excluding oil) in the period 1987–9

	Manufacturing companies		*Non-manufacturing companies*	
	Small	*Large*	*Small*	*Large*
	(Average per cent 1987–9)			
1 *Fixed assets*				
Net tangible assets	30.2	34.2	26.4	52.4
Intangibles	0.4	3.3	0.9	3.4
Investments	0.9	7.0	3.5	3.4
Total net fixed assets	31.5	44.4	30.9	59.2
2 *Current assets*				
Stock and work in progress	19.6	19.8	25.0	14.0
Trade and other debtors	37.9	23.6	36.0	19.3
Investments	1.0	2.8	0.6	1.7
Cash and short-term deposits	9.9	9.3	7.9	5.8
Total current assets	68.5	55.6	69.1	40.8
Total current and fixed assets	100.0	100.0	100.0	100.0
3 *Current liabilities*				
Bank overdrafts and loans	11.3	6.1	11.0	4.4
Directors' short-term loans	0.5	0.0	2.7	0.0
Other short term loans	0.3	1.1	1.1	1.3
Trade and other creditors	35.3	23.6	41.9	21.9
Dividends and interest due	0.3	1.7	1.3	1.5
Current taxation	7.1	4.8	4.4	3.9
Total current liabilities	55.0	37.3	62.4	33.1
Net current assets	13.5	18.3	6.8	8.3
Total net assets	45.0	62.7	37.6	67.5
4 *Long-term liabilities*				
Shareholders' interests*	36.1	42.0	26.8	47.4
Minority interests and provisions	2.3	6.5	1.1	2.8
Loans **	3.2	11.5	6.3	15.4
Other creditors and accruals	3.4	2.7	3.5	1.9
Total capital and reserves	45.0	62.7	37.6	67.5
Total capital and liabilities	100.0	100.0	100.0	100.0
5 Long-term loans as per cent all loans	20.5	61.7	29.4	72.9
All loans as per cent shareholders' interest	42.4	44.3	78.7	44.5
Interest expense as per cent earnings before tax	15.4	12.4	21.4	14.7
6 Pre-tax return on Net Assets	15.9	19.6	19.1	14.4
Pre-tax return on Total Assets	12.4	14.3	13.0	17.6
Pre-tax return on Equity	10.4	19.1	18.8	13.3

Source: *Business Monitor* MA3 Company Finance, Various Issues; Hughes (1992)
Notes: *Ordinary, plus preference plus capital and revenue reserves.
**Directors' loans, bank loans, convertible and debenture loans, all of which have a duration of over one year.

There have, however, been some clear changes in the growth in importance of 'new' types of finance. Illustrations of this are leasing and hire purchase, both of which have increased their role. A helpful review is provided by Berry *et al.* (1990). The key difference between the two is that equipment purchased through leasing remains the property of the leasing company, whereas that purchased through hire purchase ultimately is owned by the purchaser. Berry *et al.* show there was a spectacular growth in both during the 1980s, but that usage of both leasing and hire purchase was much more characteristic of the larger than the smallest of small firms. They found that 75 per cent of new investment during the 1987–90 period in equipment acquired by the firms they studied was financed by either leasing or hire purchase, in approximately equal shares. The Cambridge Small Business Research Centre (1992) survey also highlights the importance of hire purchase and leasing, which was used by 45 per cent of firms which had obtained new finance over the previous three years.

Changes in the profitability of small firms

Section 6 of Table 7.1 shows that, for all three measures, the profitability of small manufacturing companies is below that for large manufacturing companies. However, for non-manufacturing companies, for two of the measures, small companies appear to be more profitable than large. Hughes examines these measures of profitability for UK smaller companies throughout the 1980s and finds that in the manufacturing sector, according to all three measures, large manufacturing companies are more profitable than small manufacturing companies.

Hughes shows that these results contrast with those obtained earlier by both the Bolton Committee (1971) and the Wilson Committee (1979). The latter found that small manufacturing companies in the late 1960s, and up to the mid-1970s, were consistently *more* profitable than large. However, this seems to have reversed by the late 1970s so that, during the 1977–89 period, only in 1988 is small company profitability higher than that for large firms using the return on total assets (ROTA) measure. For the return on net assets (RONA) measure the same pattern is observed, except that it is not until 1979 that small company profitability falls below that of large.

For the non-manufacturing sector the results are more variable, and no clear or consistent pattern emerges, other than that during the 'boom' period between 1986 and 1989 the profitability of large companies rose markedly faster than for small companies.

It is, however, appropriate to point to the limitations of these official figures. The first is that the concept of profitability in small firms is likely to differ sharply from that in a large firm. Keasey and Watson (1993) and Watson (1990) show the measures of profitability in Table 7.1 are *after* directors' remuneration, which constitutes 65 per cent of gross profit margins. The lack of strict comparability occurs because in small firms profitability is more 'discretionary', and includes a larger element of 'return' on owners' equity than is the case for large firms. In short, there is likely to be greater variety in the accounting procedures employed by small firms than by large.

Financial awareness amongst small business owners

The variety of accounting procedures employed in small firms emerges clearly from the work by Nayak and Greenfield (1994). They show that in businesses with less than ten employees, formal monitoring of profits takes place in only one-third of businesses.

Nayak and Greenfield examined 200 micro-businesses in the West Midlands and were struck by the lack of financial awareness of those operating these firms. Only 34 per cent of firms used any form of budgeting, with the most frequent strategy being to keep information in the head of the proprietor.

Several other important findings emerged from this study:

- The first was that those firms which professed to be performing at least satisfactorily were those which maintained the best records – i.e. those most likely to know their profitability and to engage in regular budgeting.
- The second was that the single-proprietor business was the least likely to hold information on paper or in the computer; those businesses which had more than one proprietor were more likely to keep better records.
- Thirdly, it emerged that, perhaps surprisingly, it was manufacturers who were less likely to be able to estimate profitability figures than those in the service industries.
- Finally, 16 per cent of firms with debtors kept *no* debtor records.

The overall impression which emerges is that, whilst the majority of small business owners do maintain adequate record-keeping, there still remains a significant minority who profess to no formality in this area. It cannot be surprising, therefore, to find the high rates of business failure amongst such tiny firms, and an unwillingness on the part of the financial institutions to extend them credit.

Small firms and their banks

Total lending by banks to businesses with a turnover of less than £1m. was approximately £43.6 billion in November 1992. This constituted a 3 per cent fall from that of nine months previously (Bank of England 1993). At that time the total number of small business accounts was estimated to be 4.1 million, this figure having fallen 7 per cent compared with nine months previously. It was suggested by Bannock and Doran (1991) that, although there was a slight fall in bank lending to smaller firms (those with less than £1m. turnover) in the 1992/93 period, this was a very modest reversal of the huge growth which took place in bank lending to this sector from the mid-1980s onwards. They suggest (p. 51) that bank lending to small firms in 1992 was perhaps twice that (in real terms) of the mid-1980s.

Bannock and Doran also remark that, certainly since the Bolton Committee (1971) report, there has been a fairly continuous growth in the relative importance of term loans to small businesses, and conversely a lower dependence upon overdrafts. Bannock and Doran point out that, in May 1991, 30 per cent of National Westminster Bank's total lending to small firms was in the form of term loans. At the time of the Bolton Committee, however, such term loans were almost unheard of.

These findings are confirmed in surveys by Binks, Ennew and Reed (1992), Cowling, Samuels and Sugden (1991) and by Cambridge Small Business Research Centre (1992). Binks *et al.* found that 37 per cent of respondents had fixed-term loans whereas, in the Cowling *et al.* survey, 31 per cent of those seeking a loan of any description requested a fixed-term loan. Cambridge SBRC (1992) shows that, for manufacturing and business services firms, there has been a marked increase since 1971 in the proportion seeking external finance, and markedly fewer failing to find finance at all. It also shows that these types of businesses in the 1990s are much more dependent upon term loans than was the case twenty years ago.

The margins charged by the banks on base rate-related lending are shown in Table 7.2, which is derived from the Bank of England (1993). It tabulates the aggregate response to questions asked of the major UK clearing banks in 1992. For businesses with a turnover of less than £1m., about 80 per cent pay a margin above base rate of 4 per cent or less. For somewhat larger small firms, with a turnover of between £1. and £10m., 96 per cent pay a margin over base of 4 per cent or less. This demonstrates clearly that, even within the small firm sector, it is the larger firms which are more likely to obtain lower rates of interest than the very smallest firms. It suggests that, at least across

Table 7.2 Bank lending to smaller businesses

	Turnover <£1m.		*Turnover £1–10m.*	
	June 1991	*Nov 1992*	*June 1991*	*Nov 1992*
Margin bands				
0–2 per cent	21	20	56	35
2–4 per cent	59	61	40	61
4–6 per cent	16	16	3	3
6–8 per cent	4	3	1	1
>8 per cent	–	–	–	–

Source: Bank of England (1993)

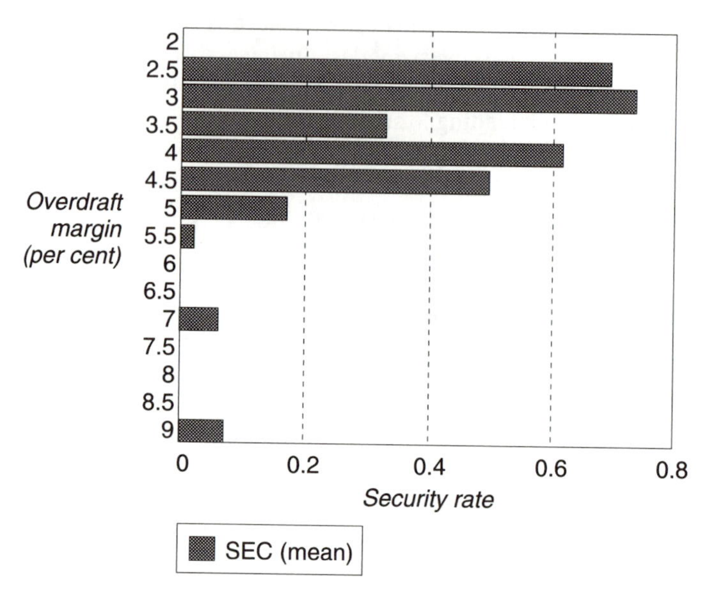

Figure 7.1 Start-up overdraft security rates, 1988
Source: Cressy (1992)

broad risk classes, banks do vary their interest rates in response to perceived higher risk.

Cressy (1992), in his analysis of start-up businesses, shows there is a strong relationship between the margins over base which are charged by banks to new businesses, and the extent to which security is provided. Whilst Cressy's security data are binary, and so do not reveal the value of security pledged, from Figure 7.1 it can be seen that approximately 70 per cent of start-up businesses charged an overdraft margin of 3 per cent or less provided security, compared with less than 10 per cent of the businesses charged an overdraft margin in excess of 5 per cent. This again suggests that interest rates are higher for high-risk projects.

Security ratios – defined as the value of the security divided by the value of the loan – have also been examined in empirical work. Binks, Ennew and Reed point to the problems which arise in calculating security ratios where property is involved. To overcome these problems in their most recent (1992) survey, property values were estimated, net of outstanding mortgage. Binks *et al.* show the role of security to overdrafts is approximately 4.4, whereas that on term loans is between 2.7 and 3.0. These ratios appear to be significantly higher than obtained by comparable surveys in the United States (Dennis *et al.* 1988).

In summary, it is clear that bank lending to small firms rose particularly sharply in the 1980s. Much of that lending was short-term and the interest rate was used by banks to reflect perceived high-risk projects.

The growth of venture capital

Venture capital has been defined by Shilson (1984) as 'A way in which investors support entrepreneurial talent with finance and business skills to exploit market opportunities and thus to obtain long term capital gain.' Using this definition, Dixon (1991) identifies three distinguishing features of venture capital as:

- the provision of capital for entrepreneurs;
- the provision of business skills;
- the obtaining of long-term capital from the investment, rather than income from dividends.

The 1980s saw a major increase in the size and scale of the UK venture capital industry. To some extent this is reflected in Table 7.3, which shows the actual investments made in UK-based companies by the UK venture capital industry. Unfortunately, it is not possible to obtain adequate time series data on this topic, because it was only from 1987 onwards that the United Kingdom's major venture capital organisation – 3i – was included in the data. Nevertheless, it is clear from the table that actual investment in UK-based companies by the UK-based venture capital industry rose from £66m. in 1981 to £480m. in 1986. Once 3i are included in the data from 1987, it is also clear that investment rises significantly, to reach £1,420m. in 1989, but then falls away to £989m. in the recessionary conditions of 1991. It should be noted that the figures quoted exclude investments made by UK venture capital companies overseas. The total sums invested by UK venture capital firms,

Table 7.3 Venture capital investments in the United Kingdom

	1981	*1982*	*1983*	*1984*	*1985*	*1986*	*1987*	*1988*	*1989*	*1990*	*1991*
Actual investment in UK-based companies (£m.)	66	110	166	228	279	480	934	1,298	1,420	1,106	989
Actual investment in start-ups (£m.)				25	32	68	75	70	86	76	35
Other early stage (£m.)				13	18	28	45	60	129	52	23
Per cent of amount invested in early stage				17	18	20	13	10	15	12	6

Sources: 1981–90 data: Bannock and Doran (1991: Table 4.3); 1991 data: British Venture Capital Association, 'Report on Investment Activity', p. 9
Note: 3i data included only for 1987 onwards.

including their overseas operations, was £1,153m. in 1991 – i.e. 14 per cent of their investments in that year were overseas.

It would, however, be incorrect to assume that the bulk of these monies was in the form of investments in smaller businesses. Table 7.3 makes it clear that investments in start-ups and other early stage developments have never exceeded more than one-fifth of the total actual investments.[3]

It can also be seen from Table 7.3 that, in the period prior to the inclusion of 3i in the data, the proportion of investments made in early stage businesses was rather higher than after 1986. Furthermore, it is apparent that particularly in 1991 not only was there a substantial fall in actual investments made, but there was an even more rapid fall in the importance of early stage investments. In that year only 6 per cent of venture capital investments, by value, were in early stage businesses. Although there are clear discontinuities in the data, it does suggest that, since 1986, non-3i venture capitalists have become even more reluctant to invest in small firms than was the case in the early 1980s.

The bulk of the investment funds from the UK venture capital sector is devoted to management buy-outs or buy-ins. A management buy-out is defined as where funds are provided to enable the current operating management and investors to acquire an existing product line or business, whereas a management buy-in is defined to be where a manager or group of managers from outside the company is able to buy that business.[4]

In 1991, 55 per cent of the total sum invested by UK venture capitalists was in management buy-outs or buy-ins. The comparable percentage for 1990 was 53 per cent; that for 1989 was 61 per cent. Hence the bulk of funds made available by the formal venture capital industry in the United Kingdom do not focus upon the smaller firm sector. This is illustrated in Table 7.4, which shows investments made by the industry between 1987 and 1990, according to the size of those investments. In all years, more than half of the total

Table 7.4 UK venture capital: investment by size range, 1987–90

Size range (£'000)	*1987 per cent*	*1988 per cent*	*1989 per cent*	*1990 per cent*
0–99	1.0	1.0	<1.0	<1.0
100–199	2.0	1.0	<1.0	1.0
200–499	13.0	6.0	2.0	5.0
500–999	17.0	10.0	5.0	8.0
1,000–1,999	12.0	14.0	6.0	12.0
2,000 +	55.0	68.0	87.0	74.0
Total	100.0	100.0	100.0	100.0

Source: Bannock and Doran (1991)
Notes: Data from 3i Ventures are included for the years 1983 to 1989. 3i regions are excluded. The 1989 size range data are thought to contain errors.

amount invested was in sums exceeding £2m., and only 2 or 3 per cent of amounts invested were in sums of less than £200,000.

The formal venture capital industry, primarily because of the large sums which it chooses to invest in a single business, is therefore virtually irrelevant to the vast bulk of small and medium enterprises in the United Kingdom. This is reflected in the BVCA (1991) data which show that, for the United Kingdom as a whole, the number of venture-backed companies in 1991 was 7 per 10,000 registered for VAT. The Cambridge Small Business Research Centre (1992) survey primarily of small limited companies in the manufacturing and business service sectors found a much higher proportion of firms seeking new finance in the previous three years (6.5 per 100) had used venture capital.

Despite its infrequent use, it would be unwise to assume that the impact of venture capital has necessarily been small. As the current author has argued elsewhere (Storey 1993), the major economic contribution of the small firm sector is made by a tiny proportion of rapidly growing businesses. It is these businesses which are much more likely to be attractive to venture capitalists since, in principle, they offer the prospect of capital gains, and are more likely to be seeking external equity involvement as a way of financing growth. In this sense the formal venture capital industry can play an important role in maximising the economic contribution of the SME sector. This is also illustrated in the Cambridge SBRC study, which shows that the most likely users of venture capital are medium-sized but fast-growth businesses (Cosh and Hughes 1994).

It is therefore appropriate to reflect upon the expected changes and challenges which face the formal venture capital sector. Murray (1993), in his review of the sector, concludes that during the 1980s it experienced the type of massive growth often characteristic of a new industry. Furthermore, as Bannock and Doran (1991) point out, the growth of venture capital in the United Kingdom meant that by the early 1990s it was, relative to GDP, at least as large as that for the United States,[5] and significantly larger than for all other European countries. By the early 1990s, the venture capital industry was seen by Murray as experiencing the characteristics of the onset of maturity. He points to a slowing of the rate of industry growth – almost certainly accelerated by world-wide recessionary conditions. He shows the industry grew markedly faster in the early to mid-1980s than the UK economy as a whole, but then contracted much faster during the recessionary conditions of 1989-92. Other indications of greater maturity are greater market concentration and an intensification by leading firms in the industry in a search for ways to differentiate the product which they provided.

Probably the clearest illustration of this is the increasingly clear distinction between 'hands-on' and 'hands-off' funds. This is most easily illustrated by reference to the definition of venture capital used by Dixon at the start of this section. The 'hands-on' investor would place considerably more emphasis upon the provision of business skills – the second item – than the 'hands-off' investor. The 'hands-off' investor assumes that the most knowledgeable person able to run the business is the existing management team, and that if the firm's performance falls below expectations, these individuals have to be replaced. The view of the 'hands-on' investor is that venture capitalists can make a significant contribution in strategic areas to the performance of the business. For this reason they expect to be more heavily involved in strategic decision-making than the 'hands-off' investor.

Despite these clear distinctions, research by Fredriksen, Olofsson and Wahlbin (1990) on the performance of 'hands-on' and 'hands-off' investors failed to identify any clear difference in the performance of investee companies. A similar result is obtained by MacMillan, Kulow and Choylian (1989) for the United States.

Murray, in his discussions particularly with smaller UK venture capitalists, finds many believe that greater 'hands-on' involvement with their clients will lead to faster growth and to significant capital appreciation for the venture capitalist. The extent to which the venture capitalist can be 'adding value' to investee businesses appears to be leading to product differentiation within the industry. Murray sees this as an illustration of increasing industry maturity in a market characterised by increasingly well-informed 'customers' for venture capital and increasing competition between suppliers.

We now turn away from the formal to the informal venture capital sector. The latter can be considered to be direct private external equity, compared with the formal sector discussed above which primarily is established financial institutions taking an equity share in a business.

The informal venture capital sector has been investigated most intensively in the United States. Gaston (1989) and Wetzel (1987) estimated that total equity investment from informal sources was between two and five times greater than that from the formal venture capital industry.

The authoritative research on this subject in the United Kingdom has been conducted by Richard Harrison and Colin Mason (1992, 1993). They estimated the United Kingdom's informal risk capital pool to be in the range of £2–4bn, which marginally exceeds the amount invested by the formal venture capital sector in the United Kingdom during the 1980s. However, as we have pointed out above, at least 50 per cent of the latter investment is in the form of financing management buy-outs and buy-ins. If Harrison and Mason are correct, then the amount invested by the informal venture capital sector (sometimes called 'business angels') is probably rather higher than that which has been invested in smaller firms by the formal industry. For example, Bannock and Doran estimated that the formal venture capital industry has invested about £1.25bn in small firms, which suggests that the informal market is one and a half to three times larger (Harrison and Mason 1993).

One central difference between the formal and the informal venture capital sector is in the typical sums invested. As noted in Table 7.4, less that 3 per cent of the sums invested by the formal sector are less than £200,000 per head. However, Mason, Harrison and Chaloner (1991) in their study of the UK informal investment sector found the median amount invested per investor during the previous three years in terms of both loans and equity to be in the range of £22–100,000. The median amount invested per firm was between £10–30,000.

The central value of the Mason and Harrison research has been in identifying the characteristics of business angels:

- These individuals invest relatively infrequently, with most making not more than one investment per year.
- They prefer early stage ventures which are located close to where they live and work.
- In most cases the 'angels' have been in business before as an owner.
- In a substantial number of instances they have sold their former business and seek to reinvest a proportion of their capital in a small portfolio of businesses.

Nevertheless, these broad patterns serve to mask the considerable diversity of the group.

From the viewpoint of the investee business, Harrison and Mason (1992) find venture capitalists and informal investors make contributions to a broadly similar range of functions, with financial issues, and acting as advisers, being the most important. However, business angels seem to have different investment 'motives' from formal venture capitalists. They appear to place considerable importance upon non-financial rewards – notably the ability to play an active role in the entrepreneurial process. Perhaps the most surprising result derived by Mason and Harrison, however, is that it is the informal investors who are most likely, according to the investee companies, to make *no* contribution whatever to the management of the business. 'Angels' make their most significant helpful contribution in serving as a sounding board to the management team. Where there are differences between formal and informal investors, and these are only marginal, it is the venture capitalists who appear to focus heavily upon monitoring and control functions, whereas informal investors appear rather more involved with market development issues.

The role of the public sector

The 1980s saw a considerable growth in the number of public sector initiatives which were designed to overcome perceived problems in the financing of small businesses. For the purposes of this section these will be broadly subdivided between initiatives taken by central government and those taken by local government.

The three topics to be covered in the review of the role of central

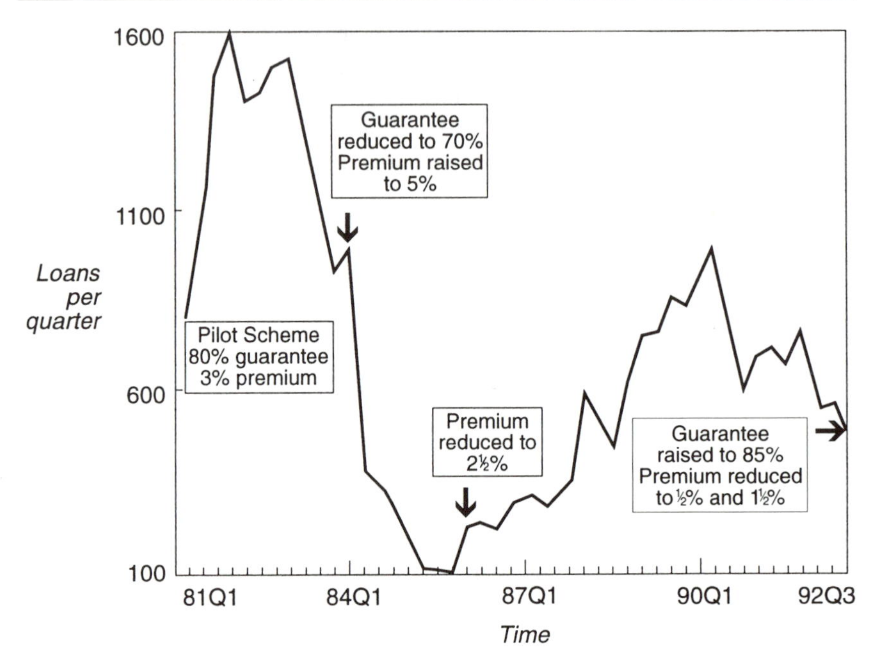

Figure 7.2 The Loan Guarantee Scheme

government in the financing of small businesses are: the Loan Guarantee Scheme, the Business Expansion Scheme and the taxation environment. This is certainly not to imply that these are the only areas where central government policy has impacted upon the establishment or viability of small firms. Other public initiatives, such as the Enterprise Allowance Scheme and the provision of subsidised consultancy, are discussed in Chapter 8, on the grounds that they are not primarily financing initiatives, even though they do have implications for the financing of small businesses and do incur public costs.

The Loan Guarantee Scheme (LGS) was introduced on a pilot basis in June 1981 to overcome a perceived gap in the availability of loan finance for smaller firms. This followed the Wilson Committee (1979) recommendations, even though a National Economic Development Office sub-committee 'were unable to advise the committee on the available evidence of whether there is a clear need for a Loan Guarantee Scheme' (National Audit Office 1988). Under the Loan Guarantee Scheme the government provides a guarantee to the banks on specified loans to potentially viable small firms which would not otherwise receive debt finance on commercial terms, primarily for lack of adequate assets to use as security (National Economic

Research Associates 1990). In return for this access to finance, firms pay an interest-rate premium on loans provided. The guarantee to the bank is only made for a proportion of the loan, and not for the loan in full. Use of these schemes was restricted to those either without personal assets which could be pledged as collateral, or where the personal assets were being used to cover other forms of financing.

Figure 7.2 shows that the terms and conditions of the Loan Guarantee Scheme have been varied quite substantially since it began, and that this has had a major effect upon use of the scheme. Even so, in the peak years of 1982/83, when there were approximately 6,000 LGS loans, this constituted only a tiny proportion of all bank loans to small businesses. Taking the most conservative assumptions, there are at least one million small business accounts which are borrowing from the bank at any one time. Hence, at its peak, the Loan Guarantee Scheme was relevant to perhaps 0.6 per cent of small firms.

Figure 7.2 shows the take-up of LGS has varied considerably, with sharp falls being observed when the proportion of the loan guaranteed fell from 80 per cent to 70 per cent, early in 1985. At the same time the interest rate premium was raised from 3 per cent to 5 per cent, and this seems to have had the effect, in the long term, of cutting the take-up of LGS by virtually a factor of ten.

The outcome suggests that, whilst in 1985 the guarantee was reduced and the premium was raised, it was the former which had the greater impact upon take-up. This is because when the premium was reduced to 2½ per cent early in 1986, the long-term effect was only to raise take-up by a factor of between three and four. Econometric analysis of these changes by Cowling (1993) suggests that the rise in the premium from 3 per cent to 5 per cent, and the reduction in the guarantee from 80 per cent to 70 per cent, had similar effects in reducing take-up rate. To some extent these were offset by increases in self-employment which took place during the 1980s.

In 1993 the LGS was significantly modified, with the premium on fixed rate loans being reduced to only 0.5 per cent and that on variable rate loans being charged at 1.5 per cent. The proportion of the loan guaranteed was allowed to rise from 70 per cent to 85 per cent. Following these changes it is to be expected that take-up of the LGS will rise sharply.

A thorough assessment of the impact of the Loan Guarantee Scheme was conducted by National Economic Research Associates (1990), after interim and partial reviews had been made earlier by Robson Rhodes (1984). NERA's conclusion was that the Loan Guarantee Scheme may have been effective in the early 1980s in providing a demonstration to the clearing banks that there were opportunities for profitable lending in the small business sector. However, by the end of the 1980s, when the clearing banks had markedly increased their lending to smaller firms, NERA appeared to have become sceptical about the impact of the scheme on the economy as a whole. Their recommendations focused upon lowering the default rate, on the grounds that influencing the 'additionality' of the scheme would be difficult.

As noted in the above paragraph, the Government's response in 1993 was to do precisely the opposite. It has encouraged the take-up of LGS by lowering the premium and increasing the guarantee, even though the effect of these changes will certainly lead to a sharp increase in the percentages of loans which fail and incur a public sector cost. This is clear from National Audit Office (1988) data which show that, when take-up of LGS was at its lowest in 1984, failure rates on loans were approximately 5 per cent, compared with an average of 10–12 per cent during the earlier and later periods.

Overall, the assessment of the Loan Guarantee Scheme must be that, given the current level of banking involvement with small businesses, its impact on the small business sector as a whole is minimal. The changes implemented in 1993 suggest that utilisation of LGS will increase sharply, that failure rates of the guaranteed businesses will lead to an escalation of public sector costs because of its low 'additionality', but that the net effect on economic activity makes it difficult to justify the costs involved.

In many respects the variations in the Business Expansion Scheme have an even more chequered history. The Business Expansion Scheme (BES) was introduced in 1983 as a follow-up to the Business Start-up Scheme (BSU). The purpose of BES was to provide tax relief to individuals investing in qualifying unquoted companies with which they were not connected. Tax relief was granted at the highest marginal rate, so providing an incentive to high-income earners to make such investments. It was felt that these investments were likely to be of the relatively small sums of equity which we have observed are characteristic of business angels – generally in the region of £10–50,000. The scheme was intended to provide an incentive for individuals who wished to invest, and hence make it easier for smaller companies to obtain external equity participation.

In 1992 it was announced that BES was to be abolished at the end of 1993, following a decade in which a laudable idea had been transformed into a tax avoidance vehicle for the wealthy. As the Chancellor of the Exchequer said at the time:

> When it was introduced in 1983 the venture capital industry was in its infancy, and there was a concern that the investment needs of small firms were not well understood and provided for.... Britain now has a venture capital industry the equal of anywhere in the world, outside the United States and nowadays only a small part of the BES goes to small businesses.
>
> (November Budget Speech, 1991)

In the early 1980s, however, BES had seemed to be serving the purposes for which it was introduced. The review by Peat Marwick (1986) examined a sample of companies in receipt of BES and then attempted to estimate the cost in terms of tax relief of the BES finance received. It also attempted to estimate the impact on employment of investee businesses by speculating about what the employment levels in these firms would have been in the absence of equity through BES. Their results suggested that the scheme was effective in terms of generating additional jobs, at a cost to the Exchequer of between £8,000 and £13,000.

Yet, by the mid to late 1980s, the scheme had become the subject of powerful criticism from a range of external observers. It was noted that significant tranches of investment were in non-productive areas, such as the storing of fine wines, art treasures, or racehorses. Although these loopholes were subsequently closed, Mason and Harrison (1991) note that the average size of investment under BES rose sharply from £147,000 in 1983–4 to £245,000 in 1987–8. They note that over the 1983–8 period, only 9.5 per cent of BES funding was in amounts of £50,000 or less. The specific purpose of BES was to increase the supply of small amounts of equity capital, primarily to productive businesses. It clearly failed to achieve this objective at a satisfactory cost to the taxpayer.

But it was the changes introduced in the Finance Act of 1988 which ultimately led to the collapse in credibility of BES, and subsequently to its abolition. For reasons which are unclear, the 1988 Finance Act allowed residential property for letting under assured tenancy schemes to be included within BES. This led, within a year, to assured tenancies being in receipt of nearly 90 per cent of the moneys raised in BES, even though this 'unproductive' sector was never the original target for BES funds.

As Mason (1993) pointed out, BES did have three 'symbolic' benefits: it encouraged financial institutions to take an interest, for almost for the first time, in small firms. It also encouraged private investment in small firms, and it may have educated some small business owners in the benefits of external equity.

The alternative view of the Business Expansion Scheme illustrates that, however worthwhile it may appear to be, any scheme which offers tax relief to high-rate taxpayers incurs a high risk of having its original objectives distorted in order to yield the maximum tax avoidance potential at the lowest possible risk.

Given this history, and particularly the comments made by (a different) Chancellor of the Exchequer in 1992, it seems barely credible that in 1993 the scheme was effectively reintroduced. Called the Enterprise Investment Scheme (EIS), it was virtually identical to BES, except in two respects: the rented housing sector was specifically excluded, and investors were able to exercise a managerial function in those businesses where they owned shares.

The only possible explanation for such a turnaround in policy after one year has to be the effective influence of the small business lobby organisations. Their role is discussed in Chapter 8.

Looking now more widely at the question of small business taxation, we draw upon the helpful review by Chittenden (1991), who argues that the Bolton Committee (1971) made two key recommendations in the taxation field. The first was that the overall burden of taxation be reduced, and the second was that the focus of taxation be moved away from direct tax towards indirect tax. Chittenden's review of changes over the last twenty years indicates that, whilst there has been a move towards the relatively greater importance of indirect taxes, there has been no change in the overall tax burden.

In the 1970s it was argued that high rates of income tax were a powerful disincentive to effort, particularly on the part of small business owners. High rates of taxation were thought to lead to a reluctance on the part of the entrepreneur to work additional hours and obtain additional income. This was thought to be particularly important where the marginal rates of taxation were high for any additional hours worked. Such logic was a driving force underlying the priorities which a Conservative administration gave to lowering both the standard rate of income tax and also the highest rates of tax.

The work of Rees and Shah (1993), however, casts doubt upon the impact which these taxation changes had upon the hours worked by the self-employed. They estimate a model which examines the hours worked by the self-employed and other groups, based primarily upon wage rates and human capital characteristics such as age, education, marital status, number of children, etc. They show that the self-employed, when these personal characteristics were taken into account, worked less hours in the 1980s than they did in the 1970s. Their results are not compatible with the view that lowering the rates of personal taxation provides an incentive to individuals to work harder. They support the views of Curran (1986), who suggested that small business owners are more powerfully motivated by achieving a given level of income and seeking other sources of satisfaction from owning a business – most notably a sense of independence. The only 'indirect' impact of tax changes could be that more people are attracted to become entrepreneurs *because* they believe that those in self-employment work *less* hard.

Bannock and Peacock (1989) argue that the prime (undesirable) influence of the UK taxation regime, in so far as it influences small firms, is that it provides greater incentives to business owners to invest in pensions, domestic property and other schemes than to invest in their own businesses. As noted earlier, Watson (1990) finds that tax-minimisation behaviour by small business owners is a powerful explanation of personal remuneration policy. As Storey *et al.* (1987) show, reinvestment in small companies is strongly correlated with subsequent (employment) growth, suggesting that tax incentives to remove moneys out of smaller firms are highly counter-productive.

Overall, the evidence suggests that attempting to use the taxation system to encourage 'desirable' behaviour from the small business sector in the United

Kingdom has not been successful. The evidence from BES and from income tax changes is not encouraging. It is for this reason that current proposals to provide tax incentives to encourage individuals to invest more heavily in their own businesses, whilst a highly desirable objective, do not have the support of this author.

Finally, in our review of public sector financial developments we note that the 1980s also saw the growth of local and regional sources of equity capital, provided initially by public sector institutions. Several Labour-controlled local authorities, together with the Development Agencies in Scotland and Wales, saw the establishment of Enterprise Boards as a way to improve their local economies. Hence London, West Midlands, West Yorkshire, Lancashire and Merseyside all established Boards, whose function was primarily to make equity investments in local businesses.

The abolition of the Metropolitan councils in 1984 meant that the Enterprise Boards were no longer able to obtain access to capital from the local authorities. Even so, the Boards survived and continued to make a modest contribution to the sources of equity capital in their areas. By the early 1990s the total invested by the Boards was only about 1 per cent of that of the UK venture capital industry, although they were somewhat more significant as a supplier of small sums of capital of less than £100,000 (Mason and Harrison 1991).

Taken as a whole, public sector financial intervention to support small firms cannot be viewed as successful. The use of the taxation system to achieve 'desirable' objectives demonstrates that the effects have either been counter-productive, or have been used as tax avoidance vehicles. The only scheme which did serve a clearly useful function was the Loan Guarantee Scheme in the early 1980s; once its 'demonstration effect' had been exercised, however, it became an anachronism.

IS THERE COMPETITION IN THE PROVISION OF LOAN CAPITAL?

A number of criticisms have been made by small businesses and their pressure groups against the clearing banks in the United Kingdom. This section asks whether these criticisms reflect a fundamental lack of competition in the provision of funds for smaller firms.

Table 7.5 sets out six main areas in which the UK banks have been criticised by smaller firms. On the left-hand side of the table is a specification of the criticism, and on the right-hand side is the author's own judgement of the validity of that criticism.

During the late 1980s and early 1990s there have been a number of surveys of small businesses, asking about their attitudes to, and involvement with, their banks (Binks, Ennew and Reid 1990, 1992, Cowling *et al.* 1991). For example, Cowling *et al.* asked about firms' 'most significant concern with

Table 7.5 Criticisms of banks by small firms

Criticisms	*Comments*
1 Bank charges:	
• too high;	Difficult to assess.
• the customer doesn't get itemised charges;	In 1992/93 most banks introduced itemised charges;
• frequently calculated incorrectly;	Private computer programs now available to check charges.
2 Base rate reductions are not passed on immediately to customer;	Not a justified criticism.
3 Banks only lend against collateral;	Not wholly correct. 80 per cent of start-up loans are not collateralised.
4 Banks are less willing to lend to high-risk/high-return borrowers;	Broadly correct.
5 Banks close down a business 'too early' if it gets into difficulties;	Not proven.
6 Banks have an 'attitude' problem and don't understand small firms;	Less true than in the past. Staff training and reorganisation have led to improvements.

existing banking practices'. Of the items identified, the single most frequently specified concern related to bank charges. Even so, from survey evidence it is often difficult to distinguish the element within bank charges which is the prime source of complaint. The impression from the survey by Binks *et al.* is that the charges are deemed to be too high, with only 26 per cent of respondents seeing bank charges as providing good value for money. We find it difficult to assess the validity of this criticism, except in the overall context of the extent to which the small business sector is an area in which banks compete. Judgement will therefore have to be suspended until the end of this section.

The second criticism associated with bank charges is that, until recently, the small business customer did not even receive an itemised statement of bank charges. The chairman of the House of Commons Treasury and Civil Service Committee raised this point with the chairman of Barclays Bank, Sir John Quinton on 17 July 1991.

> Chairman: 'There is no other business which deducts the money without sending you the bill.'
>
> Sir John: 'There is no other business which has the capability to do it. The fact is that we hold the money.'
>
> (House of Commons Treasury and Civil Service Committee 1991)

This particular quote received extensive coverage in the financial press at the time, since it was argued to reflect the reluctance of banks to enter into the type of market relationship with their customers that was characteristic of firms elsewhere in the economy. Indeed, it was seen by some as encapsulating the 'attitude problem' which is referred to in item 6 of the table. Nevertheless, shortly after this statement the banks recognised they would make changes in this area and, in 1992, all the major clearing banks issued customer charters, one component of which was a recognition that itemised charging was necessary.

The third component of the first criticism of bank charges is that in a number of instances they have been incorrectly assessed. As a response to this, private sector consultants have developed computer packages which now enable the small business easily to check whether bank charges imposed are correct or not.

The second criticism of banks by small firms is that, when base rates fall, these reductions in interest rates are not passed on immediately to small firm customers. Despite the publicity given to this during the summer of 1991, the Bank of England (1993) firmly rebutted any suggestion that base rates are not passed on to customers within one or two days. It points out that banks' computer systems mean that changes are inputted centrally, and the banks cannot pick and choose which of their customers should receive the change.

The third criticism levelled at the banks is either that they lend only against collateral, or that the amount of collateral required to cover a loan is excessive. Dealing with the first of these criticisms, it is clear from Cressy (1992) that, so far as start-ups are concerned, most are not collateralised. Cressy shows that approximately 80 per cent of those borrowing from National Westminster Bank at start-up are not required to provide collateral, and there is no reason to believe that this rate differs markedly for other banks. A more complex argument is whether or not the ratio of collateral provided, to loan, is excessive. This is more difficult to assess since, as noted earlier in the chapter (p. 209), the valuation of the security varies between the bank and the small business customer. Nevertheless, it is clear from Binks *et al.* that, based on customer estimates, security ratios on overdrafts can be in excess of 4:1, and that ratios on fixed-term loans are virtually 3:1. This appears to be significantly higher than required by banks in the United States.

The fourth criticism of banks is that they are less willing to lend to high-risk/high-return borrowers, than to low-risk/low-return borrowers. This could be a quite serious criticism since, if the high-risk small firms turn out to be successful, they make a major contribution to the economy. Storey, Watson and Wynarczyk (1989), in their study of fast growth businesses in Northern England, found that it was this type of business which was most likely to have experienced problems with their banks, whereas the slower-growing firms were more likely to have had a satisfactory relationship.

However, as was pointed out earlier (pp. 211–12), given the role of supplying primarily loan capital which banks play in the United Kingdom, neither criticism 3 nor criticism 4 is unexpected. Both derive directly from the assumption of the nature of the contract which the bank has with the small business customer. It will be recalled that the bank gains when a successful project leads to the interest and the principal being repaid. It does not gain directly from an increase in the valuation of the firm; the prime gainer from increased valuation is the business owner, via his/her ownership of equity. Hence it is entirely appropriate for the owner to bear the business risk associated with these upside gains.

The fifth criticism of the banks is that, particularly during recessionary times, they seek to close a business and obtain their security, rather than allowing the business to continue to trade and so giving it a chance to rescue itself. The evidence on this tends to be rather anecdotal and highly subjective. Nevertheless, it is quite understandable, given the nature of its contract with the firm, for the bank to be primarily concerned with protecting its security. Since the bank gains relatively little from any improvement in the firm's overall position, it is hardly surprising that it seeks to protect its sources of income. Of course, if the business is viable, then it is most clearly not in the interests of the bank for the business to be closed down.

It can be seen that criticisms 3, 4 and 5 are in some senses inevitable, given the nature of the contractual relationship between the small firm and its bank. It would be much more surprising if such criticisms were made if the bank also participated in the upside gains of the business – i.e. if it were an equity shareholder. But, given that most business owners do not wish to share equity with the bank, and that banks in most instances do not wish to be equity shareholders, criticisms 3, 4 and 5 are the likely outcome of the contractual arrangement into which the parties enter.

Finally, Table 7.5 shows a sixth criticism of banks made by small businesses relates to their 'attitude', and lack of understanding. We have already observed that the powerful position of 'holding the money', which the bank has in relation to small businesses, causes some resentment. It is also the case that the uncertain position of the small business owner contrasts starkly with the perceived security of the bank employee. The banks, however, have now become aware of this issue and have begun to implement changes. Small business advisers have been appointed in many bank branches to improve communications with the small firm sector, extensive programmes of staff training to provide a better understanding of small firms have been implemented, bank managers have been seconded to voluntary organisations such as Business in the Community in order to increase their understanding of the position of small business customers, and loan officers themselves are now much more likely to be visiting clients in their own premises than was the case in the past.

Overall, of the six criticisms identified in Table 7.5, it is criticism 4 on high-risk/high-return borrowers which has the greatest implications for the economy, whilst criticisms 3 and 5 stem directly from the nature of the contractual relationship between bank and small firm.

The central question is whether these criticisms can be overcome by a combination of a greater willingness on the part of the banks to obtain an equity shareholding in the businesses and hence participate in the upside gains, together with a greater willingness of the firms themselves to share ownership with external financial institutions. Alternatively, do these problems stem from an absence of competition amongst the financial institutions in the small business finance market?

Table 7.6 attempts very briefly to synthesise the five most frequently heard arguments relating to the extent to which there is competition in the small firm finance market-place. On the left-hand side it presents five arguments which suggest that the market is competitive, while the right-hand side presents five arguments which suggest the market is uncompetitive. We shall review each of these groups of arguments in turn.

The market for small business loan finance is extremely highly concentrated. Binks, Ennew and Reed (1992) showed that 82 per cent of the small firms in their survey bank with either National Westminster, Barclays, Midland or Lloyds. The two largest – National Westminster and Barclays – each have approximately 25 per cent of the market-place. These institutions therefore have considerable 'market power', and there is a clear *a priori* case for suggesting that there may be a lack of competition in the market-place. However, successive Treasury Committees and Bank of England reports have produced no evidence to suggest collusion between the banks occurs with a view to increasing the profitability of the market, or to exclude new entrants.

A second indicator of lack of competition in the market-place might be if banks were generating excessively high profits in this area. A number of assertions have been made by external observers, suggesting that the market is likely to be lucrative, but the banks do not publish information on their profitability in the various market-places in which they operate. In part, this is because of the problems the banks themselves have of identifying the costs associated with the small business market in a branch, compared with the

Table 7.6 Is the market for small business loan finance competitive?

	Yes	*No*
1	No evidence of collusion.	80 per cent market share held by four banks.
2	Profitability of market is not known, but major losses in recession.	Profitability of market not known, but presumed to be high.
3	High product differentiation.	No 'single price'.
4	Every bank branch is a competitor.	Customers have no choice.
5	Extensive local information through Advice Agencies and 'grapevine'.	Firms don't change banks because of lack of information.

costs associated with the personal banking sector or large corporates in the same branch. In short, the allocation of fixed costs throughout the banking network to the separate market-places in which banks operate makes it difficult to assess the profitability to the bank of 'markets' such as small businesses.

On the other hand, during times of recession, banks have been able to identify the extent to which their bad debt provision is attributable to the small business market. For example, during 1992, the chairman of Barclays Bank stated that bad debt provision was running at approximately £1m. per working day – £250m. per year. This clearly contrasted with conditions during the prosperous mid-1980s, but it does point to the need to take macroeconomic conditions into account when making assessments of profitability in the small firm market-place.

A third characteristic of an uncompetitive market-place is the ability of the seller both to differentiate the product on offer and to sell into 'separate' market-places at high prices. It can be argued that this is a characteristic of the small business finance market-place, in the sense that there is no single price at which finance is made available. Interest rates can vary, even for small businesses, according to the Bank of England (1993), from between zero to 8 per cent above base rates, although 61 per cent of firms borrow in the margin of 2–4 per cent above base. The response of the banks to this criticism is to point out that the absence of a single price in fact lies at the heart of the competitive process. They argue that the ability of a bank, and of an individual bank manager, to compete is a reflection of their ability to judge the riskiness of a small business. If the risk is overestimated, then the customer is likely to go elsewhere and the bank will incur the loss of not having repaid to it the interest plus principal of the forgone loan. But to charge too low an interest rate would mean that the bank had insufficient interest income to cover its potential bad debts and to yield it a profit.

It should not be assumed that the interest payment is the only charge which banks impose. The Bank of England (1993) document makes it clear that bank charges vary widely from one bank to another. Table 7.7 shows these charges at the end of 1992, and how they had changed over the previous eighteen months. The Bank of England makes it clear that in recent times 'there seems to have been a more thoroughgoing attitude to implementing charges', so that the small business customer has to be aware not only of the interest rate charged, but all the other associated charges of borrowing money.

Turning back to Table 7.6, the fourth argument is that small business customers, in practice, do not have a choice of bank. This is because the occasion on which firms most want to move banks is when they have been denied credit facilities. Yet this is precisely the time when the business is in most difficulties and will look least attractive to an alternative banker. The banks themselves recognise this, as is illustrated by Sir John Quinton's comments to the Treasury Select Committee. He said:

Table 7.7 Bank charges

	Credit		*Debit fee*		*Management fee p.q.*		*Arrangement fee*		*Returned cheque*		*Night safe p.a.*		*Unauthorised borrowing*		*Next review*
	June	*Dec*	*June*	*Dec*	*June*	*Dec*	*June*	*Dec*	*June*	*Dec*	*June*	*Dec*	*June*	*Dec*	
	1991	*1992*	*1991*	*1992*	*1991*	*1992*	*1991*	*1992*	*1991*	*1992*	*1991*	*1992*	*1991*	*1992*	
BoS	42p	47p	42p	57p		£7.50	1%	1%		£20		£50	15% ob	up to 25%	Dec 1993
Barclays	63p	66p	63p	66p	£5	£6		1.25%	£20	£25		£24–40	15% ob	22%	May 1993
Lloyds	70p	75p	70p	75p	£7.50	£7.50	1%	1%	£25	£25		£40	31.2%	28.8%	1994
Midland	74p	74p	74p	74p	£7.50	£7.50		1.25%	£20	£20		£15–30	36.7%	32%	March 1993
Natwest	64p	66p	64p	66p	£6	£7	1.5%	1.5%	£20	£27.50		£80	37.6%	36.3%	Dec 1993
RBS	*	*	*	*	*	*	*	*		£20		£50	7% ob	25%	March 1993
TSB	63p	67p	48p	53p	£4	£6		up to 1.5%	£15	£20		£144#	26.5%	30%	April 1993
Average		66p		65p		£6.90		1.25%		£22.50		£60			

Key:
* Negotiable
# Includes all lodgement fees
ob over base rate
BoS Bank of Scotland
RBS Royal Bank of Scotland
TSB Trustee Savings Bank

> We find, as a matter of experience, something like half of our bad debts are from customers we have taken on from other banks in the last year or two, so we have issued instructions for a number of years from the centre, and I have no doubt other banks have done the same if they are sensible, saying if you get offered business from another bank look at it hard, once, twice, three times, before you take it. That you may regard as an oligopoly but I do not. I regard it as a matter of assessment of risk. That would apply equally if there were fifty banks or five.
>
> (House of Commons Treasury and Civil Service Committee 1991)

The interesting point of this statement is that it reflects precisely the expected outcomes from theoretical models of asymmetric information discussed earlier in the chapter (pp. 205–6). Nowhere is this better illustrated than in Stiglitz and Weiss (1981),who say almost exactly the same thing:

> Let us assume that banks make higher expected returns on some of their borrowers than on others: they know who their most creditworthy customers are, but competing banks do not. If a bank tries to attract the customers of its competitors by offering a lower interest rate, it will find that its offer is countered by an equally low interest rate when the customer being competed for is a 'good' credit risk, and will not be matched if the borrower is not a profitable customer of the bank. Consequently banks will seldom seek to steal the customers of their competitors, since they will only succeed in attracting the least profitable of those customers.

Customer choice, therefore, is likely to be extremely limited when the business is performing poorly, but it is the case that competition exists both between banks and even within banks. Thus if a business is clearly performing well, but is receiving an inadequate service and/or unduly high charges at a particular branch, it is quite feasible for it to move branches within the same bank. Overall, therefore, it is the case that small business customers do have a choice when their business is performing well, but have only a very limited choice when their business is performing poorly.

Binks *et al.*, in their 1989 survey, report that 78 per cent of respondents had either never changed their principal bank, or had not changed for the previous five years. Binks *et al.* also asked firms which had not changed banks the reason for this. The most frequent response, other than satisfaction with their current bank, was that most of them did not perceive any difference between the banks. This lack of information about the market-place could be interpreted as a reflection of market imperfection. On the other hand, the banks argue that the last decade has seen a considerable increase in information on banking practices. The growth of Enterprise Agencies, Chambers of Commerce, small business pressure groups, etc. has served to make the small business owner more aware of the alternative financial packages available. In their most recent survey, Binks *et al.* find evidence of this amongst their respondents. They also see that banks are starting to make greater efforts to differentiate their product, so that small businesses are now less likely to see the banks as homogeneous. This is particularly important at a local level for smaller firms, where an effective 'grapevine' operates about which branches of banks are likely to be supportive of proposals, and which are not.

Overall, our conclusion is that despite 80 per cent of the market-place being held by four banks, and few new major entrants to the market-place, there are clear indications that competition between the banks does exist. The interest rate charged is likely to range from project to project, the banks vary according to the costs they charge, there is no evidence of collusion between the banks and, when bank rates fall, they are fully passed on quickly to their customers. Probably the most powerful force promoting this competition is the lobby groups, accountants and small business advisers who, quite correctly, see their task as being to make the small business owner aware that the market-place for finance should be no different from those into which small firms sell their own products. Despite the severe losses which the banks experienced in the small business sector in the early 1990s, the banks' success in the market-place will depend upon their ability to make better judgements of risk than their competitors. From a UK banker's perspective, the domestic small business market is more attractive than much overseas lending, where the risks of default are extremely high. It is also more attractive than lending to large organisations, where the bank's margins are extremely thin. For these reasons the small business market is likely to be given even greater priority than in the past. For the banks to make money in this market requires them to be better judges of risk.

GAPS, MARKET FAILURE AND CREDIT RATIONING

The single most consistent theme in discussions of small business finance has been the concept of a 'gap' – defined as an unwillingness on the part of suppliers of finance to supply it on the terms and conditions required by small businesses. Expressed in its most casual form, indications of a 'gap' include the difficulties of obtaining small sums of equity capital, or the difficulties which some businesses have in obtaining bank finance.

It is often difficult to distinguish between the instances where the market for finance is working well – so that the 'good' projects are being accepted and the 'bad' projects are being rejected – and where there is market failure, where either decisions are imperfect and/or insufficient resources are provided to finance the small business sector.

The terminology used can also be extremely confusing. Thus, it is primarily non-economists who use the term 'gap', whereas economists are more likely to use the terms 'market failure' or 'credit rationing'.

Our preference is not to use the word 'gap'. This is because, even when the market is working perfectly, there will be businesses with an unsatisfied demand for finance; in that sense there is always a 'gap'. The 'gap', when the market is working perfectly, reflects either the unwillingness of the business owner to pay the higher price (interest rates) or the rejection of the project on grounds of risk by the financial institution. If the latter's judgement is a good one, then there is no market failure, even though there may still be businesses seeking finance. This type of 'gap' is not relevant to policy makers, and so we choose not to use the word 'gap' at all. Instead, the more specific terms 'market failure' and 'credit rationing' will be used.

The seminal theoretical contribution of Stiglitz and Weiss (1981) was to demonstrate that, even though the market may be in a state of equilibrium, credit could still be rationed. Stiglitz and Weiss define credit rationing in the following way:

> We reserve the term credit rationing for circumstances in which either:
> a) among loan applicants who appear to be identical some receive a loan and others do not, and the rejected applicant would not receive a loan even if they offered to pay a higher interest rate;
> or
> b) there are identifiable groups of individuals in the population who, with a given supply of credit, are unable to obtain loans at any interest rate even though with a larger supply of credit, they would.

The difficulties of operationalising these definitions are illustrated in the important study by Aston Business School (1991) of the financial constraints on growing small firms. They use the following three definitions:

> Supply Side Market Failure is defined as proposals which are turned down for reasons not connected with the viability of the proposal itself e.g. because of the firm's lack of 'a track record'.
>
> Demand Side Market Failure is defined as where firms do not properly make use the financial opportunities available, either through lack of knowledge, poor management or inadequate presentational proposals.
>
> Complete Market Failure is defined as where firms have not been offered *any* finance for reasons which were not to do with the viability of the proposal itself or the business.

Finally, severe market failure appears to be defined to include both complete market failure plus cases where institutions have offered finance, but where this has been rejected by the firms for reasons such as the cost being too high.

National Economic Research Associates (1990), in their evaluation of the Loan Guarantee Scheme, also provide a definition of financial market failure:

> The failure of the financial markets to provide finance to apparently viable

small firms. 'Viability' in this context means that the firms expected private financial benefits, encapsulated in the returns from various possible outcomes, to exceed the cost of capital resources employed in them.

The common thread in all these definitions is that the market is seen to be working imperfectly when two identical business proposals are presented to a financial institution, and one of the proposals is financed and the other is not. Unfortunately, operationalising this definition is a central problem, since it is almost impossible to compare one business proposal with another. Deakins, Hussain and Ram (1992) did attempt to overcome this problem by using the same business proposal to examine the responses of thirty bank managers. They found that the same proposal was rated very differently by the managers, with one-third scoring it at seven or nine out of ten, and one-third scoring it at less than three out of ten. This suggests a lack of uniformity in the way in which proposals are treated by bankers. To some extent this can be 'explained' by different objectives and portfolios sought by the different banks; indeed, some might see it as reflecting the diversity and richness of the market-place. The view of Deakins *et al.*, that there is a strong 'chance' element seems the more reasonable, suggesting an irrationality on the part of bankers which is incompatible with the perfect market.

However, the major empirical studies of the UK small business loan finance market do not suggest the existence of either market failure or credit rationing on a major scale. The Aston study interviewed 1,095 small firms, of which 609 indicated they were proposing to innovate or invest over the next three years. These were defined as 'growing' firms.

Figure 7.3 is taken from the Aston study and it shows the outcomes of discussions with these firms about their sources of finance in the future. Of the 609 firms, the most relevant group are the 217 firms on the left-hand side of the figure, which had already approached an external source for financing their growth. It will be recalled that the Aston authors defined market failure as occurring when a project is turned down for reasons unrelated to the viability of the proposal. These market failure boxes are shaded and, in total, constitute twenty-two cases out of 217, i.e. about 10 per cent.

The second value of Figure 7.3 is that it highlights the fact that a much higher proportion of firms are in receipt of an offer of finance, but choose to reject it. When all instances of where an offer was made, but rejected by the firm are included, then the rate rises to about one case in three. For example, of the 126 cases where an offer was made to a firm not expecting financial problems, it was accepted in only eighty-two instances. The problem of defining the presence of market failure or credit rationing in this context is that these cases where offers have been made, but rejected by the firm, could also constitute instances of market failure if the offer was set at penal rates. Rationing would therefore take place through frightening off the clientele.

Nevertheless, the careful Aston study concludes that 'small firms in Great

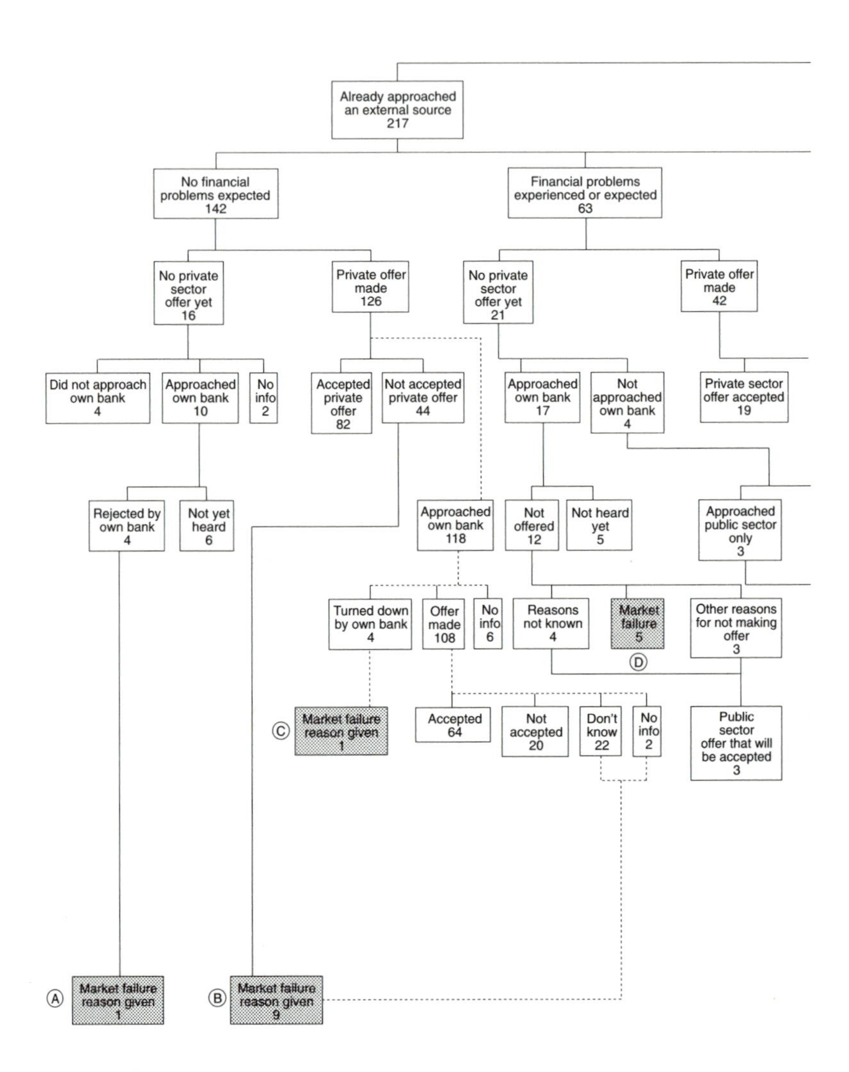

Figure 7.3 Financial constraints and market failure

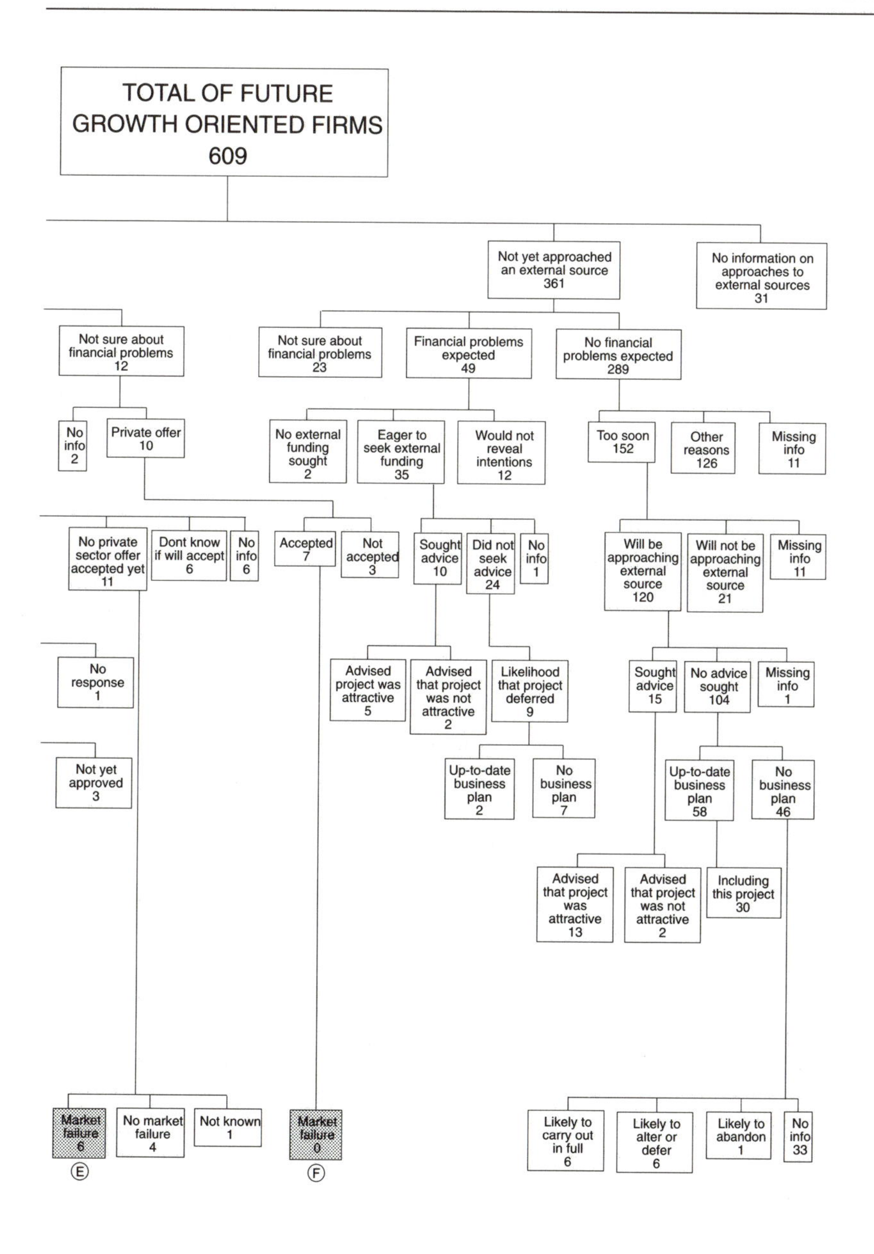
TOTAL OF FUTURE GROWTH ORIENTED FIRMS 609
Not yet approached an external source 361
No information on approaches to external sources 31
Not sure about financial problems 12
Not sure about financial problems 23
Financial problems expected 49
No financial problems expected 289
No info 2
Private offer 10
No external funding sought 2
Eager to seek external funding 35
Would not reveal intentions 12
Too soon 152
Other reasons 126
Missing info 11
No private sector offer accepted yet 11
Dont know if will accept 6
No info 6
Accepted 7
Not accepted 3
Sought advice 10
Did not seek advice 24
No info 1
Will be approaching external source 120
Will not be approaching external source 21
Missing info 11
No response 1
Advised project was attractive 5
Advised that project was not attractive 2
Likelihood that project deferred 9
Sought advice 15
No advice sought 104
Missing info 1
Not yet approved 3
Up-to-date business plan 2
No business plan 7
Up-to-date business plan 58
No business plan 46
Advised that project was attractive 13
Advised that project was not attractive 2
Including this project 30
Market failure 6
No market failure 4
Not known 1
Market failure 0
Likely to carry out in full 6
Likely to alter or defer 6
Likely to abandon 1
No info 33
E
F

Britain apparently face few difficulties in raising finance for their innovation and investment proposals in the private sector'. In our view this is the case but, for the reasons outlined above, it seems likely that rather more small firms are deterred than is apparent from the Aston study.

The Aston findings appear to contrast with those of the Cambridge Small Business Research Centre (1992) in their study of 2,000 smaller firms. They asked firms to score the significance of eleven possible constraints upon their ability to meet their business objectives. The survey, which was conducted in the early part of a long recession, indicated that the two main constraints related to finance for expansion and overdraft finance. These, for example, dwarfed other constraints such as market demand, availability of skilled labour, appropriate premises, etc. Of perhaps even greater significance is that the availability of finance appeared to be particularly characteristic of both fast-growing and newer firms.

The fact that firms identify finance as a constraint on their growth does not necessarily indicate the existence of market failure or credit rationing. Nevertheless, as shown earlier (pp. 225–8) the introduction of the Loan Guarantee Scheme in 1981 suggested that the government at that time believed the market for loan finance was imperfect. However, the NERA (1990) evaluation of the Loan Guarantee Scheme provides little support for the view that there were serious imperfections at the end of the 1980s.

One of the strengths of the NERA research is that it highlights the links between the discussion of market imperfections for both loan and equity capital. It makes the point that small firms' demand for loan capital reflects their inability or unwillingness to seek external equity. The two markets therefore cannot be divorced. We observed earlier that one frequently quoted illustration of a 'gap' was the almost total absence in the formal equity capital market of sums of £100,000 or less being provided. This 'gap' was presumed to exist for three reasons:

- The first reason is that the costs of assessing a project or proposal are broadly invariant with the scale of the proposal. This means the venture capitalists will prefer to spread costs over a small number of larger projects, rather than a large number of smaller projects.
- The second reason is that the costs of monitoring an investment from the viewpoint of the venture capitalists also do not vary markedly with the size of that investment. Again, therefore, it is in the interests of venture capitalists to have a small number of larger projects.
- The third reason is that the bulk of smaller firms are reluctant to share equity ownership with an outside financial institution. This is particularly the case when the business is young and small, when the owner feels that it would not be highly valued by the venture capitalist. As a minority shareholder, the minority venture capitalist has very limited means of controlling the actions of the owner-manager and, moreover, has almost

no means of exiting, i.e. selling the shares, except where there is a move to flotation.

This again illustrates that the existence of a 'gap' is not necessarily an instance of a market failure. The 'gap' exists for perfectly understandable market reasons, reflecting the perceived costs and benefits involved to the various parties. To demonstrate that this also constitutes market failure requires evidence of the lack of availability of small sums of venture capital having adverse wider (social) implications. For example, if it were shown that the lack of availability of small sums of venture capital was a major constraint upon the growth of smaller firms and that there is *a priori* evidence to suggest that government intervention to provide subsidised finance would be in the interests of the economy as a whole, then such action might be justified.

To some extent this reasoning is at the heart of the European Seed Capital Fund scheme (Murray and Francis 1992). Under the ESCF scheme, moneys are provided by the European Commission to twenty-four funds in the form of an interest-free advance to cover up to 50 per cent of their operating costs within the first five years of their existence. After three years, Murray and Francis found that a total of seventy-nine enterprises in Europe had received investments from the Seed Capital Fund Scheme, with an average investment per project of 127,000 ECUs. In this sense the scheme has been much more successful than BES, for example, in directing relatively small sums of equity to smaller firms. However, it is less clear that the scheme implies the existence of market failure in this area. Murray and Francis point out that two-thirds of fund managers do not believe that their funds can be self-sustaining in the longer term without external financial support. This suggests that seed capital funds cannot be operated on a commercial basis and require the use of 'social' criteria to justify their existence.[6]

Overall, this section suggests that, although there are instances where small firms are unable to obtain finance in the quantities and at the price they would like, the financial institutions in the provision of both loan and equity capital have increased their involvement with the small firm sector over the last ten years. It is very difficult now to be able to point to evidence which suggests clearly the presence of market failure and hence imply new directions for financial involvement of government. Cosh and Hughes (1994) summarise the position well:

> It is however difficult to argue that there were financial constraints on business formation as a whole in the 1980s or that there is a more pervasive market failure for small firms in the availability of funds at least in quantitative terms.

It appears that, despite the market power which the largest banks exercise in the United Kingdom, there is no clear case for government to seek to overcome market failure, subject to the two provisos which we make later.

From the point of view of the banks and financial institutions, the central focus of their developments has to be to make better lending decisions. We find the Deakins, Hussain and Ram (1992) results disconcerting, in that there can be such a wide range of decisions upon a single business proposal. As De Meza and Webb (1990) point out, such relatively poor decision making can lead to an oversupply of credit to the small business sector. The central issue is the making of good decisions, and not either the scale of resources provided to the small business sector, or the fact that some businesses are excluded (probably quite correctly) from access to loans.

TWO 'SPECIAL' CASES?

Finally, we turn to two areas where there has been a strong case presented that the existing banks and financial institutions do not provide adequate supplies of either loan or equity capital. The first is the new technology-based firms (NTBF) sector. The crucial role which innovation plays in economic development has made the high-technology sector a subject of considerable interest amongst policy makers. Of special relevance here is the finding by Pavitt, Robson and Townsend (1987) that, over the last thirty years, there has been a significant increase in the productivity of the small firm sector in terms of major innovations.

It has been suggested in the reviews by Barber, Metcalfe and Porteous (1989) and by the Advisory Council on Science and Technology (1990) that, although NTBFs play a crucial role in the economy, they find it disproportionately difficult to obtain appropriate financing from the institutions. This is because such firms are perceived to be particularly risky, for several reasons:

- The first is that they are frequently attempting to introduce products and processes which are new to, and untested in, the market-place. In the event of failure these highly specific assets and the intangible R. & D. know-how are unlikely to have a market. This implies a low residual value available to creditors and investors.
- Secondly, the firms are often in industries where rapid developments make existing technology obsolete and are often in businesses which have only a single product.
- Finally, the businesses are often owned and managed by individuals with stronger technical than business skills.

For all these reasons it is not surprising that studies such as those by Oakey (1984) in the United Kingdom and Roberts (1991) in the United States have suggested that bank finance is significantly less important at start-up for NTBFs than for conventional small businesses. Even so, these results contrast with those of Monck *et al.* (1988) which indicate little difference in the ways in which high-technology firms are initially funded, compared with small businesses as a whole.

Moore (1994) investigated this subject. He compared 292 high-technology small companies with more than 1,700 smaller companies which were not in the high-technology sector. Both groups were asked the same questions about the extent to which a range of factors had constrained the growth of their business. For both high-technology *and* conventional firms, finance constraints were seen to be the most important. In a multiple regression analysis Moore demonstrated that the businesses which are most likely to report financial constraints are those which are young, in the manufacturing sector, have below average profitability and are smaller. Holding these and other variables constant, Moore found no evidence that the high-technology business is more likely to experience difficulties in obtaining finance than its counterpart in the conventional sectors. Indeed, it appears to be the case that the small high-technology firm is, if anything, more likely to be in receipt of venture capital and support from private individuals (business angels) than is the case for the conventional firm. Even so, as we shall show in Chapter 8, the NTBF is one of the few groups of small firms where government intervention has consistently been shown to have a positively beneficial influence upon growth.

The second special case is the financing of ethnic or non-white businesses. The central issue here is whether there is evidence of the owners of these businesses being denied access to loan or equity capital on racial grounds, and whether restricted modes of financing influence the performance of the ethnic business sector.

The major research on this topic in the United States has been conducted by Bates (1991). He found that start-up businesses established by blacks tend to receive smaller loans from banks than white-owned start-ups. Secondly, he found that black-owned firms were under-capitalised, compared with white-owned firms.

Bates hypothesised that commercial banks are more likely to lend to individuals with more human capital, more equity and with demographic traits that are associated positively with business viability. In this context, human capital is likely to be reflected in the level of education of the individual, their age, whether or not they have previous managerial experience and family small business background. The first key result which Bates generated was that, even when these factors are taken into account, it is still the case that the loans made to white business start-ups exceed those made to black business start-ups.

Bates then showed that it is *lower* levels of capitalisation which are associated with higher risk of business failure. From this he inferred that at least part of the observed higher failure rate of black-owned firms reflects this lower capitalisation. Most significantly, he found that their failure rates would be no different from white-owned start-ups if they received a similar level of external loan.

Research on the financing of ethnic businesses in the United Kingdom has not made use of the very large data bases or the statistically sophisticated techniques which were employed by Bates. Nevertheless the work by Ward and Reeves (1980), Wilson and Stanworth (1987), Deakins, Hussein and Ram (1992) and Curran and Blackburn (1993) provide us with helpful insights into this topic in the United Kingdom. The most comprehensive review of the financing of both white and non-white businesses was undertaken by Jones, McEvoy and Barrett (1994), and it is the conclusions of this work which are presented here.

Jones *et al.* show that the most striking difference between the ethnic groups, in terms of mode of financing, is not between whites and non-whites, but between Asians and Afro-Caribbeans. They show that Afro-Caribbeans are perhaps twice as likely to experience problems obtaining bank loans as white applicants. They also show that the Asian business is significantly more likely to have been established using loans from family or friends than either the white or Afro-Caribbean businesses. Thirdly, they point to recent, but highly significant, changes in the ways in which Asian businesses are being financed. They suggest that, if anything, UK banks now look more favourably upon the Asian business owner than upon the white business owner. However, in a very interesting analysis of those businesses established by Asians which have been funded 100 per cent by the bank, Jones *et al.* show that these are much more likely to have been started by British-born Asians than those born overseas, and are more likely to have been established by Asians with higher educational qualifications.

It is in their comments upon how matters are likely to change that Jones *et al.* offer important policy perspectives. Although there is now clearly a much greater willingness on the part of banks to support Asian-owned businesses, there is evidence that bank support is more difficult to obtain for businesses in the non-'traditional' areas such as manufacturing than in the 'traditional' areas of food retailing and confectionery, tobacconists and newsagents (CTNs). Jones *et al.* point to the changing character of the Asian entrepreneur in the 1990s, as being more likely to be British born and educated to a high level, more likely to be seeking finance for a business outside the traditional areas and less likely either to wish to or be able to rely upon finance from family sources. Jones *et al.* are clearly sceptical of whether the banks are yet targeting, or even aware of, this type of shift.

To summarise, there does appear to be clear evidence of market imperfections in the financing of black businesses in the United States. Fully comparable work has not been conducted in the United Kingdom, but that which has does not suggest any clear market failure in the financing of Asian businesses. The only major reservation expressed both by Jones *et al.* and by Curran and Blackburn (1993) is whether banks are sufficiently aware of the 'new' type of entrepreneur emerging from the Asian community. So far as Afro-Caribbean businesses are concerned, these are clearly very different from Asian businesses and do experience significantly greater problems both in raising finance, and in their relationships with the banks. Whether this constitutes an illustration of a market failure, or whether it merely illustrates the higher risk associated with these types of business, is not clear from the research conducted thus far.

CONCLUSIONS

This chapter has attempted to summarise the debate concerning financing of smaller businesses. It has drawn upon theoretical work to yield new insights into this debate. It has then used these insights to assess the implications of the leading empirical work conducted on this topic. Unfortunately some issues, most notably the role of trade credit and the case for statutory interest to be charged upon late payment of bills, has not been the subject of any thorough empirical work. For these reasons the conclusions which we derive upon the issue are extremely speculative.

On the central themes of the chapter, however, our findings are clear. The seemingly perennial difficulties which characterise the relationship between small firms and their banks stem directly from the nature of the contract negotiated between the two, to overcome the presence of asymmetric information and lack of 'control' by the bank over the actions of the business owner. Expressed simply, under a loan agreement, the maximum gain for the bank is when it is repaid the interest plus the principal in full. If the project for which bank finance was sought turns out to be extremely successful to the firm, the bank does not share in that gain. On the other hand, if the project turns out to be unsuccessful to the firm, leading to its demise, the bank, in the absence of collateral, will lose all of its loan plus the forgone interest. In short, a loan contract involves the bank incurring full downside risk and a fixed upside gain.

There are three ways open to the bank to overcome this problem.

- The first is for it to seek collateral in order to lower its downside risk, and this procedure is employed extensively. However, this means that individual small businesses which are unable to provide collateral, even though they may have an identical business plan and prospects to other businesses with collateral, may be denied loan facilities.
- The second is for the bank to take an equity shareholding in the business and so share in the upside gain. There are three problems with this. The first is that many small business owners are reluctant to share equity with anyone, at least in part because they are unaware of the benefits. The second is that most small businesses are unlikely to grow sufficiently to yield the bank any significant equity gain. The third problem is that of

adverse selection – those entrepreneurs who are most uncertain about the prospects for their business will be most willing to share their equity, whereas those who are most certain will be least likely to share the equity. In this sense the bank would only be offered the poorest business prospects. Nevertheless, one of the major UK banks – the Midland – has implemented a series of regional pilot schemes to investigate the feasibility of equity participation, and the results will be awaited with interest (Midland Bank 1993).

- The third 'solution' is already used by banks. It is to create a portfolio of loans, representing a spectrum combining high-risk and high-return with low-risk and low-return projects. In the portfolio there will always be projects which fail, but these are 'balanced' by the survivors. However the selection of the portfolio requires good judgement, with the objective of increasing the emphasis towards high-return low-risk projects. Problems emerge in the portfolio when, because of 'external' unfavourable macroeconomic factors, the whole portfolio becomes more risky.

Difficulties in obtaining small sums of equity capital stem mainly from the cost structure of the financial institutions themselves. It cannot be surprising that small sums of equity are difficult to obtain when the costs to the equity provider of monitoring and assessment are very similar for small and for large investments.

It is therefore perfectly feasible for there to exist a 'gap' in the sense that rarely are small sums of equity provided, and yet there has been no evidence of market failure in the sense of a case for government to intervene. Indeed, the two main government interventions – the Loan Guarantee Scheme provision of loan capital and the former Business Expansion Scheme for the provision of equity – are judged to be no longer relevant. The Business Expansion Scheme was first abolished after a shabby history as a tax avoidance dodge, only to be resurrected as the Enterprise Investment Scheme. The government's own evaluation of the Loan Guarantee Scheme has pointed to a scheme currently making only the most modest social contribution and yet this was also revamped following pressure from lobbyists.

In principle, business angels do not have the same cost structure as the formal venture capital industry, and so might be expected to be used by smaller firms. Yet the problems which they experience are those of being made aware of suitable investment opportunities. From the viewpoint of the firms, the problem with informal investors is identifying and assessing their potential contribution to the business.

During the 1980s changes occurred because of an explosion in bank lending to smaller firms, so that the small business sector at the end of the decade became significantly overborrowed. The issue which now faces the banks in their lending to small firms is that of making better decisions. There is clear evidence that the sector is becoming more competitive and that firms themselves are increasingly shopping around for finance. At the heart of any bank's competitive advantage is the ability of its managers to assess risk adequately, not just in terms of whether the risk is covered through collateral, but also in terms of a judgement about the likely success of the business. The successful banks in the small business market in the 1990s and beyond will be those which are consistently able to charge the lowest interest rates commensurate with the risk to the bank. This inevitably means greater uniformity of decision making, more extensive training of personnel, and overcoming some of the 'attitude' problems which banks have been accused of in the past.

For the small firms themselves, the major conclusion has to be that one development of the 1990s is likely to be increasing pressure on the rapidly growing firms to finance further growth, partly through the sale of equity to financial institutions. Only in that way will the institutions be able to share in the upside gain with the growth of the firm, and this involvement in the business is likely to lead to better, in the sense of more informed, lending decisions. There may be some lessons to be learned in this respect from Germany and Holland (Deakins and Philpott 1993).

A second way in which firms themselves may consider providing signals to financial institutions about the risk involved in their operations is through the establishment of mutual guarantee schemes. Hughes (1992) points to their extensive use elsewhere in Europe in 'pooling their private information about project riskiness and entrepreneurial quality, and developing mutual schemes to guarantee individual loan applications to banks by members of the group, after group screening based on the pooled information'.

This chapter therefore does not point to a major role for government in improving the financing of small firms. It suggests that, as part of the competitive process, banks are now more aware of the needs of their small business customers. In short, although 'gaps' will always exist, there is little clear evidence of market failure.

Perhaps the only possible exception is over the question of late payment and education. In principle, government has been reluctant to 'interfere' over the question of late payment for fear that legislation would be ineffective; from the viewpoint of this book a better reason for caution is the absence of any high-quality research on the matter. Nevertheless, it is likely to be the case that governments, possibly at an EC level, will be pressurised to act to ensure a statutory right to interest on all late paid debts.

A second possible role for government in this area is to improve the quality and business awareness of small business owners. The work by Nayak and Greenfield (1994) shows the almost total absence of financial awareness and business planning in very small firms. The work by Watson (1990) suggests that 65–70 per cent of total profits are removed from businesses each year in the form of directors' remuneration, and the pattern of these payments suggests tax-minimising behaviour. Large falls in gross profit do not lead to swift falls in remuneration and, given the low equity base for many small firms, financial difficulties occur.

In Holland, company directors are required to pass examinations to demonstrate competence, whereas in the United Kingdom for £2 an individual may attempt to insulate himself or herself from limited liability by becoming a company director. It is surprising that the small business community cannot see that it is in the interests of the honest and trustworthy members who make up the bulk of its number to ensure that the dishonest and/or incompetent are excluded from trading. This could be the most important single step to improving the relations between financial institutions and small firms.

Chapter 8

Public policy

INTRODUCTION

This chapter examines public policy towards small firms. It draws upon material presented in the earlier chapters and can be seen as a way of unifying the key themes of the book. Effective public policy requires an understanding of the factors which influence the birth, death and growth of smaller firms; these are presented in Chapters 3, 4 and 5.

In practice, public policy towards small firms has been mainly concerned with two issues: the creation of employment in smaller enterprises and the problems which smaller enterprises experience in obtaining access to finance. Hence, to formulate public policy in this area also requires an understanding of the issues addressed in Chapters 6 and 7.

Two key themes emerge during this chapter. The first is that the growth in importance of smaller firms in the United Kingdom, over the last twenty years, means it is no longer possible to discuss economic policy without recognising the role which small firms play in the economy and in the rest of society more generally. Public policy towards small firms cannot be considered in isolation from other influences in the economy and, perhaps equally importantly, cannot be left simply to those with a particular interest in smaller firms. In short, public policy towards small firms is now so important that it cannot be formulated by small business interests alone.

The second key theme of the chapter is that, whilst there is a wide range of policy initiatives to assist small firms, governments throughout Europe have yet to formulate a coherent policy towards the sector. In no country, as far as we are aware, is there the equivalent of a 'White Paper' which articulates the range of public policies towards smaller firms which currently exist, which provides a justification for the existing configuration of policies, and which provides criteria for judging whether or not policies are successful. Instead, public policies have been developed, jettisoned, and often reintroduced on a piecemeal basis.

Of central importance is the need to specify the objectives of public policy. This chapter begins by showing that it is possible to infer a large number of rather different objectives from small firm policies. The key issue is that the ultimate objectives of policy have to be clearly specified in such a way as to determine to what extent targets are being met. This is rarely done.

The chapter then undertakes a review (pp. 263–301) of some of the key instruments of public policy in the United Kingdom. There is a very brief review of their operation, but the section concentrates primarily on the assessments of their effectiveness which have been undertaken. The purpose is to reach some form of judgement, based upon good-quality empirical research, as to the effectiveness of the instruments of policy. Such a review is, of course, difficult since in many instances the objectives of policy are not clearly specified. Nevertheless, a judgement is reached in the chapter by implying objectives where these are not clearly specified.

To obtain an understanding of how this 'patchwork quilt' collection of policies has come about, a schema of small firm public policy making in the United Kingdom is provided. This highlights the key influences upon public policy, in order to explain, at least in part, how some elements of policy which seem to have questionable economic effectiveness, continue to be pursued.

It is, however, inappropriate to examine policy towards small firms in the context only of the United Kingdom. A fuller picture is only available by understanding the European and international policy making framework which influences the operations of small firms in the United Kingdom. This is reviewed in the final part of the chapter (pp. 301–3), followed by the conclusion.

Any discussion of the role of public policy towards smaller firms in a market economy has to be prefaced by asking why such policies should exist. We begin with this in the next section.

WHY HAVE PUBLIC POLICY?

In an earlier review of public policies to assist small firms, the current author (Storey 1982a) felt it important to understand the rationale for such public policies. It is still important to address this matter.

Economists justify government intervention in a market economy when there is evidence of 'market failure'. Liberal economists, however, would argue that the presence of market failure is a necessary, but not sufficient, condition for government intervention. For liberals, intervention can only be justified where post-intervention welfare improvements can be demonstrated, after taking account of the costs of bureaucratic intervention (Rowley and Peacock 1975).

Describing this philosophy, the current author wrote (1982a):

> Those favouring a market approach to economic problems argue that, subject to certain qualifications, the free market would provide an optimal number of new firms. New firms will be created in industries where there is an opportunity for profit and firms will disappear from industries where

> demand for the final product has declined. Government intervention is legitimate only where the social and private costs and benefits of new firm formation diverge, or where it is believed that the existing income distribution significantly reduces the extent to which willingness to pay reflects an individual or group's demand for a good or service.
>
> It is not immediately clear to what extent subsidising the formation of new firms (and thus increasing, *ceteris paribus*, the existing stock of small firms) can be justified on any of these bases.

More than ten years later, and following a huge number of policy interventions, it may seem a contradiction that a government can be committed to 'free markets' and at the same time have active policies to promote smaller firms. What is perhaps even more surprising is that, with a few notable exceptions such as the Loan Guarantee Scheme or technology policies, very little justification is provided by the UK government, in terms of market failure, for these policies. It continues to be the case today, as the current author noted twelve years ago, that:

> Subsidies by government to those wishing to establish their own firm results in the increased number of new firms and leads to increased employment in the small firm sector. But subsidies to one group have to be raised by increased taxes or reduced reliefs to other groups, and it has never been shown that the *net* effect of subsidising small firms is to create more wealth in the community. In essence the argument must always return to the basic issue that, if there are economic factors which currently favour the small firm, these would be exploited by that sector *without* the assistance of government.
>
> (Storey 1982a)

It is then appropriate to examine carefully the arguments which have been presented by the Government in support of its small firm policies. Probably the most frequently heard, but least sophisticated, is that small firms have been shown to be a major source of job creation. Hence it is argued that, during times of high unemployment, such firms should be the focus of policies both to increase the number of firms and to add to the number of jobs within each firm. Yet such policies can only be justified in a market economy where it can be demonstrated that the effect of government intervention is to lead to an overall net improvement in welfare to the economy as a whole. If small firm policy intervention leads to an increase in the number of small firms, but also to a compensating, or more than compensating, reduction in employment in large firms, then it is difficult to justify such policies on welfare grounds. Despite the increased focus upon small firm policies, macroeconomic studies of the impact of policies still do not exist. Reaching an informed judgement about the overall impact of policy is therefore difficult.

The second, and somewhat more sophisticated, argument is that there is a market failure peculiar to small firms, because of their comparative weakness in the market-place and their relatively high unit cost of compliance with government regulations (Bannock and Peacock 1989). Bannock and Peacock argue that small firms merit support from government, not to give them an unfavourable advantage over other sizes of enterprise, but simply to offset the disadvantages which they experience by their small size and to offset the perverse effects of other government policies. For example, they show that the cost of compliance with VAT requirements is 2.5 per cent of turnover for those businesses with sales of less than £15,000 per annum, but only 0.07 per cent for those with an annual turnover in excess of £2m. Bannock and Peacock argue that similar, though less extreme, differentials in compliance costs apply to other forms of legislation and taxation. Finally they argue that additions to the stock of small firms through new firm formation is the key to ensuring that competition exists in market-places. Where there is a continuous stream of new entrants, existing (large) firms are under continuous threat, inhibiting them from obtaining excessive profits through an ability to raise prices and/or be X-inefficient.

These arguments have some validity. On grounds of equity alone, small firms should not be penalised by incurring substantially higher compliance costs with government regulations than the larger firms with which they compete. However, in deciding the extent to which cost differences emerge 'naturally' through size is a tricky issue. For example, large firms may obtain inputs at a lower cost because they purchase in larger quantities. In this sense, scale economies occur 'naturally'. Yet legislative compliance costs, which operate in much the same way, are deemed by some to be 'unnatural'.

The problem emerges even more clearly when the recommendation is that small firms should be exempt from particular items of legislation, on the grounds that costs of compliance are 'excessive'. Those making such proposals, however, frequently take little account of the impact on the rest of society of this legislative exemption. This again illustrates a reluctance to examine the *net* effect of public policies to assist smaller firms.

A third issue relates to recognition that the indicator of demand in the market-place is willingness to pay, but that this, in turn, is influenced by income distribution. Hence government intervention in a market economy is often justified on the grounds of providing assistance and services to those without market power – i.e. those on low incomes. Classic examples of this are the provision of public health services and public housing which will be 'consumed' by those on relatively low incomes.

Distribution of income arguments are unlikely to provide any justification for small firm policies. Table 8.1 shows the distribution of earnings according to job status for employed and self-employed full-time workers in 1986 in the United Kingdom. It shows the arithmetic mean earnings level of the full-time self-employed to be virtually 25 per cent higher than that for the full-time employed workers. Interestingly, it also shows that the variance of income is

Table 8.1 Relative frequency distributions of earnings by job status (full-time workers, £ 1986 prices)

	Self-employed	*Employed*
£5,000 and under	8.6	0.8
£5,000 but less than £10,000	21.5	28.9
£10,000 but less than £15,000	25.8	49.2
£15,000 but less than £20,000	10.2	13.7
£20,000 but less than £25,000	14.0	4.2
£25,000 and over	19.9	3.2
Mean	16,441	12,663
Standard deviation	10,134	5,191
Coefficient of variation	62%	41%

Source: Dolton and Makepeace (1990)

very much higher for the self-employed than for the employed, with virtually 9 per cent of the self-employed earning less than £5,000 per year, compared with less than 1 per cent of the employed population. However, amongst higher earners – those with earnings in excess of £20,000 per year – one-third of self-employed workers featured, compared with only 7 per cent of employed workers. Whilst recognising that some of this 'income' for the self-employed includes a 'return' upon investment of their capital within the business, it is difficult to justify, on equity grounds, policies which focus upon providing public assistance to an already relatively more wealthy group.

Policy interventions by government to assist small firms therefore have to be examined very carefully. To justify intervention in a market economy it is necessary to identify precisely where the market failure exists, and whether it is possible to rectify that market failure through intervention. The costs of the intervention have to be carefully assessed and the benefits estimated. It is also important to assess who are the beneficiaries of the intervention and who are the losers. Ideally this has to be placed within a macroeconomic framework to yield an overall assessment. As will be demonstrated in the subsequent sections of this chapter this is rarely, if ever, undertaken in European countries. If it is, it does not appear in a public document.

THE OBJECTIVES AND TARGETS OF SMALL FIRM POLICY

There has been no UK White Paper about the objectives and targets of public policy towards SMEs. Instead, policies have been introduced on a piecemeal basis, often in response to pressure from small firm lobby organisations and to changes in the macroeconomy. It is therefore necessary to guess at the objectives of policy, rather than being able to view each initiative as clearly fitting into an overall conceptual framework.

The United Kingdom is far from unique in Europe in this respect. The authoritative review by de Koning, Snijders and Vianen (1992) pointed to four main objectives in SME policy pursued by EC member states. These were:

- competition;
- strengthening the production chain;
- diversification;
- creation of employment.

De Koning *et al.* saw competition as a focus for public policy, since market competition presupposes a large number of participating enterprises. They saw the strengthening of the production chain as reflecting the role which small firms play in both providing inputs to large firms as subcontractors and in the distribution of the products of large firms as wholesalers, transporters and retailers. Thirdly, they saw small firms as a valuable provider of different products and services, leading to greater diversification of the market-place. Encouragement of this role could therefore be seen as an objective of public policy. Finally, the role which SMEs play in employment creation and in the reduction of unemployment is seen as a clear objective of policies towards firms in this sector.

However, de Koning *et al.*, as we shall see later, note that 'Only a few countries select employment creation as an objective. None of them emphasise the competition, diversification or strengthening of production chain explicitly as an objective.' The key point is that de Koning *et al.*, once they have completed their review of policies, have to *infer* that the objectives of policy are competition, diversification, etc. The fact that it is only possible to infer objectives by observing the policies in operation, rather than these being clearly stated as a coherent response to an agreed role which government plays within the market-place, is a severe criticism. If the objectives of policy are not specified, then it is impossible to specify policy targets. If targets are not specified it is impossible to decide whether or not the policies are in some sense 'successful'. Hence, reaching a judgement on the effectiveness of public policies in this area is fraught with difficulty.

Like de Koning *et al.*, we also have to infer objectives from observing public policy in this area. Our inferences suggest there are both 'intermediate' and 'final' objectives of policies to support SMEs in the United Kingdom. This is illustrated in Table 8.2, which shows six possible objectives of small firm policy. These objectives may be considered to be either 'intermediate' or 'final'. Taking the first row, the table shows that increases in employment may be considered either as an 'intermediate' or as a 'final objective' of small firm policy. Thus the effectiveness of a particular policy may be judged in terms of its impact either on increases in employment directly attributable to the policy, or upon reducing unemployment. Unfortunately, these two measures are by no means the same; indeed it is quite possible that a policy may have a much greater impact on employment than upon reducing unemployment.

An example of this is reported by Scott (1993), who evaluates the impact of loans and grants to small firms in Northern Ireland. He shows policies have had a strong impact upon survival and employment creation in assisted firms, but that the impact upon unemployment has been more modest. This is because reducing unemployment depends not only upon increases in employment, but also upon other factors such as migration patterns, activity rates and 'discouraged workers'. The Northern Ireland example shows that the effect of small firm job creation directly attributable to subsidies has been to lower rates of out-migration and to raise activity rates, rather than to impact primarily upon unemployment rates.

Measurement problems also arise in attributing changes in unemployment to particular policy initiatives (Storey 1990a). For example, in making an assessment of the impact of policies it is necessary to determine what would have happened in the absence of the policy. Policy impact can only be correctly assessed by removing from what actually did happen that which would have happened without the policy. The latter is called 'deadweight'. In the context of small firms the classic example, which we discuss in the next section, is the availability of subsidies to the unemployed to start a business. Here it would be a serious over-estimate to attribute all the employment in such new businesses to the availability of subsidies, since some individuals would have started their own businesses even if the subsidies had not been available.

A second measurement problem, particularly relevant to small firm policies, is that of 'displacement'. Taking the example discussed in the paragraph above, it would be unwise to assume the impact of the subsidy is the number of jobs created in subsidised firms after taking account of deadweight. The reason is that, in a fixed market-place such as may exist locally for hairdressing or possibly taxi services, the entry of a subsidised firm almost certainly leads to the exit of an unsubsidised firm. Clearly not all markets are of this type, but the 'forced exit' or 'displacement' effect also has to be taken into account in evaluating the employment-creation effects of policies. Whilst it is clear that 'deadweight' and 'displacement' are relevant to making an assessment of the impact of small firm policies, it is much more difficult to estimate, in practice, their magnitude. Surveys need to be conducted to ask respondents about whether they would have proceeded without the subsidy, and estimates of the impact upon other firms have to be made by direct and indirect techniques. (For illustrations, see Elias and Whitfield 1987, Scott 1993, Wren and Waterson 1991, Robinson, Wren and Goddard 1987.)

Even so, it is easier to focus upon the direct employment impact of small firm policies than to estimate the impact which these policies have upon unemployment. In practice, as McGregor and Fletcher (1993) show, the intended beneficiaries of some small firm policies are particular groups within the unemployed, such as the long-term unemployed or those suffering

Table 8.2 Objectives of small firm policy

	Intermediate	*Final*
1	Increase employment	– Increase employment – Reduce unemployment
2	Increase number of start-ups	– Increase number of start-ups – Increase stock of firms
3	Promote use of consultants	– Promote use of consultants – Faster growth of firms
4	Increase competition	– Increase competition – Increase wealth
5	Promote 'efficient' markets	– Promote 'efficient' markets – Increase wealth
6	Promote technology diffusion	– Promote technology diffusion – Increase wealth
7	Increase wealth	– Votes

a number of forms of social deprivation. Another group whose employment prospects are of particular concern are the young unemployed (MacDonald and Coffield 1991). Reaching a judgement about the effectiveness of 'enterprise policies' to assist these 'special' groups is particularly hazardous and subjective.

The second set of 'intermediate' and 'final' objectives of small firm policies shown in Table 8.2 are those which increase the number of businesses started. In some instances this appears to be a 'final' objective, whereas in others it appears to be only an 'intermediate' objective, with the 'final' objective being to increase the total number or 'stock' of firms in the economy. For example, in 1992 the Small Firms Minister, Baroness Denton, said:

> The success of these [government small firm] policies is reflected in the unprecedented growth that the United Kingdom small business community experienced during the 1980s. For example, between 1979 and 1989, the total number of businesses in the United Kingdom grew by two-thirds – representing a net increase of almost 500 businesses for every working day of the decade. All regions and most industrial sectors benefited from growth. Even in the more difficult economic period of the more recent past the number of new firms starting up is still impressive; bankers' surveys show 450,000 for 1991 and another 200,000 in the first six months of this year.
>
> ('Gateways for Growth', Conference, Birmingham)

At the beginning of this quote the speaker cites the change in the *stock* of firms as a measure of success, whereas, later, it is the *number* of new firms which is the key point. This demonstrates the use of each measure almost interchangeably even though, as shown in Chapters 2, 3 and 4 of this book, the two are clearly very different.

The justification for regarding an increase in the relative importance of small firms as measured by the stock of firms which are small as a final objective reflects the influential views of Graham Bannock (Bannock and Peacock 1989). He argues that the large firm sector in the United Kingdom is overly dominant, compared with other comparable developed countries, and that the size and importance of the small-firm sector in the United Kingdom needs to be increased. Bannock says (p. 17):

> It seems clear to me . . . that this share is below the optimum in the United Kingdom . . . [and] below that of most other developed countries . . . so we cannot leave it to the market, and the fact that all parties in this and most other countries subscribed to special policies for small firms indicates that there is a general consensus that things cannot be left to the market.

The third row of Table 8.2 refers to objectives designed to lead to the greater internal efficiency of small firms. It is our presumption that these improvements in efficiency are likely to lead to faster growth on the part of the firm. However, policies such as the Consultancy Initiative state that 'The overall objective of the scheme is to improve management performance of small and medium sized businesses by encouraging firms to make use of consultants at full market rates' (Segal Quince Wicksteed 1991).

The above quotation could be interpreted as suggesting the use of consultants is the 'final' objective of the Consultancy Initiative. However, in their evaluation of the scheme, whilst there is a strong focus on the firms' satisfaction with the Initiative as an end in itself, Segal Quince Wicksteed (1991) suggest the scheme should have other identifiable effects. The first is upon business variables such as increased sales, efficiency, product quality or the customer base of the firm. The second is upon the way in which the firm is managed – reflected in increased delegation or emphasis upon training. Hence it is difficult to specify single ultimate objectives upon which a judgement on effectiveness can be made.

Row four of Table 8.2 refers to objectives which are apparent in observing small firm policies in operation, and correspond to one of the objectives identified by de Koning *et al.* – that of increasing competition. In many senses, seeing small firms as a force for increasing competition in the market-place is at the heart of public policies but, as Bannock and Peacock (1989) say:

> The market and competition are means and not ends. They are instruments to be used in achieving objectives. Judgement of their efficiency depends on the choice of objectives and trade-offs, the view taken of how the economy functions and how improving the operational market forces compares with other methods of intervention in the economy.

The implicit assumption is that the forces of competition within the market-place will lead to consumers within that market-place enjoying higher levels of consumption. In this sense, increased competition is an 'intermediate' objective, leading to the 'final' objective, which is that of increasing wealth.

The fifth row of the table notes that one element of public policy towards small firms is to ensure the market-place operates efficiently. Illustrations of market imperfections include situations where small firms are penalised and are subject to discrimination or forced to incur higher costs than their rivals, for non-market reasons. If firms are required to incur these costs, which are frequently the result of government legislation, they become less competitive, so the market becomes less efficient and welfare is reduced. Government's role is to ensure that these inefficiencies are not perpetuated. The UK Government, through the DTI De-regulation Unit, pursues policies to minimise 'red tape', to ensure legislative compliance costs are broadly similar according to sizes of enterprise, and to ensure that access to sources of finance is not subject to credit rationing on the basis of firm size. The issue is whether the creation of efficient markets is a 'final' or an 'intermediate' objective. If it is the latter, then the ultimate measure of success of the policy is presumably whether it leads to wealth creation.

The sixth row of the table sees a key objective of small firm policy as being to facilitate the diffusion of new ideas and products. In the recent past, small enterprises have been a major and increasing source of new innovations (Monck *et al.* 1988) and, given the role that new technology is thought to play in economic development, small high-technology firms are seen as potentially major contributors to wealth (Oakey, Rothwell and Cooper 1988). Again, however, it is not clear whether the criterion for success of such policies is wealth creation or whether it is technological diffusion.

Finally, and perhaps most contentiously, the seventh row of the table suggests that the 'final' objective of small firm policy is votes, with the only question being whether or not there is an 'intermediate' objective of increasing wealth. Expressed at its crudest the argument is that, as we shall show later, the small business owner is significantly more likely to vote Conservative than to vote Labour. Some public policies towards small firms adopted by Conservative administrations – such as lowering taxation, reducing bureaucratic burdens, etc. – will directly benefit those individuals who are currently business owners and who therefore are likely to be Conservative voters.

Since workers in large, highly unionised plants in both the public and private sectors are the least likely to vote Conservative and the most likely to vote Labour, there is a powerful incentive for a Conservative administration to ensure that voters transfer from large enterprises to small. A convenient vehicle for this allows for, or even encourages, the shedding of labour in large plants in the public or private sectors and, when those individuals become unemployed, offers them subsidies to become self-employed. In this sense, government is directly favouring its own supporters and providing subsidies to individuals who are more likely to become its supporters once in receipt of that subsidy. The policy is then viewed as directly 'buying votes' and votes are seen as both an 'intermediate' and 'final' objective.

The alternative view is that governments have the objective of being re-elected, but that this is achieved through pursuing wealth- and job-creating policies such as those identified in rows 1–6 of Table 8.2. Hence the issue is whether votes are being 'bought' directly – which would be deemed unacceptable – or whether they are being 'bought' legitimately through increased wealth and economic activity. There would be evidence to suggest that votes were being 'bought' directly if the focus of small firm policy was primarily or exclusively benefiting the owners of small businesses, rather than consumers, the economy or society more generally. Evidence which suggested that small firm policies leads to faster rates of job- and wealth-creation as an 'intermediate' objective would imply policies were being designed in the public interest.

Overall, this section has demonstrated that the objectives of public policies to assist small firms are rarely specified directly. Instead it is necessary for analysts to 'infer' the objectives by observing the range of individual measures. What does appear to be strikingly absent is a framework within which it is possible to see the extent to which objectives of policy are satisfied by individual measures. The absence of targets for small firm policies as a whole means that monitoring of performance is particularly difficult. Nevertheless, the next section will review small firm policies in the United Kingdom and reach some judgement, given the inferred objectives, of their effectiveness.

SME POLICIES IN THE UNITED KINGDOM

It is neither possible nor appropriate within the limited space available to review each and all of the UK government policies designed to assist SMEs. For example, during the 1979–83 period, more than 100 measures were introduced by the Conservative administration to assist smaller firms. Some schemes, which could not be regarded as 'small firm' policy measures, even though their major impact was on smaller firms, are also excluded from this review. Enterprise Zones are one such example.

Since 1979 there have also been many changes of policy, with some major initiatives such as the Business Expansion Scheme being introduced, then discontinued and then effectively reintroduced as the Enterprise Investment Scheme. In other cases the same or similar policies have been administered at different points in time by different organisations – the Enterprise Allowance Scheme, for example, being administered first by the Manpower Services Commission, then successively by the Training Commission, the Training Agency and the Department of Employment. More recently it has been renamed the Business Start-Up Scheme (BSUS) and is now administered by some Training and Enterprise Councils (TECs).

Unfortunately, there is no comprehensive overview, as far as this author is aware, of the history and development of small firm policy in the United Kingdom. Clearly one needs to be written, but for present purposes it is sufficient to be aware of the key elements of public policy and the ways these are delivered.

We begin our review by taking the basic structure of small firm policies as outlined by Bannock and Binks (1990) and combining it with the framework provided by Barberis and May (1993).

This combined structure of public policies is reproduced as Table 8.3, which identifies six general categories. Each of these will be discussed in turn, with references being made to the specific policy measures shown as illustrations. The purpose of the discussion is to present the specified policies and then to carefully examine evidence which assesses the extent to which the policies have met their implied objectives.

Macroeconomic policies

These policies have a major impact on the trading position of small firms. Of course, the prime objective of macroeconomic policy is not solely to assist smaller firms, but rather to provide a framework for all sizes of enterprise in the economy to flourish. Nevertheless, matters such as interest rates, taxation, public spending and inflation are seen by small firm owners themselves as key factors which influence the development of their businesses. The Cambridge Small Business Research Centre (1992) survey of proprietors of smaller firms showed that taxation and interest-rate policies were perceived to be the two government policies which had either most helped or most hindered their businesses. The Cambridge survey reported that virtually 30 per cent more firm owners thought government policies on interest rates had hindered the development of their firm rather than assisted it. On taxation, the consensus appeared to be that, whilst reductions in rates of personal and corporate taxation were welcomed as an assistance, this was effectively offset by those who felt that indirect taxation increases had hindered the development of their business.

Firms' responses to questions of this type are strongly influenced by macroeconomic conditions, so that priorities for policy change according to the state of the economic cycle. Even so, the quarterly surveys conducted by the Small Business Research Trust (SBRT) confirm that the main factors which restrict the growth of businesses relate to the macroeconomy. For much of the early 1990s the key elements were lack of demand, high interest rates and poor cash flow.

In its review, *Small Firms in Britain*, the Employment Department (1992), when it had responsibility for small firms, examined government measures in support of small firms. After the control of inflation, it appeared to place considerable emphasis on the creation of a 'beneficial' tax regime. Judging from the text, the word 'beneficial' means that taxes on those owning a small business are either lowered (income tax, corporation tax) or abolished (investment income surcharge), or reliefs are granted (on capital-based taxes). The rationale underlying these taxation changes appears to be to provide an incentive to business owners to earn (and declare) income rather than be deterred from undertaking additional work on the grounds that the taxation authorities will be the main beneficiaries. It may also be to influence the decisions of small business owners over matters such as choice of legal form or inheritance.

As noted in Chapter 7, Rees and Shah (1993) examined the hours worked by the self-employed between 1973 and 1986. They found these to depend primarily upon personal circumstances such as the age of the individual, marital status and, to a lesser extent, the number of children. Rees and Shah found that, if anything, taking account of these characteristics, the self-employed worked fewer hours after 1979 than in the earlier part of the 1970s. It is, then, interesting to note that personal tax rates fell after 1979.

This finding can be easily rationalised: the self-employed individuals, rather than seeking to maximise their income, are more likely to set out to achieve a particular *level* of income. Since their income is strongly related to the number of hours which they work, and which they have the ability to adjust, these individuals are likely to work more hours under a less 'beneficial' tax regime.

Here, then, is a classic case of a difference between what people say and what they do. If work is a disutility, then the self-employed will want to minimise their hours worked to achieve a given level of income. They will therefore claim that higher taxes are a deterrent, and seek to achieve a more 'beneficial' regime under which they will need to work less hours. However, if taxes rise this group will, in fact, work more hours rather than less, in order to achieve a given level of income.

An interpretation of Rees and Shah's careful work is to raise fundamental doubts about whether taxation policy has had the effect of stimulating number of hours worked. However, as we saw in Table 8.2, it is equally plausible to argue that small firm policy has political, as well as economic, objectives. If work is a disutility for the self-employed, then this group will look more favourably upon, and hence be more likely to vote for, a government which implements policies which mean they have to work less hours to achieve specified income levels.

Overall, there can be little doubt that government macroeconomic decisions do play a key role in influencing the viability of small firms. Interest rates and the level of aggregate demand in the economy are of prime importance, but decisions on these items are taken with a view to their impact on all sizes of firm, rather than simply on those which are small. The evidence is that taxation rates, which have been lowered at least partly to provide 'incentives' to the self-employed to work harder, do not seem to have had the desired effect.

Deregulation/administrative simplification

Within the deregulation/administrative simplification group of policies, particular emphasis has been placed upon the importance of cutting 'red tape'. We have already discussed the philosophical basis for this, and the Government has been at pains to point out that:

> the amount of regulation which new and established firms face acts as a break on enterprise and the wealth and job creating process. Deregulation means two things. First, freeing markets and increasing the opportunities for competition. Second, lifting administrative and legislative burdens which take time, energy and resources from fundamental business activity.
>
> (*Lifting the Burden* (1985), para. 1.5)

In its assessments of the impact which these burdens could have, *Lifting the Burden* reported the results of a survey by Research Associates, suggesting that amongst 200 firms contacted, fifty-two reported they had lost or not taken on an average 6.5 employees each year over the last five years, due to the inhibiting or costly effect of regulations. If these firms were typical then a massive increase in employment could take place if such burdens were limited.

By 1988, in *Releasing Enterprises*, the Government reported that it had made considerable progress on easing the bureaucratic pressures on businesses, especially small businesses. These improvements included changes to the VAT system, allowing cash accounting and annual accounting, less severe penalties for non-compliance with VAT, and simplification of registration procedures under the Data Protection Act. The UK Government was also highly influential in setting the agenda for the Small and Medium Enterprise (SME) Task Force in the European Commission, which subsequently became DG23, ensuring that this Directorate General had as a major focus the scrutiny of European legislation, to ensure that its adverse impact upon (in particular, small) business was minimised.

It is extremely difficult to assess the effectiveness of policies to cut red tape and the issuing of legislative exemptions. One crude measure of the success of policies would be the number of instances in which legislation was repealed or modified, as illustrated in the document *Releasing Enterprise* quoted in the previous paragraph. However, such a measure would be inappropriate for organisations such as DG23 in the European Commission, which have a responsibility to ensure that inappropriate legislation never reaches the statute book. Furthermore, there is, as we have seen, often a fundamental conflict of interest between what the entrepreneur sees as 'red tape' and what the workforce sees as legitimate employment rights, or the factory neighbours see as protection against environmental hazards or intrusions. Merely shifting the balance in favour of the entrepreneur does not necessarily mean there has been a real improvement for society as a whole.

These observations fundamentally conflict with the opinions expressed by some of the lobby groups. These were well summarised by Dr Ann Robinson of the Institute of Directors (IOD). In a speech in Belfast on 12 March 1993 she said:

> During its life some of the most burdensome regulations for small firms have passed through the Council of Ministers without so much as a peep from DG23. . . . The IOD believes the EC should focus more closely on the real problems that SMEs face in doing their day-to-day business and on the impact of taxation on those firms. . . . Action to reduce 'red tape' should be given a much higher priority by DG23.

It is this proposal which is the crux of the matter, since it implies that the public policy agenda for small business is set by the owners of small businesses themselves, with their opinions being voiced by lobby organisations such as the Institute of Directors.

Before critiquing such a point of view, it is important to set out the areas of consensus. First, given their role in the economy, there can be no justification for ignoring the interests of small business in the drafting of legislation. Second, there can also be no justification for the legislature being unaware of the impact of legislation on smaller firms, particularly where that impact could be eliminated or substantially reduced by a minor change, while still retaining the legislation's original purpose. Thirdly, it cannot be satisfactory that the volume of legislation relevant to operating a small business is so extensive and written in so inaccessible a form that, in practice, it is ignored by the entrepreneur.

However, matters are rarely as easy as that. We have already made the point that the entrepreneur's 'red tape' is often the same as a worker's 'right' or a neighbour's 'environment'. Secondly, as May and McHugh (1991) show, it is unclear to what extent the lobby organisations are 'representative' of small business as a whole. Their work (Coleman, McHugh and May 1991a) found that only ten out of virtually 300 firms in Stockport and Oldham had ever belonged to any of the leading small business lobby organisations. Six of these had been, or were, members of the Forum of Private Business, three had membership of the CBI, and one was a member of NFSE. The other lobby groups were not mentioned by any business.[1] Small firms, however, were much more likely to join trade associations (which have large as well as small firms amongst their membership) than small firm lobby organisations, but most did not join any organisation at all.

Thirdly, as we will argue later, the agenda of lobby organisations is designed to reflect the majority views of members, yet this may not be the view of the small proportion of small firms which are growing rapidly and making a major impact upon the economy. For example, the Cambridge Small Business Research Centre (1992) survey found that, whilst 3.1 per cent of fast-growth firms are members of the CBI, 7.5 per cent of stable/declining firms are members. A similar pattern is observed for trade association membership, but the reverse is the case for professional associations. Overall, there is then a risk that public policy may be more strongly influenced by the majority members of lobby organisations, but only weakly influenced by growing small firms which have the largest economic impact.

For all these reasons the economic case for the UK Government to give such high priority to 'administrative simplification' remains unproven. The political case is clear, in the sense that it is popular with some small business owners. What is less clear is whether policies, as currently pursued, yield major welfare improvements to society as a whole.

The third element of deregulation and simplification in Table 8.3 is legal form. Freedman and Godwin (1994), show that government needs to review the incentives which influence the legal form of a small business. They argue there are powerful incentives for a small business to choose corporate status and limited liability, even though this legal form is often inappropriate for a very small firm. They point out that, whilst the owners of small businesses believe limited company status provides them with credibility in the market-place, and protects their home from the debts of the business, the latter advantage disappears when banks require personal security. In addition, choice of limited company status imposes additional costs upon the owner of a small firm – most notably those of the conduct of a statutory audit and the lodging of publicly available information with Companies House. In many instances, Freedman and Godwin argue, business owners misguidedly choose limited company status, but then find that it is expensive, complex and a move which is open to misinterpretation to switch back to becoming either a sole proprietor or partnership. For these reasons, the research team indicated that if it was public policy to make limited liability available to smaller firms at lower cost, then the requirements of statutory audit should be lifted.

Partly in response to this, the Government announced proposals for lifting the statutory audit requirements for companies with an annual turnover of under £90,000. For those with a turnover of between £90,000 and £350,000 there is only a need to produce a 'compilation report'. There seems to be more reluctance to pursue the alternative option of 'educating' firms about the benefits of being unincorporated businesses, although this is thought to be part of the Hamilton review of Company Law. Government also has been reluctant to create new legal forms for essentially self-employed workers who work either through an agency or for a very limited number of clients.

As Freedman and Godwin (1994) say:

> Our empirical findings therefore support the analysis of Halpern *et al.* (1980), that an unlimited liability regime would be the most efficient for

Table 8.3 UK Government SME policies

1 *Macro policies*
- Interest rates
- Taxation
- Public spending
- Inflation

2 *Deregulation and simplification*
- Cutting 'red tape'
- Legislative exemptions
- Legal form

3 *Sectoral and problem-specific policies*
- High-tech firms
- Rural enterprises
- Community enterprises
- Co-ops
- Ethnic businesses

4 *Finance assistance*
- Business Expansion Scheme/Enterprise Investment Scheme
- Loan Guarantee Scheme
- Enterprise Allowance Scheme/Business Start-Up Scheme
- Grants

5 *Indirect assistance*
- Information and advice
- Business Growth Training/other training
- Consultancy Initiative

6 *Relationships*
- Small firm division
- Lobbyist/policy formulation

small, tightly held companies to avoid creating moral hazard, transferring uncompensated risk to creditors and inducing costly attempts to reduce these risks.

Overall, the role of government in ensuring that it is not a 'burden on business' is a vexed issue. Government has to decide the level of resources it should devote to ensuring that the voice of the small business is heard when legislation is being considered. But government also has to take into account other interests – the public, employees, its own internal efficiency and the impact upon the economy more widely. The extent to which it shifts the balance or emphasis is likely to depend, at least in part, on the objectives of public policy, specified earlier in this chapter.

Sectoral and problem-specific policies

Table 8.3 identifies five illustrations of sectoral and problem-specific policies where the prime beneficiaries are small firms. The common feature of these policy areas is that they are *not* focused on *all* small firms. Instead, they either examine a sub-group of small firms – such as high-technology small firms or community enterprises – or target certain groups of enterprises or geographical areas where the vast bulk of firms is likely to be small. Illustrations of geographically based policies are those which support enterprises in rural areas, whereas illustrations of groups of firms primarily comprising smaller businesses include co-ops or ethnic businesses. This section reviews the problems faced by such types of firms and reaches a judgement on the extent to which government policies have been effective in promoting their development.

The first group of small firms identified in Table 8.3 is the small high-technology firm. Here, government intervention is justified through market imperfections caused by the problem of 'appropriability'. This occurs for two reasons. The first is because the individual inventors, and their financial backers, are unable to ensure they appropriate to themselves all the benefits of their invention. This makes inventors less likely to seek inventions and financiers less likely to supply resources, and hence causes a public loss. On the other hand, competition in R. & D. can lead to duplication through 'patent races', with 'excessive' R. & D. being required to achieve given levels of innovation (Stoneman 1985).

The response of government has been to introduce policies to overcome what are perceived to be market failures in the supply of finance. It is argued that new and small firms in high-technology sectors require substantial capital to develop novel research ideas. This funding is generally required *before* any product is available for sale.

These firms are therefore high-risk, but also possibly high-return, ventures. They are high risk because they often do not have a clearly identifiable product at the time at which they start to trade. Indeed, there is a real risk that they may never have such a product but the costs of, for example, assembling a prototype, can be considerable. Secondly, the newer or more novel the product, the more difficult it is to assess the scale of the potential market. Thirdly, because of the scientific and technical skills necessary to develop the product, it is often felt by financiers that the business and managerial skills of the business owner(s) may be questionable. On the other hand, the returns from such ventures, if successful, can be extremely high.

For these reasons the UK Government during the 1980s felt it was appropriate to introduce a number of financial schemes to assist the formation and development of new technology-based firms. For example, in 1982 it introduced the Support for Innovation (SFI) scheme, which provided 33 per cent grants for innovative projects. By 1986 this had been replaced with LINK, where firms which collaborated with universities or other businesses in pre-competitive research received grants of up to 50 per cent. Thirdly, Small Firms Merit Awards for Research and Technology (SMART) was introduced in 1986, providing 75 per cent funding for small research projects where the objective was to bring existing ideas to the market-place.

In addition to these financing schemes, the 1980s also saw major growth in the number of science parks in the United Kingdom. At the start of the decade only two such parks existed – those at Cambridge and Heriot Watt – whereas by the end of the decade only a handful of UK universities did not have a science park, either on their premises or close by.

Whilst the development of science parks is by no means exclusively the province of smaller firms, such developments provide an opportunity for academics to become entrepreneurs through commercialising the results of their research. From the viewpoint of local small firms, location on a science park enables better links to be forged with specialist staff. The importance of smaller enterprises on science parks is demonstrated by Monck *et al.* (1988) who show that, at that time, 55 per cent of firms on science parks were single-plant independent enterprises, and only 20 per cent were subsidiaries.

Assessments of the effectiveness of technology-based policies have generally been positive. Moore (1990), in what was admittedly a very small sample of twenty-three firms, found clear evidence that provision of government grants had been a major factor in a number of technology-based firms overcoming market failure:

> Provision of government funds does appear to be some sort of watershed in the company's life. Three of the companies have received substantial risk capital from market sources *after* the grants were received. [Also] . . . by enabling the company to develop innovative technology where it was unable to do so before, the company's product range is enhanced and thus offers the possibility of moving the growth of the firm onto a different trajectory.

The role of government finance in this respect is to reduce the risk to the firm in two ways. The first is simply that the external funding directly improves the business's financial position. The second, and equally important, is the implied guarantee, following the investigations government undertakes before grants are paid, that the technology is worth backing. In this sense it cuts the costs of assessment necessary before external private financiers can make their decisions. As Moore shows, the provision of the award is taken as a positive 'signal' by the financial institutions and frequently leads to significant additional funding.

Assessments of the impact of science parks have also been broadly positive. Monck *et al.* (1988) report the major growth in numbers of new science parks created in the 1980s and a growth in the number of tenant firms. Parks, therefore, were clearly satisfying a demand both from academics as a way of commercialising their research and for enterprises to be located in high-quality accommodation close to centres of learning.

More recently science parks have been subject to some criticism from Massey, Quintas and Wield (1992). They argue that a 'linear' model of scientific research which leads on to industrial innovation contributes to social and geographical polarisation. On the basis of the same data used by Monck *et al.* (1988), they question whether science parks can play a key role in local economic development.

The most recent review of science parks is by Westhead and Storey (1994). Their key finding is that high-technology small firms have higher growth rates and lower failure rates than small businesses in the more 'conventional' sector. They argue that the key issue is to increase the 'supply' of such firms and that the founders of today's high-technology firms require the highest possible academic qualifications. Technologies are advancing so rapidly that only those with a deep understanding of technology are able to ensure its commercial exploitation. Hence the supply of such individuals through the education system has to be at least maintained and preferably accelerated.

Since technology-based firms grow significantly faster than the typical UK small business, public policy has to facilitate the continued creation and development of these types of firm, illustrating yet again that small business policy cannot be divorced from other areas of public policy. These results provide a justification for extending financial support to small technology-based enterprises, through schemes such as SMART awards. More fundamentally, it points to the number of new technology enterprises in the future being dependent upon today's schoolchildren in their choice of subjects to study. It also means that public budgets for higher education, and for science in particular, should be at least maintained. Restrictions on that budget today lead to fewer individuals having the technical capacity to establish businesses which will use the technologies of the twenty-first century (Oakey 1991).

A second group of small firms identified in Table 8.3 are those located in rural areas. It is interesting to compare both their performance, and the role which public policy plays, with broadly comparable firms in urban areas. Interest in rural firms occurs because the bulk of firms in such areas are small.

An overall review of small firms in urban and rural environments in the United Kingdom is provided by Curran and Storey (1993). They point to a number of research findings which suggest that, for manufacturing small firms, those located in 'accessible' rural areas generally outperform comparable firms in urban areas. In many respects these variations in performance reflect the differences in motivations for establishing businesses in rural areas. Keeble (1993) and Keeble *et al.* (1992a) emphasise that many businesses established in rural areas are started by relatively highly educated individuals who are in-migrants to the area and who seek a higher quality of life. Townroe and Mallalieu (1993) confirm this, pointing out these are often arts- and crafts-based businesses. Firms set up in 'remote' rural areas do not appear to perform as well as those in 'accessible' rural areas (Keeble *et al.* 1992a). These firms are likely to increasingly become the target for agencies such as the Rural Development Commission.

The prime public policy challenge to facilitate the development of accessible small rural businesses relates to property and the impact of industrialisation within the countryside. Here a choice has to be made: on the one hand, rural businesses in manufacturing appear to be more likely to seek and achieve growth in employment than their urban counterparts (North and Smallbone 1993), but this growth ultimately leads on to a pressure to seek new premises. The key point which emerges from Smallbone, North and Leigh (1993b) is that rural business owners are more reluctant to move out of their existing town or village than urban owners; they have a commitment to location in a particular village and yet the opportunities for expansion are likely to be restricted by planning controls which are intended to prevent rural areas from becoming industrialised. On the other hand, in order to prevent out-migration, it is necessary for these small firms to be allowed to develop in order to provide employment for local workers. The research therefore identifies an explicit public policy trade-off which has to be made. It also involves providing explicit encouragement to certain types of small businesses – those whose adverse environmental consequences are least, but whose ability to provide employment opportunities in the locality are greatest, should be favoured.

Accessible rural areas have generally been amongst the most prosperous parts of the United Kingdom, whereas the inner-urban areas of the main cities are amongst the most disadvantaged. Here, unemployment rates are well above the national average and there are heavy concentrations of the long-term unemployed – those individuals who have been unemployed for more than one year. In earlier discussions of the objectives of small firm policy in Table 8.2, we pointed to a role which small firms could play both in employment creation and in the reduction of unemployment. However, we noted that the objective of small firm policy may not be simply to reduce the *numbers* of individuals who are registered as unemployed, but to focus upon particular *groups* within the unemployed who are deemed to be in particular need of assistance. One such group may be the long-term unemployed in areas of extreme economic, physical and social disadvantage.

McGregor and Fletcher (1993) examined the experience of 'enterprise policies' in such areas. They focus upon two initiatives: the first is the promotion of community enterprises (CE) and the second is the development of managed work space (MWS). Both types of initiative have been in receipt of significant sums of public money.

McGregor and Fletcher define community businesses as:

> A form of organisation set up specifically to assist disadvantaged communities and individuals, typically through the creation of employment and training opportunities, but also by providing local services. It is distinguished from conventional small businesses in so far as no individual can take profit out of the business. Profits are recycled or

reinvested for the benefit of the community.

On the other hand, MWS is a form of property development which provides premises from which conventional small businesses can trade. MWS provides certain core activities such as secretarial and office services and offers security and business advice for which the tenant pays. Public subsidies may then be used to cover any rent income shortfall. Pioneered in the United Kingdom, primarily by British Steel (Industry) Ltd, the concept has been implemented by a number of local authorities and is even the basis for specialised developments such as incubator units on science parks.

In their evaluation of both CEs and MWS, McGregor and Fletcher examined the cities of Belfast, Bristol, Glasgow, London, Manchester and Newcastle. Their conclusions were that if the objective of policy was to maximise job creation, or to ensure the maximum number of jobs were created per pound of public subsidy, then unquestionably MWS is a more efficient use of public funds than CEs. In this sense MWS 'offers a more cost effective means of enhancing the employment base of disadvantaged urban areas than the Community Enterprise model' (McGregor and Fletcher 1993). Nevertheless, the jobs created in MWS are less likely to be filled by individuals from the immediate locality than is the case for jobs created by CEs. This raises the question, yet again, of the objectives of policy. If policy is designed to maximise job creation, or even to reduce levels of registered unemployment, then clearly MWS is superior. If the objective is to provide an experience of enterprise to those individuals who are least likely to be re-employed in the immediate future – the long-term unemployed – then public funding of CEs might be considered more favourably. The objectives of policy need to be clearly specified before a fully informed judgement can be reached.

A fourth group of firms identified in Table 8.3, the vast bulk of which are small, and towards which some public policy has been directed, are workers' cooperatives. Cooperatives differ from conventional small private companies because they are democratic organisations, in the sense that each member of the cooperative has one vote, whereas in small private companies a particular individual or group of individuals has the bulk of the shares of the business. Cooperative membership normally, but not always, coincides with those working in the business.

Workers' cooperatives in the United Kingdom have a somewhat tarnished image, associated with the poor performance of those established during the late 1970s by the then Labour administration. It is for this reason that, despite the efforts of the Cooperative Development Agency, there are only about 2,000 currently operating in the United Kingdom.

This is not the case in other EC countries. As Bartlett (1993) shows, there may be as many as 50,000 workers' cooperatives in Italy, and more than 3,000 in Spain. In almost all the cases, the cooperatives are small. The central question which Bartlett asks is whether there are differences in the economic performance – most notably in terms of the creation of employment – between cooperatives and comparable small private firms in both Italy and Spain. If there are, and there is evidence to suggest that cooperatives are a more efficient way of creating jobs, then this could be the basis for a recommendation that such types of enterprise be supported by public policy in the United Kingdom.

Bartlett's findings, however, do not point unambiguously in this direction. Instead, they yet again emphasise the importance of deciding what are appropriate objectives of public policy towards smaller firms. He shows that cooperatives in both countries increase employment less rapidly than private firms in relation to a given increase in demand. This indicates that cooperatives are not likely to be a useful vehicle for crude job creation policies, although a corollary of the findings is that, over the business cycle, stability is likely to be greater in cooperatives than in private firms. The key issue is that the quality of the jobs undertaken by members of cooperatives was clearly much superior to that of those undertaken by workers in small private firms. Both the Spanish and the Italian cooperatives had virtually three times as many workers as a proportion of their labour force on training courses than small private firms in those countries. There also seems to be evidence that productivity growth both in Italian and Spanish cooperatives exceeded that of comparable small private firms in those countries – although output per head was currently higher in the private enterprises. Bartlett attributes the recent growth in productivity amongst cooperatives to their greater likelihood of reinvesting their surpluses in plant and machinery and investment in workforce training.

An assessment of the potential importance of cooperatives stresses the need for clarity in the objectives of public policy: if the objective is simply to maximise job creation in the short run, then cooperatives appear to yield no clear advantage over small private firms. If the objective is more long-term, and with an emphasis upon the quality of jobs created, then the evidence from southern Europe is that the promotion of cooperatives could yield some significant benefits.

The final sub-group of smaller firms, identified in Table 8.3, which have been the focus of public policy attention are ethnic minority businesses. Following rioting in Brixton and other inner-urban areas in 1981, one of the key recommendations of Lord Justice Scarman's report (Scarman 1981) was that ethnic minority business ownership should be promoted to avert 'the perpetuation in this country of an economically dispossessed black population' (quoted in Jones and McEvoy 1992).

In the United Kingdom, many ethnic businesses – regarded primarily as those where the owners themselves or their immediate families originally migrated from India or the Caribbean – are located in large urban areas, and the issues relating to them are in many ways similar to those relating to the stimulation of enterprise in disadvantaged areas in general. The additional problem facing ethnic firms is that many suffer from problems of racism.

As Jones, McEvoy and Barrett (1993a) demonstrate, particular problems emerge in designing public policies to assist ethnic enterprises. For example, both Afro-Caribbean and Asian businesses are significantly more likely to use unpaid family labour than white businesses in the same sectors. This again means that it is necessary to be clear about the objectives of public policy – whether it is designed to promote job creation, and if so, for whom. In part, this emphasis on family labour may be because ethnic business owners feel alienated or intimidated in dealing with agencies such as Job Centres but, in part, it also reflects the tighter-knit family communities which can exist amongst ethnic groups. A related issue is the findings of Marlow (1992) that advisory services to the ethnic business community are much more likely to be utilised when provided by ethnic individuals or ethnic-based organisations. Even so, Jones and McEvoy (1992) find ethnic business founders are more likely to use public support than white-owned firms.

Although both are regarded as 'ethnic' businesses, significant differences between the Afro-Caribbean and South Asian groups are apparent. Although Jones *et al.* are anxious to avoid racial stereotyping, it is the case that Afro-Caribbeans have much lower rates of self-employment than Asians. The latter, in turn, seem heavily concentrated in retailing, whilst the major area for Afro-Caribbean enterprise is in hairdressing and the music industry. One key public policy objective is to raise self-employment rates amongst the Afro-Caribbean community. For Asians, the crucial development is to move away from 'long hours, dead-end' retailing towards the provision of products and services which yield a higher added value.

One familiar theme which emerges from the work of James Curran over many years is the diversity of the small firm sector and, by implication, the difficulty of having a 'small firm policy'. Nowhere is this better illustrated than in this section, where the focus has been upon public policy directed towards a diverse group of small firms – varying from high-technology enterprises to community enterprises, but including ethnic-owned corner shops and workers' cooperatives. Common to all are problems with financing, premises and management, which the Government, through its agencies, is trying to address. The problems, however, differ from group to group, from firm to firm, and locality to locality. Furthermore, the objectives of public policy are rarely specified and appear to reflect the need 'to do something' or 'to be seen to be responding', rather than as part of a coherent agenda designed to achieve clear objectives.

Financial assistance

The discussion so far has examined small firm public policies concerned with macro-policy, deregulation and administrative simplification and with sectoral and problem-specific policies. The next two sections focus upon financial assistance policies which are most clearly directed towards smaller firms, with a distinction being made between those where financial payments are made to the firm and policies explicitly designed to improve the efficiency of the firm – referred to as indirect assistance.

This section deals with financial payments, but it needs to be read in conjunction with Chapter 7 on financing, where the Loan Guarantee Scheme and the Business Expansion Scheme/Enterprise Investment Scheme were discussed. Here discussion is limited to the role of the Enterprise Allowance Scheme and its successor, the Business Start-Up Scheme (BSUS), with the purpose again being to conduct an appraisal of the effectiveness of these schemes.

It is with mixed emotions that the current author has to report on the history of the Enterprise Allowance Scheme (EAS). In earlier writings on public policy towards small firms (Storey 1982a,b) this author pointed to the anomaly in which an individual who was unemployed could not earn in excess of £0.75 per day from any activity without fully forfeiting unemployment pay for that day. At that time, I wrote:

> If the unemployed were allowed their full unemployment pay for a period up to 12 months when they were starting their business, provided that business paid all its taxes, this would have a number of benefits. First it would encourage those people, who currently find it too risky, to start a business by giving them 12 months to determine whether their idea is viable. The Government will gain by receiving some tax revenue where it previously obtained none, and it would be able to reduce its employment of enforcement officers. Consumers would gain by having a greater variety of goods and services provided at competitive prices.

Whilst these words were in print the Government introduced a pilot scheme, known as the Enterprise Allowance Scheme, in line with these recommendations. Under this scheme, £40 per week was paid over a fifty-two week period to individuals wishing to start their own business. The allowance was set to correspond broadly to a married person's supplementary benefit (£37.50 at that time, plus Class 2 National Insurance contributions at £3.40). The objective was to help unemployed people create viable new businesses which would not otherwise exist.

A review of the Enterprise Allowance Scheme was undertaken by the National Audit Office in 1988. Table 8.4, taken from the National Audit Office report, with later updated information, shows the rapid rise in the numbers of entrants to the scheme. These rose from 2,500 in the pilot stages during 1982–3, peaking at 106,300 between 1987 and 1988. Possibly associated with the overall fall in unemployment in the economy as a whole, numbers on the scheme then fell fairly continuously until shortly before the budget for the scheme was transferred to local Training and Enterprise Councils (TECs) in 1991–2.

Table 8.4 Enterprise Allowance Scheme: expenditure and entrants

Year	*Expenditure £m.*	*Target no. entrants*	*Entrants*	*Drop-outs*	*Drop-out rate (per cent)*
1982–3	2.4		2,500	365	14.6
1983–4	23.2	25,000	27,600	3,730	13.5
1984–5	76.7	50,000	46,000	5,060	11.0
1985–6	103.9	62,500	60,000	7,800	13.0
1986–7	143.4	85,900	86,800	13,450	15.5
1987–8	195.9	102,500	106,300	17,000	16.0
1988–9	196.7		98,500		
1989–90	170.9		77,900		
1990–1	132.9		60,300		
1991–2	105.2		49,600		
1992–3	N/A		40,500		

Sources: National Audit Office: 1982–3 until 1987–8; Employment Department: 1988–9 until 1992–3

It can also be seen that the targets of numbers of entrants were broadly met in each year and that the gross expenditure on the scheme at its peak was virtually £200m. Finally, the table shows that around 14 per cent of those entering the scheme failed to survive during the year in which the subsidy was paid.

The transfer to TECs of responsibilities for EAS led to several changes:

- the scheme was renamed the Business Start-Up Scheme (BSUS);
- applicants no longer needed to be in receipt of unemployment benefit;
- applicants no longer needed to have £1,000 to invest in the business;
- TECs could vary the level and duration of the payments;
- TECs could impose their own entry criteria.

One very useful aspect of EAS and BSUS, from the point of view of researchers, is that panels of entrants have been tracked over a period of time to see how their businesses performed. This information can then be used to determine the extent to which the scheme was 'successful'. The Employment Department stated that the objective of the scheme was to 'help unemployed people in receipt of benefit to start their own business and thereby create new businesses which would not otherwise exist'. We may also infer that its objectives included the creation of employment and the reduction in the numbers of registered unemployed.

It is possible to examine the 'success' of EAS according to all three criteria. The author's own estimates are provided in Table 8.5.

EAS entrants have been tracked, both eighteen months after starting on the scheme and two years after completing the scheme (i.e. three years after starting). The most recent eighteen-month study of BSUS has been completed by Tremlett (1993), and the most recent three-year study of EAS is by Maung and Erens (1991). These studies are used in the subsequent analysis.

Table 8.5 shows the eighteen-month and three-year data in the boxed columns, to make it clear that it is *actual* survey data, and to distinguish it from the other columns which are author's interpolations or forecasts. The eighteen-month study is used only as a device to obtain more accurate estimates of changes after one and two years. Hence the number of jobs in row 6 of the table for the eighteen-month assessment is not included in the total number of jobs in row 7.

The table assumes that 100 businesses are started and subsidised by the Enterprise Allowance Scheme. Row 1 shows that at the end of year 1, eighty-seven businesses are still trading (NAO 1988), but this falls to fifty by the end of year 3 (Maung and Erens 1991). This is a rather lower survival rate than would be expected from an examination of VAT-registered businesses (Daly 1991). We estimate that, given the trends of VAT-registered businesses, perhaps forty businesses would be surviving at the end of year 5, but no five-year survival cohorts of EAS firms have been studied.

Row 2 of the table estimates the number of jobs created in these 100 business starts. In all cases it is assumed the owner's job is created and that, in 90 per cent of cases, this is a full-time job (Maung and Erens 1991). Tremlett (1993) finds that, after eighteen months, job creation is fifty-five jobs per 100 surviving firms. However, thirty-nine of these jobs are part-time jobs and only sixteen are full-time jobs. After three years, Maung and Erens find the total number of jobs are eighty-four per 100 surviving firms, with twenty-six being part-time. In estimating the total number of jobs created, we have assumed that a part-time job is the equivalent of 0.5 full-time jobs.

Given the survival rate of firms in row 1, row 2 is then able to calculate the total number of full-time equivalent jobs in subsidised firms between year 1 and year 5. Taking the eighteen-month data as an example, the calculation is as follows:

$$[(39 \times 0.5) + 16] \times 0.71 = 25 \text{ workers}$$
$$25 \text{ workers} + 67 \text{ FTE proprietors} = 92 \text{ jobs}$$

The table shows that after the end of the subsidy in year 1, the surviving firms have created 102 jobs, and this falls only slowly to year 5. This is because although a number of the firms cease to trade, those which survive increase their employment, so partially offsetting these losses.

However, it is unreasonable to attribute the whole of this growth in employment to the provision of the Enterprise Allowance. This is because a number of individuals starting a business would have done so even if EAS/BSUS had not been available. This is conventionally referred to as 'deadweight'. It was originally estimated by the Employment Department itself that approximately half of the individuals entering self-employment would have done so without the scheme being available; this estimate has now risen to 67 per cent.

Table 8.5 Economic impact of Enterprise Allowance Scheme

		End Year 1	End Yr 1.5	End Year 2	End Year 3	End Year 4	End Year 5
1	Number of firms	87+	71	59+++	50++	44++++	40++++
2	Employment owner * FTEs	82	67	56	47	42	39
	workers ** FTEs	20	25	30	35	36	35
	total FTEs	102	92	86	82	78	74
3	Deadweight rate ***	50%	52.5%	55%	60%	65%	70%
	Employment after deadweight	51	44	39	33	27	22
4	Employment after displacement (50%) ****	25	22	19	17	14	11
5	Impact on registered unemployed °	9	11	9	8	7	6
6	Discounted (NPV) effect °°	9	10	8	6	5	3
7	Cost £60,000 °°°						
	Total fall in no. unemployed	31					

Key assumptions: + NAO (1988) says 13 fail to survive until the end of Year 1. ++ Maung and Erens (1991) say 58 per cent survivors after 2 years. +++ Estimated from Maung and Erens (1991) Table 106. ++++ Inferred from VAT-based death rates.
* Maung and Erens (1991) show, Table 314, that 10 per cent of owners are part-time. ** Maung and Erens (1991) Tables 319 and 321 find after three years, surviving firms have 58FT + 26 PT per 100 firms. Assuming PT = 0.5FT then 71FTE per 100. *** Deadweight rates inferred from Gray (1990). **** Displacement rates of 50 per cent reported by NAO (1988).
° It is assumed that only the full-time jobs created lead to a potential fall in registered unemployed. This is then converted at 0.5 to a fall in registered unemployed. °° Using an annual discount rate of 10 per cent. °°° Assuming 20 per cent of EAS starters would have gone back to work after three months and a further 10 per cent after six months. The additional benefit paid is £40,000. In addition the fixed costs of administering EAS (including training for all) are estimated and unmarried individuals obtain higher levels of benefit under EAS than from other forms of benefit. For all these reasons we estimate a £60,000 cost.

The work by Gray (1990) and by Gray and Stanworth (1989), together with that of the National Audit Office (1988) and Corry (1987), all suggest that employment creation takes place in relatively few of the EAS-assisted firms. For example, NAO reports that 'About two thirds of EAS business owners do not employ anyone and less than 4 per cent of them are responsible for more than 60 per cent of all the jobs created.'

When the scheme was being piloted, Corry (1987), in his unpublished analysis of EAS firms, found it was much easier to identify factors which 'explained' those firms which grew in terms of employment, than to explain the factors influencing survival. This is because the 'survivors' are in two distinct categories – those who barely survive, but continue in the scheme because of a lack of alternative employment opportunities, and those who perform well.

Corry showed that the firms most likely to grow in terms of employment were those where the personal investment of the owner was higher, where there was a strong motivation to make money and where bank finance was obtained. This confirms the results of Gray (1990), who says: 'Two thirds of the participants who took the Enterprise Allowance Scheme, but intended to start whether or not EAS existed, had high survival rates, employed more people and earned more than other EAS participants.'

It is for these reasons that row 3 of the table assumes the deadweight rate rises from 50 per cent to 70 per cent between the end of year 1 and the end of year 5.

Each row of the table takes into account that a number of the businesses assisted by the Enterprise Allowance Scheme will, because of being in receipt of the subsidy, be able to undercut the prices charged by existing firms. In a finite market this leads to existing firms being forced out of business through price competition. This is called 'displacement'. The jobs created in the subsidised firms can therefore only be considered a net gain to the economy when the jobs lost in the unsubsidised firms are taken into account. Despite the significant theoretical contributions made by Elias and Whitfield (1987), it continues to be difficult to devise a method of estimating accurately the extent of EAS displacement. Certain parameters are clear: that displacement is likely to be higher when the product or service is sold locally, particularly where that market is fully satisfied currently. Asking EAS participants about the impact which their business has upon their rivals has been unreliable, the answers probably telling the researcher more about the comparative awareness different respondents have about their rivals than about the actual impact! The lack of a better figure has led to the convention that displacement is 50 per cent, and this figure is used in calculations in row 4.

Row 5 estimates the impact which the scheme has, not in creating employment, but in reducing unemployment. Two assumptions are made. The first is that any part-time jobs can be eliminated on the grounds that these individuals were unlikely to be registered as formally unemployed. The second is that it requires two full-time jobs to be created for each one person removed from the register. This is because a number of the new jobs created will be filled as a result of increases in activity rates – women entering or re-entering the labour force, juveniles being less likely to stay on for further education, fewer people retiring early, etc. Furthermore, in areas of relatively high unemployment, additional job creation leads to lower rates of out-migration, rather than to a fall in unemployment. (See, for example, work on Northern Ireland reported by Scott 1993.) Making these assumptions, row 5 shows the impact upon registered unemployed over the five-year period of job creation.

Row 6 of the table then attempts to take into account the fact that benefits in the future are less valuable than the same level of benefit today. Hence a crude discounting measure is used in which each successive year after the end of year 1 exhibits a cumulative 10 per cent fall in utility.

Finally, row 7 shows that the estimated cost of the Enterprise Allowance Scheme is approximately £60,000 for the 100 firms. This assumes that if each individual is receiving only the same level of benefit under EAS as they would expect to receive on alternative schemes, then the scheme is in fact costless. Yet for those people who are proposing to establish a business, whether or not they are in receipt of EAS, the state does incur additional costs. This is because the rational entrepreneur will stay on the Enterprise Allowance Scheme for the full fifty-two weeks and hence impose a cost on the state, when, if the scheme did not exist, he/she would have started the business without the subsidy.

We estimate, and we have little empirical basis for this, that 20 per cent of EAS starters would have gone back to work after three months and that a further 10 per cent would have gone into employment after six months. The 'additional' benefit paid is therefore £40,000. In addition, the state pays more to young and unmarried individuals under the EAS than under other state benefit schemes. Finally, and this appears to be ignored in almost all the valuations, there is a cost of administering EAS/BSUS. In recent years all participants were expected to spend a day undertaking training, particularly on business planning. For all these reasons, it is probably reasonable to attribute a £60,000 cost per 100 firms which start in the scheme.

If this is the case, then the gross costs can be divided by the number of individuals removed from the unemployment register which we estimate to be thirty-one, suggesting that, at about £2,000 each, despite its imperfections, the scheme does seem to be cost-effective. This is even more the case when account is taken of the fact that these individuals will make payments, whilst at work, to the Exchequer in the form of additional tax and National Insurance contributions.

Even so, a number of reservations may be expressed about the scheme. The first is that it was originally designed primarily to rectify an anomaly in the taxation/benefit system. It clearly was undesirable for individuals wishing to start a business to be effectively penalised by being unable to earn more than £0.75 per day without losing their benefits. Such a rule either encouraged growth in the black economy or, where the risks of this were perceived to be too high, provided a disincentive to starting in business at all. Prior to the introduction of EAS, unemployed individuals wishing to start a business were therefore subject to economic discrimination. Yet five years later, as Table 8.4 shows, more than 100,000 individuals were entering self-employment by this route. EAS had moved from rectifying a modest anomaly in the taxation/benefit system, to become the spearhead of the 'enterprise culture'. By 1988 the unemployed were entering the scheme on an unprecedented scale.

Table 8.5 shows that the effect of the scheme, in terms of job creation and reductions in unemployment were less significant than at first sight. The scheme undoubtedly meant that a number of individuals who were unemployed became business owners for a year or more. In this sense they experienced the 'enterprise culture', which was an (unspecified) objective of the scheme.

Two main criticisms remain.

- The first is that the observed relatively high failure rate of EAS participants, once the subsidy had been removed, was an inefficient use of public funds and one which perhaps could be rectified to some extent by the provision of training and information. From 1987 onwards participants in EAS were generally provided with a single day's training/counselling before starting in business. As a result of that training a number of potential entrants chose not to start a firm. However, as in other aspects of training for small firms, there appears to be little evidence that small firms which invest in training perform better than those which do not. The first insight into this was provided by Corry (1987), who found for EAS firms in the scheme pilot phase that a fairly consistent influence upon non-survival was their use of the Small Firms Service. He attributes this to small firms which are in difficulty being more likely to contact the service, since he finds the opposite relationship for EAS clients which exhibit employment growth. Nevertheless the Government did introduce some training for EAS participants and, by the time the scheme was implemented by Training and Enterprise Councils, 54 per cent of those starting BSUS had been on some form of training scheme prior to start-up. Tremlett (1993), however, finds that of the six types of scheme provided, in every case there were marginally, but not significantly, higher rates of failure for those who went on the courses than for those who did not.
- The second criticism of EAS levelled by both National Audit Office and by Colin Gray stems from the NAO finding that more than 60 per cent of the jobs created in surviving firms after three years under EAS were in 4 per cent of those businesses which originally started. The Office

> believed this provided a strong justification for focusing EAS-type assistance more closely. NAO felt more efforts should be directed towards individuals on EAS who were more likely to be successful in business, with a view to avoiding expenditure on other groups. In one sense the work by Corry (1987) can be seen as a step in this direction, since it examines the personal and other characteristics of EAS business owners, with a view to identifying characteristics of those owners whose business survived, those which grew in terms of employment, and those which grew in terms of the income generated. His results were in many senses disappointing. Whilst the factors influencing survival and growth are broadly similar to those which we identified in Chapters 3 and 5, he was not able to forecast, with acceptable levels of accuracy, the characteristics of 'winners' or 'losers' on EAS.

EAS therefore was never a 'targeted' initiative. This was partly because of the technical problems of targeting – the difficulty of painting an identikit picture of a successful entrepreneur before the business begins – but it may also be because EAS was deemed to have a social and political role. If the purpose of the Enterprise Allowance Scheme was to act as a conduit enabling people to move from employment in large (often highly unionised) enterprises towards being self-employed, then it was entirely appropriate not to restrict access to the initiative. Again, there are strong political grounds for having, as an objective of policy, a strategy to maximise the number of individuals who were subsidised to make this transition. Even if it were possible to make the initiative more cost-effective in terms, for example, of cost per job, through eliminating certain groups, this might have been deemed unattractive for 'political' reasons.

EAS provides a fascinating insight into public policy towards small enterprise in the United Kingdom. On economic grounds the scheme appears to be cost-effective in terms of job creation, or removing individuals from the unemployment register. Yet Storey and Strange (1992) report that in areas of high unemployment, such as the county of Cleveland where in the 1980s more than 40 per cent of those starting businesses were unemployed, the net effect in terms of job creation has been extremely modest. Whilst the county experienced a major rise in rates of new firm formation, firms which were established were much smaller than those established in the pre-EAS period. This suggests a rise in business volatility but little identifiable increase in net employment. In short, there is a rise in the quantity of firms, but there is a virtually compensating reduction in their quality.

The challenge of the 1990s, as we shall argue in Chapter 9, is to implement public policies which specifically address the question of small business quality. What is clear from this chapter, and from Chapter 5, is that there is no accurate 'identikit picture' of a successful entrepreneur which can be constructed from information about that individual, or group of individuals, prior to them establishing in business. Whilst it is possible to favour certain groups, such policy is likely to make significant errors in individual cases. The high risks associated with start-ups is a key element in support of the concept that local policy initiatives should be increasingly focused on established businesses with a trading record (Storey 1993).

The change from EAS to BSUS reflects at least a tacit acceptance of the need for targeting. The relatively healthy survival rates (71 per cent after eighteen months) suggest the TECs have had some success in ensuring better performance amongst start-ups. Nevertheless, it remains open to serious question as to whether public policies designed to increase rates of new firm formation are in the long-term interest of the UK economy (Storey 1993).

Table 8.3 refers to grants as part of the UK Government SME policies. Such grants are normally distributed by local or regional agencies, rather than by central government, although grants are available to firms locating on Enterprise Zones and as part of regional policies.

The small business community generally appears unenthusiastic about the role of grants. For example, Coleman, McHugh and May (1991), in their questioning of firms in Oldham and Stockport, asked about particular measures that government could take to help small businesses. The most frequently referred to measure was lower interest rates – referred to by 40 per cent of firms; the next most frequent response, by 27 per cent of respondents, was that there was nothing the government could do. Making money available for grants or the provision of loans at low interest rates was referred to by only 10 per cent of respondents – slightly higher than the 8 per cent who referred to the need to reduce red tape, but slightly lower than the 12 per cent who thought that the lowering of taxes was the most important. Similar priorities are identified in the Cambridge Small Business Research Centre (1992) study referred to earlier in the chapter.

Despite this, evidence on the effectiveness of grants to small firms is provided by Owen (1992), who examined state aid to small firms in three EC areas – South Yorkshire in England, Nord-Pas-de-Calais in France, and the Hainant region of Belgium. He found that in all three areas the provision of grants had led to additional economic activity. For example, he found in Rotherham that local additionality was at least 60 per cent, with somewhat lower rates in France and Belgium. Wren and Waterson (1991) also report that the provision of grants, primarily to smaller firms in northern England, through regional policy and local economic agencies can be effective in job creation. Whilst the cost per job varies quite markedly from one type of grant to another, they find (p. 132) 'considerable support for the notion that financial assistance can create employment'. The overall effectiveness of grants, however, appears to vary markedly according to macroeconomic conditions so that, for example, the cost per job created by Regional Selective Assistance was seven times higher in the prosperous 1975–8 period than during the recessionary 1978–81 period.

Finally, Keeble, Walker and Robson (1993) in their examination of spatial variations in formations and dissolutions also produce some evidence of the effectiveness of financial assistance. They show that those counties in the United Kingdom which exhibited increases in the stock of manufacturing firms had Enterprise Agencies with direct access to loan or grant funds. The particularly interesting point is that this is virtually the only example of public policy variables appearing as significant in influencing spatial variations in new firm formation or dissolution in the United Kingdom in the 1980s.

The overall pattern which emerges from UK policy of direct assistance to small firms is that the Enterprise Allowance Scheme and other grants do have an identifiable effect. The criticisms of EAS are that is focuses exclusively upon start-ups of generally 'low quality' businesses and probably has a greater 'political' than 'economic' effect but, in its own terms, the scheme is an efficient use of public money. Similarly, the use of grants does seem to induce changes which would not have occurred otherwise.

Indirect assistance

As well as providing financial assistance to overcome market imperfections – as in the case of EAS and other grants discussed above – public small firm policy has been directed towards subsidising improvements in the internal efficiency of small firms. These are referred to as 'indirect assistance' and stem from a perceived need to overcome information imperfections. For example, the small firm is deemed to be unaware of the benefits of training or using external consultants. Most fundamentally it is unaware of how to obtain information and advice.

One of the major recommendations of the Bolton Committee (1971) was the creation of what they referred to as:

> a pure signposting or referral service ... whose function should be to provide information in response to queries, and assistance on technical, financial and management problems by providing introductions to the appropriate sources of professional, commercial or official advice.

This idea of a referral service became the basis for the Small Firms Counselling Service – whose function, as Bolton emphasised, is not directly to provide information, on the grounds that this was a legitimate function of the private sector, but merely to provide guidance to the small business owner as to where that advice could be obtained.

In making any assessment of the effectiveness of counselling or advisory services, there appear to be three main questions:

- Is the service used?
- Do the users find it helpful?

Table 8.6 Public support services for small firms

Source			*Total*	
1 Jones and McEvoy (1992)	Use of any support Agency by:	– White owner	– 7%	8%
		– Asian owner	– 6%	
		– Afro-C owner	– 17%	
2 Coleman, McHugh and May (1991)	Use of Small Firms Service:	– Oldham firms	– 7%	5%
		– Stockport firms	– 3%	
3 Storey and Strange (1992)	Use of any public agency when trading in 1980s:	– Cleveland	– 26%	
	Use of Small Firms Service:	– Cleveland	– 1%	
4 Storey (1982)	Use of any public agency when trading in 1970s:	– Cleveland	– 7%	
	Use of Small Firms Service:	– Cleveland	– 2%	
5 Smallbone, North and Leigh (1993b)	Receipt of assistance from public and semi-public agencies (mature firms):	– London firms	– 5%	
		– Rural firms	– 55%	
6 Cambridge (1992)	Use by manufacturing and business service firms:	– Small Firms Service	– 7%	
		– Enterprise Agencies	– 7%	
		– Enterprise Initiative	– 33%	

- Does use of the service seem to improve the performance of the business?

The majority of assessments of counselling and advisory services have concentrated upon the first two of these questions (CEI/BIC 1985, Enterprise Dynamics 1987). Ignoring the third question arises partly because of the difficulties of making such a judgement, but it also may be that it is feared the answers might be unpalatable.

The evidence on the use of advisory services suggests that, amongst the small business population as a whole, usage is low, although it has probably become more common to use the services in more recent times. This is documented in Table 8.6, which reports the results of six separate surveys which have attempted to address this question. First, the study of white-owned and ethnic-owned businesses conducted by Jones and McEvoy shows that use of any public support services by small firms in a variety of urban locations throughout Britain is approximately one in twelve. The interesting finding is that the Afro-Caribbean business owner is significantly more likely to utilise support from an agency than either white-owned or Asian-owned firms.[2]

A second study by Coleman, McHugh and May (1991) of firms in Oldham and Stockport is specifically about the use of the Small Firms Service. Whilst there are differences in the responses of firms in the two towns, only 5 per cent of firms overall claimed to have used the Service, although more than half of the respondents were aware of its existence.

The third and fourth studies reported in Table 8.6 refer to the county of Cleveland, which probably has as large a range of support services for small firms as anywhere in the United Kingdom. Here, the Storey and Strange (1992) survey suggested that 26 per cent of new businesses established in the 1980s had at some time used a public agency. This is higher than most other studies, and is likely to reflect the substantial network of assistance available to firms in that area. Given that, it is interesting to note the use of the Small Firms Service is only referred to by 1 per cent of start-ups. The fourth study reports the results of asking identical questions of firms established in Cleveland in the 1970s – i.e. a decade earlier than the above study. It is clear that, during the 1970s, a substantially lower proportion of smaller firms were seeking advice and information than was the case in the 1980s.

The fifth study, by Smallbone *et al.* (1993b), highlights differences in the use of support services between urban and rural areas. They show that, amongst mature small firms only, 6 per cent of firms in London claim to have used these public support services – a figure which is broadly similar to that of the other studies in the table. Yet usage is very much higher amongst firms in rural areas, where the Rural Development Commission, in particular, is used extensively.

The final study, by the Cambridge Small Business Research Centre (1992), is the only national study in the table. It reports the findings of (primarily) limited companies in the manufacturing and business service sectors. It shows that, whilst the figures for the use of their Small Firms Service and Enterprise Agencies is similar to that elsewhere in the table, there does appear to have been extensive use made of the Enterprise Initiative.

Overall, these studies suggest that usage of publicly funded advice and signposting agencies by small firms is quite low but, as awareness rises, usage also increases. It is probably also the case that sector differences exist, with usage being higher amongst manufacturing firms. Finally, the Cambridge study suggests that, amongst their firms, usage of the Consultancy Initiative was high.

A number of studies have attempted to address the second key question, which is the extent to which clients of the organisations are satisfied with the service or information they received. The general impression from a number of studies is that these support services are found to be useful by the clients.

For example, the Centre for Employment Initiatives (1985) in their study of Local Enterprise Agencies in Britain found that 19 per cent of firms said the advice and assistance which they received was crucial to employment in their business and a further 38 per cent said it was useful. The Storey and Strange (1992) study of firms in Cleveland reported that 78 per cent of firms which used a public support agency in its first year of trading were satisfied with the service which they received. They also found that the satisfaction expressed with such agencies was markedly greater in the 1980s than in the previous decade, suggesting the agencies themselves were becoming more 'professional' and client-orientated.

This does not, however, imply that the services which small firms receive from public agencies are superior to those provided by private sector support organisations. Storey, Watson and Wynarczyk (1989) find small firms report higher levels of satisfaction in their relationships with both their accountants and their banks than in those with public support organisations.

The much more difficult third question is whether firms perform better as a result of using publicly available information and support services. Measures of performance would include the survival of the firm, its growth in terms of income for the owner or employment. Here the central analytical problem is to determine whether any better performance which is observed is *caused* by the provision of the assistance, rather than merely being associated with it. Conversely it may be that firms experiencing difficulties may be more likely to use agencies.

Evidence on the negative side includes the work by Corry (1987), which suggested that EAS-assisted businesses, other things being equal, were less likely to survive if they had used public agencies such as the Small Firms Service and the Scottish and Welsh Development Agencies as a source of advice. Conversely, Corry showed that the major factor positively associated with survival is the use of a private sector accountant. Using univariate analysis, Tremlett (1993) obtains the same results for the most recent cohort of individuals tracked under the Business Start-Up Scheme. Corry, however, also shows that EAS-assisted businesses which grew significantly in terms of employment were also more likely to have approached the Small Firms Service once the allowance had ceased. This relationship is not tested for by Tremlett (1993).

An apparently more positive finding emerged from Enterprise Dynamics (1987) in their assessment of the effectiveness of Enterprise Agencies. They reported: 'Even on the most cautious interpretation . . . there seems little doubt that small firms assisted by Enterprise Agencies have a significantly better survival rate than the national average.'

Unfortunately, such a conclusion is not robust, given the methodology of the study, for three reasons. The first is that Enterprise Agencies themselves conducted the survey, the second is that the comparison ('the national average') is VAT deregistrations, which were shown in Chapter 4 to approximate only loosely to small firm death rates, and thirdly, no other variables, which are known to influence death rates of firms, were held constant.

Potentially more persuasive evidence is presented in the Cambridge Small Business Research Centre (1992) survey. This shows that usage of Enterprise Agencies and the Enterprise Initiative was greater amongst fast-growing firms than amongst medium-growth firms, with the latter's usage being higher than that of stable/declining firms. Unfortunately, this analysis was only conducted in a univariate framework, so it was not possible to take account of other influences, most notably firm age. Since it only examined surviving firms, the study could not test whether the use of agencies was a factor influencing survival. Even so, the association between agency use and growing businesses is interesting.

Research which investigates factors influencing business cessation generally finds the use of public support agencies is not a significant factor, once other factors have been included in analysis. As shown in Chapter 4, the key influences upon business survival relate to its absolute size, rate of prior growth, its age and to a lesser extent the sector in which it operates. Secondary influences, particularly for younger firms, are the way in which the business is financed and the human capital provided by the owner(s). Once these elements are included, we are not aware of any studies which demonstrate that the provision of information and advice is a significant factor influencing the survival of the business.

Two different interpretations upon these findings as a whole can be put forward:

- The first is that the contribution of the 'Enterprise Industry', as MacDonald and Coffield (1991) call it, can be over-estimated. Whilst it may offer satisfying comfort to its client base, its impact in terms of influencing the performance of assisted small firms remains unproven.
- The alternative interpretation is that it is unreasonable to expect agencies to influence significantly the performance of small firms, since this depends upon a myriad of factors of which they are only one. Furthermore, the measures of firm performance which the studies have used may be too crude to isolate precisely the role played by information and advice.

Of the two arguments, the second looks the weaker. If a policy is incurring public expenditure, then it has to be judged in terms of its effectiveness in achieving particular objectives. The research evidence assembled here suggests the 'enterprise industry' has yet to demonstrate clearly its effectiveness in terms of significantly influencing the performance of small firms. In part this may reflect inappropriate objectives which the 'industry' sets itself. Specifically, it continues to use numbers of clients as one important measure of its 'success'. This seems inappropriate since, if the purpose is to make an observable impact upon firm performance, maximising the number of users of the service may mean that the 'jam is spread so thinly' that no one can taste it. The resulting lack of an observable effect inevitably suggests the effect is minimal.

The provision of information and advice is deemed to be compatible with the governments 'level playing field' objective, since it is designed to enable markets to operate more efficiently as a result of more parties having access to information. The problem is that there is currently little persuasive evidence that, for the small proportion of firms which use public information and advice services, their performance is improved as a result.

A second major 'indirect' small firms policy initiative identified in Table 8.3 concerned policies which are focused upon improving the quality of management within small firms, either by provision of training of, generally, the owner-manager, or by the subsidised use of external expertise. Two assessments of the impact of these schemes are reported here. The first is the assessment made of Business Growth Training (BGT), Option 3 of which scheme was introduced in 1989 by the Training Agency. The scheme was designed to overcome the perception that smaller firms were less likely to train their workers, primarily because of scepticism on the part of owner-managers as to the value of this training. To overcome this, BGT Option 3 provided smaller firms with up to half of the cost, to a maximum of £15,000, of employing a consultant to train and develop their management staff. One objective was to persuade small firms of the benefit of such training so that, once the subsidy had been paid, firms would choose to continue to purchase training at full market rates. Another objective was to observe improvements in firm performance associated with the provision of training.

An assessment of BGT is provided by Marshall *et al.* (1993). Their assessment clearly demonstrates the provision of the subsidy led to a significant one-off rise in the quantity of training undertaken by small firms. There also appears to have been some effect in encouraging firms, once the subsidy had been exhausted, to continue with a higher level of management training than had been the case prior to the provision of the subsidy. Yet, on the key area of whether training influenced firm performance, the researchers are much more equivocal:

> We were less successful in demonstrating that human resource development thereby improves business performance . . . and the lack of a clearly demonstrable link between training and firm performance is one of the reasons why many firms are reluctant to invest in human resources.

The failure of careful research such as that by Marshall *et al.* to isolate an influence of training upon *small* firm performance parallels virtually all of the robust research findings in the United Kingdom on this topic. For example, Wynarczyk *et al.* (1993) were unable to find a link, once a variety of variables were held constant, between firm performance and the provision of training.

They were also unable to find a link between salaries paid to managers in small firms and whether those managers had undergone training. As we observed earlier, Corry (1987) was unable to point to a link between the use of public advisory services and firm survival under the Enterprise Allowance Scheme. Analysis of data in more recent years of survival under the Enterprise Allowance Scheme, when training became more common, also fails to isolate an influence (Tremlett 1993, Maung and Erens 1991).

The Cambridge Small Business Research Centre (1992) survey was also unable to demonstrate a clear link between firm growth and whether training was undertaken. Indeed this study reported 49 per cent of firms to be *not* satisfied with the quality of government-sponsored agency training, and only 4.5 per cent to be very satisfied.

These findings are clearly at odds with 'received wisdom'. Illustrations of such received wisdom include CBI (1993), Midland Bank (1992) and Small Business Bureau (1993). All three documents make virtually identical statements. CBI (1993) may be regarded as typical:

> In the SFC 1988 report it was recommended that lending should be made on more favourable terms to businesses whose managers had undertaken prescribed training. This carrot and stick approach is justified by figures from the DTI which showed that failure rates could fall from one in three in the first three years, to one in ten where training was undertaken.

The efforts of the author to locate the ultimate source of this information have proved unsuccessful. The closest study results seem to be those referred to by the National Audit Office (1988), who say:

> A detailed follow up by the Training Commission of the first 200 trainees on the New Enterprise Programme found that 82 per cent had started in business and of these only 2 per cent failed after three years.

Whilst these figures do not precisely correspond to those being quoted in 1993, their orders of magnitude are broadly similar. Hence, it is disconcerting that 'received wisdom' has to rely upon the New Enterprise Programme which dealt with people starting their businesses at the end of the 1970s as a justification for current training policies. Instead, the more justifiable inference from robust research in this area is that it is difficult to isolate an impact which training has upon small business performance.

A number of reasons may be put forward for this:

- The first may be the quality of the training provided, which is inappropriate to the needs of smaller firms. Associated with this may be the fact that the training is provided by individuals or organisations who may lack an understanding of the particular problems facing small firms.
- The second is that training is provided in a wide variety of different ways: one-day courses, distance learning, nights and weekend specialised

courses, use of external consultants, etc. It is also provided by a variety of different institutions, such as consultants, educational institutions, trade associations, etc. It is provided to a variety of different types of firm in different sectors, of different sizes, of different stages in their development – pre-start-up, start-up, growth training, etc. It may therefore be that some types of training, provided by some types of institution, are effective, whereas others are not.

- The third reason may be that the research undertaken so far has been insufficiently targeted towards the question of assessing the impact of training. This seems the least likely explanation, since it the most sophisticated research which yields the most ambiguous results.
- Fourthly, and probably most importantly, formal external training is irrelevant to the needs of small firms. As argued in Chapter 6, and in Wynarczyk *et al.* (1993), small firms rely heavily upon 'poaching' workers, whereas large firms undertake training as part of their 'internal labour market'. Thus the large firm trains workers to enable them to undertake work according to the norms and standards of the company. The focus, particularly amongst managers, is that the individual will be promoted into a more senior position and the training both gives a wider perspective on the firm, so enabling the current job to be undertaken better, and also prepares the individual for future posts. The training is also often highly specific to the business and so reduces the external 'marketability' of the trainee. Yet these 'large firm' reasons do not apply to small firms. The small business owner has a short time horizon and is less willing to invest in long-term matters such as training. The small firm worker is much more likely to be subsequently employed in another firm, rather than to be promoted 'in-house'. Hence there is less value to the worker/manager in a small firm seeking training and expecting it to be paid for by the firm.

For all these reasons considerable doubts over the effectiveness of small business training have to be registered and contrasted with 'received wisdom' in this area. Bearing in mind the size of the small firms enterprise training 'industry', it does seem curious that more careful scrutiny of small firm training has apparently not taken place.

A third major public policy initiative during the 1980s designed to improve the internal efficiency of small firms was the Consultancy Initiative (CI). This provides small and medium-sized firms with financial assistance towards the cost of purchasing external consultancy to supplement internal expertise in the areas of marketing, design, quality assurance, manufacturing assistance, business planning and financial and information systems. As with Business Growth Training, one objective of the scheme was to improve overall business performance through making use of these consultants. It was hoped the scheme would raise awareness of the value of such individuals through what was referred to as 'a demonstration effect'.

Evaluation of the Consultancy Initiative was conducted by Segal Quince Wicksteed (1989, 1991a, 1991b). The evaluations yielded broadly similar results to those of BGT. They indicate that, for example, 83 per cent of the firms rated the scheme as satisfactory or better in terms of their share of the consultancy cost. Segal Quince Wicksteed also found that the vast bulk of firms had implemented the consultants recommendations, or were intending to do so.

The much more contentious area is whether the provision of the CI led to improvements in performance which would not otherwise have occurred. The measures used by Segal Quince Wicksteed in their evaluation of CI differ from those of Marshall *et al.* in their assessment of BGT. The latter, in order to assess additionality, conducted interviews with 'comparison' firms – which were similar to the BGT-assisted firms, except that they had not participated in the scheme. Marshall *et al.*'s measure of additionality was the difference between the performance of the assisted firms and that of the non-assisted.

Segal Quince Wicksteed did not adopt this strategy. Instead, their additionality was measured by asking firms whether they would have gone ahead with the project if the consultancy had not been available. It has to be said that this is a significantly inferior methodology. The problem is the difficulty which the firm has in making this calculation, as there are inevitably a large number of variables which influence firm performance and which the firm owner has difficulty taking into account when calculating additionality. The value of the Marshall *et al.* methodology is that it specifically takes account of four of these variables – size, industry, location and ownership – which, as we have seen from earlier chapters, are key influences upon small business performance.

Hence the measures of 'additionality' estimated by Segal Quince Wicksteed in their assessments of the Consultancy Initiative are open to question. On the other hand, their reported satisfaction levels of firms which had participated in this scheme appear to be broadly similar to those of other studies, as reflected in high usage of the scheme reported by the Cambridge Small Business Research Centre (1992). What does appear to be the case is that identifying impacts on firm performance through the use of 'matched pairs' schemes is a much more severe test of additionality than asking the firms themselves to estimate the likelihood of going ahead with a particular scheme.

The overall impression from the studies which have assessed the impact of 'indirect' assistance to small firms, designed generally to improve their internal efficiency, is that, whilst the assistance is generally appreciated by the small firm, it is more difficult to link it to improvements in performance.

Too often there are 'findings' from questionable research which have entered 'received wisdom', and which are quoted by the 'enterprise industry'. This is disconcerting because government has been aware for some years, on the basis of its own research, that a substantial 'unproven' verdict hangs over policies in this area.

Relationships

One of the key issues addressed by the Bolton Committee (1971) was the relationship between government and small firms. The Committee reported that 'Many statements made to us in evidence . . . suggested that Westminster and Whitehall were on the lookout for every opportunity to destroy some element of small business.' Bolton rejected this view, but recognised that such a viewpoint was understandable, since there was no minister or department with a special responsibility for small businesses. It therefore recommended that a Small Firms Division be created within the Department of Trade and Industry, headed by a junior minister. Shortly after publication of the report this recommendation was implemented.

The Division continues to exist today as the Small Firms and Business Links Division, having recently moved from the Employment Department back to the Department of Trade and Industry. Our purpose in this section is to utilise the concepts of 'policy community' and 'policy network' to explore the influences upon small firms policy and specifically the Small Firms Division. In this we draw heavily upon the work of May and McHugh (1989a,b) and Barberis and May (1993).

The basis for this discussion is Figure 8.1, which attempts to chart the significance and direction of major influences upon small business policy making. The direction of influences is shown by the arrows, and their thickness is intended to reflect the strength of the influences, the thickest arrows being equated with the strongest influences.

The two major influences upon small firm policy making, shown at the top of the figure, are small firms themselves and large firms. It may seem surprising that large firms are included as important influences, but it is unquestionably the case that many items on small firms policy agenda could only be implemented at the expense of large firms. Examples include legislation on late payment, where large firms are seen to be the 'culprits', or problems over financing where the 'culprits' are the banks, or problems relating to the use of market power by larger firms.[3]

The 'policy community' is shown in the subsequent two levels of Figure 8.1. The first level shows four circles, each of different sizes, again designed to reflect the strength of influence which they exert on policy making. The largest circle, and by implication the greatest influence, is exercised by lobbyists. These lobbyists are primarily 'membership organisations', some of which only have the small firm as members, such as the Forum of Private Business and the Association of Independent Businesses, whereas others lobby on behalf of the business community generally but, as in the case of the CBI, have a small firms committee.

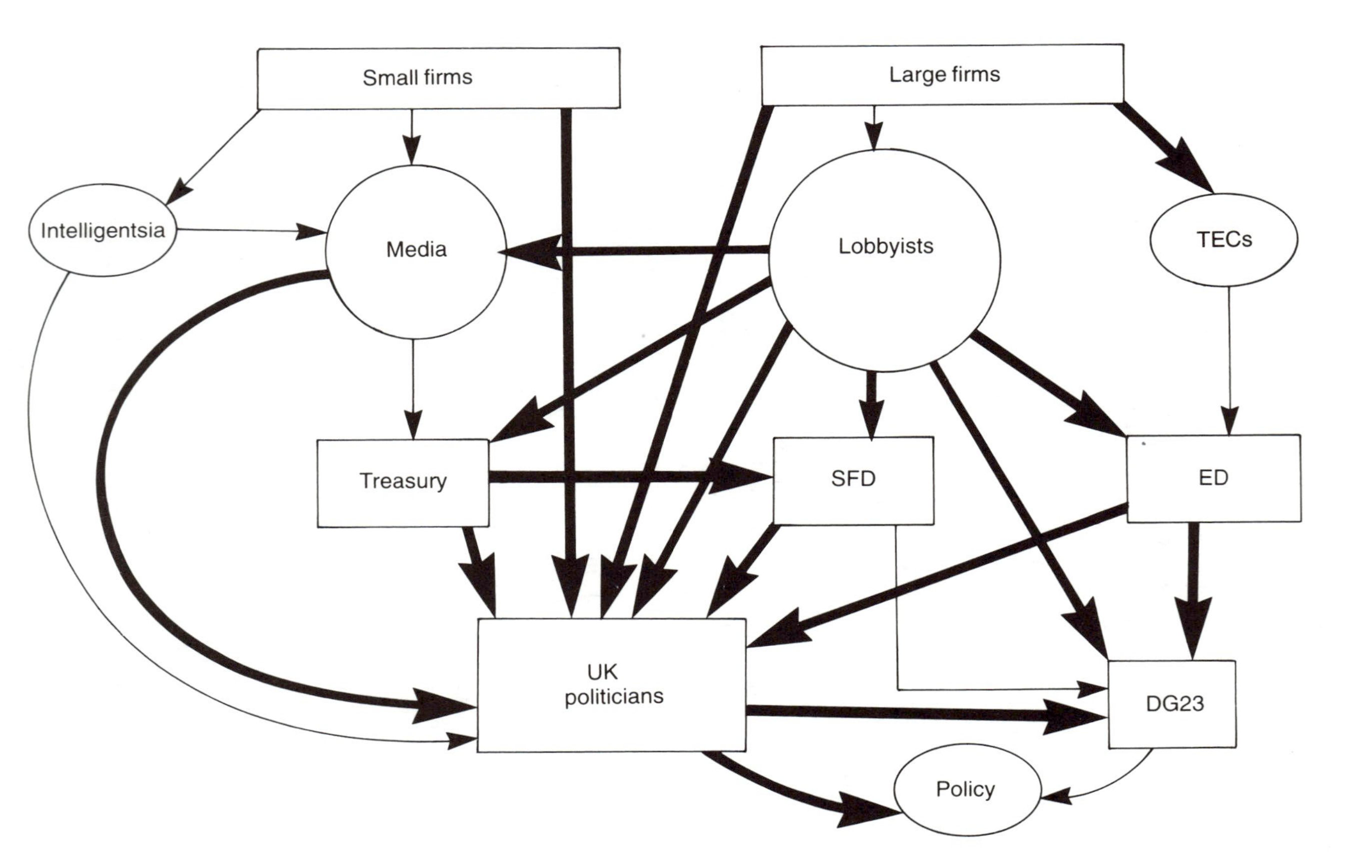

Figure 8.1 Small firm policy-making framework in the United Kingdom

For this reason Figure 8.1 shows that the prime influence upon the lobbyists is small firms, but that large firms also operate through the lobby organisations and influence small firm policy in this way. The key point here, however, is that lobby organisations are not homogeneous. Lobbyists range from national trade associations, where firms are of very different sizes but are all members of the same sector, to local chambers of commerce, where the vast bulk of the members are small and membership includes a wide variety of different sectors. Professional associations might also be placed in this category.

Lobby organisations also have different 'styles'. The Forum of Private Business and the Institute of Directors are seen to conduct highly public campaigns on particular topics, whereas the Union of Independent Companies seems closely allied to the Conservative Party and to exercise this influence at a more personal level with ministers and Members of Parliament.

A second member of the 'policy community' is the media. This includes both national newspapers, radio and television and specialist journals. Figure 8.1 implies the media has a strong impact directly upon UK politicians, as well as upon the relevant government departments and their officials, as shown in the third level of the diagram. The media is also a clear focus of attention for lobbyists, but derives some information directly from the small firms. The media also relies to some degree on the intelligentsia.

The latter may be considered as the third element of the 'policy community' and includes those undertaking academic research in this area and, to a lesser extent, 'think tanks'. Figure 8.1 shows the intelligentsia relies primarily upon small firms for information. It is probably appropriate to make a distinction between the academic component of the intelligentsia, where the prime dissemination, as it affects policy, is through the media, and the 'think tank' element which has much more direct access to politicians.

The fourth element of the 'policy community' is Training and Enterprise Councils (TECs). The characteristic of TECs is that, although they have local responsibility for enterprise training in small firms, they also have wider labour market responsibilities for training in general. It is perhaps for this reason that the industrialists who constitute the bulk of the board members of TECs are drawn primarily from large employers in the locality. Figure 8.1 therefore shows a large arrow from the large firm box as an influence on TEC policies. It may also seem curious that the other three elements within the policy community – intelligentsia, media and lobbyists – are not regarded as major influences upon TECs. Casual observation, however, suggests such is not the case. Since their establishment, many Training and Enterprise Councils appear to have asserted a fierce independence, taking to heart the need to ensure that their policies suited local, rather than national, needs. In so doing, however, many have tended to 'reinvent the wheel', and so to date have had only a very indirect impact upon small firm policy making.

The fifth component of the 'policy community' is the traditional government departments concerned with small firms. These are shown as the third level in Figure 8.1. We have already made reference to what has now become the Small Firms and Business Links Division within the Department of Trade and Industry. Responsibilities for overall monitoring of, for example, BSUS and some training activities remain with the Employment Department and so this is included as a major government 'player' in small firms policy making, although it has become much less influential than in the past. Finally, all small firm policy matters having financial implications, and particularly those relevant at budget time, are the responsibility of the Treasury. Lobbyists therefore focus their attention heavily upon these three government departments. They also seek to influence these departments less directly, through pressure from the media.

In no sense is this an exclusive list of government departments or agencies with an interest in small firms. For example, the Department of the Environment has prime responsibility for inner-city policies where the employment-creation role of small firms is important. The Home Office has an interest in ethnic businesses, whilst organisations such as the Health and Safety Executive are heavily involved in the debates over safety and 'red tape' in small firms.

Policy which emerges from these sets of influences reflects decisions which are made both in the United Kingdom and the European Community. The fourth level of Figure 8.1 reflects these influences. It shows that UK politicians are subject to a number of very powerful influences. The first, and probably most important, is directly from small firms themselves. This pressure comes from the small firm owner as a voter. Blanchflower and Oswald (1992) reported that 56 per cent of the self-employed identify with the Conservative Party, compared with 18 per cent who identify with the Labour Party. This contrasts with employees, 36 per cent of whom identify with the Conservative Party and 33 per cent with the Labour Party. These data are taken from the British Social Attitudes Survey 1983–7 and 1989. Curran (1992) finds even more striking results. In a survey of small business owner-managers, he found that 52 per cent regarded the Conservative Party as best for business, compared with only 11 per cent for Labour at the time of the 1992 election. Heath, Jowell and Curtice (1985) also reported that in the 1983 election, 71 per cent of those engaged in mainly small-scale economic activities voted Conservative.

This direct influence is exercised primarily through letters written by small firm owners either directly to their MPs or to the relevant minister. Recent occupants of the role of small business minister, such as Baroness Denton, have been particularly keen to ensure they received a stream of evidence about individual cases supplied directly by the firms themselves, when discussing public policy. Direct access to politicians is therefore a key influence upon policy making in this area.

However, it is difficult for civil servants and ministers to gauge the significance of particular issues through direct contact with the small firm community, beyond issues such as interest rates or tax policy which can be discerned without any contact at all. This is primarily because there are three million such individuals, many of whom have differing opinions on the same subject. Officials and politicians therefore rely heavily upon information supplied to them from the media and are particularly dependent upon the information 'processed' for them by lobbyists. The problem, as noted on p. 267, is that relatively few small firms are members of any of the lobby organisations and therefore there is a question over the extent to which information presented is 'representative'. The second problem is that the lobbyists themselves are in some senses competitors with one another and have different responses to issues – such as concerning late payment. Each competes for members and assumes their membership will be impressed with being able to demonstrate that a particular victory has been achieved through their own efforts.

Figure 8.1 also shows that the European Commission is an influence upon the environment in which small firms operate. Within the Commission, Directorate General 23 (DG23) has special responsibility for smaller firms, and has four main tasks.

- The first, and most important, is to scrutinise European Community legislation to ensure the interests of small firms are taken into account.
- Secondly, DG23 is concerned with information dissemination, primarily across the boundaries of member states, and has established opportunities for links between firms such as BC-Net.
- Thirdly, the Commission is concerned to encourage the trading by small firms across boundaries of member states and organises symposia such as Europartinariate.
- Finally, it sees itself as a repository for information about the effectiveness of policy in member states – the production of the annual European Observatory Report for SMEs being an illustration of this role.

The central influences on the agenda of DG23 are the lobbyists themselves, such as the European Chambers of Commerce Association, with whom DG23 consults regularly. It also has an 'Article 4' committee, on which are represented the UK government departments of Employment and Trade and Industry. Finally, of course, members of the European Parliament also exercise influence over the agenda of DG23.

This description of policy making in Figure 8.1 cannot be comprehensive. It is certainly possible to point to additional relationships, other than those identified in the figure, between elements of the policy community. For example, the intelligentsia does have links with politicians, government departments, TECs, DG23 and with the lobbyists. Nevertheless, it is unquestionably the case that UK politicians are much more strongly influenced in delivering policy in this area by lobbyists, small firms themselves and the media, than they are by the intelligentsia. The absence of arrows between boxes and circles is then not to be interpreted as 'no relationship', but also includes only weak relationships.

Finally, we recognise that large firms have an influence upon UK politicians in implementing small firm policies. As noted earlier, tensions exist between the competing interests of small and large businesses and, if the media are to be believed, strong advocates of causes dear to small firms can antagonise the large firm sector. For example, it was reported in the *Daily Telegraph* of 3 October 1993 that the then Small Firms Minister, Baroness Denton, was moved to an alternative post because she had 'gone native', upsetting larger firms and the banks by 'unduly' championing the interests of small firms.

The complexity of the policy-making framework for small firms in the United Kingdom reflected in Figure 8.1 is perhaps best summarised in words by May and McHugh (1989a):

> The small business policy community is rather like an extended family or tribe in which there is a degree of shared kinship. The nature of the particular relationship between the participants varies from the close and intense to the rather tenuous and even strained. Exactly which parts of the tribe participate in which family occasions will depend on the occasion in question. On some occasions many will be engaged while in others fewer will be involved. Similarly the role and importance they assume will vary, although some like the Small Firms Division will tend to be consistent and significant participants. Just as the tribe reflects the existence of a number of different family groups, so the policy community contains a variety of policy networks. The variety of networks reflects in turn particular preoccupations, interests and perceptions of different segments of the small business sector. In trying to make sense of small business policy making it is important to recognise there are particular segments which cover the heterogeneous nature of the sector as a whole.

Our overall purpose in this section has been to provide an understanding of the framework of small business policy making in the United Kingdom. It has emphasised the importance of the various lobby groups, but it has also stressed the 'political' nature of this process. It has emphasised, particularly under a Conservative administration, the importance of the direct links between votes and the small business community. This description is intended to provide a deeper understanding of the nature of the existing public policy UK framework described in this section.

Even in a UK policy context, the role of European Community is clearly present, through DG23. One key role of both the Directorate-General, and the increasing importance of international organisations such as the Organisation for Economic Cooperation and Development (OECD), is to provide a forum to better understand which small firm public policies are effective and which are less so. We therefore turn briefly to summarising the findings of de Koning, Snijders and Vianen (1992), who review such policies in the European Community.

SME PUBLIC POLICIES IN THE EUROPEAN COMMUNITY

In the section earlier in this chapter on the objectives of SME policy (pp. 254–7), there was a reference to the study of public policies towards SMEs in EC countries made by de Koning *et al.* (1992). The study inferred there were four major objectives of such policy: competition, strengthening the production chain, diversification of products and services and creation of employment.

This section summarises the key findings of that paper, so as to provide a brief overview of SME policy instruments in EC countries.[4] De Koning *et al.*'s central findings are summarised in Table 8.7 below. This shows the twelve EC countries as the columns of the table, and shows fourteen policy fields as the rows. The prime purpose is to provide a very crude 'count' of the number of measures in each policy field in the twelve member states.

The key to the table is shown below, but the casual reader need only note that the greater the number of + signs, the more instruments there are available for SME policy. It is therefore possible to construct a numerical index based on summing these + signs which gives a measure of the policy fields in which there are most instruments – shown as the numbers in the final column – and as the total number of instruments in each country – shown as the final row of the table.

Taking, then, the crude measure of the number of instruments per policy field, the final column of the table shows technology and R. & D. to be the field in which countries are most likely to have more than a single policy instrument. Luxembourg is the only country with less than three policy instruments in this area. All countries have financing instruments for R. & D. and technology and many in addition have information and training activities. Amongst the leaders are Denmark, which established Technical Information Centres (TICs), and France with the ATOUT programme which was designed to support the diffusion of new technologies in smaller firms.

The second two most frequently referred to fields are those of start-ups and financing. The United Kingdom and France are the countries which have most instruments focused upon start-ups, whereas the countries which have most financing instruments are Germany and Ireland.

At the other end of the scale, despite the crucial role which small firms play in this respect, subcontracting is not a frequent policy field. There is a special law on subcontracting in France, and the Netherlands has developed a special programme on supplying, but this is about all. Similar comments apply to administrative simplification, cooperation and environment and energy.

Turning now to examine the intensity of programmes according to various

Table 8.7 Instruments per policy field in twelve EC countries

Policy field	*Country*												
	B	*DK*	*F*	*G*	*GR*	*IRL*	*I*	*L*	*NL*	*P*	*SP*	*UK*	*Total*
General tax facility	++	o	+	++	+	+	o	+	++	o	+	++	13
Regional development	+	+	++	++	++	+++	++	o	+	+	+	++	18
Technology/R. & D.	++	++	+++	+++	+++	+++	++	+	++	++	++	++	27
Suppliers and contractors	+	o	+	+	+	+	o	o	+	+	+	+	9
Export	++	++	++	++	++	+++	++	+	++	+	+	++	22
Employment	++	+	o	+	+	++	+	o	+	+	++	++	14
Start-ups	+	++	+++	++	++	++	+	+	++	++	++	+++	23
Information and counselling	++	++	+++	++	+	++	++	+	+	+	+	++	20
Financing	++	+	++	++	+++	+++	++	++	+	++	++	+	23
Training	++	+	+++	+	+	+++	++	+	++	+	+	+++	21
Business licensing *	++	+	+	+++	o	o	+	+++	++	+	o	o	14
Administrative simplification	+	o	+	+	+	+	+	o	+	o	++	+	10
Cooperation	o	+	+	+	+	+	+	o	o	+	++	++	11
Environment/energy	o	o	o	+++	o	+++	o	o	++	+	++	o	11
Total	20	14	23	26	19	28	17	11	20	15	20	23	236

Key:
o = no instruments
+ = 1 or 2 instruments
++ = 3, 4 or 5 instruments
+++ = more than five instruments
Source: de Koning *et al.* (1992)
Note: *Here the intensity of the licensing is indicated (see de Koning *et al.*, *Policy on Small and Medium-Sized Enterprises in Countries of the European Commission*, (1991).

countries, it is clear that, in general, the larger countries have more instruments of policy. The exception is Ireland, which has more instruments of public policy (twenty-eight) than any of the other countries, but it is quite closely followed by Germany (twenty-six), and France and the United Kingdom (twenty-three). Countries with relatively few policy instruments, particularly taking account of their size and nature of economic development, are Italy (seventeen) and Denmark (fouteen).

Whilst it is a helpful indicator of the *number* of instruments, Table 8.7 does, however, have significant limitations:

- The first is that simply counting the number of instruments does not provide an adequate indication of the effectiveness of policies. Thus there may be relatively few policies, but their effectiveness, in terms of achieving specified objectives, may be high.

- Secondly, policies and instruments may exist, but small firms may be unaware of them and hence take-up rates may be relatively modest.
- Thirdly, the number of instruments may be an inadequate proxy of the levels of subsidy or value of the schemes.
- Fourthly, in some policy areas, it is difficult to isolate what constitute policy instruments and what is part of 'good government'. Illustrations of this are the relatively small number of instruments attributed to administrative simplification, which may be so well integrated into government policy formulation that there is little need to establish units such as the United Kingdom's Deregulation Unit or the Industrial Costs Monitoring Group (ICMG) in Ireland.
- Finally, the table provides no indication of the effectiveness of policy, nor of the extent to which the different policy fields are co-ordinated. For example, this chapter has been critical of the lack of coherence of UK policy towards small and medium-sized enterprises, but it is equally the case that none of the EC countries has yet produced any policy document which clearly sets out objectives of SME policy and how its configuration of policy instruments sets out to achieve these objectives.

The value of Table 8.7 is to provide a 'first stab' at the distribution of policy instruments across fields of activities. In so doing it points to fields in which most countries have policies, and to others where some countries have a number of policies and others have few. Its purpose is to begin debate as to which configuration of policies is appropriate for a particular country. The next stage is to reach some agreed assessment of the effectiveness of policies and conclude whether it is appropriate to divert resources away from one field and into another, or to reduce the level of resources altogether. In the case of the United Kingdom it is possible to make these judgements on the basis of research evidence on the effectiveness or otherwise of policy measures. This is examined in the final section in Chapter 9 dealing with implications for government.

CONCLUSIONS

There are a number of key conclusions to this chapter. First, the small firm sector in the United Kingdom has now reached a size and importance in which public policy towards it cannot be left entirely to those with a vested interest in smaller firms. Enterprise policy is relevant to those looking to achieve economic development in urban areas experiencing high levels of deprivation. It is appropriate to employees of smaller firms and appropriate to those whose environment is influenced by the activities of smaller firms. This means public policy towards the sector has to examine the implications of small firm policies within a wider framework than has been the case in the past. Within an economic context an assessment has to be made of the macroeconomic implications of small firm policy measures. In the social context an assessment has to be made of both the 'losers' and the 'gainers' from particular initiatives.

Unfortunately, this is unlikely to happen until government imposes greater consistency in this policy area, rather than adding to the 'patchwork quilt' of policies which currently exists. It is vitally important that government produces a White Paper on this topic which sets out the objectives and targets of policy in measurable terms. It also needs to clarify how the current policies fit together to achieve those overall objectives. No such document exists currently. Only when targets are clearly specified will it be possible to determine accurately whether policies are successful and, if not, what alterations in the portfolio of policies should be implemented.

Despite the absence of such a document, the existing research findings provide a guide to appropriate public policies in this area. Several powerful themes emerge: the first is that the key influences upon the development of small firms lie in government macropolicy. Firms themselves regard the key role of government as its influence on the levels of aggregate demand in the economy, rather than as the provider of the many support schemes which currently exist. However, as pointed out earlier, it is not solely the opinions of small firms which should be the driving force behind small firms policy. Nowhere is this better illustrated than in the key finding that, despite the creation of a more 'beneficial' tax regime during the 1980s, the self-employed between 1979 and 1986 worked fewer hours, given their circumstances, than in the 1970s. Yet the 1980s was a decade in which personal taxation rates were deliberately cut in the United Kingdom, at least partly to provide an incentive for smaller enterprises and the self-employed to work harder. This finding demonstrates the importance of distinguishing between what people say and what people do.

Secondly, there appear to be three areas of existing policy towards small firms where the 'returns' currently are unproven.

- The first relates to the question of deregulation and administrative simplification. From the viewpoint of the firms, government initiatives in this area appear to have had some effect, even if these changes are grudgingly appreciated and there are powerful voices demanding further action. From the viewpoint of society as a whole, however, it has yet to be demonstrated that policy intervention in this area leads to welfare improvements.
- The second area is that of training: here it has still to be demonstrated that the considerable public expenditure on training of owners, managers and workers within small firms exerts a significant influence upon the internal performance of the firm. Specifically, careful research has yet to show that undertaking training influences either the rate of growth or the survival rate of smaller firms.

- The same finding appears to be true for the provision of information and advice. Despite the growth of the 'enterprise industry', careful research has failed to demonstrate a clear link between the provision of information and advice and the better performance of the firm.

The justification from research for small firm policies in these areas is therefore open to question.

Turning now to the positive side, there are two elements of public policy which seem to be effective:

- Probably the most important of these relates to technology policies under which high-tech firms receive financial and other forms of support. The research evidence presented in this chapter suggests that the support received is a key influence upon the development of these businesses. However, it is not only through direct assistance that government can support the growth of new technology-based businesses. A key influence upon these types of firm, which have significantly faster growth rates than typical small businesses, appears to be the public expenditure decisions which government makes, both in supporting science in higher education and in encouraging schoolchildren to take science-based subjects. Quite simply, if government wishes to ensure that in the twenty-first century there is a high rate of formation of technology-based businesses, the Westhead and Storey (1994) research suggests the supply of doctorates in science-based subjects needs to be increased. A Ph.D. is, in future, likely to become the 'entry qualification' for the high-tech entrepreneur.
- A second area which does seem to have some effect upon small firm performance is financial grants. The evidence here suggests that firms and jobs are created by regional and local grants and also, at relatively modest costs, by the Enterprise Allowance Scheme (Business Start-Up Scheme).

Although the EAS is cost-effective in job creation, two criticisms are made of it:

- The first is the high failure rate and the high displacement rate of assisted businesses – raising the question of whether it is possible to be more selective about those who enter the scheme. A review of the evidence suggests that selectivity on EAS or BSUS is not feasible because of the difficulties of identifying the characteristics of individuals who are going to be successful in business, prior to start-up.
- The second problem with EAS/BSUS is that it provides the wrong signal to policy makers – suggesting that the emphasis should be on encouraging the number of business starts, rather than focusing assistance upon existing businesses with growth potential. As the current author has argued elsewhere, the latter strategy would appear to yield rather greater

public returns than the former (Storey 1993).

To summarise, therefore, there is a clear need for a statement about objectives and targets for small firm public policy. This should be in the form of a government White Paper, so that targets can be identified and measured. Research also suggests that on economic grounds there appears to be justification for 'soft pedalling' on initiatives relating to start-ups, training, information and administrative simplification. Conversely, a much greater emphasis needs to be placed upon setting the appropriate macroeconomic environment technology policy, grants and targeting policies towards existing firms with growth potential.

As we show in the chapter, however, small firm policy is not exclusively part of economic policy. If account is taken of the political significance of smaller firms, then the current emphases in the policy agenda can be much more easily understood. Current policies reflect the interaction of small firms, large firms, lobby groups, politicians and civil servants. To rearrange government priorities towards the small firm sector in the ways suggested, whilst it would have significant economic benefits, could have electoral implications.

Chapter 9

Conclusions

OVERVIEW

It is appropriate at this point to remind the reader that the title of this book is *Understanding the Small Business Sector*. To achieve such an understanding, this book has not only to describe what is happening, but must also provide an explanation of why it is happening. It has been our intention in the previous chapters to provide that understanding. This chapter draws upon that understanding and examines the implications for three key actors: small firms themselves, the financial institutions (most notably the banks), and government. Yet to do this without sketching in some of the consistent themes which have emerged in this volume would lead to recommendations unrelated to understanding. For this reason the chapter will reiterate two key themes which have emerged, and then link these to policy matters.

Even so, it is not our objective to forecast what is likely to happen to smaller firms in the United Kingdom over the next decade or so. The reader interested in informed speculation should consult the work of Grayson (1990). He argues that amongst the megatrends likely to influence the development of small businesses are the increasing importance of older people in the workforce, the increased role of females as entrepreneurs, the move towards a higher proportion of total employment being in the service sector, and greater emphasis upon part-time but often highly skilled occupations. There seems no reason from the research conducted to challenge these forecasts.

Our purpose here is to repeat two key findings as the context for policy makers. The first is to emphasise that small firms in most developed economies are currently more important in terms of contribution to GDP and employment growth than was the case twenty years ago. However, it is a fallacy to assume that those countries which have a higher proportion of their employment in smaller firms have necessarily performed better than countries with economies which are more dominated by large firms. It is also a fallacy to assume that those countries which have experienced the most rapid increases in new firm formation (measured in terms of increased self-employment) are those which have experienced the fastest increase in employment creation. Instead, the evidence suggests that increases in self-employment are generally unrelated to increases in employment (OECD 1992). The only interesting contrary observation is that, during the post-1979 period, countries with high increases in self-employment tended to have somewhat lower increases in (registered) unemployment.

Chapter 6 shows that it is not justifiable to assume that, because small firms have been creating jobs at a time when large firms have been shedding jobs, an increase in the number of small firms therefore leads to increased employment or lower unemployment. It is not even justifiable to infer that such trends necessarily justify a greater focus in policy in favour of small firms and away from large firms.

The second issue is one with which the Bolton Committee was concerned in 1971. This was whether the decline in the relative importance of the small firm which had taken place over the previous twenty years in the United Kingdom was likely to continue. Bolton made the interesting point that, 'In considering this question we have found no help in published academic research and little in the statistics which we collected.' Nevertheless the Committee concluded that, in its phrase, 'given a fair crack of the whip', the small firm sector would continue to fulfil an important economic role. This is generally taken to be one of Bolton's most far-sighted forecasts, since it implied that it did not expect the sector to decline further. This proved to be a correct assessment, although even Bolton was not bold enough to forecast the turnaround in fortunes which the sector was to experience over the following twenty years. We now have to ask ourselves a similar question to the one which Bolton asked. Given that the small firm sector has increased its importance over the last twenty years, do we believe that this is likely to continue?

The evidence in this book is not conclusive, and requires careful weighing. There clearly are trends which suggest that small firms are likely to continue to play an increasingly important role in the economy: for example, the movement towards a higher proportion of employment being in the service sector, where traditionally small firms have been dominant, the trend towards higher levels of income leading to increased demand for 'one-off' goods and services, which are more likely to be provided by smaller firms. There is also an increased demand for more flexible working arrangements – for example tele-working, where directly employed staff are externally located at 'distant' work-stations (Stanworth, Stanworth and Purdy 1993). This would lead to more people being classified as self-employed.

On the other hand, the evidence presented by Acs *et al.* (1991) suggests that economic development is associated with lower, rather than higher, levels of self-employment. Indeed the rapid increase in self-employment which the United Kingdom experienced between 1980 and 1986 appears to have been associated primarily with increased levels of unemployment, the availability of government schemes to promote 'enterprise' and the relatively low levels of state benefits available to the unemployed. In short, Acs *et al.* imply that a reduction in unemployment and alterations in government policy would do much to slow down or even reverse the growth in the numbers of small firms. It is also the case that the United Kingdom, certainly at the start of the 1980s, had a relatively low level of self-employment, so some of the increase can be attributed to a 'catching up' factor.

On balance, the case made by Acs *et al.* seems persuasive, suggesting that growth in self-employment and increased importance of smaller enterprises is likely to slow, particularly in the event of a change in UK government policy. Given that context, the remainder of the chapter examines lessons for public policy makers and financial institutions. It begins, however, with some lessons for small firms themselves.

SOME LESSONS FOR THE SMALL FIRM COMMUNITY

With higher rates of new business formation, the 1980s saw publication of a large number of books which were aimed at a small businesses readership and designed to communicate effectively the lessons for successful small business management. Good examples of these 'how to do it' books include works by Colin Barrow and others, such as Barrow *et al.* (1992), Clegg and Barrow (1984), Barrow (1989), Morris (1985) and Hargreaves (1983).

The current book is not of the 'how to do it' type. It does not seek to inform small business owners about how best to manage their businesses. However, in achieving an understanding of the small business sector, there are certain themes which emerge from the research reviewed and which are highly relevant to the small business owner. Table 9.1 has been constructed to provide a brief summary of these themes, in so far as they relate to small business owners. It does not aim to be a complete 'check-list' of issues influencing the performance of smaller firms – for that, the reader is advised to see the references above. It certainly does not claim that any of these findings are particularly 'new'. Although the issues are placed in order, it also does not even necessarily imply that some need to be given greater priority than others. Furthermore, some issues appear in the 'Dos' column and the converse in the 'Don'ts' column, whereas others appear only in one. Again, no inference can be made in terms of giving greater priority to the messages which appear in both columns.

The first row of Table 9.1 emphasises the importance of directors' remuneration in influencing both the survival of the firm and its growth. Research referred to in Chapters 5 and 7 shows that those businesses which survive and grow are those where the owner has reinvested heavily within the business and been frugal in removing moneys from the business for personal consumption purposes. There is a strong temptation for small business owners to remove moneys in 'good' years, but this leads to their businesses being under-capitalised and hence perceived as high-risk during more difficult

Table 9.1 Dos and don'ts for small firms

	Dos	*Don'ts*
1	Invest in your own business	Don't take out large sums in 'good' years
2	Talk to the bank	Don't 'surprise' the bank
3	Get private sector advice	Don't blame everyone except yourself
4	Keep and use current financial data to make key decisions	
5	Be prepared to consider selling equity	Don't be greedy
6	Grow if you want to survive	
7	If you want to grow, the key elements are: • Product innovation • Management team building • Personnel policy • Marketing	

trading conditions. This finding has encouraged researchers to point to the need to encourage entrepreneurs to invest in their own businesses, rather than making investments in personal equity plans (PEPs), pension schemes, property, etc. (Bannock and Peacock 1989). The evidence from Chapter 7, however, is that tinkering with the taxation system to provide 'incentives' for small business owners has not been successful and should not continue to be a focus of policy. Instead, the lesson has to be learnt by business owners themselves that reinvestment is the key to survival and growth.

A second theme which emerges from Chapter 7 is the importance to the small firm of maintaining good relationships with its bank. This means regular dialogue with the bank is essential if the bank, for its part, is to maintain a long-term relationship with the firm. The simple message for the firm is that its relationship with its bank is likely to be a lot smoother if the bank is kept aware of developments and is not 'surprised' by sudden requests for additional finance.

The third row of the table indicates the importance of obtaining good-quality private sector advice – most notably from accountants, banks and solicitors. The research reported in Chapters 4 and 8 suggests this is influential in explaining why some businesses survive and others do not. The research in Chapter 4 suggests business owners are likely to blame a variety of 'external' factors and events for the failure of their business. On the other hand, the liquidator, who may by viewed as taking a more objective view, is much more likely to lay the blame squarely with the business owner. These two findings are associated, since the external adviser is likely to make it clear what action the business owner needs to take in order to ensure the survival of the business.

Given the advent of modern computers, the availability of spreadsheet packages, etc., it is surprising that so many small firms appear to keep inadequate financial information on which to run their businesses. Even those which do, use this information for making few key decisions about the business. Research in Chapter 7 suggests that, probably linked to point three, the more successful firms are those which keep and use financial data with which to make key business decisions.

A further theme which emerges from the research is the reluctance of business owners to even consider the sale of a proportion of the equity of their business to outsiders. This is generally because they believe this would lead to a dilution of their managerial control. Yet the evidence from Chapter 5 suggests that, where equity is shared, the business is likely to exhibit rather faster growth than where equity is held exclusively by the owner-manager. Although this is not clearly demonstrated, it implies that the owners of businesses where equity is shared with outsiders are wealthier, even though they own less than 100 per cent of the shares of the business. The implication of the right-hand side of the table is that, even where owners consider selling equity to outsiders, the 'price' they wish to charge for that equity is unrealistically high, bearing in mind the perceived risk from the viewpoint of the venture capitalist.

The sixth row of Table 9.1 emphasises it is unwise for owners to assume that, by not growing, there is a higher probability of their business surviving. Research evidence from the United States, reported in Chapters 4 and 5, suggests the reverse is the case. Those small businesses which grow in terms of employment are more likely to survive than small businesses which do not grow.

Although growth is clearly not an objective, probably for the bulk of UK small businesses, those which both set out to and achieve growth appear to share four common characteristics:

- The first is that over time they shift, often only relatively marginally, the product markets in which they operate, and are rarely in the same market-places a decade later.
- Second, the ability to develop managerial teams appears to be a skill of the growing businesses. Businesses which grow are more likely to recruit individuals who are managers and who have previously worked in large firms, and to recruit from outside, rather than to promote internally.
- Even so, businesses with between ten and fifty workers have the greatest difficulty in the recruitment of staff; their personnel procedures and practices are often weak and this is a barrier they have to surmount to achieve growth.

- Finally, the more rapidly growing small businesses generally have particular expertise in marketing when the business begins.

It is again appropriate to conclude this subsection by re-emphasising that few of these findings are particularly new. Instead, they are offered as insights which complement our purpose of examining the implications of small firm research for financial institutions and for public organisations.

IMPLICATIONS FOR FINANCIAL INSTITUTIONS

Table 9.2 identifies six implications for banks, which will be the prime financial institution considered in this section, on the grounds that their contact with small business is more frequent. The first of these implications may seem like a truism: to make better and more consistent lending decisions. Yet it has two very practical dimensions:

- The first is to encourage the bank to give greater weight to the merits of the trading business, and rather less weight to the value of the collateral, when the entrepreneur is seeking funding. To do this requires the bank to have a much clearer understanding of the characteristics of those small businesses which survive and grow, compared with small businesses which fail to survive. Chapter 5 of this volume provides a review of the types of indicators that banks need to take into account in making these judgements.
- The second dimension is that lending decisions by banks need to become more consistent. Whilst account needs to be taken of local circumstances, there are marked differences even between managers within the same bank in their attitudes to identical proposals, which is in the interest of neither the bank nor the entrepreneur. Greater uniformity in bank decision making means diminished discretion of local managers to take into account particular circumstances; conversely, it means an increase in the use of computerised credit-scoring techniques and a movement of decisions away from local branch manager level, to discretion being operated by 'specialists' at head or regional office. Although this can lead to frustration amongst older entrepreneurs who hark back to the days when they were able to 'talk round' their bank manager, the benefits which the system yields to the bank in terms of greater consistency are worthwhile.

The problem facing the banks is that they are large and inevitably bureaucratic organisations dealing with huge numbers of customers, only the largest of which can justify significant amounts of staff time. Banks, however, have the accumulated experience of dealing with large numbers of small firms. Hence it is inevitable that they will draw upon that experience by employing relatively simple rules in dealing with individual small businesses. The

Table 9.2 Implications for the banks

1	Make better lending decisions.
2	Develop long-term relationships with small business clients.
3	Change spectrum of lending towards longer-term financing.
4	Avoid market share competition.
5	Develop 'angels' network.
6	Improve manager training/awareness.

research in Chapters 4 and 5 is likely to form the basis for computerised credit-scoring techniques. This should enable the banks to make marginal shifts away from their current emphasis upon collateral-based lending.

Given the banks' size, these changes have to take place through improved staff training. Most of the major banks now ensure that managers responsible for small businesses participate in training courses to provide them with a heightened awareness of the problems faced by smaller firms. Banks have also consistently seconded staff to organisations such as Enterprise Agencies, where they can see matters 'from the other side of the fence'. Both of these initiatives are in the long-term interests of the banks and are likely to continue.

The second item in Table 9.2 requires a major philosophical shift on the part of the banks. It is to consider their relationship with their small business clients as one which is likely to last into the long term – the so-called 'relationship banking'. The elements of this long-term relationship are that, as noted in item 3, less emphasis is placed upon the short-term overdraft facility and more upon term loans and, in some cases, equity participation. The central problem with the use of the overdraft as the main conduit between bank and firm is that it may be withdrawn at any time with the minimum of warning. It does not provide the bank with an incentive to monitor what is going on in the business, whereas such an incentive would exist if the bank knew it could not withdraw the facilities immediately. It is also the case that, from firms' point of view, although the overdraft is not designed for this purpose, it can and is used for the purchase of fixed assets. For these reasons, the overdraft, whilst extremely useful in its own terms, provides the wrong signals in the relationship between the bank and the smaller firm. Instead, if the fixed-term loan became the norm, this would provide the bank with a greater incentive to obtain a better understanding of the business.

Another implication of making better lending decisions is reflected in the fourth point of the table. It warns against the banks each seeking to increase their market share as an objective of policy. It certainly was the case that, during the mid- to late 1980s, a number of the banks, regarding small businesses as a potentially profitable market-place, sought to increase their market share, often at the expense of the quality of the lending which they made. The recession at the end of the 1980s and in the early 1990s led to huge bad debts and substantial losses to the banks. Even so, such lessons may quickly be forgotten in improved trading conditions. Making better lending decisions does *not* mean accepting all requests for lending. Although rejecting requests for funding from small firms does leave the banks open to charges that there is a 'finance gap', Chapter 7 demonstrates there is little evidence of 'market failure' in the current provision of loan finance for small firms. Instead, the bank has to emphasise that the reasons why proposals are rejected is because they have an inadequate expected return. The rejection of proposals is not necessarily a reflection of a 'finance gap'. The evidence in Chapter 7 is that relatively few projects were unable to secure finance. With bank bad debts from small businesses of £1m. per day in 1992, the implication is that an even higher acceptance rate of small business proposals in the mid- to late 1980s could have undermined the whole financial system in the early 1990s.

Table 9.2 also refers to the development of a network for business angels, discussed in Chapter 7. Here banks can make a significant new economic contribution by bringing together those of their clients who wish to become informal investors in small businesses, with those businesses seeking external equity. A bank could charge for this service but, since it would have both sets of clients on its books, it does seem the most suitable intermediary to exercise this function.

Several of the recommendations in Table 9.2 are being implemented to some degree, with various levels of enthusiasm, by the major clearing banks in the United Kingdom. In this sense they are not wholly novel recommendations. The speed with which banks are moving does vary. In a number of cases the broad philosophical basis of the recommendations in Table 9.2 has been accepted by senior staff, but implementing changes 'on the ground' within large organisations such as the banks is a slow and somewhat *ad hoc* process. Hence, probably the greatest challenge facing the banks in this area is to ensure that philosophical changes embraced by senior staff are actually delivered to the small business customer 'at street level'.

IMPLICATIONS FOR GOVERNMENT

This section discusses the implications for government of the results of the research. Table 9.3 summarises the findings and makes a distinction between items in the top and bottom halves of the table. In the top half of the table are general themes which broadly reflect current government policy in this area, but where some refocusing would be helpful. The lower left-hand half of the table identifies policy areas where there is little research evidence of their effectiveness and hence a case is made for reduced emphasis in policy making. On the lower right-hand side are policies where there is evidence of effectiveness and which merit consideration for additional support.

The basic message to government is that, in its dealings with small firms, it needs to do less and better, rather than more and worse. The very clear

Table 9.3 What government should do

1	Concentrate on creating a suitable macroeconomic framework.
2	Publish a White Paper on objectives and targets of small firm policy.
3	Continue with devolving policy to the local level (TECs).
4	See small firm policy as integral with economic, employment and social policy.

Reduce emphasis in policy on:		*Increase emphasis on*:	
1	Tax	1	Selectivity/targeting
2	Deregulation	2	Technology/science
3	Training	3	'Special' groups
4	Start-ups	4	Financial assistance
5	Information/advice	5	Encouraging dialogue
6	Short-term 'tinkering'		

message which comes across from discussions with small firms is that the key role which government can play is in creating a suitable macroeconomic framework within which firms can prosper. Again, at the risk of producing a truism, small firms seek an environment in which there is low inflation, low interest rates, economic growth and a high level of aggregate demand. It is the ability of a government to deliver these macroeconomic conditions which is the main influence upon its judgement of competence by the small firm community.

In practice, of course, every government would like to achieve these objectives, not only for small firms but for all sizes of firms in the economy. Nevertheless the macroeconomic framework appears to be the 'acid test' by which small firms judge the economic effectiveness of government.

Turning now to the more 'conventional' elements of small firm policy, item 2 of Table 9.3 emphasises the importance of producing a White Paper on the objectives and targets of policy. No such policy document has been produced in the United Kingdom, or in any other EC country. Production of such a paper, which specified the objectives and targets of the small firm policy, would serve a number of valuable functions.

- The first would be to make clear the objectives of policy for government as a whole, rather than for each separate government department. As shown in Chapter 8, it is often difficult to determine the objectives of policy instruments, or how these various instruments combine to achieve policy objectives.
- The second objective of a White Paper would be to specify clear targets of policy, so that it would be possible to monitor the extent to which targets are met, and hence determine whether policies are successful. It would also generate a discussion of whether or not targets are appropriate and whether they fit into the overall objectives of government economic policy. It would be of particular concern to ensure that targets were

'output' measures, such as improved small firm performance, survival, etc., rather than 'input' measures, such as the number of firms in receipt of assistance, the number of individuals trained, etc.

- The third component shown in the top half of Table 9.3 refers to the need to continue with the current policy of delivering assistance at a local level. The concept by which Training and Enterprise Councils (TECs) and Business Links (BLs) operate at a local level and take account of local circumstances seems entirely sensible, bearing in mind that most small firms sell into and purchase primarily from local markets.

Two reservations, however, from the small firm point of view, about local policies are firstly that relatively few of the members of governing boards of Training and Enterprise Councils are employed by, or have experience of, small firms. The second reservation is that, whilst some TECs have been extremely imaginative and innovative in their approach, others have been much more pedestrian. There will also always be variability in any locally delivered system but, on balance, this seems a price worth paying in terms of ability to tailor national policies to a local context.

The final general recommendation for government in developing its small firm policies is shown in the top half of Table 9.3. It is somewhat more contentious and stems from a recognition that small firm and enterprise policies are now so central to economic, employment and social policy issues that they cannot be left to a dialogue with the small firm interest groups alone. Examples include policies to encourage ethnic minority groups to establish their own enterprises in deprived inner-city areas. These have as much to do with combating social unrest and crime as with 'creating enterprise', but responsibility for these issues does not lie with the DTI. Equally, discussions about legislative exemptions for smaller firms relating to employment protection, health and safety, environmental issues, etc. require a wider input than simply listening to small firms' lobby groups complaining about 'red tape'. In short, small firms are now such an important source both of existing employment and new employment opportunities in the future that discussions about public policy towards them have to involve wider sections of the community than small firms themselves discussing these matters with DTI.

Table 9.3 then subdivides between the issues on the left-hand side which are currently part of the public policy agenda towards small firms, but where the research is unable to point to clear benefits, and the right-hand side of the table where there is evidence of the effectiveness of policy. The items on each side of the table are not numbered in a sense of ordering of priorities. It is also the case that reduced emphasis on some issues on the left-hand side of the table implies an increased emphasis upon items on the right-hand side.

There are six items on the left-hand side of the table which are currently part of government small firm policy but, on the evidence presented from research in this volume, are either counter-productive, ineffective or have an unproven impact upon the role which small firms play in economic development. Whilst they may yield some desirable political benefits, which it is appropriate for politicians to take into account in public policy making, the economic case for their support is currently comparatively weak.

Taking each of these items in turn, the case for reducing the rates of personal taxation as an incentive for people to work harder appears unproven. The evidence referred to in Chapter 8 suggests that during the 1980s, when personal rates of taxation were lowered, the self-employed actually worked less hours than during the 1970s. A second example of a taxation scheme designed to induce changes in behaviour which also proved unsuccessful was the Business Expansion Scheme. Here, an appropriate objective such as increasing the supply of equity capital for smaller businesses was in fact used primarily as a tax avoidance vehicle for the wealthy. Its impact upon small businesses was so limited that it was abolished. One year later, however, the scheme was effectively reintroduced, with two major alterations, as the Enterprise Investment Scheme. This followed pressure from lobbyists, rather than independent research evidence.

The research evidence suggests government has to look very carefully at proposals to use the taxation system to provide 'incentives' to modify the behaviour of individuals who own small businesses. Currently, it is unanimously recognised that small business owners have to invest more heavily in their own businesses, rather than being excluded from doing so, as was the case with the BES. For example, the research evidence consistently shows that individuals who do not reinvest sufficiently in their own businesses run a much higher risk of business failure. However, the history of BES is one of desirable objectives of small firm policy being the focus of taxation exemptions, for these only to be used as tax avoidance vehicles. Our recommendation would therefore be to avoid, wherever possible, the use of the taxation system to provide incentives in this area. Instead we feel that government would be best advised to use its powers of persuasion, possibly through collaboration with banks and accountants, to emphasise the investment message. The message that excessive withdrawals from the business are likely to lead to its failure has to be drilled home to small business owners, rather than emphasis being on the provision of tax breaks for the wealthy.

The 1980s saw a strong emphasis upon deregulation and avoidance of red tape, etc. in small business policy making. It is unquestionably the case that small firms are disadvantaged in this area. For example, there are considerable quantities of legislation which relate to starting up in business, about which probably the bulk of firms are blissfully unaware. It is also the case that legislators, when drawing up legislation, are themselves unaware that compliance is comparatively more expensive for smaller than for larger firms. Finally, it is an understandable source of irritation for entrepreneurs who seek to take speedy decisions to find themselves in conflict with government departments, whose response often seems extremely slow. Nevertheless, as we said in Chapter 8, one person's red tape is another person's employment protection, safety at work or environment. The research in this volume suggests that the 'easy' solution of offering exemptions from certain types of legislation for smaller firms has yet to be shown to be in the interests of society as a whole. This area is one that requires the most careful scrutiny, on a case-by-case basis, to ensure an appropriate balance is struck between the freedom of entrepreneurs and the benefits to the rest of society. In our view, the 1980s saw the interests of the entrepreneur more loudly proclaimed than had been the case in the past. The time has now come to take stock of these issues.

The third issue on the lower right-hand side of Table 9.3 relates to the provision of training for entrepreneurs. The research presented in Chapter 8 suggests it is difficult to identify a clear impact upon small firm performance of entrepreneurs in receipt of training, either at start-up or at some other stage in their development. On the other hand, the evidence in Chapter 5 suggested that the educational attainment of the business owner is positively associated with entrepreneurial success. The inability to demonstrate an impact of training either owner or workforce on small firm performance is serious, bearing in mind the large public sums which have been, and which continue to be, spent in this area. The careful studies conducted by the National Institute of Social and Economic Research which have compared Britain and Germany suggest that the quality of workforce training provided in Germany is both significantly superior to that in the United Kingdom, and a powerful reason for Germany's superior economic performance (Prais 1993). Hence it may seem curious that small firm studies in the United Kingdom are unable to isolate an impact of entrepreneurial training. The reasons for this may be the poor quality of the training provided, the fact that it is often too short to exert an influence upon the firm, that perhaps some forms of training are more effective than others, or that some providers are better than others, but that the poorer providers dominate the rest. Chapter 8 makes the case that training in small firms is undertaken for fundamentally different reasons from training in large firms, and that whilst training may yield clear benefits for large firms, it is less likely to yield benefits to the small firm. Whatever the reason, there is now a strong case for government to look closely at small firm training with a view to making changes which will lead to improved value for money.

For much of the 1980s the focus of small business policy was to encourage the start-up of new firms. By the early 1990s, in response at least in part to the research evidence, this became less central to policy. This was partly because of the high rate of business failure among business start-ups, and also due to difficulties of identifying the characteristics of successful start-ups. Furthermore, as noted earlier, the international research evidence suggests that there is no consistent association between those countries which experience rapid increases in self-employment (which in turn are likely to reflect high rates of business start-ups) and those countries which have increased employment. This does not imply that the starting up of new businesses is to be discouraged, but that subsidising start-ups is likely to be ineffective, compared with using those same resources in other areas of policy.

The fifth row on the left-hand side of the table relates to the public provision of information and advice for small firms. Following the report of the Bolton Committee in 1971, a Small Firms Counselling Service was established. This provided a signposting service to small firms who were unaware of the appropriate private sector sources of advice available from accountants, lawyers, consultants, etc. Whilst there is evidence that small firms which use professional private sector advisers are more likely to survive, there does not seem to be the same consistent evidence suggesting a key influence is played by public agencies. These organisations are used by only a small proportion of the business population, although awareness of them is high and rising, and those who do use them appear broadly satisfied with the service they receive. The research presented in Chapter 8 suggests that the impact of public information and advice services on the performance of small firms is broadly unproven. As in the training area, it may be that some providers are better than others and have a bigger impact, but overall the results suggest government would be unwise to invest further in these services without a careful stock-take.

Finally, in line 6 on the left-hand side of Table 9.3, we refer to short-term 'tinkering'. Even the most casual observer of the small business scene cannot fail to be struck by the clamour on the Budget, in the period immediately before decisions are made, for the introduction of 'pet schemes' by the small business lobbyists. Unfortunately, the desire by government to be seen to be doing something[1] to assist the small business community at Budget time, in our view, dominates the political scene and moves the emphasis away from the long-term strategic purposes which small firm policy should have, and which need to be encapsulated in a White Paper. It is virtually impossible to assess the impact upon small firms of the myriad of minor changes at Budget time. Our recommendation would be that if a White Paper were produced on objectives and targets, only changes which were compatible with the objectives, and which specified clear monitorable output-based targets, would be appropriate for inclusion.

We now turn to the items on the lower right-hand side of Table 9.3. These refer to areas where there seems from the research evidence to be a case for more intensive policy, primarily because these policies seem to have had some desirable impact in the past.

The first item refers to a greater emphasis upon selectivity and targeting. Much of the research evidence in this volume suggests that the most cost-effective way of maximising the economic and employment impact of small firms would be to concentrate public assistance upon existing small firms which have grown rapidly, and which demonstrate a wish to continue growth. The direct implication of this is that, since these firms constitute a relatively small proportion of the total small business population, the remainder of small firms would not be the focus of public policy. In essence, targeting means providing a much higher level of assistance to certain firms which are constrained in their growth, and the removal of assistance from the vast bulk of smaller firms.

The justification for such policies is simple: employment growth is heavily concentrated in a tiny proportion of small firms. Most small firms do not wish to grow and the provision of public assistance to them is therefore likely to be ineffective. The emphasis upon existing firms as a focus for policy is that it is not possible to target effectively public assistance to start-ups, since the ultimate performance of small businesses cannot easily be forecast at start-up, whereas forecasting is considerably easier once the business has a track record.

It is envisaged that selective policies would be introduced at a local level and the criterion for success would be not the number of firms assisted, but rather the impact upon performance of the assisted firms. The key elements of a selective policy would be that, at local level, fast-growing independent firms between three and seven years old would be identified from a comprehensive trawl of local businesses. On the basis of this identification, the firms would be approached to see whether they had particular problems or barriers to growth which they were currently experiencing, and where public policy could make a significant difference to them being overcome. The difference between current policies and that proposed here is that the firm is not offered a choice from a pre-ordained package of assistance. Instead, it is able to set the framework for required assistance itself. The difference is between an individual entering a restaurant and being presented with a menu, as opposed to being asked what he or she would like to eat. The package of assistance will therefore vary markedly from one firm to another but might have, for example, elements of information, advice, financial assistance, provision of managerial resources, assistance with obtaining new premises, removal, etc. The key role of the local provider of these services, which in the current context might be Business Links, would be first to derive a population of rapidly growing firms, to visit these firms and find out what the problems were and *then* to determine whether it was possible to provide assistance to the businesses.

Of course, it is recognised that a number of the businesses either may not require or may reject public assistance of this type. This, in fact, makes the allocative problem easier since there would inevitably be businesses which were prepared to participate in the schemes, and so low participation rates would actually be helpful. A full description of the merits of a selective scheme, together with a firm rebuttal of the familiar arguments against it, and a description of how it might work in practice are found in Storey (1993).

It will be apparent that the public policy recommendations so far encourage a movement away from the criterion of maximising the number of start-ups and towards the promotion and development of existing businesses. This is referred to as emphasis upon 'quality' rather than 'quantity'. There are, however, some important exceptions to this and these are identified as items 2 and 3 on the lower right-hand side of Table 9.3. The first of these, shown as item 2, relates to science and technology-based small firms. The research evidence suggests these types of firm generally have lower failure rates and higher growth rates than 'typical' small businesses. Secondly, science-based firms are much more likely to export and to provide high-quality employment opportunities. For all these reasons there is a case that the group deserves special attention. If the ultimate objective of small firms policy is to increase the quality, rather than the quantity of small firms, then science and technology-based businesses must play a key role. There is a strong economic case for public policies which add to the number of these firms. There is also evidence that existing public policies in this area are effective, but could be more effective if better resourced. This supports the case for an extension and development of schemes such as SMART awards, encouraging links between local firms and universities and the commercialisation of advanced research.

However, policies to develop science-based small firms will only be fully effective if they are combined with major changes in other aspects of government policy. In the years to come, the only individuals likely to be able to establish, or possibly even manage, high-technology businesses will be those with the highest possible educational qualifications. In short, a PhD in a scientific subject is increasingly becoming a necessary 'passport' for businesses formation in this area. If government is to facilitate an increase in the number of these types of key start-up, its policies need to address a much more wide-ranging set of issues than is normally addressed as part of small firms policy. The size of government expenditure on higher education, and in particular the size of the science budget, is a key element influencing the supply of potential entrepreneurs in this area. At an even earlier stage, there is the importance of the choice of subject made amongst schoolchildren to the supply of high-technology entrepreneurs in the future. This illustrates, yet again, that the influences upon small firms are much wider than the elements generally viewed as appropriate for small firms policy making.

Line three of the right-hand side of Table 9.3 refers to 'special' groups. In some senses high-technology entrepreneurs may be thought of as a 'special' group, but their potential impact is clearly within the areas of economic policy. Nevertheless, Chapter 8 emphasised that small firms policy has wider implications, suggesting the involvement of groups other than the small businesses themselves and the government. The types of 'special' groups which we have in mind are ethnic minorities, disadvantaged residents in inner-cities, the long-term unemployed, etc. It is the case that, during the 1980s, the 'enterprise culture' was seen as a way of overcoming problems besetting these groups. Following the Brixton riots, efforts were made to encourage urban-based Blacks to form businesses as a way of knitting together the social and economic fabric of their communities. Enterprise policy was closely entwined with urban policy. Research examined in this volume suggests that the problems experienced by these disadvantaged groups continue into the 1990s. One central decision which has to be taken is whether it is appropriate to use public funds to 'encourage' these individuals, many of whom may lack the human capital to become effective small business owners, to become entrepreneurs. The clear alternative, instead of encouraging them to become business owners, with all the attendant risks, is to opt for a more selective policy of facilitating the growth of small businesses in the locality which appear to have growth potential, and ensure the disadvantaged can fill the jobs created. In our view, the problems of urban areas of crime, poverty, homelessness, etc. are so great that it would be unwise to dismantle the existing enterprise support framework which currently exists in these areas. For these reasons, although it may not be hugely effective, there are arguments which suggest that an abolition of business start-up schemes would be unwise in this context for these groups.

The fourth item on the right-hand side of Table 9.3 refers to the role of financial assistance. It is the case that the bulk of small business owners in the United Kingdom, philosophically, do not favour the use of government financial incentives, other than through the taxation system. Reference is often made to the importance of government ensuring there is a 'level playing field'. Financial assistance provided to some groups of firms but not to others is seen as being incompatible with that objective. On the other hand, the research evidence is that it is easier to identify an impact on small firm performance of schemes which provide financial assistance than of those providing information, advice or training. For example, although in our view it offers the wrong signal in the sense of being focused upon start-ups amongst unemployed individuals, the Enterprise Allowance Scheme clearly did lead to job creation at a relatively low cost per job. It was also seen in Chapter 4 that the only observable impact of public policy on the birth/death rate of firms was in those areas where Enterprise Agencies were able to provide finance to small firms. Similarly, regional grants have been shown to be effective in creating jobs, particularly during favourable macroeconomic circumstances. The research evidence is that, although it may not be 'politically correct', provision of financial assistance to small firms does appear to have had observable impacts. For this reason it has to be included as an area where increased emphasis can be justified.

Finally item 5 on the right-hand side of Table 9.3 suggests that government needs to place an even greater emphasis upon encouraging dialogue between the small business community on the one hand and what in Chapter 8 is referred to as the 'policy community', on the other. This does not imply that government departments are currently unaware of the importance of such dialogue, or that government does not exercise such a role currently. The suggestion is that this role of encouraging dialogue could be given even greater priority in helping to overcome a number of the problems identified. For example, the general thrust of the research reviewed in Chapter 7 on the financing of small enterprises suggested that, whilst there was evidence that not all small businesses received financing in the way and at the cost they would choose to receive it, it was difficult to point to any clear market failures within the financial system. There we argued that banks and smaller firms had to enter into a more long-term and trusting relationship than has been characteristic of relations in the United Kingdom to date. Government could exert a very powerful moral influence in encouraging the parties to trust one another and in being seen to be speaking out against efforts by either side to destroy the build-up of confidence.

If government were to accept the recommendation that the objectives and targets for small firm policy were clearly stated, this would imply a need to discuss with all parties in the policy community what those targets were to be. In this sense, the government would be committed to bringing groups together, rather than allowing the guerrilla warfare between banks and small businesses over financing, and between small businesses and large businesses over late payment of debts, to continue.

This emphasises that, whilst small and large firms are clearly different, it is counter-productive to infer that somehow small firms can prosper almost at the expense of other sizes of enterprise. Much of the discussion in Chapter 6 about what size of firm 'creates jobs' suggests that it is small firms that are major sources of job creation. However, in making these types of calculation it is, at a macro level, important to recognise the mutual interdependence of different sizes of enterprise. Similar arguments apply in the area of technological innovation, where small firms are often argued to be more innovative, but as leading researchers such as Roy Rothwell have pointed out (Rothwell 1983), it is the interrelationship between small and large firms which is crucial to technological development. For these reasons, although the Small Firms Division of government clearly has to look after the interests of smaller businesses, it should not do so in a way which is perceived to be adversarial and against the interests of medium- and large-sized enterprises.

Notes

CHAPTER 1 INTRODUCTION

1 'St Nicks'' is the local mental hospital.

CHAPTER 2 SMALL FIRMS: DEFINITIONS, DESCRIPTIONS AND PATTERNS

1 More precisely, small firms have a higher share of major innovations than their share of employment. However it is *not* the case that there is a higher probability that an individual small firm will introduce a new product than that an individual large firm will introduce a new product. This is because, as Table 2.5 shows, 88 per cent of businesses in the United Kingdom have five or less workers, and provide only 22 per cent of employment.

2 The judgement is exercised because employment and turnover are in 'bands' and the distribution within the band is not known. However, what is known is total employment and total number of firms having turnover within the band. Hence, the theoretical Pareto distribution which is used has to be subjectively adjusted in order to ensure that the rows and the columns balance. For this reason it is not appropriate to state formal margins of error for the estimates.

3 It is not suggested that the self-employed are identical to business owners. As Jim Curran has pointed out to me, some individuals who are classed as self-employed are little different to employees, and only have self-employment status for the tax and legislative exemptions which benefit their 'employers'. Classic examples of this occur in the construction and hotel sectors.

4 During the 1960s and 1970s the United Kingdom's manufacturing productivity growth was lower than that of Japan, Italy, France, the United States, Canada and Germany. In the 1980s its productivity growth was higher than all of these countries, although its productivity levels remained below those of most of these countries.

International comparisons: productivity

Whole economy productivity: rates of annual percentage change

1960–70		*1970–80*		*1980–90*		*1979–89*	
Japan	8.9	Japan	3.6	Japan	3.0	Japan	2.9
Italy	6.3	Italy	3.2	UK	2.0	Italy	2.0
France	4.6	Germany	2.9	France	2.0	France	2.0
Germany	4.3	France	2.7	Italy	1.8	UK	1.9
UK	2.5	Canada	1.5	Germany	1.4	Canada	1.2
Canada	2.4	UK	1.3	Canada	1.3	Germany	1.2
US	2.0	US	0.4	US	1.2	US	1.1
G7	3.4	G7	1.7	G7	1.7	G7	1.6

Manufacturing productivity: rates of annual percentage change*

1960–70		*1970–80*		*1980–90*		*1979–89*	
Japan	8.8	Japan	5.3	UK	4.7	UK	4.2
Italy	6.2	France	3.2	US	4.1	US	3.8
France	4.5	US	3.0	Japan	3.2	Italy	3.3
Germany	4.1	Canada	3.0	France	3.1	Japan	3.3
US	3.5	Germany	2.9	Italy	2.8	France	2.9
Canada	3.4	Italy	2.5	Canada	2.7	Canada	2.2
UK	3.1	UK	1.6	Germany	2.3	Germany	2.0
G7	4.4	G7	3.2	G7	3.5	G7	3.4

Sources: OECD, CSO, IMF
Note: *Exact coverage differs between countries.

CHAPTER 3 THE BIRTH OF FIRMS

1 Firms may choose to register even if they do not meet that threshold.
2 One influence which is frequently referred to, but which is not explicitly included in the analysis, is regional culture. For example, some areas have a 'tradition' or culture of enterprise, whereas others do not. In Sweden, for example, the Gnosjö area is amongst the former (Karlsson and Larsson 1993). Conversely, existing Glasgow firms were supposed to exert an influence on their locality similar to the effect of the upas tree, which poisons surrounding trees (Checkland 1976). In the case of Glasgow the city was dominated by large firms and in the case of Gnosjö the area is dominated by small firms, and it may be that the firm size is some form of proxy for 'culture'. In this sense, because firm size is included in the analysis, it can be argued that the tradition or culture of enterprise is also incorporated.
3 It is the case, as Colin Mason pointed out to me, that there are marked differences within the service sector. For example, in the United Kingdom, there are high levels of concentration – and presumably scale economies – in the estate agency, insurance broking and retailing sectors.
4 Foreman-Peck (1985) reaches a similar conclusion in a study of business formation during the inter-war years 1919–38. Using the Register of Business Names, he showed that increases in unemployment were associated with increases in rates of new business formation – most notably those in the service sector.

CHAPTER 4 THE DEATH OF SMALL FIRMS

1 The reason often given is that whilst small firms have a higher failure rate, the *amount* of finance 'at risk' is substantially higher for larger firms. The implication is that the potential value of the losses for large firm failure is greater.
2 Assuming that 60 per cent of UK businesses are registered for VAT, of which 30 per cent are limited companies. Of those businesses not registered for VAT, 95 per cent are assumed to be sole proprietorships.
3 The actual data, together with other measures of business failure, are presented in the table at the end of Chapter 4.
4 The year 1987 was a 'boom' year. It might be expected that in recessionary times a higher proportion of businesses deregistered for VAT through going out of business, whereas in more prosperous times, the proportion of acquisitions would be higher.
5 The extent to which it is closer to 500,000 is a matter of dispute. Freedman and Godwin (1994) make a powerful case that there may be up to 300,000 companies whose turnover is below the VAT threshold. These are effectively one-person businesses, possibly designed as tax management vehicles, but which are clearly 'trading'. It is interesting to note that, if Freedman and Godwin are correct in this, then the proportion of truly 'dormant' companies is much closer to that found by Scott (1982a,b) in the 1970s.

   It should be emphasised that this is, in fact, a matter of some significance, since the number of companies which will benefit from the abolition of statutory audit for those with a turnover below £90,000, as announced in the 1993 Budget, need to be identified.
6 See Table 7 of Daly (1991).
7 The data used by Gallagher and Stewart, at that time, had relatively weak coverage for the service sector, compared with manufacturing. It seems likely that the Phillips and Kirchhoff results are more robust.
8 The latter is also a finding of Cressy (1992).
9 Michael Godwin's view on this, expressed in a letter to me on 9 September 1993, was that the Freedman and Godwin (1994) research had shown that, on balance, proprietors of unincorporated firms had made a bigger personal financial commitment to the business than the founders of limited companies. For this reason it was easy to see the small limited company as being undercapitalised, which might lead to early failure. The problem was that the lack of formalities with starting an unincorporated business meant that there were many which could not be classified as 'serious' businesses. In this sense, short-life failure rates were likely to be high for both incorporated and unincorporated businesses.
10 Expressed in more technical terms, Altman used multiple discriminant analysis (MDA) to distinguish between failed and non-failed firms. This statistical technique identifies the best linear combination of variables (ratios) which maximises the (Mahabolis distance) difference between the two groups of failed and non-failed firms.

CHAPTER 5 THE GROWTH OF SMALL FIRMS

1 This study provides a complete enumeration of new single-plant enterprises which appeared in government statistical records such as the Annual Census of Employment (Storey *et al.* 1985).
2 VAT deregistrations data suggest that, in fact, only 30 per cent of new firms survive for one decade but since, as noted in Chapter 4, VAT deregistrations data include

firms which deregister for reasons other than ceasing to trade, we have used a higher survival figure.

3 O'Farrell and Hitchens (1988) suggest there are four groups of theories of small firm growth – the industrial economics approach, the stochastic model, stage models and the strategic management perspective. They also imply that, since researchers come from only one of these disciplines, the variables used in testing are also limited to one approach. The fact that the three components which we identify – the entrepreneur, the firm and strategy – are rarely all tested in the same analysis suggests O'Farrell and Hitchens are correct.

CHAPTER 6 EMPLOYMENT

1 The reason why births become an increasing proportion of gross job gains as the period increases can be illustrated by taking the case of job generation analyses which spread over a two-year period, compared with those over a 100-year period. During the latter, very few firms will survive for the century period and would be included in the expansions column, whereas over the period the vast majority of firms in existence to the end of the period will have been born during the previous century and their current employment will be classified as births. Similarly in assessing the contribution of deaths to contractions over a 100-year period, the majority of firms in existence that started the period will have died by the end of the period. Their employment will therefore appear in the deaths column, rather than the contractions category. The contrast with the two-year period can be seen in the sense that births will make a relatively modest contribution to gross job gains, since the firms will have had relatively little opportunity to create new jobs and therefore the expansions element is likely to be significantly greater. Equally, contractions of firms would be expected to make a larger contribution to gross job losses, the shorter the time period in question.

2 The evidence is provided in *Labour Market Quarterly* research, from which the following table is drawn.

Net job generation 1982–91 (millions)

	Size band		*Total*
Period	1–19	20+	
1982–4	+1.00	–0.75	+0.25
1985–7	+0.50	0.00	+0.50
1987–9	+0.50	+0.50	+1.00
1989–91	+0.40	0.00	+0.40

3 In a private communication, dated 21 October 1993, Professor Curran emphasises that whilst his conclusions may be similar to those of Bolton, the logic or interpretation is very different. He argues that in the service sector, even small firms have to handle relations with employees in a harmonious manner. This is because the worker in the service sector is much more likely to have direct customer contact and it is that contact which the customer is purchasing, at least in part. Put crudely, and Jim Curran does *not* put it this way, the bar owner cannot afford to fall out with staff since there is a real risk that they will react by taking it out on the customer. Since the consequences of unhappy staff are more direct in service, small firm labour relations have to be

better than in manufacturing.

4 The extent to which small firms have benefited from outsourcing is, however, questioned by Curran and Blackburn (1994). They find that the prime beneficiaries are medium- and large-sized firms, which are more likely to be regarded as 'suitable' suppliers. Greater reliance on BS5750 accreditation has also served to exclude many small firms.

CHAPTER 7 FINANCE

1 Bannock and Doran (1991) show that only between 2 per cent and 10 per cent of proposals to UK venture capitalists are accepted. For those seeking loan capital, acceptance rates are much higher; Cowling *et al.* (1991) show that only 16 per cent of firms in their sample had been rejected for additional loan facilities on the last occasion they had sought such facilities.

2 It should be noted that in their evaluation of the Loan Guarantee Scheme (to be discussed later) National Economic Research Associates (1990) discussed the willingness of bank managers to use interest rates to 'compensate' for higher-risk projects. NERA observed that there was a reluctance to use interest rates for this purpose, but not for reasons of either 'adverse selection' or 'moral hazard'. Instead, the bank managers referred to a reluctance to use interest rates in this way because it was thought to be bad public relations to charge high interest rates. They preferred not to grant the loan at all than to charge a high interest rate, on the grounds that to do the latter would get the bank a reputation for usury.

3 The British Venture Capital Association (BVCA) define 'start-up' to be:

> Finance provided to companies for the use in product development and initial marketing. Companies may be in the process of being set up or may have been in business for a short time, but have not sold their product commercially.

4 The Centre for Management Buyouts at Nottingham University produces UK data on this topic. For a review of trends, see Wright *et al.* (1992).

5 Data for the UK industry, as ACOST (1990) point out, includes buy-outs, which are excluded in the US data.

6 Of course, market failure implies a divergence between social and private benefit. The argument here, however, is that there is no reason to believe that, if the market for the provision of finance were made more perfect, this would lead to the more extensive provision of seed corn equity, without the provision of public subsidies. Another illustration of this point is provided by the Informal Investment Demonstration Projects, which receive public funds on the grounds that they could yield social benefits.

CHAPTER 8 PUBLIC POLICY

1 Curran, Blackburn and Woods (1991) report somewhat higher figures in their study of service sector firms. They found that 8.9 per cent of owner-managers belonged to one of the national small business associations/bodies.

2 This finding is also supported by Curran and Blackburn (1993). They show that Afro-Caribbean business owners are very much more likely to have used both an Enterprise Agency and the Small Firms Service than either the Bangladeshi or Greek-Cypriot business owner.

3 Judith Freedman, however, pointed out to me an example of where the pressure for change in small firm legislation was championed by large firms. The example is over

pressure for the abolition of the statutory audit for small companies where, she believes, the large accountancy firms were probably more influential than either the small firm lobbyists or the intelligentsia.

4 A document by Graham Bannock (1993) covering twenty-one European countries – including several from Eastern Europe – has also addressed a number of the same issues. Bannock asked national respondents about which SME policy they feel to be most effective. He reports that only eight replied! Of these, four referred to grants, whilst the Germans emphasised the key importance of good general economic policy. Both of these conclusions are compatible with the evidence presented in this chapter for the United Kingdom.

CHAPTER 9 CONCLUSIONS

1 The same point was made by Charles Batchelor, in reviewing six years as a small business writer for the *Financial Times* (*Financial Times*, 26 October 1993).

References

Abbott, B. (1993) ‘Small Firms and Trade Unions in the 1990s’, *Industrial Relations Journal*, Vol. 24, No. 4, December.

Abbott, B. (1993) ‘Patterns of Privatisation and Market Trends in Local Government Services’, Kingston Business School Working Paper.

Acs, Z. and Audretsch, D. (1989) ‘Births and Firm Size’, *Southern Economic Journal*, Vol. 55, pp. 467–75.

Acs, Z.J., Audretsch, D.B. and Evans, D.S. (1991) *The Determinants of Variations in Self Employment Rates Across Countries and Over Time*, National Economic Research Associates, Cambridge, Mass.

Advisory Council on Science and Technology, (1990) *The Enterprise Challenge, Overcoming Barriers to Growth in Small Firms*, HMSO, London.

Allen, S. and Truman, C. (1993) *Women in Business: Perspectives on Women Entrepreneurs*, Routledge, London.

Altman, E.I. (1968) ‘Financial Ratios, Discriminant Analysis and the Prediction of Corporate Bankruptcy’, Journal of Finance, Vol. 23, No. 4, September. pp. 589–609.

Altman, E.I., Avery, R.B., Eisenbeis, R.A. and Sinkey, J.F. (1981) *Application Classification Techniques in Business Banking and Finance*, JAI Press, Greenwich, Conn.

Apilado, B.P. and Millington, J.K. (1992) ‘Restrictive Loan Covenants and Risk Adjustment in Small Business Lending’, *Journal of Small Business Management*, Vol. 30, No. 1, January, pp. 38–48.

Argenti, J. (1976) *Corporate Collapse: The Cause and Symptoms*, McGraw-Hill, Maidenhead.

Armington and Odle (1982) ‘Small Business – How Many Jobs?’, *Brookings Review*, Winter, pp. 14–17.

Ashcroft, B., Love, J.H. and Malloy, E. (1991) ‘New Firm Formation in the British Counties with Special Reference to Scotland’, *Regional Studies*, Vol. 25, pp. 395–409.

Aston Business School, (1991) *Constraints on the Growth of Small Firms*, Department of Trade and Industry, HMSO, London.

Atkinson, J. and Meager, N. (1994) ‘Running to Stand Still: The Small Business in The Labour Market’, in J. Atkinson and D.J. Storey (eds) *Employment, The Small Firm and the Labour Market*, Routledge, London.

Atkinson, J. and Storey, D.J. (1993) *Employment, the Small Firm, and the Labour Market*, Routledge, London.

Baden-Fuller, C.W.F. (1989) ‘Exit from Declining Industries in the Case of Steel Castings’, *Economic Journal*, December, Vol. 99, pp. 949–61.

Bank of England (1993) *Bank Lending to Smaller Businesses*, The Bank of England, London.

Bannock, G. (1981) *The Economics of Small Firms*, Basil Blackwell, Oxford.

Bannock, G. (1993) 'The Promotion of Small and Medium Sized Enterprises in Europe', Committee of Experts on the Development of Small and Medium Sized Enterprises, Council of Europe, 3rd Meeting 13–14 May.

Bannock, G. and Binks, M. (1990) *Appropriate Strategies for the Promotion of SME's in the Development Process*, Graham Bannock and Partners, London.

Bannock, G. and Doran, A. (1991) *Venture Capital and the Equity Gap*, National Westminster Bank, London.

Bannock, G. and Partners (1989) *Small Business Statistics: A Feasibility Study Prepared for the Department of Employment*, Graham Bannock and Partners, London.

Bannock, G. and Peacock, A. (1989) *Government and Small Businesses*, Paul Chapman Publishing, London.

Barber, J., Metcalfe, J.S. and Porteous, M. (1989) *Barriers to Growth in Small Firms*, Routledge, London.

Barberis, P. and May, T. (1993), *Government, Industry and Political Economy*, Open University Press, London.

Barkham, R. (1992) 'Entrepreneurial Characteristics and the Size of the New Firm: A Model and an Econometric Test', paper presented at the International Conference on Birth and Start-up of Small Firms, Bocconi University, Milan, 11–19 June.

Barrow, C. (1989) *The Small Business Guide*, 3rd edition, BBC Books, London.

Barrow, C., Barrow, P. and Brown, R. (1992) *The Business Plan Work Book*, 2nd edition, Kogan Page, London.

Bartlett, W. (1993a) 'Employment in Small Firms: Are Co-operatives Different? Evidence from Southern Europe', in J. Atkinson and D.J. Storey (eds), *Employment, Small Firms and the Labour Market*, Routledge, London.

Bartlett, W. (1993b) 'The Evolution of Workers' Co-operatives in Southern Europe: A Comparative Perspective', in C. Karlsson, B. Johannisson and D.J. Storey (eds), *Small Business Dynamics: International, National and Regional Perspectives*, Routledge, London.

Bates, T. (1990) 'Entrepreneurial Human Capital Inputs and Small Business Longevity', *Review of Economics and Statistics*, Vol. 72, No. 4, November, pp. 551–9.

Bates, T. (1991) 'Commercial Bank Financing of White and Black-owned Small Business Start Ups', *Quarterly Review of Economics and Business*, Vol. 31, No. 1, Spring, pp. 64–80.

Batstone, S. (1989) 'New Business Service Firms: An Explanatory Study', UK Small Firms Policy and Research Conference, London.

Beaver, W.H. (1966) 'Financial Ratios as Predictors of Failure', Empirical Research in Accounting: Selected Studies, *Journal of Accounting Research*, Supplement to Vol. 5 (1967), January, pp. 71–111.

Berger, A.N. and Udell, G.F. (1990) 'Collateral, Loan Quality and Bank Risk', *Journal of Monetary Economics*, Vol. 25, pp. 21–42.

Berry, A., Jarvis, R., Lipman, J. and Macallan, H. (1990) 'Leasing and the Smaller Firm', Chartered Association of Certified Accountants, Occasional Research Paper No. 3, London.

Berryman, J. (1983) 'Small Business Failure and Bankruptcy: A Survey of the Literature', *International Small Business Journal*, Vol. 1, No. 4, pp. 47–59.

Besanko, D. and Thakor, A. (1987) 'Collateral and Rationing: Sorting Equilibria in Monopolistic and Competitive Credit Markets', *International Economic Review*, Vol. 28, pp. 671–89.

Bester, H. (1985) 'Screening vs. Rationing in Credit Markets with Imperfect Formation',

American Economic Review, Vol. 75, pp. 850–5.

Bester, H. (1987) 'The Role of Collateral in Credit Markets with Imperfect Information', *European Economic Review*, Vol. 31, pp. 887–99.

Binks, M.R. (1991) 'Banks and the Provision of Finance to Small Businesses', in Stanworth, J. and Gray, C. (eds), *Bolton, 20 Years On: The Small Firm in the 1990s*, Paul Chapman Publishing, London.

Binks, M. and Jennings, A. (1986) 'Small Firms as a Source of Economic Rejuvenation', in J. Curran, J. Stanworth and D. Watkins (eds), *The Survival of the Small Firm*, Vol. 1, Gower, Aldershot, pp. 19–37.

Binks, M.R., Ennew, C.T. and Reed, G.V. (1990) *Small Businesses and their Banks*, Forum of Private Businesses, Knutsworth, Cheshire.

Binks, M.R., Ennew, C.T. and Reed, G.V. (1992) *Small Businesses and their Banks: 1992*, Forum of Private Business, Knutsworth, Cheshire.

Birch, D. (1979) *The Job Generation Process*, MIT Programme on Neighborhood and Regional Change, Cambridge, Mass.

Birch, D.L. and McCracken, S. (1981) 'Corporate Evolution: A Micro-based Analysis', prepared for the Office of Advocacy of the US Small Business Administration, January.

Birley, S. and Westhead, P. (1990) 'Growth and Performance Contrasts Between "Types" of Small Firms', *Strategic Management Journal*, Vol. 11, pp. 535–57.

Birley, S. and Westhead, P. (1992) 'A Comparison of New Firms in "Assisted" and "Non-Assisted" Areas of Great Britain', *Entrepreneurship and Regional Development*, Vol. 4, pp. 299–338.

Black, J., De Meza, D. and Jefferies, D. (1992) 'House Prices, the Supply of Collateral and the Enterprise Economy', Department of Economics, University of Exeter (mimeo).

Blackburn, R.A. (1990) 'Job Quality in Small Businesses: Electrical and Electronic Engineering Firms in Dorset', *Environment and Planning*, A, Vol. 22, pp. 875–92.

Blackburn, R. and Curran, J. (1993) 'In Search of Spatial Differences: Evidence from a Study of Small Service Sector Enterprises', in J. Curran and D.J. Storey (eds), *Small Firms in Urban and Rural Locations*, Routledge, London.

Blanchflower, D.G. and Meyer, B.D. (1991) 'Longitudinal Analysis of Young Entrepreneurs in Australia and the United States', *National Bureau of Economic Research*, Inc. Working Paper No. 3746, Cambridge, Mass.

Blanchflower, D.G. and Oswald, A.J. (1990a) 'Self Employment in the Enterprise Culture', in R. Jowell, S. Witherspoon and L. Brook (eds), *British Social Attitudes: The Seventh Report*, SCPR, Gower, Aldershot.

Blanchflower, D.G. and Oswald, A.J. (1990b) 'What Makes a Young Entrepreneur?', Working Paper No. 3252, National Bureau of Economic Research.

Blanchflower, D.G. and Oswald, A.J. (1992) 'Entrepreneurship and Supernormal Returns: Evidence from Britain and the US', paper presented at International Conference on Birth and Start Up of Small Firms, Milan, 18–19 June.

Blau, D.M. (1987) 'A Time Series Analysis of Self Employment in the United States', *Journal of Political Economy*, Vol. 95, No. 3, pp. 445–6.

Bögenhold, D. and Staber, U. (1991), 'The Decline and Rise in Self Employment', *Work, Employment and Society*, Vol. 5, pp. 223–39.

Bögenhold, D. and Staber, U. (1992) 'Self Employment and the Institutional-Political Framework', Mimeo.

Bolton, J.E. (1971) *Report of the Committee of Inquiry on Small Firms*, Cmnd.4811, HMSO, London.

Bradburd, R.M. and Ross, D.R. (1989) 'Can Small Firms Find and Defend Strategic Niches? A Test of the Porter Hypothesis', *Review of Economics and Statistics*, Vol. LXXI, May, No. 2, pp. 258–62.

Brough, R. (1970) 'Business Failures in England and Wales', *Business Ratios*, pp. 8–11.

Brown, C. Hamilton, J. and Medoff, J. (1990) *Employees Large and Small*, Harvard University Press, Cambridge, Mass.

Bulow, J.I. and Shoven, J.B. (1978) 'The Bankruptcy Decision', *Bell Journal of Economics*, Vol. 9, No. 2, Autumn, pp. 437–56.

Burrows, R. (ed.) (1991) *Deciphering the Enterprise Culture: Entrepreneurship, Petty Capitalism and the Restructuring of Britain*, Routledge, London.

Cambridge Small Business Research Centre (1992) *The State of British Enterprise*, Department of Applied Economics, University of Cambridge.

Campbell, M. and Daly, M. (1992) 'Self Employment: Into the 1990s', *Employment Gazette*, June, pp. 269–92.

Carter, S. and Cannon, T. (1989) 'Female Entrepreneurs: A Study of Female Business Owners, their Motivations, Experiences and Strategies for Success', Department of Employment Research Paper No. 65.

Casson, M. (1982) *The Entrepreneur: An Economic Theory*, Martin Robertson, Oxford.

Casson, M. (ed.) (1990) *Entrepreneurship*, Edward Elgar, Aldershot.

Centre for Employment Initiatives (1985) *The Impact of Local Enterprise Agencies in Great Britain: Operational Issues and Policy Implications*, Business in the Community, London.

Chan, Y.S. and Kanatas, G. (1985) 'Asymmetric Valuations and the Role of Collateral in Loan Agreements', *Journal of Money, Credit and Banking*, Vol. 17, February, pp. 84–95.

Checkland, S.G. (1976) 'The Upas Tree: Glasgow 1875–1975', University of Glasgow.

Chell, E., Haworth, J. and Brearley, S. (1991) *The Entrepreneurial Personality: Concepts, Cases and Categories*, Routledge, London.

Chittenden, F. (1991) 'Taxation', in J. Stanworth and C. Gray (eds), *Bolton 20 Years On: The Small Firm in the 1990s*, Paul Chapman Publishing, London.

Churchill, N.C. and Lewis, V.L. (1983) 'The Five Stages of Small Business Growth', *Harvard Business Review*, Vol. 6, No. 3, pp. 43–54.

Clarke, R. (1985) *Industrial Economics*, Blackwell, Oxford.

Clegg, G. and Barrow, C. (1984) *How to Start and Run Your Own Business*, Macmillan, London.

Clifton, R. and Tatton-Brown, C. (1979) 'Impact of Employment Legislation on Small Firms', Department of Employment Research Paper No. 6, London.

Coase, R.M. (1937) 'The Nature of the Firm', *Economica*, Vol. 4, pp. 386–405.

Coleman, T., McHugh, J. and May, T.C. (1991a) ESRC – *Stockport Data*, Manchester Metropolitan University.

Coleman, T., McHugh, J. and May, T.C. (1991b) ESRC – *Oldham (Survey Results)*, Manchester Metropolitan University.

Confederation of British Industry (1993) *Finance for Growth: Meeting the Financing Needs of Small and Medium Enterprises*, CBI, London.

Corry, D. (1987) 'What Factors Determine Success? Factors Associated with the Survivability of Firms Set up under the Enterprise Allowance Scheme', Employment Department (unpublished).

Cosh, A. and Hughes, A. (1994) 'Size, Financial Structure and Profitability: UK Companies in the 1980s', in A. Hughes and D.J. Storey (ed.), *Finance and the Small Firm*, Routledge, London.

Covin, J.G. and Slevin, D.P. (1989) 'Strategic Management of Small Firms in Hostile and Benign Environments', *Strategic Management Journal*, Vol. 10, pp. 75–87.

Cowling, M. (1993) 'Modelling Take up Rates on the Loan Guarantee Scheme', SME Centre Working Paper, University of Warwick.

Cowling, M., Samuels, J. and Sugden, R. (1991) *Small Firms and the Clearing Banks: A*

Sterile, Uncommunicative and Unimaginative Relationship, Association of British Chambers of Commerce, London.
Creedy, J. and Whitfield, K. (1988) 'The Economic Analysis of Internal Labour Markets', *Bulletin of Economic Research*, Vol. 4, No. 4, pp. 247–67.
Cressy, R. (1992) 'Loan Commitments and Business Starts: An Empirical Investigation on UK Data', SME Centre Working Paper No. 12, Warwick Business School.
Cross, M. (1981) *New Firm Formation and Regional Development*, Gower, Farnborough.
Curran, J. (1986) *Bolton 15 Years on: A Review and Analysis of Small Business Research in Britain, 1971–1986*, Small Business Research Trust, London.
Curran, J. (1991) 'Employment and Employment Relations', in J. Stanworth and C. Gray (eds), *Bolton 20 Years On: The Small Firm in the 1990s*, Paul Chapman Publishing, London.
Curran, J. (1992) *Small Business Survey: February*, Small Business Research Centre, Kingston Business School, London.
Curran, J. and Blackburn, R. (1993) 'Ethnic Enterprise and the High Street Bank: A Survey of Ethnic Businesses in Two Localities', Small Business Research Centre, Kingston University.
Curran, J. and Blackburn, R.A. (1994) *Small Business and Local Economic Networks: The Death of the Local Economy?*, Paul Chapman, London.
Curran, J. and Burrows, R. (1988a) *Enterprise in Britain: A National Profile of Small Business Owners and the Self Employed*, Small Business Research Trust, London.
Curran, J. and Burrows, R. (1988b) *Small Business Owners and the Self Employed in Britain: A Secondary Analysis of the General Household Survey, 1979–84*, report for the Economic and Social Research Council.
Curran, J. and Burrows, R. (1988c) 'Ethnicity and Enterprise: A National Profile', Small Firms Policy and Research Conference, Cardiff.
Curran, J. and Stanworth, J. (1979) 'Self Selection of the Small Firm Worker – A Critique and an Alternative View, *Sociology*, Vol. 13, No. 4, pp. 427–44.
Curran, J. and Storey, D.J. (1993) 'The Location of Small and Medium Enterprises: Are there Urban/Rural Differences?', in J. Curran and D.J. Storey (eds), *Small Firms in Urban and Rural Locations*, Routledge, London.
Curran, J., Blackburn, R. and Woods, A. (1991) 'Profiles of the Small Enterprise in the Service Sector', paper presented at University of Warwick, 18 April.
Curran, J., Kitching, J., Abbott, B. and Mills, V. (1993) 'Employment and Employment Relations in the Small Service Sector Enterprise – A Report', ESRC Centre for Research on Small Service Sector Enterprises, Kingston Business School.
Cuthbertson, K. and Hudson, J. (1990) 'The Determinants of Compulsory Liquidations in the UK, 1972–1989', Department of Economics, University of Newcastle upon Tyne (mimeo).
Daly, M. (1987) 'Lifespan of Businesses Registered for VAT', *British Business*, 3 April, pp. 28–9.
Daly, M. (1991) 'VAT Registrations and De-registrations in 1990', *Employment Gazette*, November, pp. 579–88.
Daly, M. (1992) 'Business Failure Statistics', Statistical Services, C4, Employment Department, unpublished paper, July.
Daly, M. and McCann, A. (1992) 'How Many Small Firms?', *Employment Gazette*, February, pp. 47–51.
Daly, M., Campbell, M., Robson, G. and Gallagher, C. (1991) 'Job Creation 1987–9: The Contributions of Small and Large Firms', *Employment Gazette*, November, pp. 589–96
Daniel, W. and Millward, N. (1983) *Workplace Industrial Relations in Britain*, Heinemann, London.
Deakins, D. and Philpott, T. (1993) 'Comparative European Practices in the Finance of

Small Firms: UK, Germany and Holland', Research Report and Occasional Working Paper, Small Business Research Group, University of Central England Business School, Birmingham.

Deakins, D., Hussain, G. and Ram, M. (1991) 'Risk Assessment by Bank Managers', Birmingham Polytechnic Business School, December, mimeo.

Deakins, D., Hussain, G. and Ram, M. (1992) 'Finance of Ethnic Minority Small Businesses', University of Central England in Birmingham.

de Koning, A.C.P., Snijders, J.A.H. and Vianen, J.G. (1992) 'SME Policy in the European Community', paper presented at Gateways to Growth – Opportunities for Smaller Firms in the EC.

de Meza, D. and Webb, D. (1987) 'Too Much Investment: A Problem of Asymmetric Information', *Quarterly Journal of Economics*, Vol. 102, May, pp. 281–92.

de Meza, D. and Webb, D. (1990) 'Risk, Adverse Selection and Capital Market Failure', *Economic Journal*, Vol. 100, No. 399, March, pp. 206–14.

Dennis, W.J. (Jnr) *et al.* (1988) *Small Businesses and the Banks: The United States*, National Federation of Independent Businesses, Washington, D.C.

Denyer, S. (1991) *Traditional Buildings and Life in the Lake District*, Victor Gollancz Ltd – Peter Crawley, London.

Department of Trade and Industry (1988) *Releasing Enterprise*, Cmnd.512, HMSO, London.

Desai, M. and Montes, A. (1982) 'A Macroeconomic Model of Bankruptcies in the British Economy, 1945–1980', *British Review of Economic Issues*, Vol. 4, pp. 1–14.

de Wit, G. (1993) 'Models of Self Employment in a Competitive Market', *Journal of Economic Surveys*, Vol. 7, No. 3, pp. 367–97.

Dixon, R. (1991) 'Venture Capitalists and the Appraisal of Investments', *Omega*, Vol. 19, No. 5, pp. 333–44.

Dolton, P.J. and Makepeace, G.H. (1990) 'Self Employment Amongst Graduates', *Bulletin of Economic Research*, Vol. 42, No. 1, January, pp. 35–53.

Dunkelberg, W.G. and Cooper, A.C. (1982) 'Patterns of Small Business Growth', *Academy of Management Proceedings*.

Dunkelberg, W.G., Cooper, A.C., Woo. C. and Dennis, W.J. (1987) 'New Firm Growth and Performance', in N.C. Churchill, J.A. Hornaday, B.A. Kirchhoff, C.J. Krasner and K.H. Vesper (eds), *Frontiers of Entrepreneurship Research*, Babson College, Boston, Mass.

Dunne, P. and Hughes, A. (1989) 'Small Business: An Analysis of Recent Trends in their Relative Importance and Growth Performance in the United Kingdom, with some European Comparisons', Working Paper No. 1, Small Business Research Centre, University of Cambridge.

Dunne, P. and Hughes, A. (1992) 'Age, Size, Growth and Survival Revisited', Working Paper No. 23, Small Business Research Centre, University of Cambridge, September.

Dunne, T., Roberts, M.J. and Samuelson, L. (1989) 'The Growth and Failure of US Manufacturing Plants', *Quarterly Journal of Economics*, November, pp. 671–98.

Elias, P. and Whitfield, K. (1987) 'The Economic Impact of the Enterprise Allowance Scheme: Theory and Measurement of Displacement Effects', Institute for Employment Research, University of Warwick, October.

Employment Department (1992) *Small Firms in Britain*, HMSO, London.

ENSR (1993) *The European Observatory for SMEs*, EIM, Zoetermeer, Netherlands.

Enterprise Dynamics (1987) *The Contribution of Enterprise Agencies, Small Firms: Survival and Job Creation*, Business in the Community, London.

Evans, D.S. and Leighton, L.S. (1990) 'Small Business Formation by Unemployed and Employed Workers', *Small Business Economics*, Vol. 2, No. 4, pp. 319–30.

Foreman-Peck, J. (1985) 'Seedcorn or Chaff: New Firm Formation and the Performance of the Interwar Economy', *Economic History Review*, Vol. XXXVIII, pp. 402–22.

Forlai, L. (1991) 'Subfornitura a Distretti Industriali', paper given at STOA, Naples, 10 May.

Fothergill, S. and Gudgin, G. (1982) *Unequal Growth*, Heinemann Educational Books, London.

Fredriksen, O., Olofsson, C. and Wahlbin, C. (1990) 'The Role of Venture Capital in the Development of Portfolio Companies', paper for the SMS Conference: Strategic Bridging, Stockholm, September.

Freedman, J. and Godwin, M. (1992) 'Legal Form, Tax and the Micro-Business', in K. Caley, E. Chell, F. Chittenden and C. Mason (eds), *Small Enterprise Development: Policy and Practice in Action*, Paul Chapman Publishing, London.

Freedman, J. and Godwin, M. (1994) 'Incorporating The Micro-Business: Perceptions and Misperceptions', in A. Hughes and D.J. Storey (eds) *Finance and the Small Firm*, Routledge, London.

Freeman, C. (ed.) (1983) *Long Waves in the World Economy*, Butterworths, London.

Fritsch, M. (1992) 'Regional Differences in New Firm Formation: Evidence from West Germany', *Regional Studies*, Vol. 26, No. 3, pp. 233–41.

Gallagher, C.C. and Miller, P. (1991) 'New Fast Growing Companies Create Jobs', *Long Range Planning*, Vol. 24, No. 1, pp. 96–101.

Gallagher, C.C. and Stewart, H. (1985) 'Business Death and Firm Size in the UK', *International Small Business Journal*, Vol. 4, No. 1, Autumn, pp. 42–57.

Gallagher, C., Daly, M. and Thomason, J.C. (1990) 'The Growth of UK Companies 1985–87 and their Contribution to Job Creation', *Employment Gazette*, February, pp. 92–8.

Ganguly, P. (1985) *UK Small Business Statistics and International Comparisons*, Harper and Row, London.

Garofoli, G. (1994) 'New Firm Formation and Regional Development: The Italian Case', *Regional Studies* (forthcoming).

Gaston, R.J. (1989) 'The Scale of Informal Capital Markets', *Small Business Economics*, Vol. 1, No. 3, pp. 223–30.

Ghemawat, P. and Nalebuff, B. (1985) 'Exit', *Rand Journal of Economics*, Vol. 16, No. 2, pp. 184–94.

Goss, D. (1991) *Small Business and Society*, Routledge, London.

Goudie, A.W. and Meeks, G. (1991) 'The Exchange Rate and Company Failure in the Macro-micro Model of the UK Company Sector', *Economic Journal*, Vol. 101, May, pp. 444–57.

Gray, C. (1990) 'Some Economic – Psychological Considerations on the Effects of the Enterprise Allowance Scheme (EAS)', *Piccola Impresa*, No. 1, pp. 111–24.

Gray, C. and Stanworth, J. (1986) *Allowing for Enterprise, A Qualitative Assessment of the Enterprise Allowance Scheme*, Small Business Research Trust, London.

Gray, C. and Stanworth, J. (1989) 'Dangers to Enterprise in the Enterprise Allowance Scheme', in P. Rosa, S. Birley, T. Cannon and K. O'Neill (eds), *The Role and Contribution of Small Business Research*, Avebury, Aldershot.

Grayson, D. (1990) 'Small Business 2001 Megatrends', speech given at Small Firms Policy and Research Conference, 16 October, Business in the Community, London.

Gudgin, G., Brunskill, I. and Fothergill, S. (1979) 'New Manufacturing Firms in Regional Employment Growth', Centre for Environmental Studies, Research Series No. 39.

Haines, G., Riding, A. and Thomas, R. (1991) 'Small Business Bank Shopping in Canada', *Journal of Banking and Finance*, Vol. 15, pp. 1041–56.

Hakim, C. (1989) 'Identifying Fast Growth Small Firms', *Employment Gazette*, January, pp. 29–41.

Hall, G. (1989) 'Lack of Finance as a Constraint on the Expansion of Innovatory Small Firms', in J. Barber, J.S. Metcalf and M. Porteus (eds), *Barriers to Growth in Small*

Firms, Routledge, London.
Hall, G. (1992) 'Reasons for Insolvency Amongst Small Firms – A Review and Fresh Evidence', *Small Business Economics*, Vol. 4, No. 3, September, pp. 237–50.
Hall, G. and Young, B. (1991) 'Factors Associated with Insolvency Amongst Small Firms', *International Small Business Journal*, Vol. 9, No. 2, pp. 54–63.
Hall, P. (1991) 'Small Business Outcomes', paper presented at 14th Small Firms Policy and Research Conference, Blackpool, 20–2 November.
Halpern, P., Trebilcock, M. and Turnbull, S. (1980) 'An Economic Analysis of a Limited Liability Incorporation Law, 30', *University of Toronto Law Journal*, Vol. 30, pp. 117–50.
Hargreaves, R. (1983) *Starting a Business*, Heinemann, London.
Harris, D. (1991), 'Salaries Lag Behind Smaller Firms', *The Times*, Friday 22 March.
Harrison, R.T. and Mason, C.M. (1992) 'The Roles of Investors in Entrepreneurial Companies: A Comparison of Informal Investors and Venture Capitalists', Venture Finance Research Project, Working Paper No. 5, University of Southampton (Urban Policy Research Unit, Department of Geography) and University of Ulster (Ulster Business School).
Harrison, R.T. and Mason, C.M. (1993) 'Finance for the Growing Business: The Role of Informal Investment', *National Westminster Bank Review*, May, pp. 17–29.
Heath, A., Jowell, R. and Curtice, J. (1985) *How Britain Votes*, Pergamon Press, Oxford.
Hendry, C., Jones, A., Arthur, M. and Pettigrew, A. (1991) 'Human Resource Development in Small to Medium Sized Enterprises', Employment Department, Research Paper No. 88, London.
Higham, R. (1993) *Employment: Where do the New Jobs Come From?*, Department of Management Studies and Labour Relations, University of Auckland.
Hillier, B. and Ibrahimo, M.V. (1993) 'Asymmetric Information and Models of Credit Rationing', *Bulletin of Economic Research*, Vol. 45, No. 4, pp. 271–304.
House of Commons Treasury and Civil Service Committee (1991) 'The Availability of Bank Credit and Interest Rates', Minutes of Evidence, 6th Report, 17 June.
Hudson, J. (1986) 'An Analysis of Company Liquidations', *Applied Economics*, Vol. 18, pp. 219–35.
Hudson, J. (1987a) 'Company Building in Britain and the Institutional Environment', *International Small Business Journal*, Vol. 5, No. 1, pp. 57–69.
Hudson, J. (1987b) 'The Age, Regional and Industrial Structure of Company Liquidations', *Journal of Business Finance and Accounting*, Vol. 14, No. 2, pp. 199–213.
Hudson, J. and Cuthbertson, K. (1992) 'The Determinants of Bankruptcies in the UK, 1971–1988', *Manchester School*, Vol. 61, No. 1, pp. 65–81.
Hughes, A. (1992) 'The Problems of Finance for Smaller Businesses', Working Paper No. 15, Small Business Research Centre, University of Cambridge.
Hughes, P. (1989) 'The Economic Contribution of Small Firms', Employment Department (unpublished).
Hughes, A. and Storey, D.J. (1994) *Finance and the Small Firm*, Routledge, London.
Jensen, M.C. and Meckling, W.H. (1976) 'Theory of the Firm: Managerial Behaviour, Agency Costs and Ownership Structure', *Journal of Financial Economics*, Vol. 3, pp. 205–60.
Johnson, P.S. (1989) 'Employment Change in the Small Establishment Sector in UK Manufacturing', *Applied Economics*, Vol. 21, pp. 251–60.
Johnson, S. (1989) 'Employment Change in Small Business: Results from a Follow up Survey', report to the Department of Employment, Institute for Employment Research, University of Warwick.
Johnson, S. (1991) 'Forecasting Small Business Employment Growth: Some Survey Findings for the UK', paper presented to the 21st European Small Business Seminar, Barcelona, 1991.

Johnson, S., Lindley, R. and Boulakis, C. (1988) 'An Exploratory Time Series Analysis of Self Employment in Great Britain', Project Report, DE Programme, Institute for Employment Research, University of Warwick.

Jones, M. (1991) 'Employment Change in Small Firms: A Cohort Analysis from 1985, 1988 and 1991 Survey Findings', paper presented to 14th Small Firms Policy and Research Conference, Blackpool, 20–2 November, 1991.

Jones, T. and McEvoy, D. (1992) 'Small Business Initiative: Ethnic Minority Business Component', end of award report to Economic and Social Research Council.

Jones, T., McEvoy, D. and Barrett, G. (1993) 'Labour Intensive Practices in the Ethnic Minority Firm', in J. Atkinson and D.J. Storey (eds), *Employment, the Small Firm and the Labour Market*, Routledge, London.

Jones, T., McEvoy, D. and Barrett, G. (1994) 'Raising Capital for the Ethnic Minority Small Firm', in A. Hughes and D.J. Storey (eds) *Financing the Small Firm*, Routledge, London.

Jovanovic, B. (1982) 'Selection and the Evolution of Industry', *Econometrica*, Vol. 50, pp. 649–70.

Kalleberg, A.L. and Leicht, K.T. (1991) 'Gender and Organisational Performance: Determinants of Small Business Survival and Success', *Academy of Management Journal*, Vol. 34, No. 1, pp. 136–61.

Karlsson, C. and Larsson, J. (1993) 'A Macro-view of the Gnosjö Entrepreneurial Spirit', in C. Karlsson, B. Johannisson and D.J. Storey (eds), *Small Business Dynamics*, Routledge, London.

Keasey, K. and Watson, R. (1987) 'Non Financial Symptoms in the Prediction of Small Company Failure: A Test of the Argenti Hypothesis', *Journal of Business, Finance and Accounting*, Vol. 14, No. 3, pp. 335–54.

Keasey, K. and Watson, R. (1991) 'The State of the Art in Small Firms Failure Prediction: Achievements and Prognosis', *International Small Business Journal*, Vol. 9, No. 4, July–September, pp. 11–29.

Keasey, K. and Watson, R. (1992) *Investment and Financing Decisions in the Performance of Small Firms*, National Westminster Bank, London.

Keasey, K. and Watson, R., (1993) *Small Firm Managers: Ownership, Finance and Performance*, Basil Blackwell, Oxford.

Keeble, D. (1993) 'Small Firm Creation, Innovation and Growth and the Urban–Rural Shift', in J. Curran and D.J. Storey (eds), *Small Firms in Urban and Rural Locations*, Routledge, London.

Keeble, D., Bryson, J. and Wood, P. (1992a) 'Small Firms, Business Services Growth and Regional Development in the United Kingdom: Some Empirical Findings', *Regional Studies*, Vol. 25, No. 5, pp. 439–57.

Keeble, D., Bryson, R. and Wood, P. (1992b) 'The Rise and Role of Small Business Service Firms in the United Kingdom', *International Small Business Journal*, Vol. 11, No. 1, pp. 11–22.

Keeble, D., Walker, S. and Robson, M. (1993) *New Firm Formation and Small Business Growth: Spatial and Temporal Variations and Determinants in the United Kingdom*, Employment Department, Research Series No. 15, September.

Keeble, D., Tyler, P., Broom, G. and Lewis, J. (1992) *Business Success in the Countryside: The Performance of Rural Enterprises*, HMSO for Department of Environment, London.

Kets de Vries, M.F.R. (1977) 'The Entrepreneurial Personality: A Person at the Crossroads', *Journal of Management Studies*, February, pp. 34–57.

Keynes, J.M. (1930) *Treatise on Money*, Macmillan, London.

Kingston Centre (1992) *Small Business Survey*, Kingston University.

Kinsella, R.P., Clarke, W., Coyne, D, Mulvenna, D. and Storey, D.J. (1993) *Fast Growth*

Firms and Selectivity, Irish Management Institute, Dublin.
Knight, F.H. (1921) *Risk, Uncertainty and Profit*, Houghton Mifflin, New York.
Kruse, D. (1992) 'Supervision, Working Conditions and the Size–Wage Effect', *Industrial Relations*, Vol. 31, No. 2, Spring, pp. 229–49.
Lane, S. and Schary, M. (1990) 'The Determinants of Business Failure', Working Paper 90-62, School of Management, Boston University.
Leach, P. (1991) *The Family Business*, Kogan Page, London.
Leeth, J.D. and Scott, J.A. (1989) 'The Incidence of Secured Debt: Evidence from the Small Business Community', *Journal of Financial and Quantitative Analysis*, Vol. 24, No. 3, September, pp. 379–93.
Leigh, R., North, D. and Smallbone, D.J. (1991) 'Adjustment Processes in High Growth Small and Medium Sized Enterprises: A Study of Mature Manufacturing Firms in London During the 1980s', Working Paper No. 2, ESRC Small Business Research Initiative, Middlesex Polytechnic Project.
Levy, J. (1993) *Small and Medium Sized Manufacturing Enterprises: A Recipe for Success*, The Institution of Electrical Engineers, London.
Leyshon, A. (1987) 'Saturation Survey in the Greater Glasgow Area', prepared for the Department of Employment (mimeo).
Lloyd, T. (1993) 'Corporate Giantism: A Suitable Case for Treatment', Quarterly Enterprise Digest, February, 3i, pp. 8–11.
Loebl, H. (1978) 'Government Financed Factories and the Establishment of Industries by Refugees in the Special Areas of England 1937–61', University of Durham, unpublished M. Phil thesis.
Loufti, M.F. (1992) 'An Overview of Self Employment in Europe: Nature, Trends and Policy Issues', in P. Leighton and A. Felstead (eds) *The New Entrepreneurs: Self Employment in Small Business in Europe*, Kogan Page, London.
Lyons, B.R. (1991a) 'Contractability and Specific Investment by Sub-Contractors: A Transaction Cost Approach', paper presented to EARIE Conference, Ferrara, September.
Lyons, B.R. (1991b) 'Subcontracting and the Small Business', End of Award Report, ESRC, Swindon.
Lyons, B.R. (1992) 'Specialised Technology, Economies of Scale and the Make or Buy Decision: Evidence from UK Engineering', University of East Anglia Discussion Paper No. 3.
Lyons, B.R. and Bailey, (1993) 'Small Sub-Contractors in UK Engineering: Competitiveness, Dependence and Problems', *Small Business Economics*, Vol. 5, No. 2, June, pp. 101–10.
McCann, A. (1993) 'The UK Enterprise Population, 1979–91', *The NatWest Review of Small Business Trends*, Vol. 3, No. 1, June, pp. 5–13.
McClelland, D.C. (1961) *The Achieving Society*, Van Nostrand, Princeton, N.J.
MacDonald, R. and Coffield, (1991) *Risky Business: Riders, Fallers and Plodders*, Falmer Press, London.
McGregor, A. and Fletcher, R. (1993) 'Generating Enterprise and Employment in Disadvantaged Urban Areas', in J. Atkinson and D.J. Storey (eds) *Employment, the Small Firm and the Labour Market*, Routledge, London.
MacMillan Committee (1931) *Report of the Committee on Finance and Industry*, Cmnd. 3897, HMSO, London.
MacMillan, I.C., Kulow, D.M. and Choylian, R. (1989) 'Venture Capitalists' Involvement in their Investments: Extent and Performance', *Journal of Business Venturing*, Vol. 4, No. 1, pp. 27–47.
Macrae, D.J.R. (1991) 'Characteristics of High and Low Growth Small and Medium Sized Businesses', paper presented at 21st European Small Business Seminar, Barcelona, Spain.

Marlow, S. (1992) 'Take Up of Business Growth Training Schemes by Ethnic Minority Owned Small Firms', *International Small Business Journal*, Vol. 10, No. 4, pp. 34–46.

Marshall, J.N., Alderman, N., Wong, C. and Thwaites, A. (1993) 'The Impact of Government-assisted Management Training and Development on Small and Medium-Sized Enterprises in Britain', *Environment and Planning C: Government and Policy*, Vol. 11, pp. 331–48.

Mason, C.M. (1983) 'Some Definitional Difficulties in New Firms Research', *Area*, Vol. 15, pp. 53–60.

Mason, C.M. (1991) 'Spatial Variations in Enterprise', in R. Burrows (ed.) *Deciphering the Enterprise Culture*, Routledge, London.

Mason, C.M. (1993) Private Communication, 25 August.

Mason C.M. and Harrison, R. (1991) 'The Small Firm Equity Gap since Bolton' in J. Stanworth and C. Gray (eds), *Bolton 20 Years on: The Small Firm in the 1990s*, Paul Chapman Publishing, London.

Mason, C.M., Harrison, R.T. and Chaloner, J. (1991) 'Informal Risk Capital in the UK: A Study of Investor Characteristics, Investment Preferences and Investment Decision Making', Venture Finance Research Project Working Paper No. 2, University of Southampton (Urban Policy Research Unit)/University of Ulster (Ulster Business School).

Massey, D., Quintas, P. and Wield, D. (1992) *High Tech Fantasies: Science Parks in Society, Science and Space*, Routledge, London.

Maung, N.A. and Erens, R. (1991) *Enterprise Allowance Scheme: A Survey of Participants Two Years After Leaving*, Social and Country Planning Research, London.

May, T.C. and McHugh, J. (1991a) 'Government and Small Business in the UK: The Experience of the 1980s', paper presented at Government/Business Relations Panel at the Annual Conference of the Political Studies Association of the United Kingdom.

May, T.C. and McHugh, J. (1991b), 'Policy Making and Small Business in Britain', paper presented at ESRC Seminar, University of Warwick.

Meager, N. (1991) *Self Employment in the UK*, Institute of Manpower Studies, University of Sussex.

Meager, N. (1992a) 'Self Employment in the European Community: The Emergence of a New Institution and its Evaluation', paper presented at UKEMRA Conference, Southampton.

Meager, N. (1992b) 'The Characteristics of the Self Employed: Some Anglo-German Comparisons', in P. Leighton and A. Felstead (eds) *The New Entrepreneurs: Self Employment in Small Business in Europe*, Kogan Page, London.

Midland Bank (January 1993) *The Changing Financial Requirements of Smaller Companies*, Midland Bank, London.

Mills, D.E. and Schuman, L. (1985) 'Industry Structure with Fluctuating Demand', *American Economic Review*, Vol. 75, No. 4, pp. 758–67.

Minister without portfolio (1985) *Lifting the Burden*, Cmnd. 9571, HMSO.

Monck, C.S.P., Porter, R.B., Quintas, P.R., Storey, D.J. and Wynarczyk, P. (1988) *Science Parks and the Growth of High Technology Firms*, Croom Helm, London.

Moore, B. (1994) 'Financial Constraints to the Growth and Development of Small High Technology Firms', in A. Hughes and D.J. Storey (eds), *Finance for Smaller Firms*, Routledge, London.

Moore, I. (1990) 'Biotechnology and Scientific Instrument Start ups in the United Kingdom: The Role of Government Policy in a Technological Innovation', in M.C. Churchill, W.D. Bygrave, J.A. Hornaday, D.F. Muzyka, K.H.Vesper, W.E. Wetzell Jr. (eds), *Frontiers of Entrepreneurship Research*, Babson College, Boston, Mass.

Morisette, R. (1993) 'Canadian Jobs and Firms Size: Do Smaller Firms Pay Less?', *Canadian Journal of Economics*, Vol. 26, No. 1, February, pp. 159–74.

Morris, M.J. (1985) *Starting A Successful Small Business*, Kogan Page, London.
Morsman, E. Jr. (1986) 'Commercial Loan Structuring', *Journal of Commercial Bank Lending*, Vol. 68, No. 10, pp. 2–20.
Mueller, D.C. (1992) 'Entry, Exit and the Competitive Process', in P. Geroski and J. Schwalback (eds) *Entry and Market Contestability: An International Comparison*, Blackwell, Oxford.
Murray, G. (1993) 'Change and Maturity in the European Venture Capital Industry', Warwick Business School.
Murray, G. and Francis, D. (1992) 'The European Seed Capital Fund Scheme: Review of the First Three Years', report produced for DG23 of the European Commission.
National Audit Office (1988) *Department of Employment/Training Commission: Assistance to Small Firms*, report by the Comptroller and Auditor General, No. 655, HMSO, London.
National Economic Research Associates (1990) *An Evaluation of the Loan Guarantee Scheme*, Department of Employment, Research Paper No. 74.
Nayak, A. and Greenfield, S. (1994) 'The Use of Management Accounting Information for Managing Micro Businesses', in A. Hughes and D.J. Storey (eds), *Finance and the Small Firm*, Routledge, London.
Nenadic, S. (1990) 'The Life Cycle of Firms in Nineteenth Century Britain', in P. Jobert and M. Moss (eds), *The Birth and Death of Companies: An Historical Perspective*, Parthenon Publishers Group, Carnforth, Lancs.
Nenadic, S. (1993) 'The Small Family Firm in Victorian Britain', in *Business History*, (forthcoming)
NIERC (1988) *Job Generation and Manufacturing Industry, 1973–86*, Northern Ireland Economic Research Centre, Belfast.
North, D. and Smallbone, D. (1993) 'Employment Generation and Small Business Growth in Different Geographical Environments', paper presented at 16th National Small Firms Policy and Research Conference, Nottingham 17–19 November.
North, D., Leigh, R. and Smallbone, D. (1992) 'A Comparison of Surviving and Non-Surviving Small and Medium Sized Manufacturing Firms in London during the 1980s', in K. Caley, E. Chell, F. Chittenden, and C. Mason (eds), *Small Enterprise Development: Policy and Practice in Action*, Paul Chapman Publishing, London.
Oakey, R.P. (1984) *High Technology Small Firms*, Francis Pinter, London.
Oakey, R. (1991) 'Government Policy Towards High Technology: Small Firms Beyond the Year 2000', in J. Curran and R.A. Blackburn (eds), *Paths of Enterprise: The Future of the Small Business*, Routledge, London.
Oakey, R.P., Rothwell, R. and Cooper, S. (1988) *Management of Innovation in High Technology Small Firms*, Pinter Publications, London.
O'Farrell, P.N. and Hitchens, D.W.N. (1988) 'Alternative Theories of Small Firm Growth: A Critical Review', *Environment and Planning*, A, Vol. 20, pp. 1365–82.
Organisation for Economic Cooperation and Development (1992) 'Recent Developments in Self Employment', chapter in *Employment Outlook*, OECD, Paris.
Orr, D. (1974), 'The Determinants of Entry: A Study of the Canadian Manufacturing Industries', *Review of Economics and Statistics*, Vol. 58, pp. 58–66.
Owen, G. (1992) 'Aid Regimes and Small Businesses in the UK, France and Belgium', Final Report to ESRC.
Pavitt, K., Robson, M. and Townsend, J. (1987) 'The Size Distribution of Innovating Firms in the UK: 1945–1983', *Journal of Industrial Economics*, Vol. 45, pp. 297–306.
Peat Marwick (1986), *The Business Expansion Scheme*, Inland Revenue, London.
Penrose, E.T. (1959) 'The Theory of the Growth of the Firm', Basil Blackwell, London.
Peters, T.J. and Waterman, R.H. Jr. (1982) *In Search of Excellence*, Harper and Row, New York.

Phillips, B.D. and Kirchhoff, B.A. (1988) *The Survival and Quality of Jobs Generated by Entrepreneurial Firms*, US Small Business Administration, Boston, Mass.

Phillips, B.D. and Kirchhoff, B.A. (1989a) 'Formation, Growth and Survival; Small Firm Dynamics in the US Economy', *Small Business Economics*, Vol. 1, No. 1, pp. 65–74.

Phillips, B.D. and Kirchhoff, B.A. (1989b) 'Innovation and Growth Among New Firms in the US Economy', Babson Entrepreneurial Research Conference.

Pickles, A.R. and O'Farrell, P.N. (1987) 'An Analysis of Entrepreneurial Behaviour from Male Work Histories', *Regional Studies*, Vol. 21, No. 5, pp. 425–44.

Piore, M. and Sabel, C. (1984) *The Second Industrial Divide*, Basic Books, New York.

Power, M. (1993) *Business-Format Franchisees Closing or Continuing*, Power Research Associates, London.

Prais, S.J. (1976) *The Evolution of Giant Firms in Britain*, Cambridge University Press, Cambridge.

Prais, S.J. (1993) *Economic Programme and Education: The Nature of Britain's Deficiencies*, National Institute of Economic Research, London.

Rainnie, A. (1989) *Industrial Relations in Small Firms*, Routledge, London.

Rajan, A. and Pearson, R. (1986) *UK Occupation and Employment Trends to 1990*, Institute of Manpower Studies, Butterworths' Press, London.

Rassan, C. (1988) *Secrets of Success: What You Can Learn from Britain's Entrepreneurs*, Sidgwick & Jackson, London.

Rees, H. and Shah, A. (1993) 'The Characteristics of the Self Employed: The Supply of Labour', in J. Atkinson and D.J. Storey (eds), *Employment, the Small Firm and the Labour Market*, Routledge, London.

Reid, G.C. (1991), 'Staying in Business', *International Journal of Industrial Organisation*, Vol. 9, pp. 545–56.

Reid, G.C. (1993a), *Small Business Enterprise: An Economic Analysis*, Routledge, London.

Reid, G.C. (1993b), 'The Survival of Small Business Enterprise', Centre for Research into Industry, Enterprise, Finance and the Firm (C.R.I.E.F.F.) Discussion Paper 9309, University of St Andrews, Fife.

Reynolds, P.D. (1993) 'High Performance Entrepreneurship: What Makes it Different?', paper presented at Babson Entrepreneurial Conference, University of Houston, 24–7 March.

Reynolds, P.D. and Maki, I. (1991) 'Regional Characteristics Affecting Business Growth: Assessing Strategies for Promoting Regional Economic Well-being', project report submitted to Rural Poverty and Resource Program, The Ford Foundation, Grant 900-013.

Reynolds, P.D. and Miller, B. (1988) '1988 Minnesota New Firms Study: An Exploration of New Firms and their Economic Contributions', Centre for Urban and Regional Affairs, Minneapolis, Minnesota.

Reynolds, P.D. and Storey, D.J. (1993) *Local and Regional Characteristics Affecting Small Business Formation: A Cross-National Comparison*, OECD, Paris.

Reynolds, P.D., Miller, B. and Maki, W. (1992) 'Regional Characteristics Affecting Business Volatility in the United States, 1980–4', in C. Karlsson, B. Johannisson and D.J. Storey (eds), *Small Business Dynamics: International, National and Regional Perspectives*, Routledge, London.

Reynolds, S.S. (1988) 'Plant Closing and Exit Behaviour in Declining Industries', *Economica*, Vol. 55, November, pp. 493–504.

Ritchie, J. (1990) 'Enterprise Culture as an Educational Phenomenon', paper presented at the British Sociological Association, University of Surrey.

Roberts, E.B. (1991) *Entrepreneurs in High Technology: Lessons from MIT and Beyond*, Oxford University Press, New York.

Robinson, R.B. and Pearce, J.A. (1983) 'The Impact of Formalised Strategic Planning on Financial Performance in Organisations', *Strategic Management Journal*, Vol. 4, No. 3, pp. 197–207.

Robinson, R.B. and Pearce, J.A. (1984) 'Research Thrust and Small Firm Strategic Planning', *Academy of Management Review*, Vol. 9, No. 1, pp. 128-137.

Robinson, R., Wren, C. and Goddard, J.B.(1987) *Economic Development Policies: An Evaluative Study of the Newcastle Metropolitan Region*, Clarendon Press, Oxford.

Robson, M. (1991) 'Self Employment and New Firm Formation', *Scottish Journal of Political Economy*, Vol. 38, pp. 352–68.

Robson, M. and Shah, A. (1989) 'A Capital Theoretic Approach to Self Employment in the UK', Department of Economics, University of Newcastle upon Tyne (mimeo).

Robson Rhodes (1984) *A Study of Businesses Financed under the Small Business Loan Guarantee Scheme*, DTI, London.

Rosa, P., Birley, S., Cannon, T. and O'Neill, K. (1989) *The Role and Contribution of Small Business Research*, Avebury, Aldershot.

Rothwell, R. (1983) 'Innovation and Firm Size: A Case for Dynamic Complementarity', *Journal of General Management*, Vol. 8, No. 3.

Rothwell, R. (1986) 'The Role of Small Firms in Technological Innovation', in J. Curran, J. Stanworth and D. Watkins (eds), *The Survival of the Small Firm*, Vol. 2, Gower, Aldershot.

Rowley, C.K. and Peacock, A. (1975) *Welfare Economics: A Liberal Re-statement*, Martin Robertson, London.

Scarman, Lord (1981) *The Brixton Disorders 10–12 April 1981*, HMSO, London.

Schary, M.A. (1991) 'The Probability of Exits', *Rand Journal of Economics*, Vol. 22, No. 3, Autumn, pp. 339–53.

Schumpeter, J.A. (1934) *The Theory of Economic Development*, Harvard University Press, Cambridge, Mass.

Scott, M. (1982a) 'Mythology and Misplaced Pessimism: The Real Failure Record of New Small Businesses', in D. Watkins, J. Stanworth and A. Westrip (eds), *Stimulating Small Firms*, Gower, Aldershot.

Scott, M. (1982b), 'Rethinking Entrepreneurial Failure', paper presented to Small Business Management Education Association Conference, Glasgow, 9–11 September.

Scott, M. and Bruce, R. (1987) 'Five Stages of Growth in Small Businesses', *Long Range Planning*, Vol. 20, No. 3, pp. 45–52.

Scott, M., Roberts, I., Holroyd, G. and Sawbridge, G. (1989) *Management and Industrial Relations in Small Firms*, Research Paper No. 70, Department of Employment, London.

Scott, R. (1993) 'Does a Regime of Intensive Grant Assistance to Small Firms Create Jobs?', paper presented to 23rd European Small Business Seminar, Northern Ireland, 15–17 September.

Segal Quince Wicksteed (1989) *Evaluation of the Consultancy Initiatives*, Department of Trade and Industry, HMSO, London.

Segal Quince Wicksteed (1991a) *Evaluation of the Consultancy Initiatives – Second Stage*, Department of Trade and Industry, HMSO, London.

Segal Quince Wicksteed (1991b) *Evaluation of the Consultancy Initiatives – Third Stage*, Department of Trade and Industry, HMSO, London.

Sengenberger, W., Loveman. G.W. and Piore, M.J. (1990) *The Re-emergence of Small Enterprises: Industrial Restructuring in Industrialised Countries*, International Labour Organisation, Geneva.

Shearman, E. and Burrell. G. (1988) 'New Technology Based Firms and the Emergence of New Industries: Some Employment Implications', *New Technology, Work and Employment*, Vol. 3, No. 2, pp. 87–99.

Shilson, D. (1984) 'Venture Capital in the UK', *Bank of England Quarterly Bulletin*, June, pp. 207–11.

Shutt, J. and Whittington, R. (1986) 'Large Firm Strategies and the Rise of Small Units', in T. Faulkner, G. Beaver, J. Lewis and A. Gibb (eds) *Readings in Small Business*, Gower, Aldershot.

Siegel, R., Siegel, E. and MacMillan, I.C. (1993) 'Characteristics Distinguishing High Growth Ventures', *Journal of Business Venturing*, Vol. 8, pp. 169–80.

Simmons, P. (1989) 'Bad Luck and Fixed Costs in Personal Bankruptcies', *Economic Journal*, Vol. 99, March, pp. 92–107.

Small Business Administration (1991) *The State of Small Business: A Report of the President*, US Government Printing Office, Washington, D.C.

Small Business Bureau (1993) *Enhanced Loan Guarantee Scheme Report*, Small Business Bureau, London.

Small Business Research Centre (1992) *The State of British Enterprise*, University of Cambridge.

Small Business Research Trust (1992) *NatWest Review of Small Business Trends*, Open University, Milton Keynes.

Smallbone, D. (1988) 'Enterprise Agencies and the Survival of New Small Business Start Ups', *Local Economy*, pp. 143–47.

Smallbone, D. (1990), 'Success and Failure in New Business Start Ups', *International Small Business Journal*, Vol. 8, No. 2, pp. 34–47.

Smallbone, D., Leigh, R. and North, D. (1993) 'Characteristics and Strategies of a Group of High Growth SMEs in the UK, 1979–1990', paper presented at the First Venezuelan SME Management Seminar, Caracas, Venezuela, 7–11 March.

Smallbone, D., North, D. and Leigh, R. (1992) 'Managing Change for Growth and Survival: The Study of Mature Manufacturing Firms in London during the 1980s', Working Paper No. 3, Planning Research Centre, Middlesex Polytechnic.

Smallbone, D., North, D. and Leigh, R. (1993a) 'The Growth and Survival of Mature Manufacturing SMEs in the 1980s: An Urban and Rural Comparison', in J. Curran and D.J. Storey (eds), *Small Firms in Urban and Rural Locations*, Routledge, London.

Smallbone, D., North, D. and Leigh, R. (1993b) 'The Use of External Assistance by Mature SMEs in the UK: Some Policy Implications', *Entrepreneurship and Regional Development*, Vol. 5, pp. 279–95.

Solem, O. and Steiner, M.P. (1989), 'Factors for Success in Small Manufacturing Firms – and with Special Emphasis on Growing Firms', paper presented at Conference on Small and Medium Sized Enterprises and the Challenges of 1992, Mikkeli, Finland.

Stanworth, M.J.K. and Curran, J. (1976) 'Growth and the Small Firm – An Alternative View', *Journal of Management Studies*, Vol. 13, pp. 95–110.

Stanworth, J. and Gray, C. (eds) (1991) *Bolton 20 Years on: The Small Firm in the 1990s*, Paul Chapman Publishing London.

Stanworth, C., Stanworth, J. and Purdy, D. (1993) 'Self Employment and Labour Market Restructuring: The Case of Freelance Tele-workers in Book Publishing', Future of Work Research Group, University of Westminster, London.

Stanworth, J., Blythe, S., Granger, B. and Stanworth, C. (1989) 'Who Becomes an Entrepreneur?', *International Small Business Journal*, Vol. 8, No. 1, pp. 11–22.

Stiglitz, J.E. and Weiss, A. (1981) 'Credit Rationing in Markets With Imperfect Information', *American Economic Review*, Vol. 73, June, pp. 393–409.

Stoneman, P. (1985) *The Economics of Technology Policy*, Oxford University Press, Oxford.

Storey, D.J. (1982a) *Entrepreneurship and the New Firm*, Croom Helm, London.

Storey, D.J. (1982b) 'New Entrepreneurs on the Dole', *Journal of Economic Affairs*, Vol. 2, No. 2, January.

Storey, D.J. (1985) 'Manufacturing Employment Change in Northern England 1965–78: The Role of Small Business', in D.J. Storey (ed.), *Small Firms in Regional Economic Development*, Cambridge University Press, Cambridge.

Storey, D.J. (1990a) 'Evaluation of Policies and Measures to Create Local Employment', *Urban Studies*, Vol. 27, No. 5, pp. 669–84.

Storey, D.J. (1990b) 'Firm Performance and Size', in Z. Acs and D.B. Audretsch (eds), *The Economics of Small Firms: A European Challenge*, Kluwer Academic Publishers, Dordrecht.

Storey, D.J. (1991) 'The Birth of New Firms – Does Unemployment Matter? – A Review of the Evidence', *Small Business Economics*, Vol. 3, pp. 167–78.

Storey, D.J. (1993) 'Should We Abandon Support to Start Up Businesses?', Working Paper No. 11, SME Centre, Warwick University.

Storey, D.J. (1994) 'The Role of Legal Status in Influencing Bank Financing and New Firm Growth', *Applied Economics*, Vol. 26, pp. 129–36.

Storey, D.J. and Johnson, S. (1987) *Job Generation and Labour Market Change*, Macmillan, Basingstoke.

Storey, D.J. and Strange, A. (1992) *Entrepreneurship in Cleveland 1979–1989: A Study of the Effects of the Enterprise Culture*, Employment Department, Research Series No. 3.

Storey, D.J., Watson R. and Wynarczyk, P. (1989) *Fast Growth Small Businesses: Case Studies of 40 Small Firms in Northern England*, Department of Employment, Research Paper No. 67.

Storey, D.J., Keasey, K., Watson, R. and Wynarczyk, P. (1987) *The Performance of Small Firms: Profits, Jobs and Failures*, Croom Helm, London.

Thomas, A. and Cornforth, C. (1989) 'The Survival and Growth of Workers' Co-operatives: A Comparison with Small Businesses', *International Small Business Journal*, Vol. 8, No. 1, pp. 34–50.

Thomas, P. (1991) 'Safety in Smaller Manufacturing Establishments', *Employment Gazette*, January, pp. 20–5.

Thompson, M. and Wilson, A. (1991) 'Wage levels, Labour Markets and Firm Size: Evidence from Six Local Labour Markets', paper presented at the seventh ESRC Small Business Initiative Meeting, University of Warwick.

Townroe, P. and Mallalieu, K. (1993) 'Founding a New Business in the Countryside', in J. Curran and D.J. Storey (eds) *Small Firms in Urban and Rural Locations*, Routledge, London.

Treasury and Civil Service Committee, (1991) 'The Availability of Bank Credit and Interest Rates', Sixth Report, HC531, London.

Tremlett, N. (1993) *The Business Start up Schemes: 18 Months Follow up Survey*, Social and Community Planning Research, London.

United States Small Business Administration (1992) *The State of Small Business: A Report of the President*, Washington D.C.

Van der Horst, R. (1992) 'The Volatility of the Small Business Sector in the Netherlands', paper presented at the International Conference on Small Business, OECD, Montreal, Canada, 24–7 May.

Variyam, J.N. and Kraybill, D.S. (1992) 'Empirical Evidence on Determinants of Firm Growth', *Economic Letters*, Vol. 38, pp. 31–6.

Ward, R. and Reeves, F. (1980) *West Indians in Business in Britain*, HMSO, London.

Watson, R. (1990) 'Employment Change, Profits and Directors' Remuneration in Small and Closely-held UK Companies', *Scottish Journal of Political Economy*, Vol. 37, No. 3, pp. 259–74.

Watson, J. and Everitt, J. (1993) 'Defining Small Business Failure', *International Small Business Journal*, Vol. 11, No. 3, pp. 35–48.

Weiss, A. and Landau, H.J. (1984) 'Wages, Hiring Standards and Firm Size', *Journal of*

Labour Economics, Vol. 2, No. 4, October, pp. 477–99.
Westhead, P. (1993) 'Late Payment of Bills: Trade Association Pilot Initiative Evaluation', report to the Department of Trade and Industry, London.
Westhead, P. and Birley, S. (1993a) 'Employment Growth in New Independent Owner-managed Firms in Great Britain', University of Warwick.
Westhead, P. and Birley, S. (1993b) 'Environments for Business Deregistrations in the UK, 1987–90', University of Warwick.
Westhead, P. and Moyes, A. (1992) 'Reflections on Thatcher's Britain: Evidence from New Production Firm Registrations', *Entrepreneurship and Regional Development*, Vol. 4, No. 1, pp. 21–56.
Westhead, P. and Storey, D.J. (1994) *An Assessment of Firms Located on and off Science Parks in the UK*, HMSO, London.
Wetzel, W.E. Jr. (1987) 'The Informal Venture Capital Market: Aspects of Scale and Market Efficiency', *Journal of Business Venturing*, Vol. 2, pp. 229–313.
Williamson, O.E. (1975) *Markets and Hierarchies: Analysis and Anti-trust Implications*, Free Press, New York.
Williamson, O.E. (1985) *The Economic Institutions of Capitalism: Firms, Markets and Relational Contracting*, Free Press, New York.
Wilson Committee (1979) *The Financing of Small Firms*, Interim Report of the Committee to Review the Functioning of the Financial Institutions, Cmnd. 7503, HMSO, London.
Wilson, P. and Stanworth, J. (1987) 'The Social and Economic Factors in the Development of Small Black Minority Firms: Asian and Afro-Caribbean Businesses in Brent, 1982 and 1984 Compared', in K. O'Neill, R. Bhambri, T. Faulkner and T. Cannon (eds), *Small Business Development: Some Current Issues*, Avebury, Aldershot.
Wingham, D.L. and Kelmar, J.H. (1992) 'Factors of Small Business Success Strategies', School of Management Working Paper 92.01, Curtin University of Technology, Perth, Western Australia.
Woo, C.Y., Cooper, A.C. Dunkelberg, W.C., Daellenbach, U. and Dennis, W.J. (1989) 'Determinants of Growth for Small and Large Entrepreneurial Start Ups', paper presented at Babson Entrepreneurship Conference.
Wood, P.A., Bryson, J. and Keeble, D. (1993) 'Regional Patterns of Small Firm Development in Business Services: Evidence from the United Kingdom', *Environment and Planning*, A, Vol. 25, pp. 677–700.
Woods, A., Blackburn, R. and Curran, J. (1993), 'A Longitudinal Study of Small Enterprises in the Service Sector', Small Business Research Centre, Kingston University and Department of Management Studies, Brunel University, November.
Wren, C. and Waterson, M. (1991), 'The Direct Employment Effects of Financial Assistance to Industry', *Oxford Economic Papers*, Vol. 43, pp. 116–38.
Wright, M., Thompson, S. and Robbie, K. (1992), 'Venture Capital and Management-led Leveraged Buyouts: A European Perspective', *Journal of Business Venturing*, Vol. 7, No. 1, January, pp. 47–71.
Wynarczyk, P., Watson, R., Storey, D.J., Short, H. and Keasey, K. (1993) *The Managerial Labour Market in Small and Medium Sized Enterprises*, Routledge, London.

Index

Page numbers which are in italics refer to tables or figures where these are separate from their textual reference.